CW01668011

LIVING *in* COUNTRY STYLE

Brent Darby
Wink Colville

Lannoo

TABLE *of* CONTENTS

Our COUNTRY HOMES

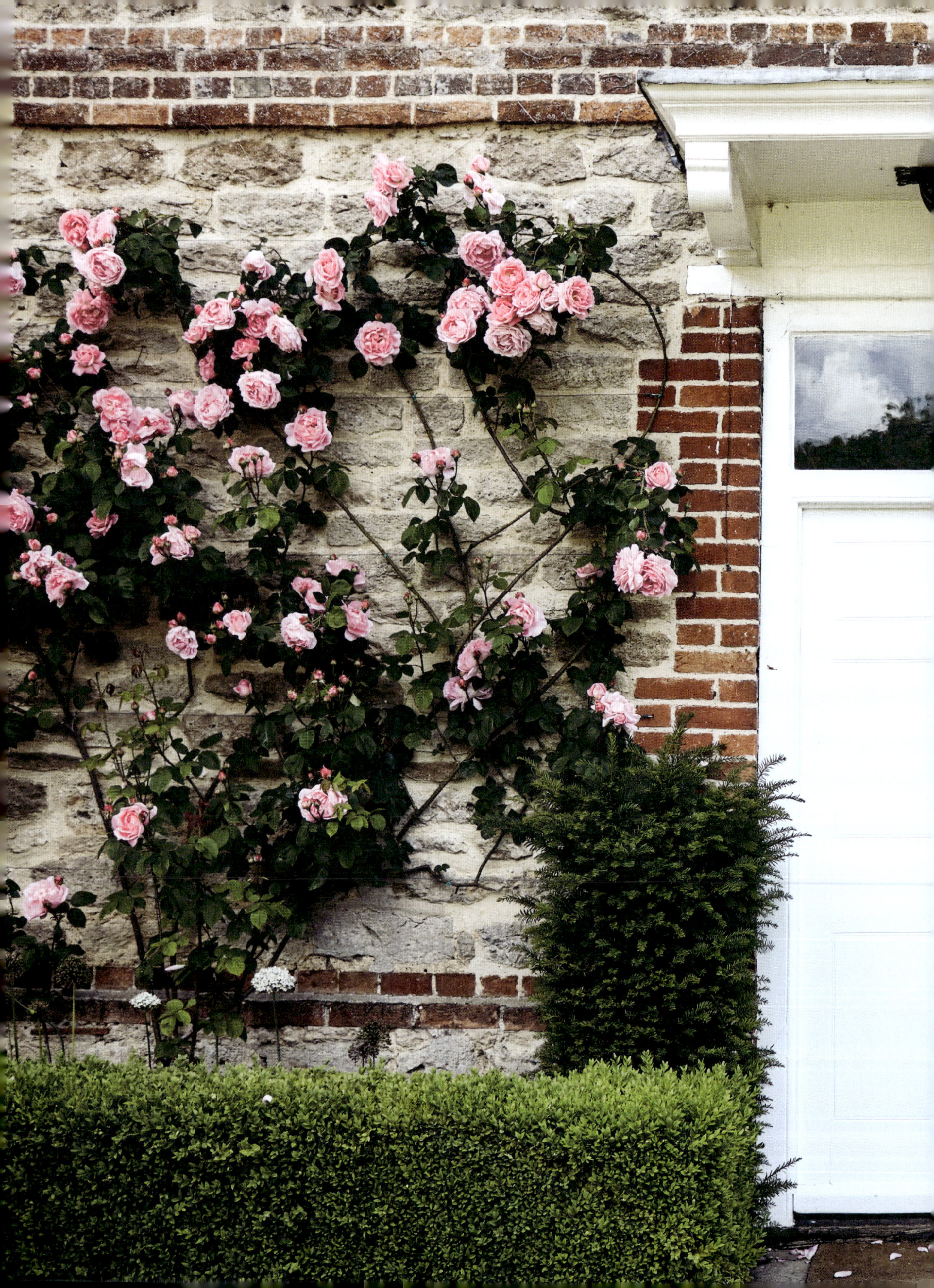

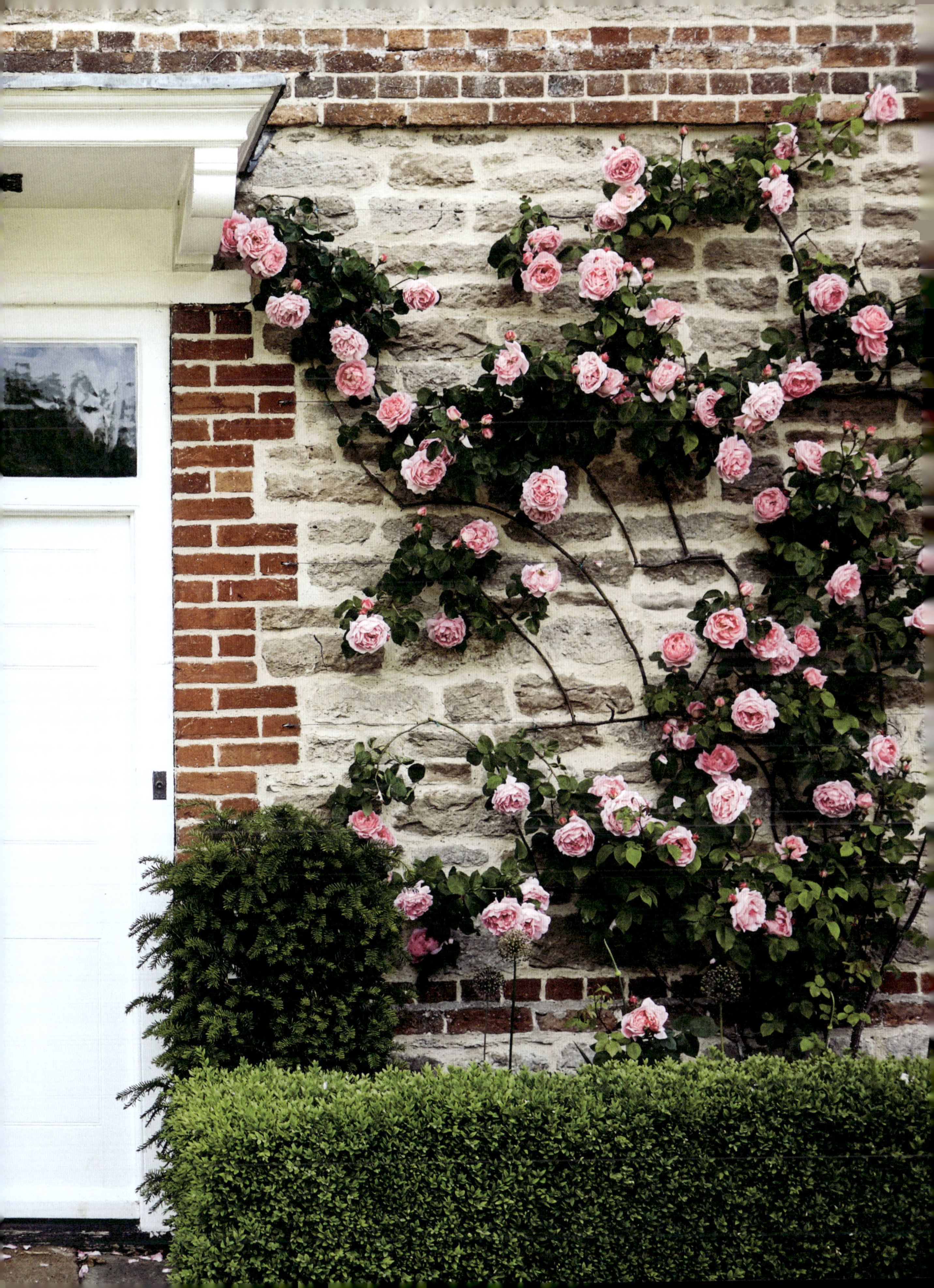

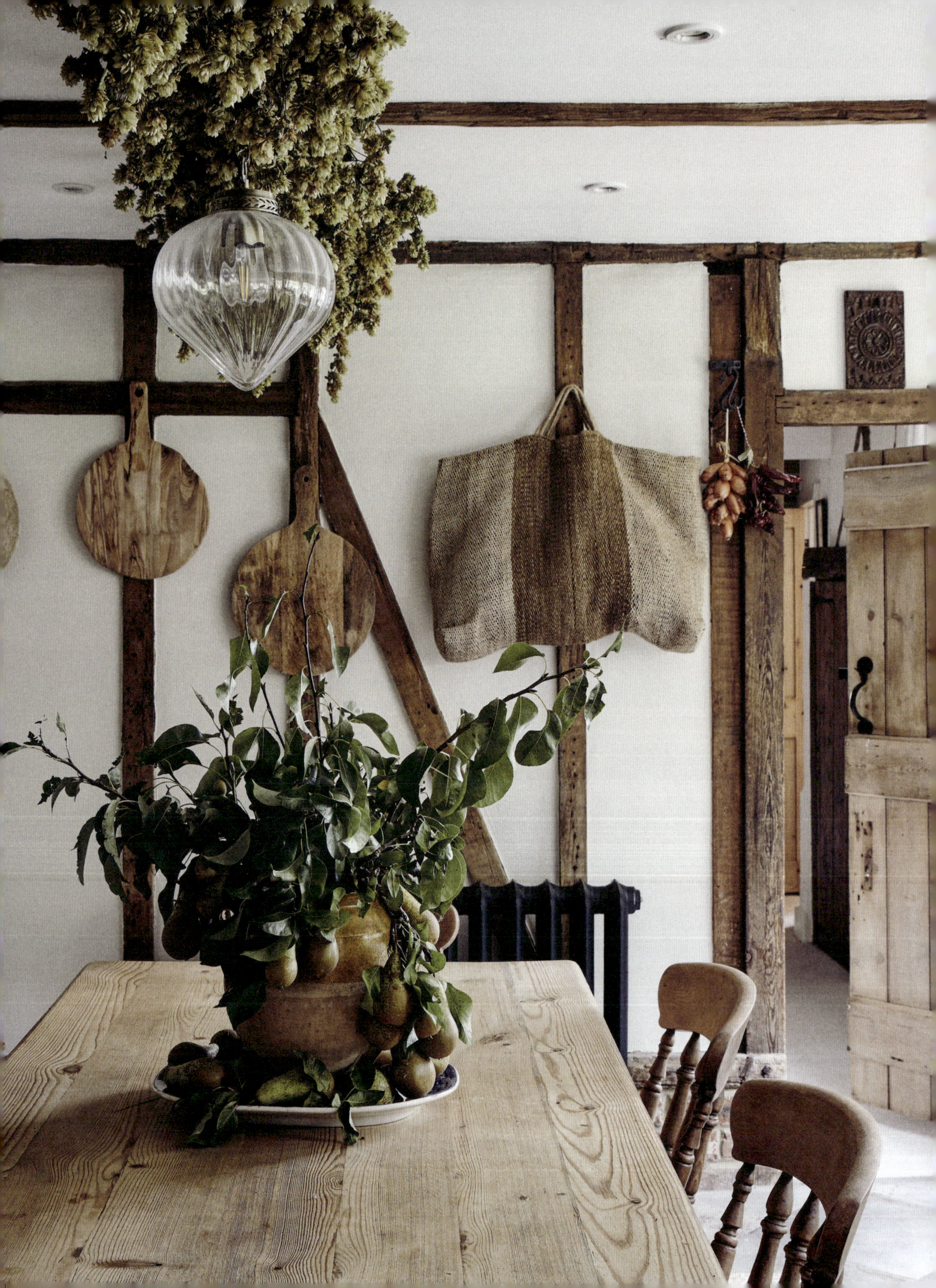

INTRODUCTION

Wink Coville

Today Brent and I photographed our last house, Heloise's stunning octagonal chapel, on a blue-skied day in May. We all agreed that, to us, it is in May that the English countryside puts on its most glorious display of all. Cow parsley froths in every verge, and hedgerows flaunt shades of green from acid to emerald. I mention this because it occurs to me that the sentiment that all the homeowners in this book share is a mutual and tireless appreciation of the natural world. While some are moved by a misty autumn morning and others by the smoke-scented chill of a midwinter night, all have a love of our magnificent rural landscapes throughout the seasons.

It was at this time of year that my family moved from London to the country. At that point, we would have bought any one of the many houses we viewed. We were bowled over by the sheer variety, and by the fact that they all had both stairs and a garden (unlike our previous Victorian conversion flats). To me they were all beautiful, and each had a unique character of its own.

Fourteen years on, I was equally impressionable while getting to know the twenty-three houses in this book. It has been a pleasure and a privilege to be introduced to them, and to hear their stories. Each one became my new favourite. I found myself repeatedly redefining my previous understanding of country style and soon accepted that there is no one size to fit all. What it involves is, I think, an ability to recognise the unique essence of a house and to enhance it.

The majority of the houses in this book have a history, and their conscientious owners have taken great pains to restore the true character and preserve the heritage of their property. And in return these places offer sanctuary and comfort to their owners. There seems to be a common instinctive urge to simplify each home before adding the layers and personal choices that bind a house to its owner. Many times I was told of the joy people felt when pulling up old carpet to reveal original floorboards beneath. Several of our homeowners went even further in uncovering the bones of their homes, taking the walls back to their original state and insulating their houses with the natural materials that would have been used centuries ago. It shouldn't have surprised me at all to learn that once buildings had been returned to their original state, such nuisances as damp and mould vanished.

In the past I've bandied the word 'character' about rather carelessly when referring to buildings. Today I have a new understanding and respect for these widely individual homes. While some have survived fires, others have been abused by past custodians and many have in the past been home to fascinating personalities - and often to livestock - they really are enriched by the history that only they truly know.

I have likewise been inspired by the beginnings of the newer builds in this book and by the diligence that homeowners have put into planning modern houses and extensions, researching ingenious ways to impact as little as possible on our planet while creating energy-efficient homes. Those newer houses have a different energy and charm, full of positive promise for the future. They are just starting their journeys, the mysteries of their own yet to unfold.

It is respect for the past and the future that has struck me most. But also important are the simple and innocent pleasures of the here and now, of day-to-day living in these houses. Laying logs on the fire, throwing open the windows, filling a jug with daffodils. Regardless of its size or grandeur, people take great comfort from their home: their safe place, their pride and joy. *Living in Country Style* I hope embodies the symbiotic relationship that people have nurtured in their country homes.

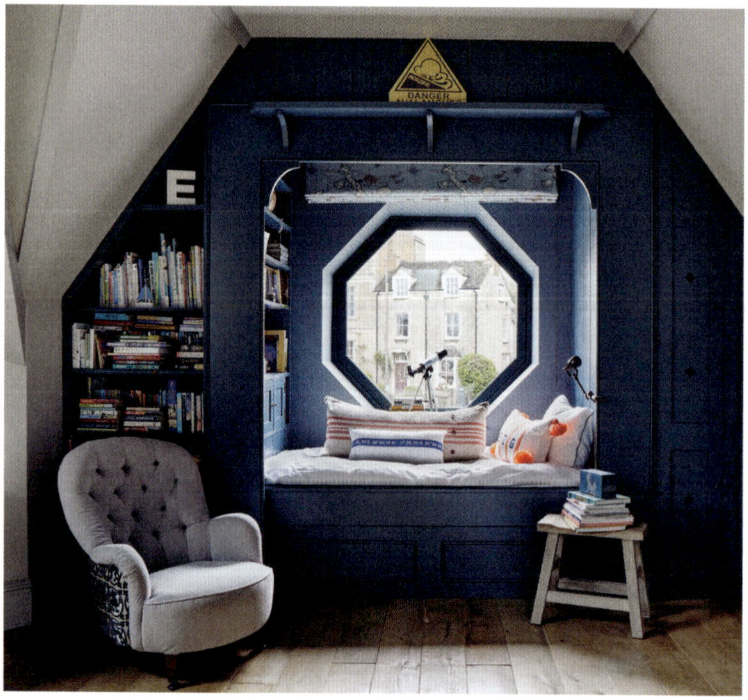

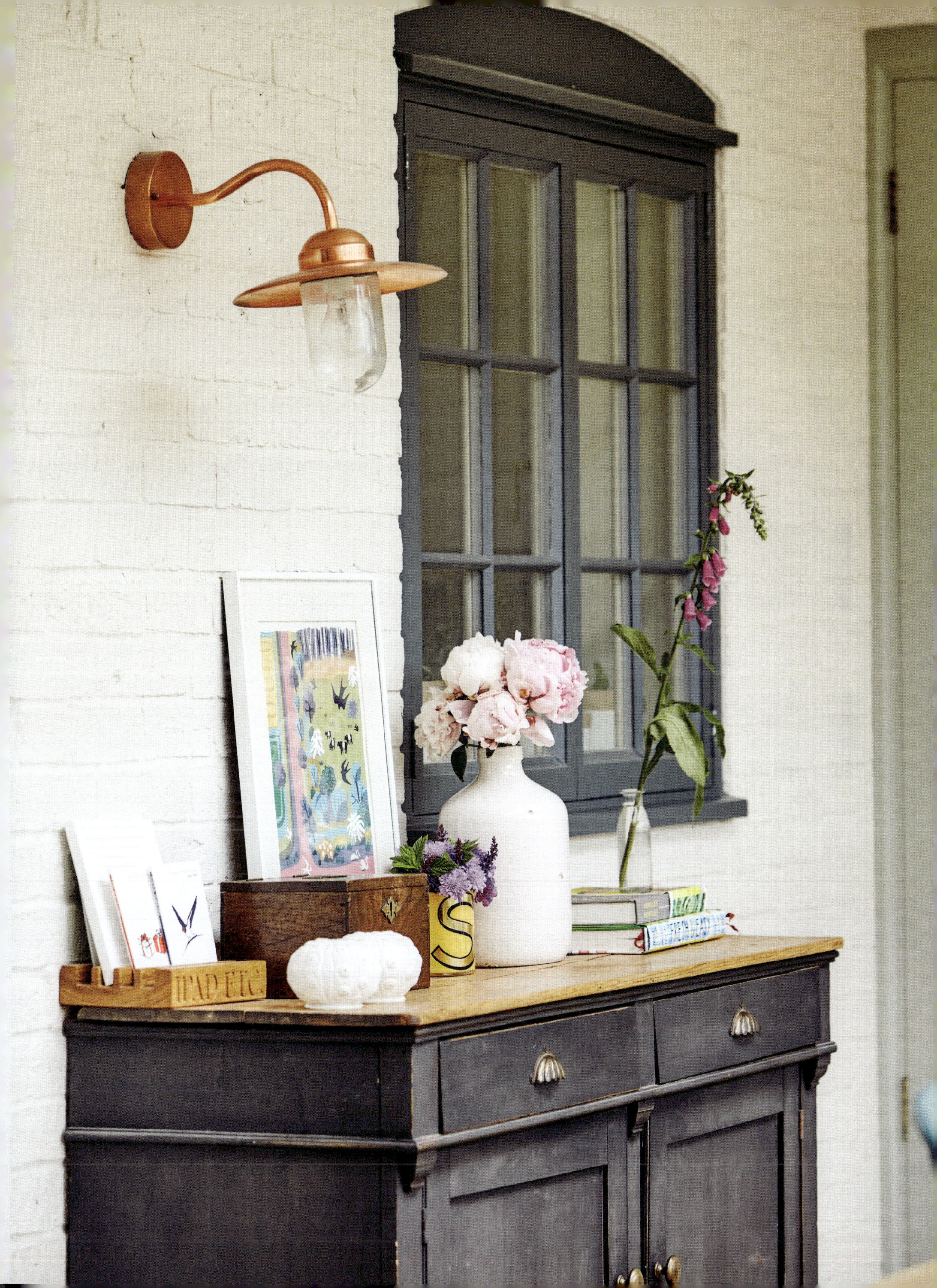
IPAD ETC.
S

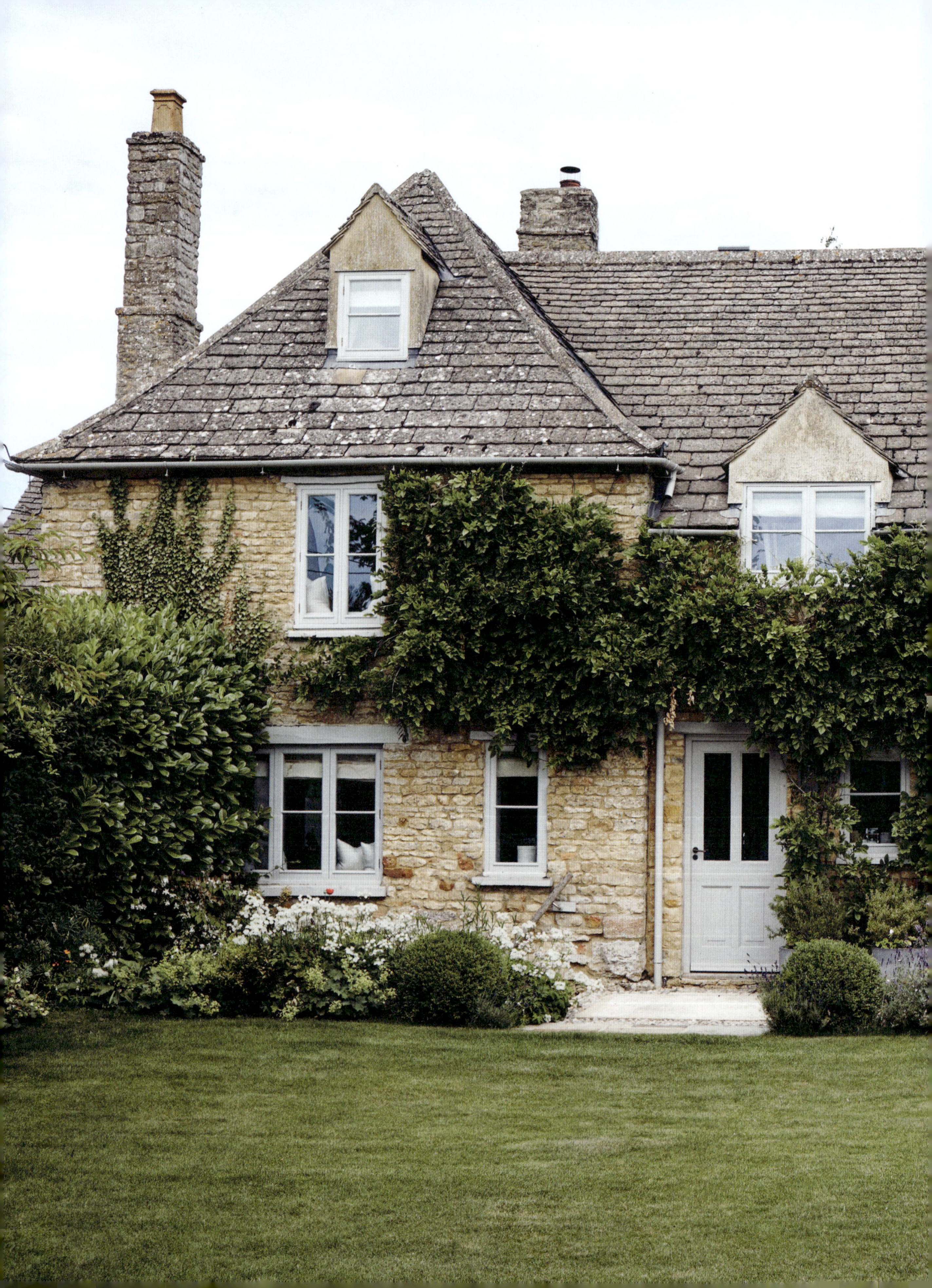

Our COUNTRY HOMES

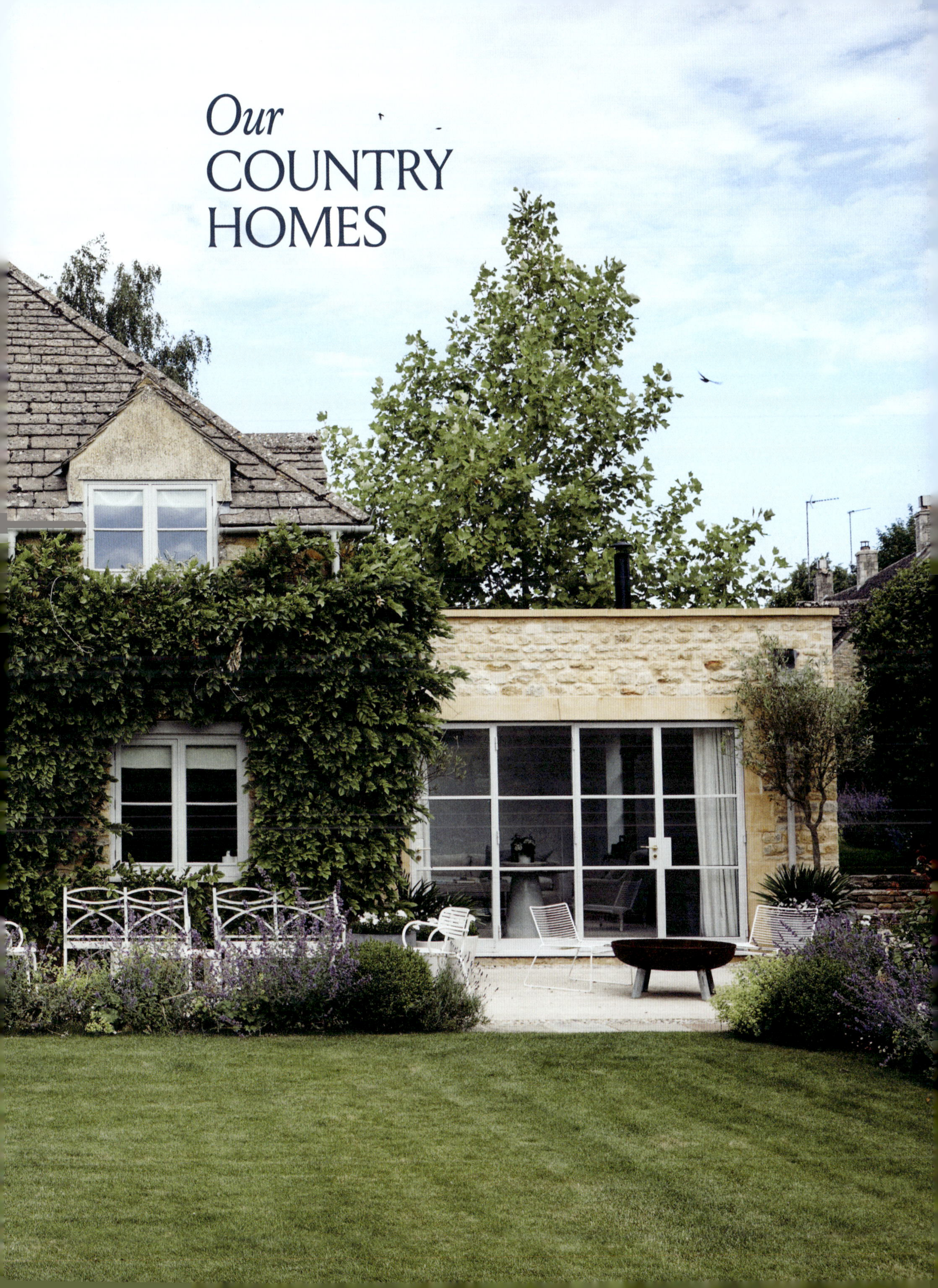

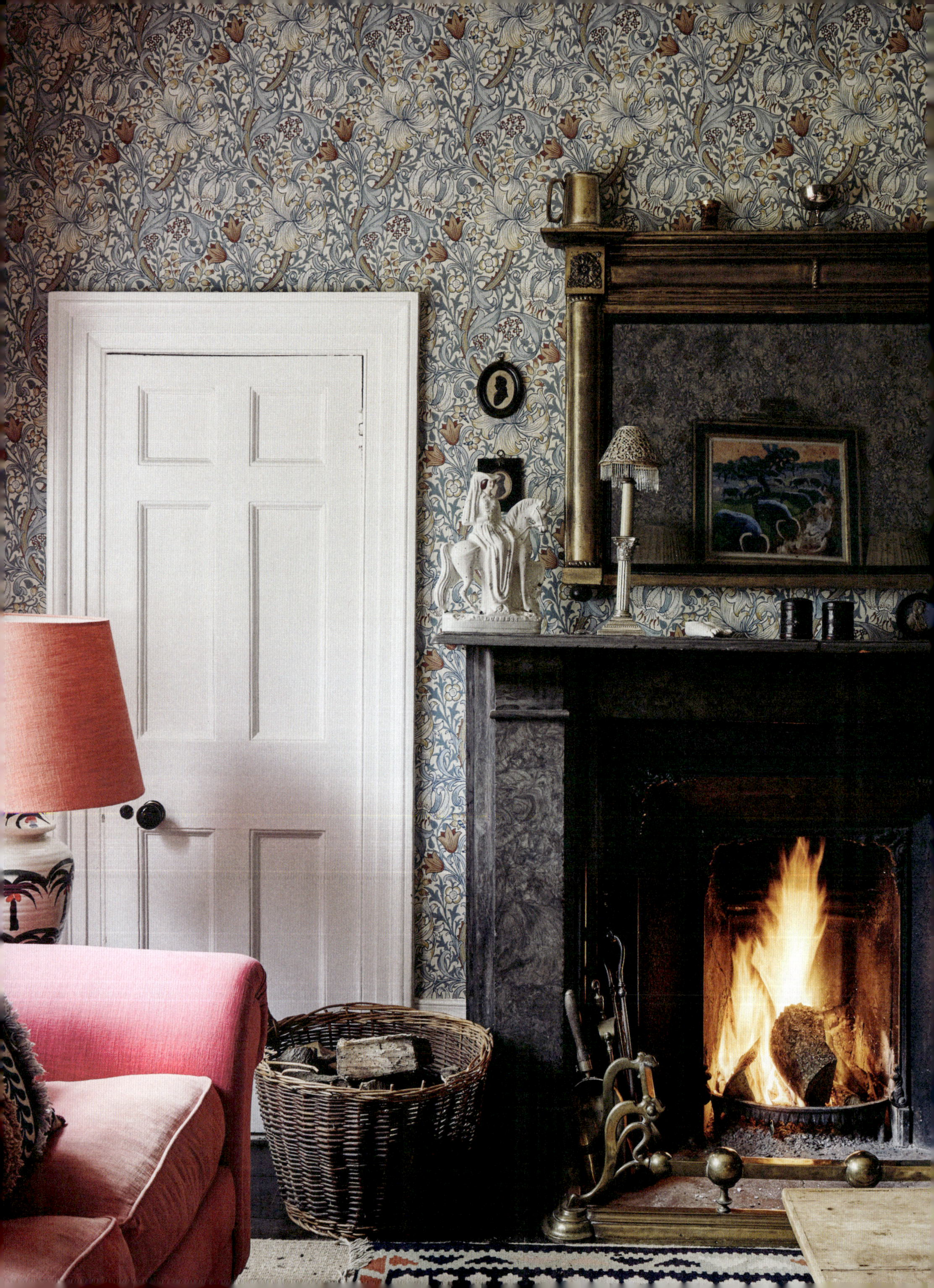

KEEP THE HOME FIRES BURNING

When the chance to move into her cherished childhood home arose, Alice Clark and her family wasted no time in moving from the capital to give their three daughters a country upbringing.

When Alice Clark thinks back to her childhood, she remembers the fresh air and freedom. 'My mother (an artist with five children needing some headspace) would open the doors each morning, and off us five siblings would set, only to return, filthy and famished, in time for tea.'

Alice's own daughters were born in London. Alice was (and still is) headmistress of The Willow Nursery in Clapham, which she founded and continues to cherish. However, she felt an urgent draw to the country and often took Molly, Rose and Lily to their grandparents' farmhouse. The little girls would unfurl in the newfound space and Alice knew that the country was the place for them. When her parents offered them the opportunity to move into the house and run the farm, it was an easy decision to make.

And so, after a decade in London, the family moved into Alice's childhood home. While the house needed some work, Alice wanted the essence to remain unchanged. The colour and art that had surrounded the family were intrinsic to the house's character, and Alice was adamant that these would never change. But the time had come to breathe in some new life. 'I wanted to freshen the house up and give it a subtle makeover,' Alice remembers.

She started with the kitchen, which three hundred years ago would have housed livestock. Its timeworn wooden stable wall and exposed beams recall the room's past as a cowshed opening onto the farmyard. In her childhood the room had been divided into two, a kitchen and a separate playroom. Alice craved a lighter, fuller space where she could see the children playing and they could all gather round a large table. She had the dividing wall removed and two RSJs disguised under beams, then had the ceiling removed to reveal the original oak joists. A light and lovely kitchen has opened up with a large play area at one end. Alice also had a window enlarged to flood the room with light.

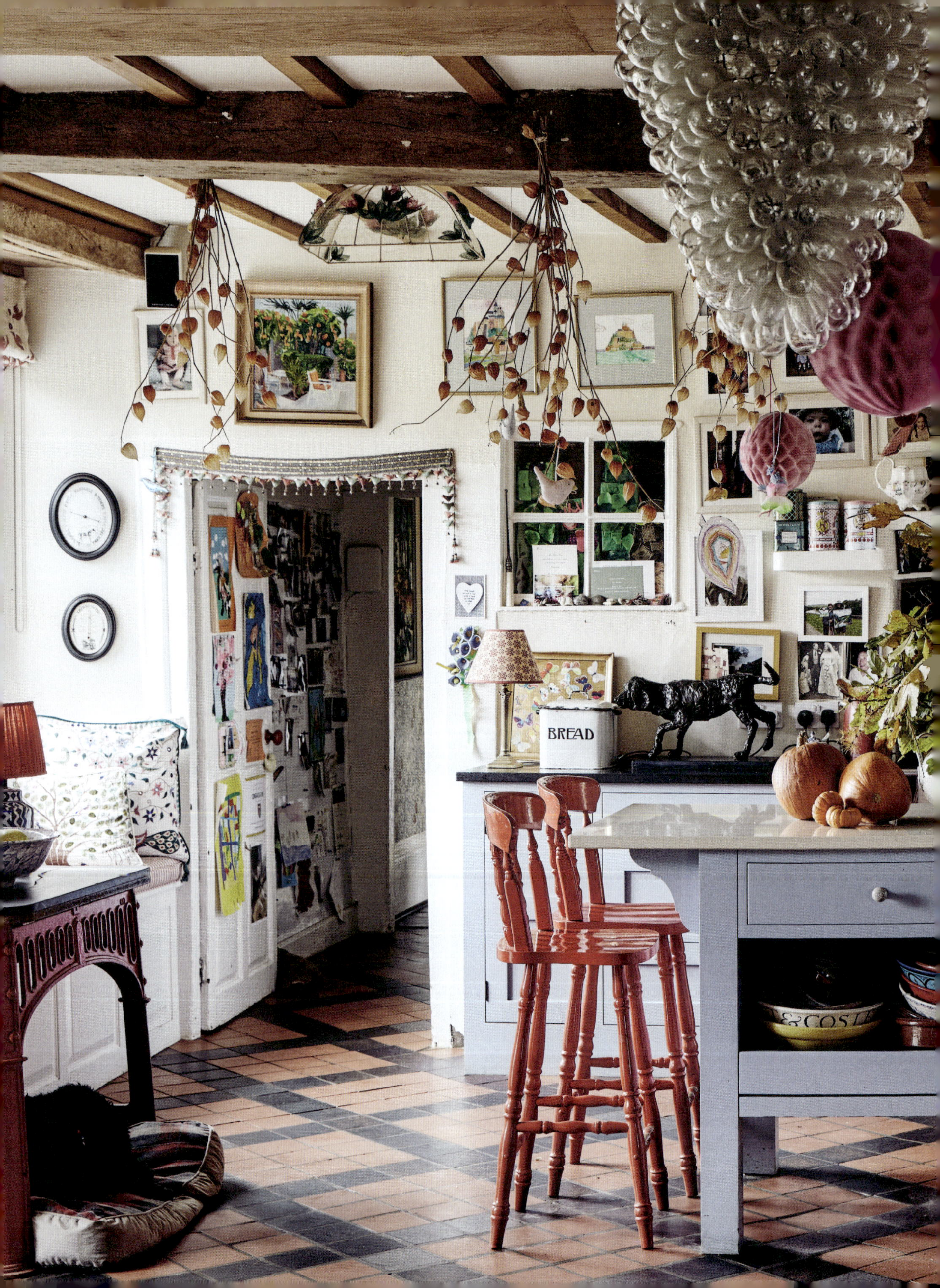
BREAD

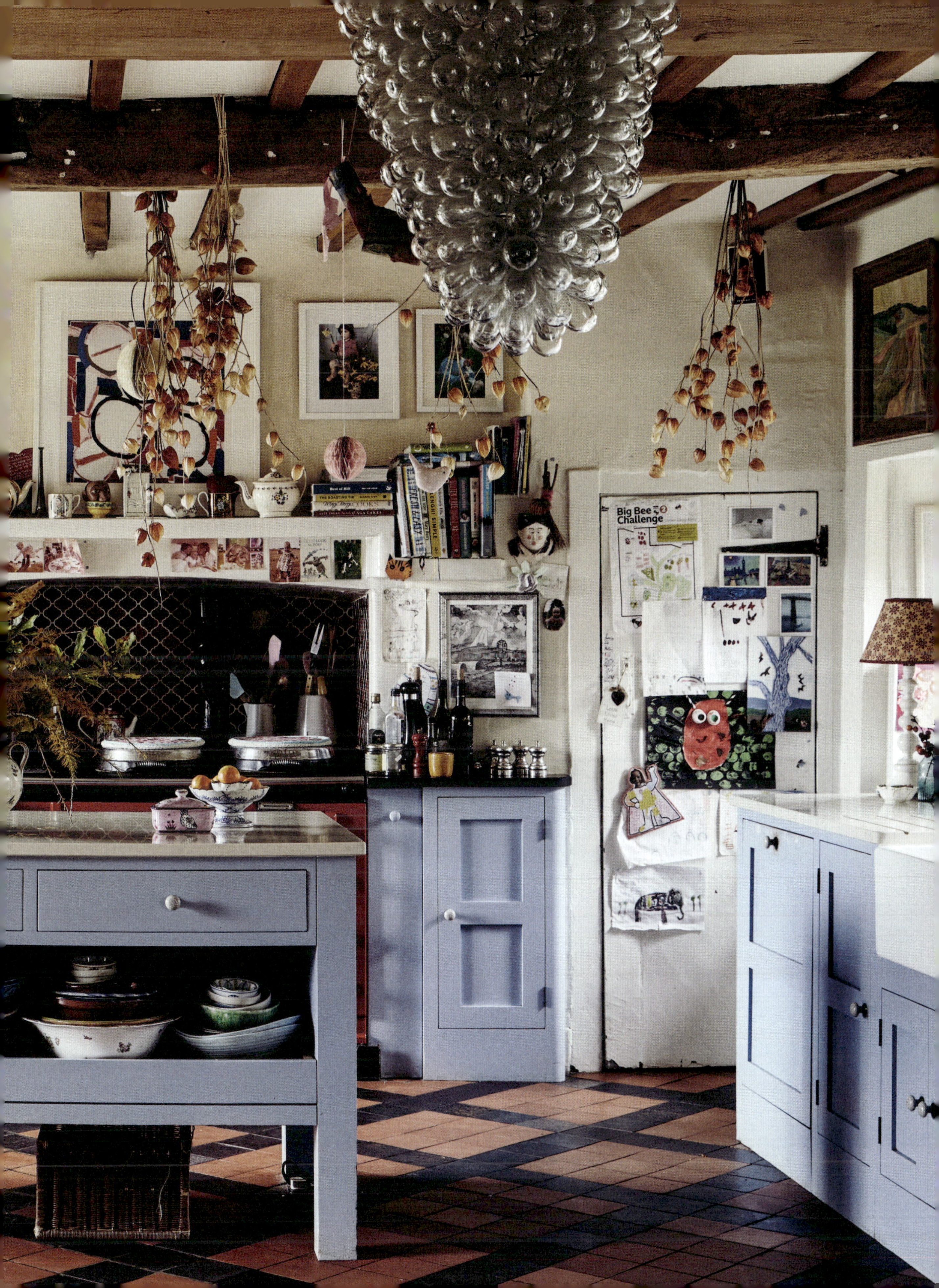
Big Bee Challenge

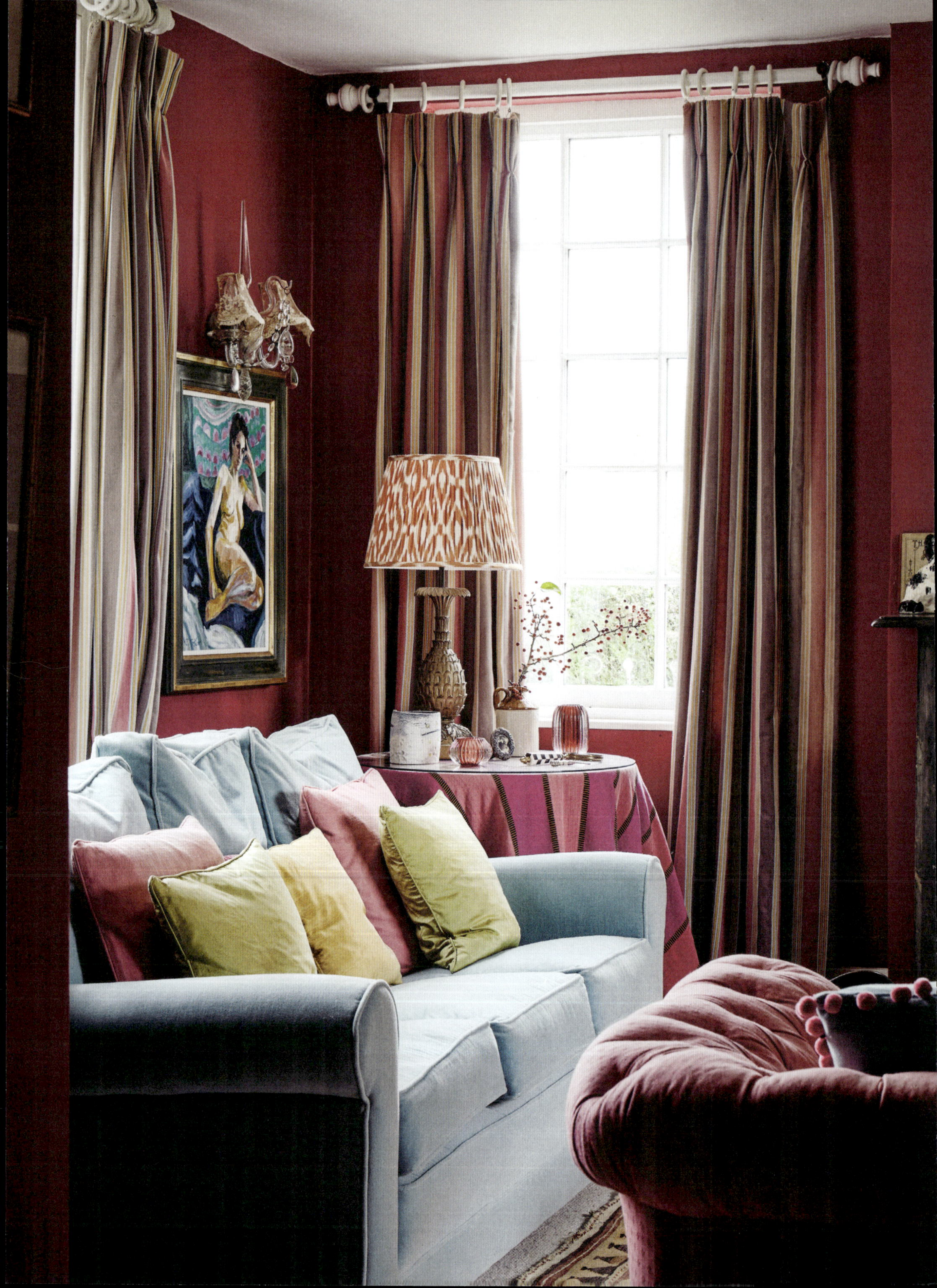

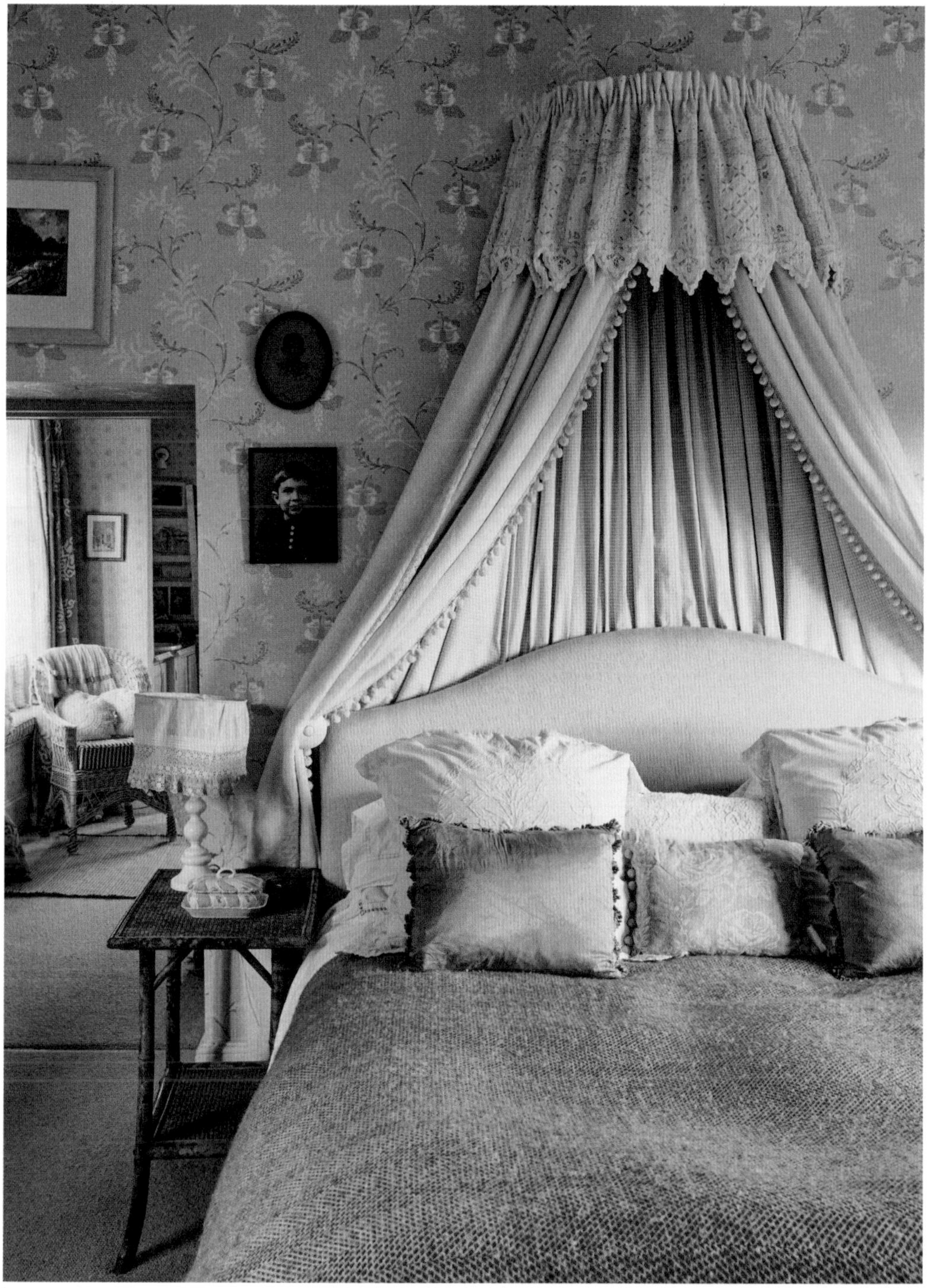

'A 300-YEAR-OLD HOUSE

has a dignity that I wanted to preserve,' explains Alice. 'While I planned to bring it up to date, I wanted to respect its age, and not lose the colour, creativity and quirky character that my four siblings and I had always cherished.'

The family inherited a great many pieces of furniture from Alice's parents' downsize. Among them are a dining table and chairs which Alice decided to move from a former dining room (which they turned into a study/sitting room) into one end of the former spacious drawing room. Alice felt that this room was better divided into two open-plan areas: a triple-aspect sitting room at one end and a dining area at the other. During her first year here, before she found premises at a nearby barn and opened the highly acclaimed Willow on the Farm, she ran her fledgling nursery from this very dining table, laying down cardboard to protect it from sticky fingers.

Alice wanted to refresh and lighten the upstairs. The long, dark corridor upstairs originally had a single 20-watt lamp to light its entirety and she remembers dashing as quickly as possible along it as a child. Years later she felt the corridor lacked an opening at the dead end and would also benefit from more light. She had a big new window put in at the darkest, creepiest stretch of the corridor, wallpapered it in a sunny yellow, added five lights where originally there had been one, and had an old staircase opened up at the far end.

Alice had always dreamed of a having a large bathroom with space for a sofa. The master bedroom did have a bathroom, but a small one with a dressing room in between. The two rooms were duly knocked into one large, luxurious bathroom with not just a sofa but a fireplace too. Three towel-wrapped girls often curl up here for bath-time chats.

Elsewhere upstairs, walls were repapered and curtains replaced, but the wonderful creaking bedsteads that Alice and her siblings had bounced on as children remained unchanged, and many pieces of furniture have not been moved for over forty years. It is a true fusion of old and new, the old embellished with a breath of new life.

As well as the free-spirited nature of her childhood, another vital ingredient of growing up here was the art and colour that had surrounded her family. Alice's mother had encouraged and inspired an artistic instinct in her children, which Alice likewise passes onto her own children. It features too in the wonderful nursery that she runs in a nearby barn. A house that has always been centred on family and fun, colour and creativity, has not changed; it has simply evolved to meet the tastes and needs of the new generation.

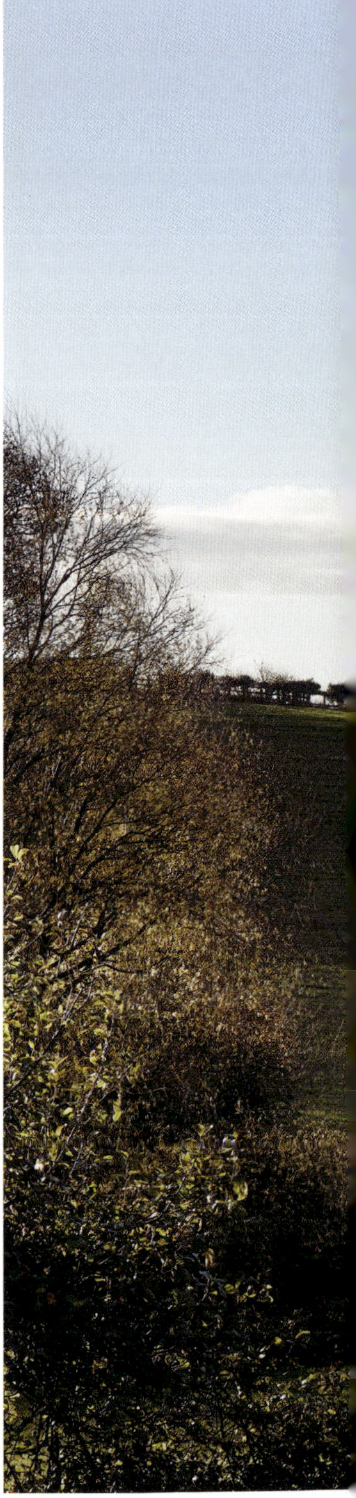

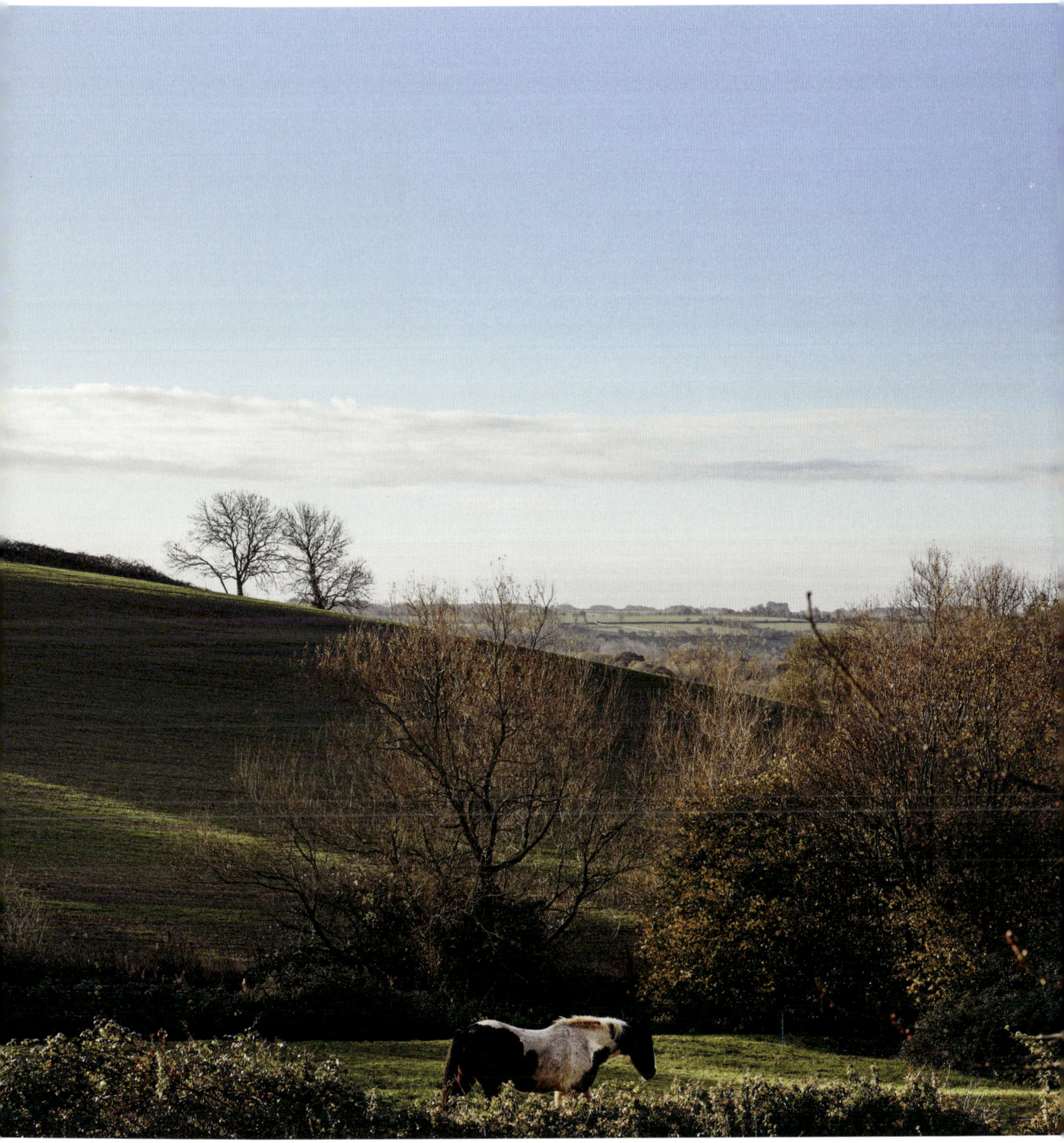

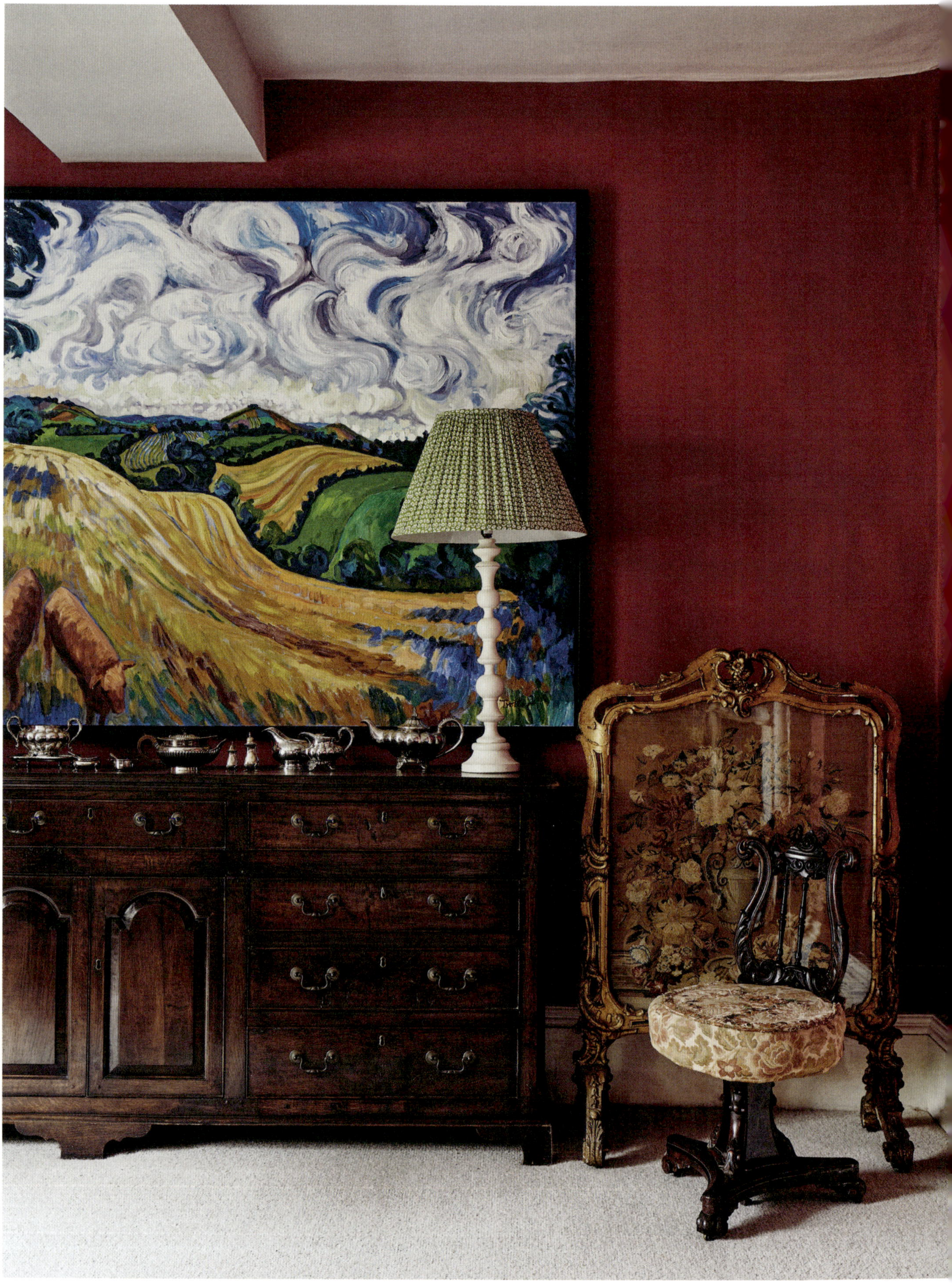

'ENGLAND'S HERITAGE IS IMPORTANT TO ME.

I try to impart to my own children, as well as the pupils in my nursery, an appreciation of what country life means: a respect for farming and livestock, history and heritage and all the glories of our rural surroundings.'

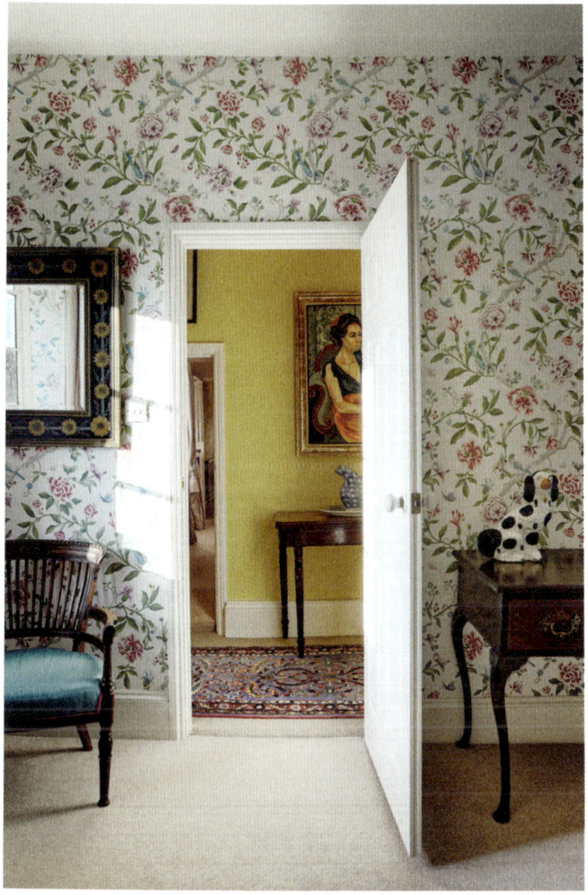

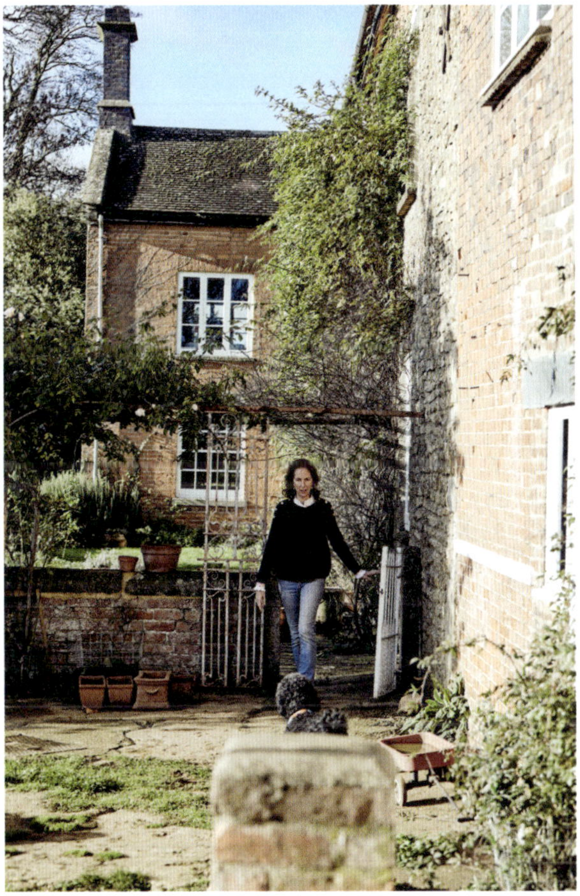

A WELL-KEPT SECRET

A magical 500-year-old thatched cottage has been sympathetically brought back to life with respect and imagination, by the creative Carlton Paget family.

It would need a happy accident to stumble upon Water Lane House. The Carlton-Paget family had rented in the village for seven years without ever clapping eyes on it. 'GPS doesn't stand a chance,' says Fi, 'because Water Lane is not in fact a road, but a footpath along a stream.' This added instant appeal for her three children, who were captivated by the 'secret house'. The house itself did not disappoint; the ancient, wonky thatched cottage smothered in roses could be straight from a children's fairy-tale.

Garden designer Fi took one look at the tangled garden and saw extraordinary potential. But the house was not a place for the faint hearted, with its sagging thatch sprouting moss and dandelions. The previous owner had been a widowed lady who had lived out her days at Water Lane House. 'It was far from a show home,' laughs Fi. Even so, the family put in an offer instantly.

On a practical level, aside from the urgent issue of rethatching certain parts, the survey showed up little that was of structural concern. Brickwork, windows and doors were in good shape, and there were plenty of redeeming features. Fi was determined to make any changes sympathetic and respectful to the house's history.

'We have tried to add to the house, rather than alter or customise it,' explains Fi. In five hundred years it must have changed hands many times, and each time evolved a little more. Its 14th-century heart was a two-up, two-down, which today makes up the kitchen and family room downstairs with two bedrooms above. Here the beams remain wonky, the staircase crooked and the walls bulging with age.

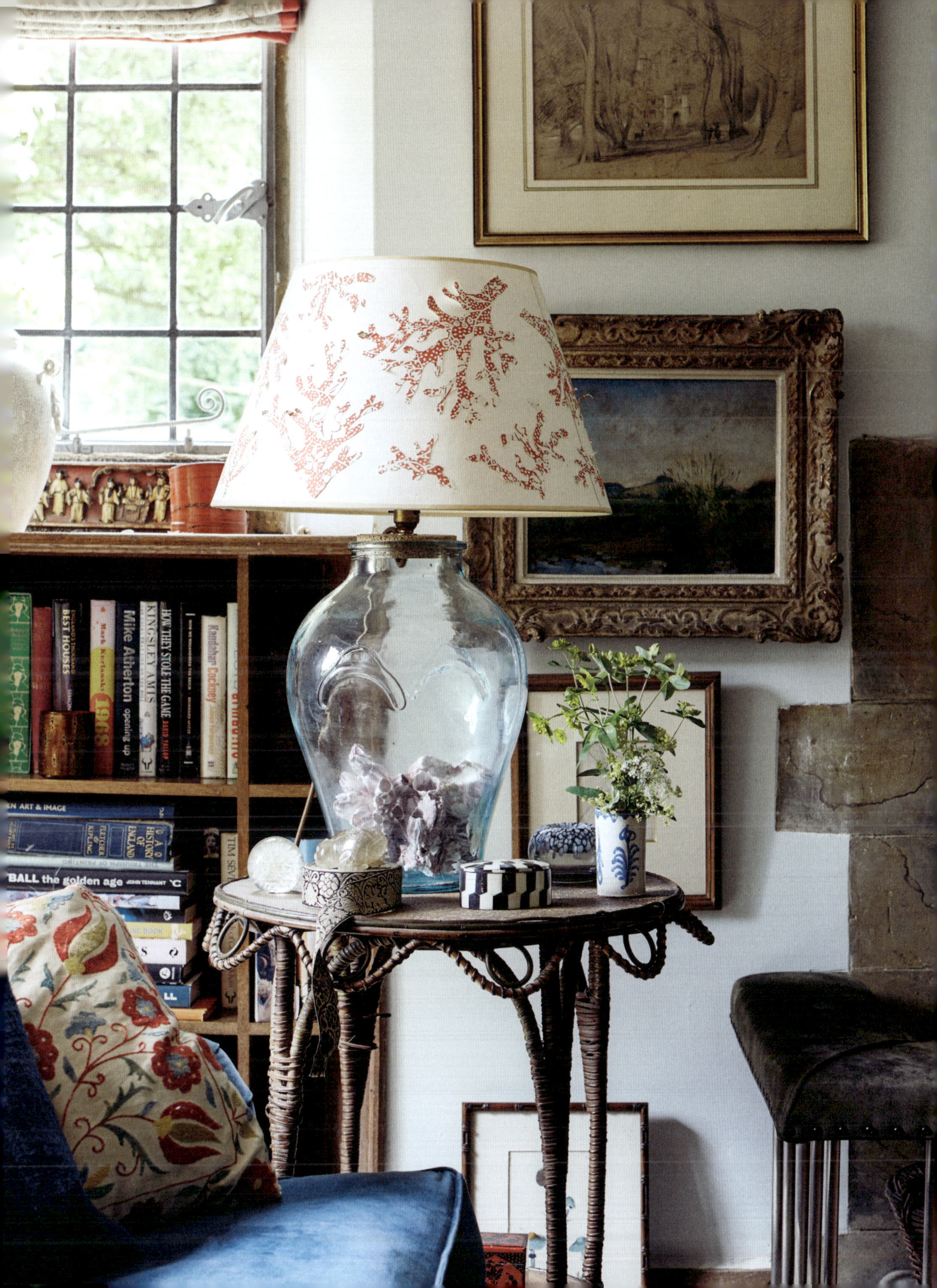
BEST HOUSES
Mike Atherton opening up
KINGSLEY AMIS
HOW THEY STOLE THE GAME
Kandahar Cockney
1968
ART & IMAGE
A HISTORY OF ENGLAND
FLETCHER & KIPLING
BALL the golden age JOHN TENNANT

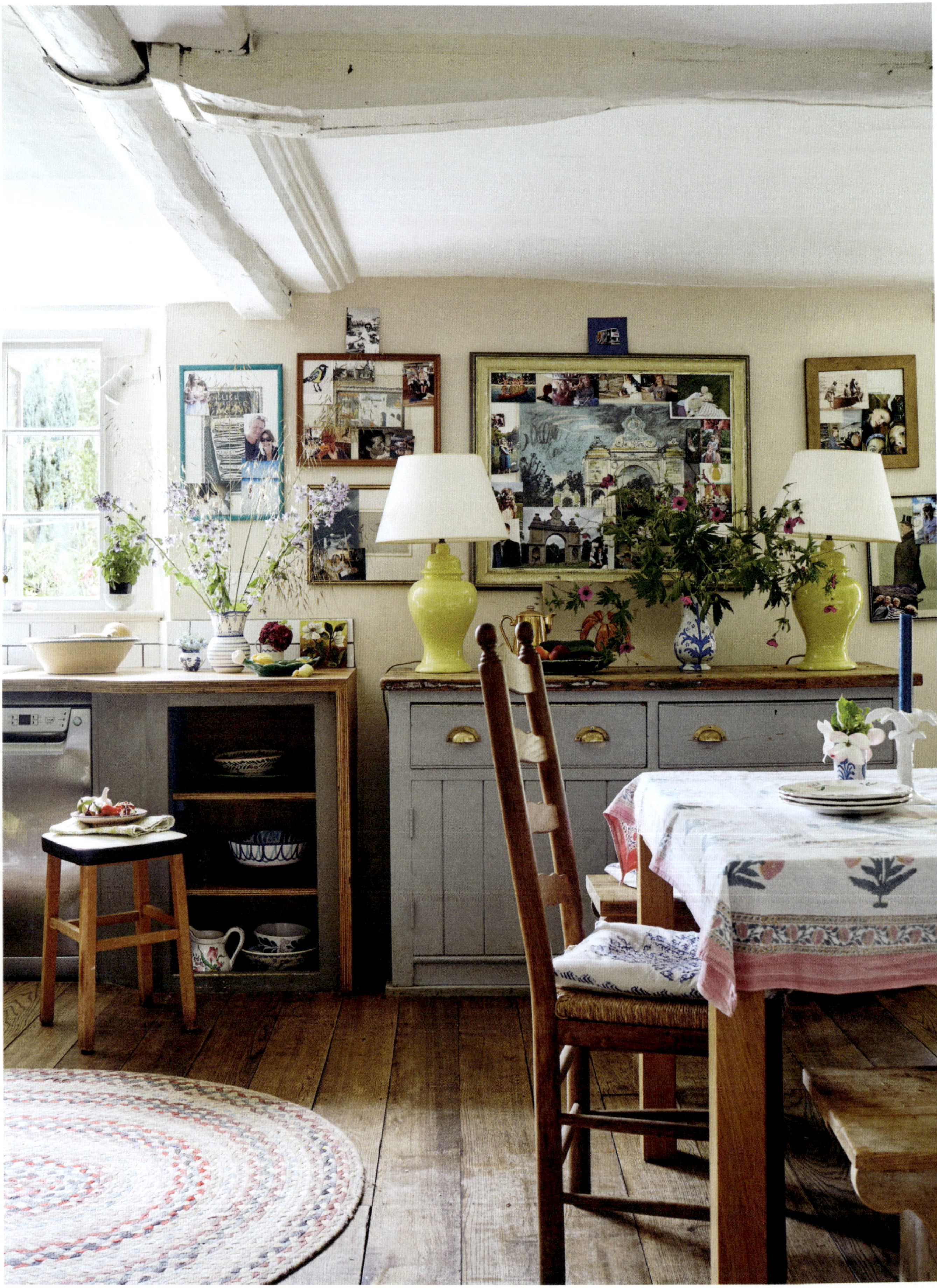

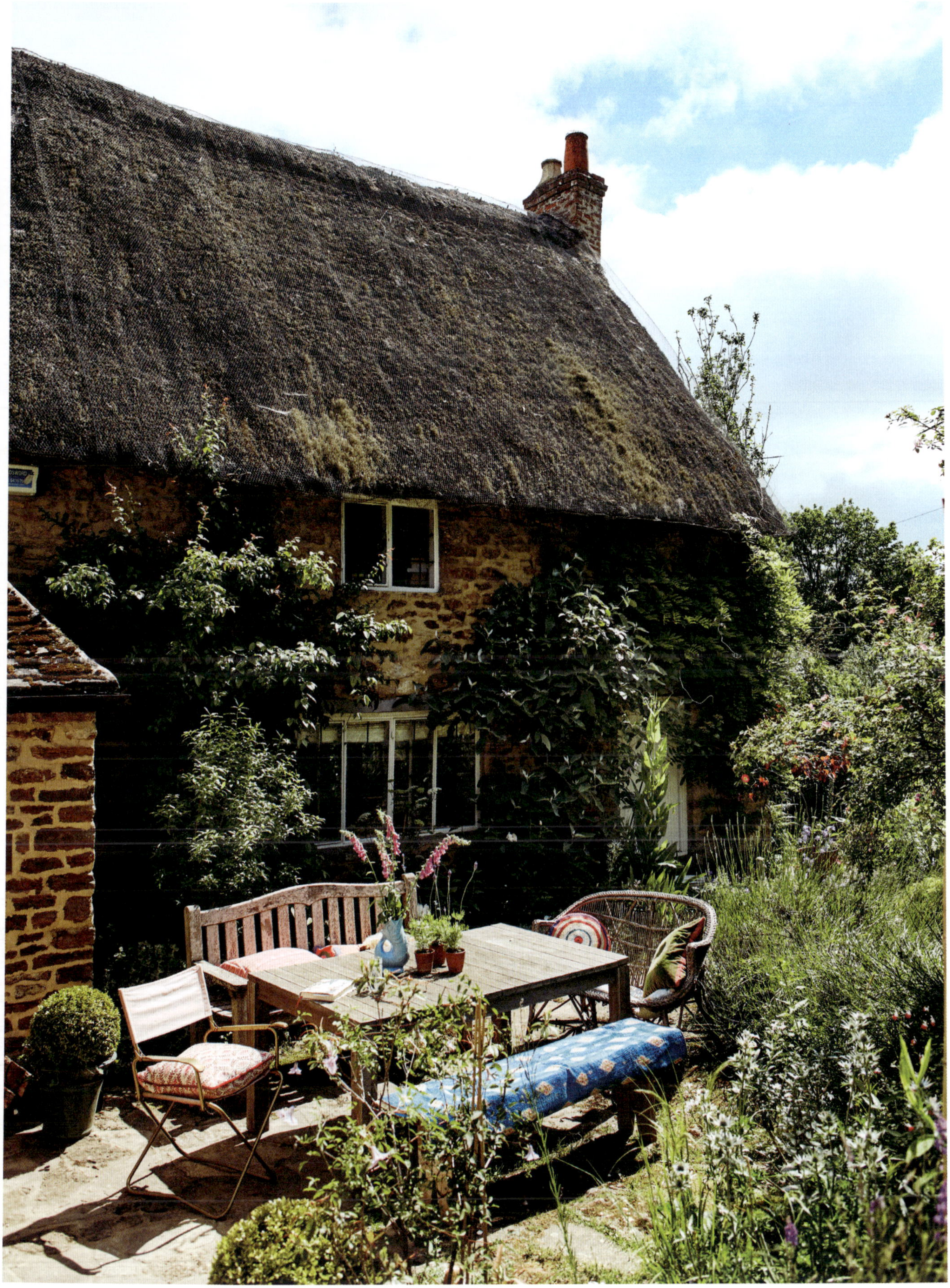

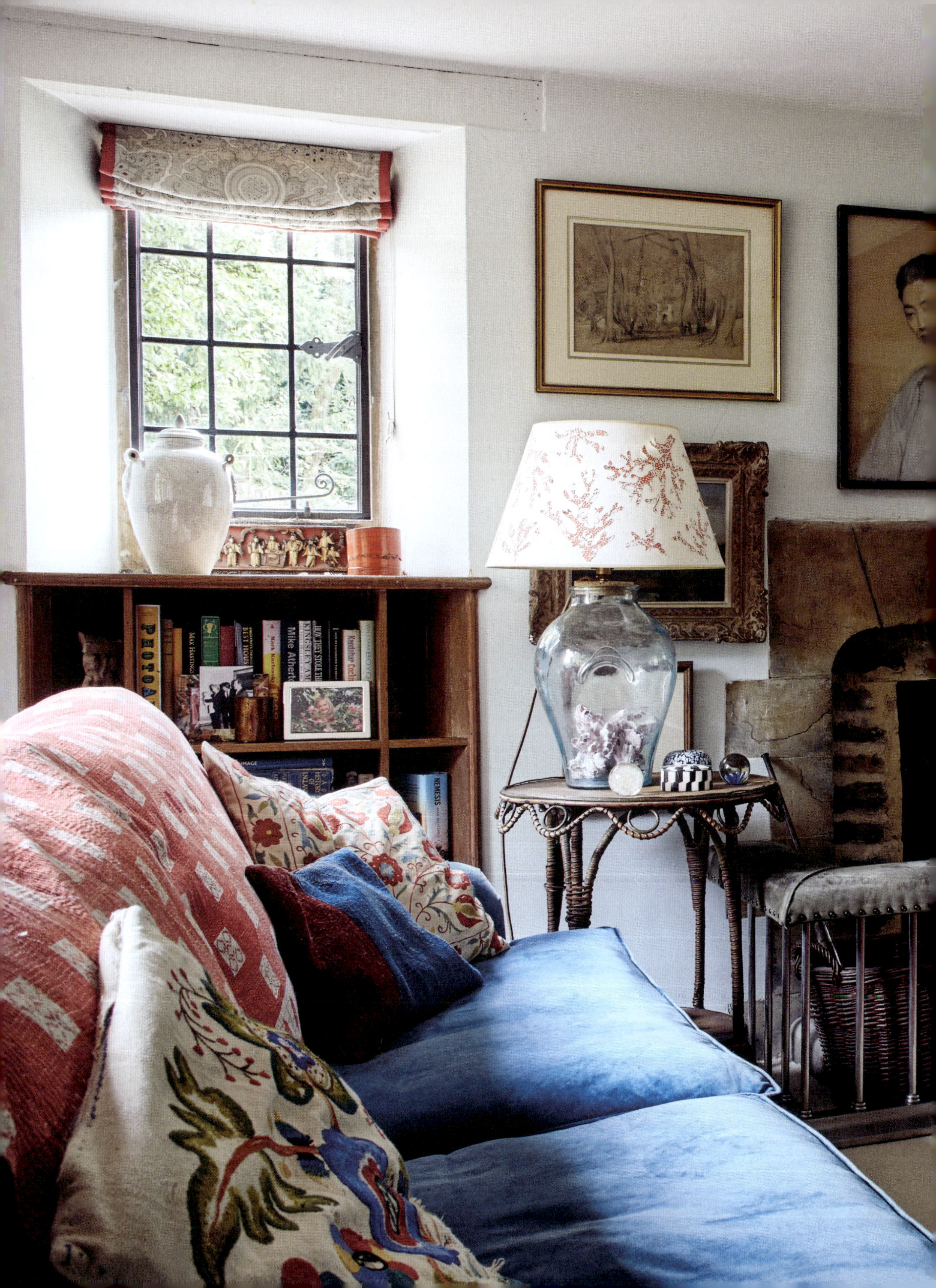
MAX HASTINGS
NEMESIS

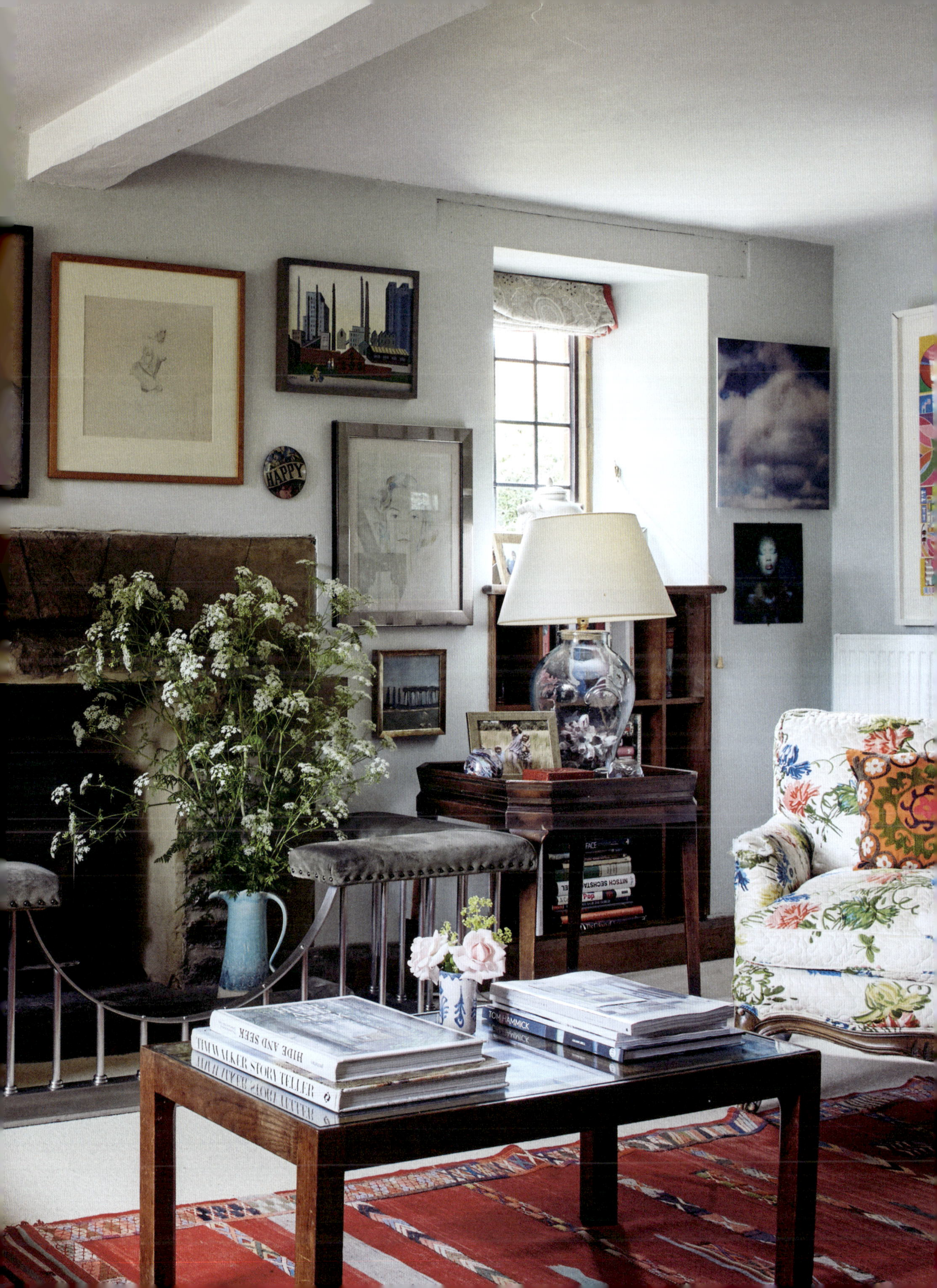
HAPPY
HIDE AND SEEK
TIM WALKER STORY TELLER
TOM HAMMICK

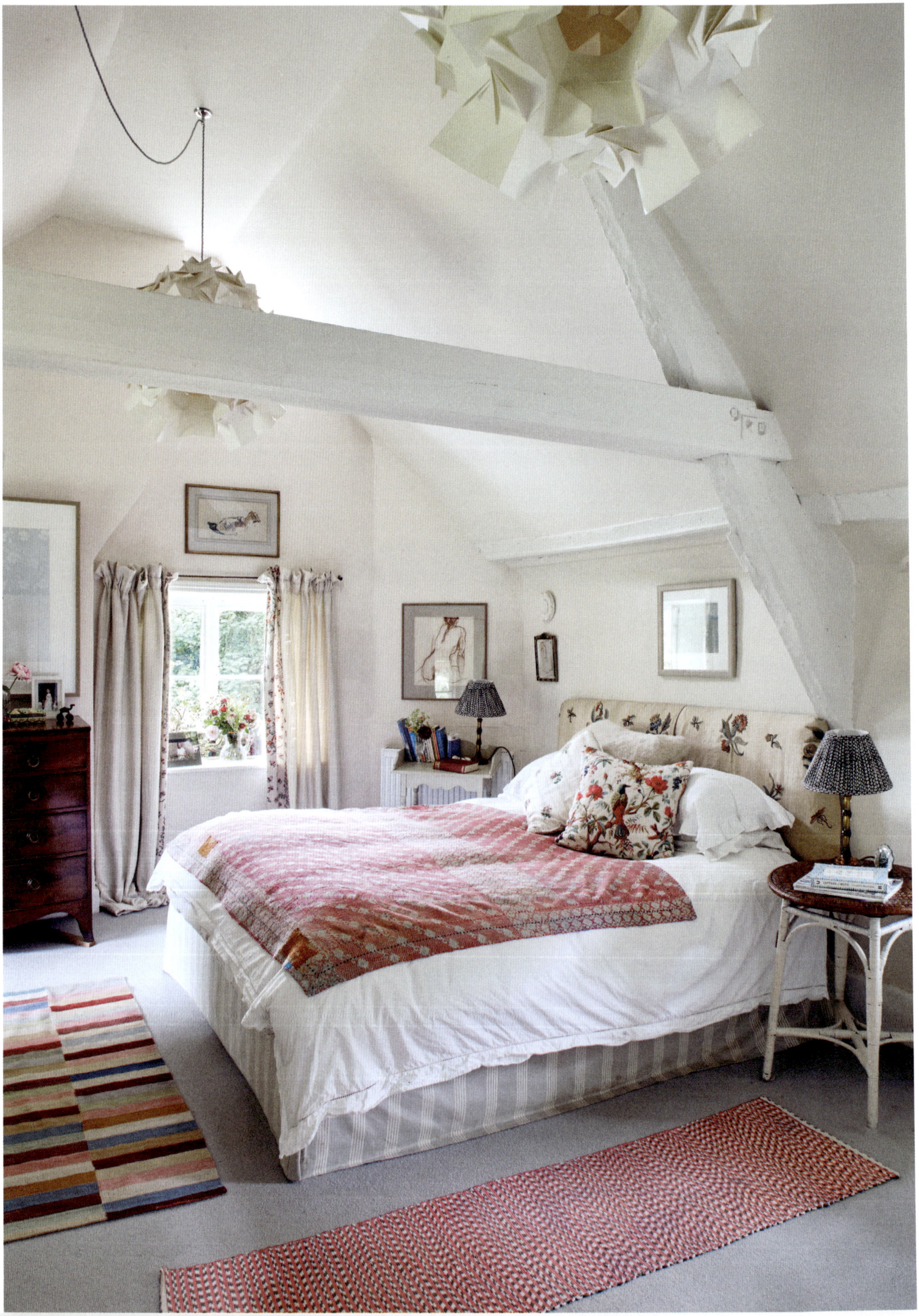

'THERE IS A COMFORTING AIR

of peace and stability here created by previous generations that have lived here and added to the spirit of the house.'

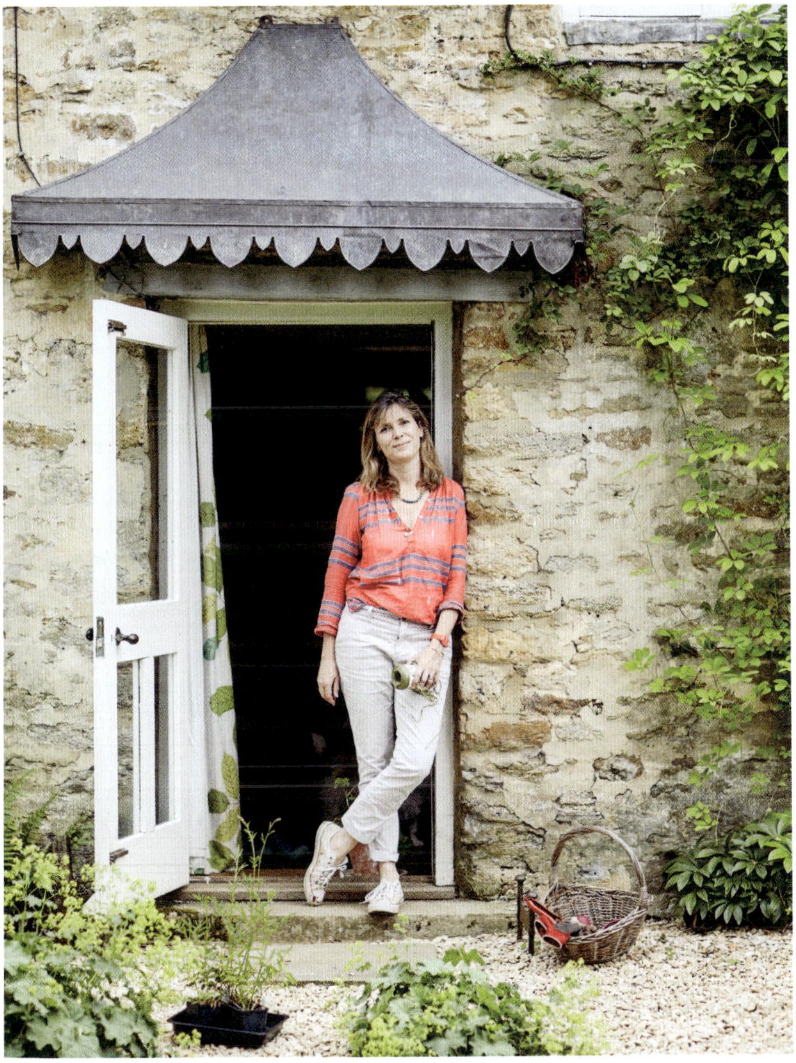

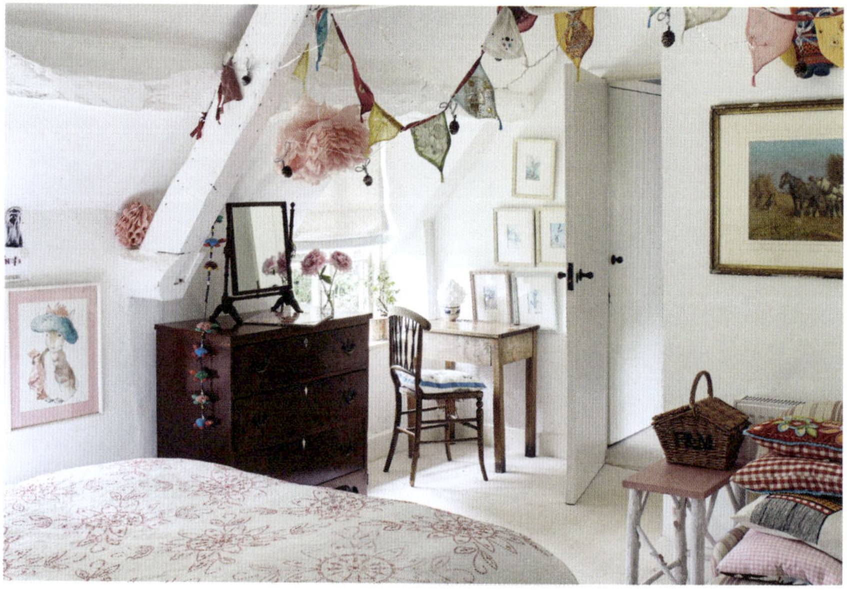

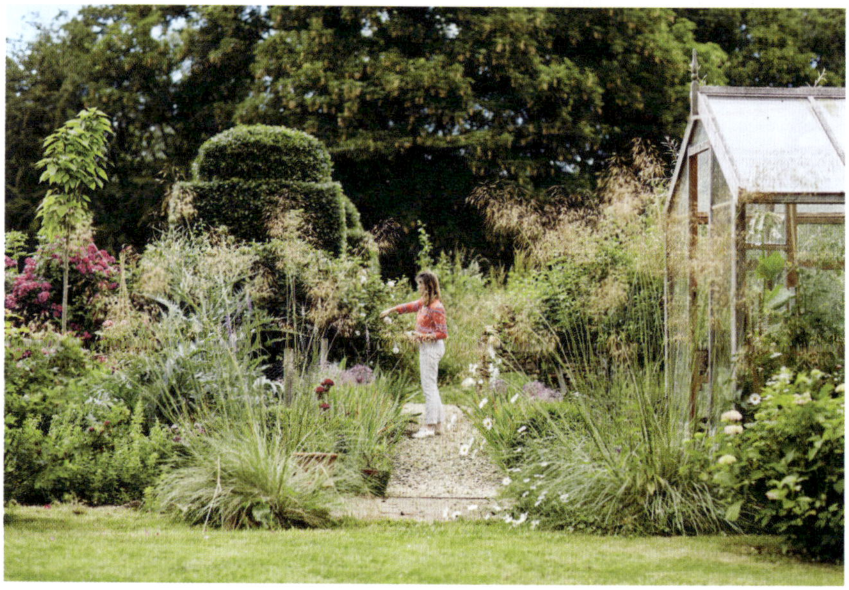

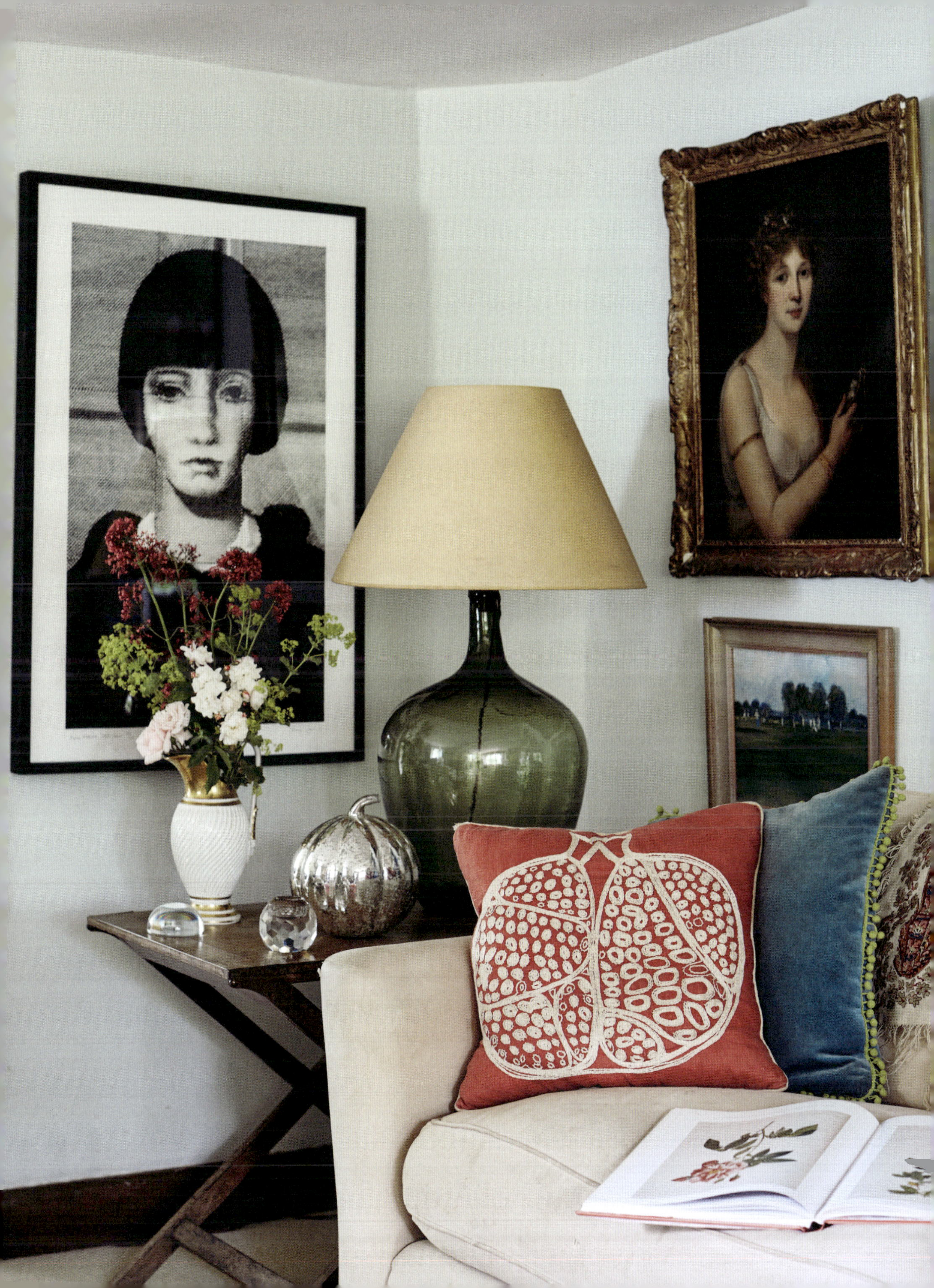

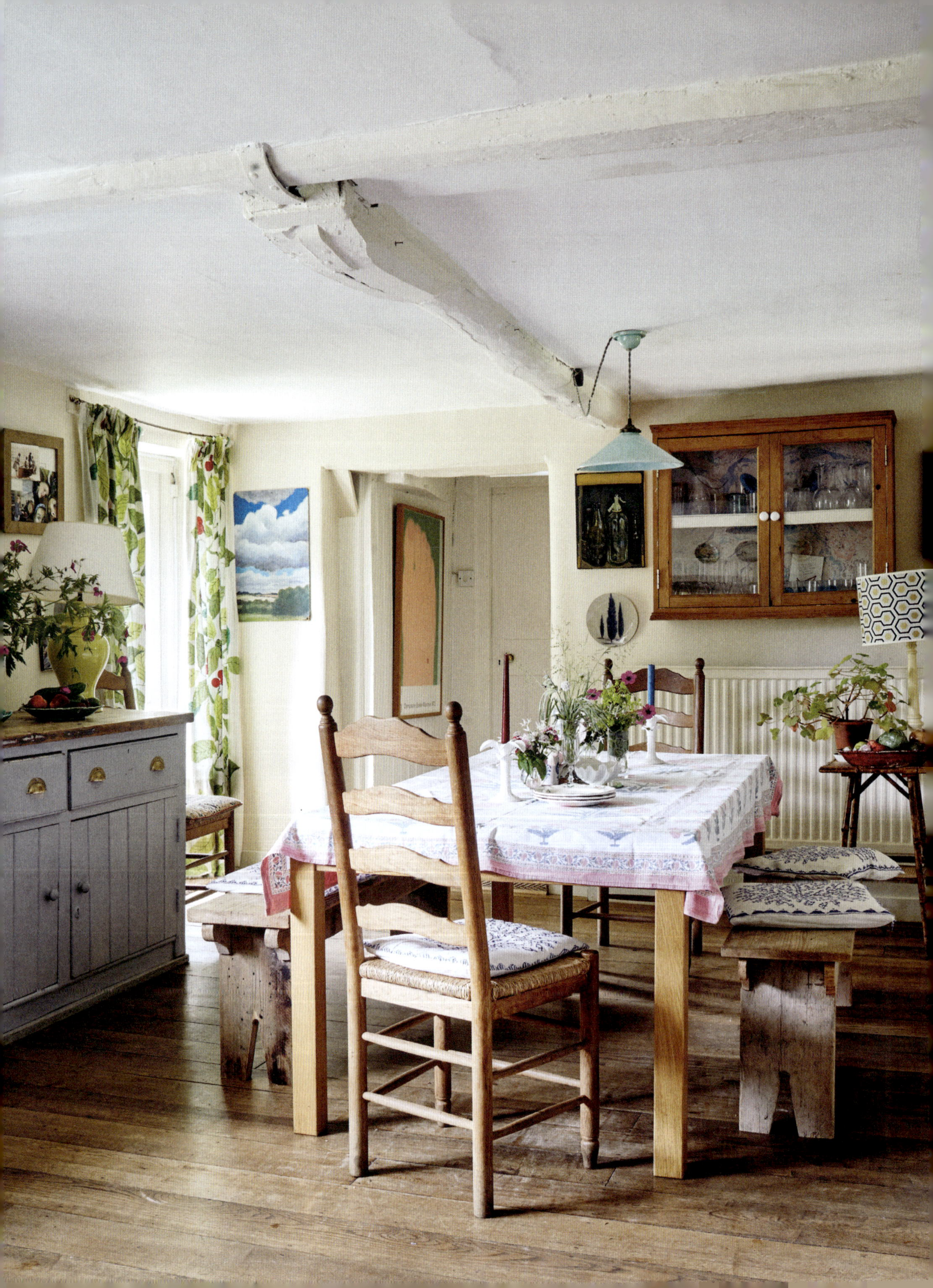

Over the centuries, the house was gradually extended. Around a hundred years ago, a cross-gable extension was added in the Arts and Crafts style, creating a large sitting room downstairs and two bedrooms above, all with intricately carved woodwork and architectural ironmongery typical of its era. In the 1960s a wooden extension was added to the end of the sitting room to use as a music room. The house seems to have adjusted gracefully, and the different eras blend easily.

Fi wanted to help the tired house without compromising its character. The careworn kitchen needed updating, but she decided against a glossy modern kitchen. Flickering strip lights and peeling Formica units were removed. She had no-frills plywood units installed and she recycled freestanding cupboards. The Aga was moved into a central position and a large mirror was hung behind it. 'The ceilings in this part are lowish, so we find ways to bring light and an illusion of space,' says Fi, who also painted walls in pale shades and whitewashed the beams.

The rest of the house was likewise given a sympathetic update rather than a drastic overhaul. Fresh paint and new carpets gave an instant facelift and Fi set about furnishing in the eclectic and laid-back style that comes naturally to her. The house had a few surprises in store for them as they discovered its history – at one point while stripping off old wallpaper before painting a wall, she came upon the loveliest floral paper. Fi pasted it back down to leave an imperfectly perfect bathroom wall.

Colour and creativity are everywhere, and despite this being a very English home there is a sense of the wider world here in the art and furnishings effortlessly put together. Fi developed an eye for oriental furnishings from her father, a renowned expert in South-East Asian antiquities and artefacts. There is confidence in the art, furnishings and colour here, in which styles, provenance and eras are mixed, apparently haphazardly.

On a summer's day the doors are flung open and pets and family stream in and out. Fi is usually to be found deep in a flower bed. Her skill is evident. There is form and subtle structure everywhere, plus vistas, mystery paths and the charm, colour and (deliberate) abandon that typifies the English cottage garden. If ever fairies might be found at the bottom of any garden, this would be the place.

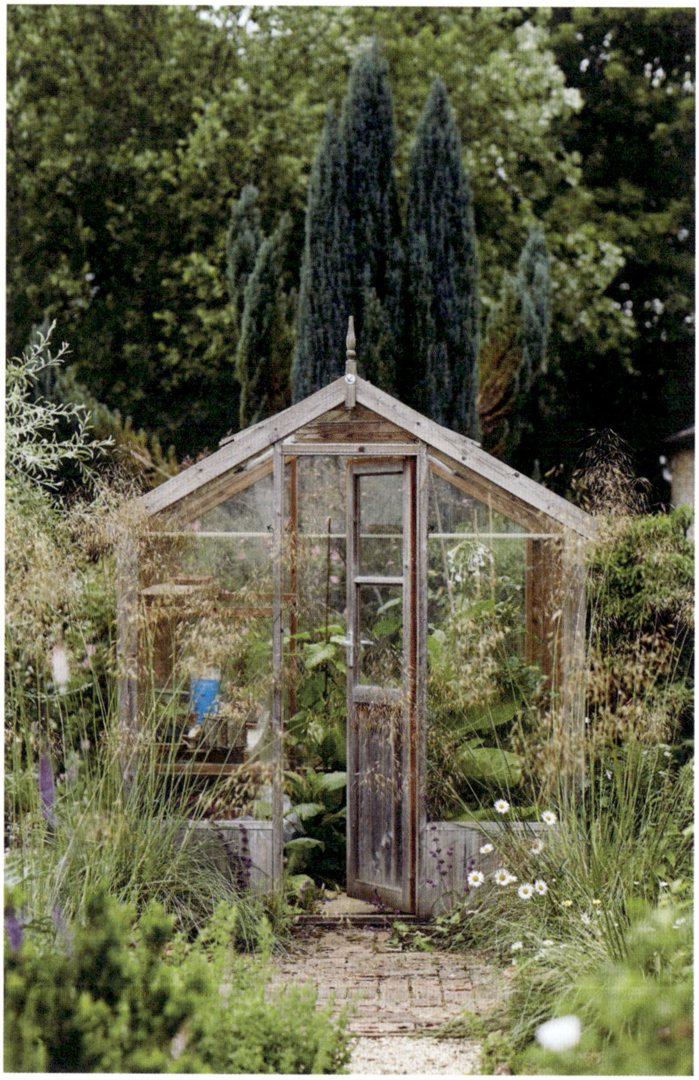

'I GREW UP IN A HOUSE

that was full of colour, art, flowers, textiles and overseas finds and the happy disarray of family life. I'm not sure if I meant to replicate it, but in many ways I have.'

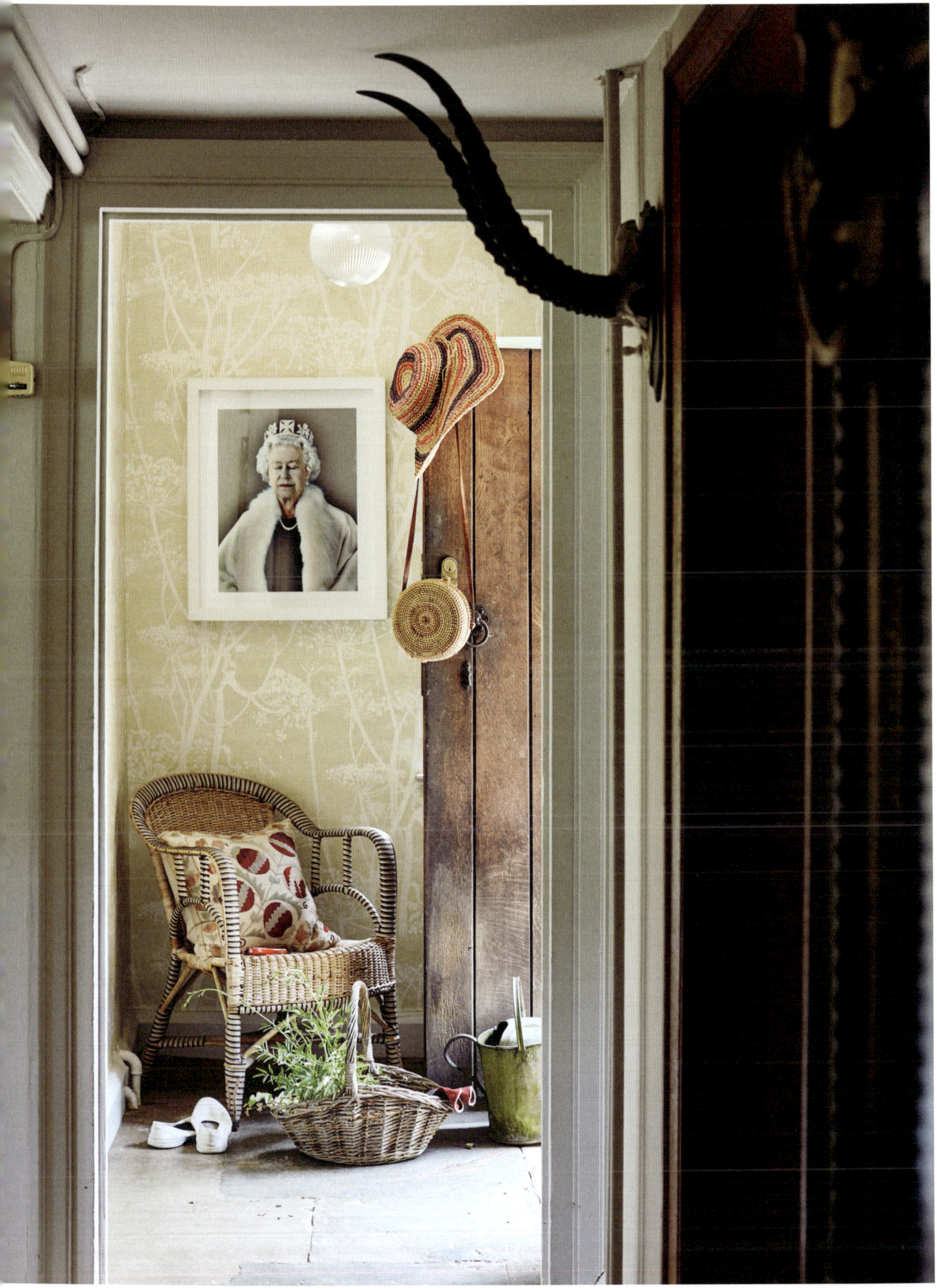

A HOME WITH HISTORY

Finding the perfect period country house for their growing family was no mean feat for Charlie and Louisa Butters, but when eventually they stumbled upon the right one, their long wait was worthwhile.

Louisa and Charlie Butters had all but given up hope of ever finding the perfect house in the country. They had started looking when Louisa was expecting their first baby, Cecilia, but after months of fruitless searching they were increasingly dispirited. It was more out of habit than real hope that Louisa found herself one Sunday night resignedly scrolling down the same old houses on Rightmove. She spotted a new one in their search area and an instinctive bolt of hope flared up. A period village house in north Buckinghamshire set over three floors, with five bedrooms and two generous reception rooms as well as a large garden.

Louisa's instincts had been spot on; this was indeed the house for them. The village was perfect: a hop and a skip to Bicester, yet rural and idyllically unspoilt, with a great pub and a wonderful farm shop. The house sat on the edge of the village, cloaked in its own secluded garden and backing onto farmland. Built in warm local stone, with 17th-century origins, it had lovely proportions, high ceilings, big windows and plenty of period features. They had an offer on the table within minutes.

It was in late June 2009 that the couple moved in. But they didn't have much time to put their feet up. Pregnant Louisa's nesting instinct went into a frenzy of home improvements. The house had recently been rewired and replumbed, which meant that initial work was purely cosmetic. They paint ed throughout and had new ceiling and wall lights fitted to replace spotlights. Louisa has a natural flair for interiors, and together with interior designer friends Bee O'Connell and Scarlett Brooksbank they enhanced the house's period character, while making it suitable for modern family life.

Structural work began a year later. The first essential job was replacing the floor-to-ceiling windows in the drawing room and master bedroom, which rattled and leaked. On close inspection the frames were found to be rotten in places. This was no simple project. The window frames were essential to the house's structure so the house had to be held up on stilts while the new windows were installed. Meanwhile Charlie unearthed some 1950s photographs of the garden, when it had been on show. The wonderful outdoor space had been neglected over the decades since, and Charlie completely redesigned it to bring it back to its former glory.

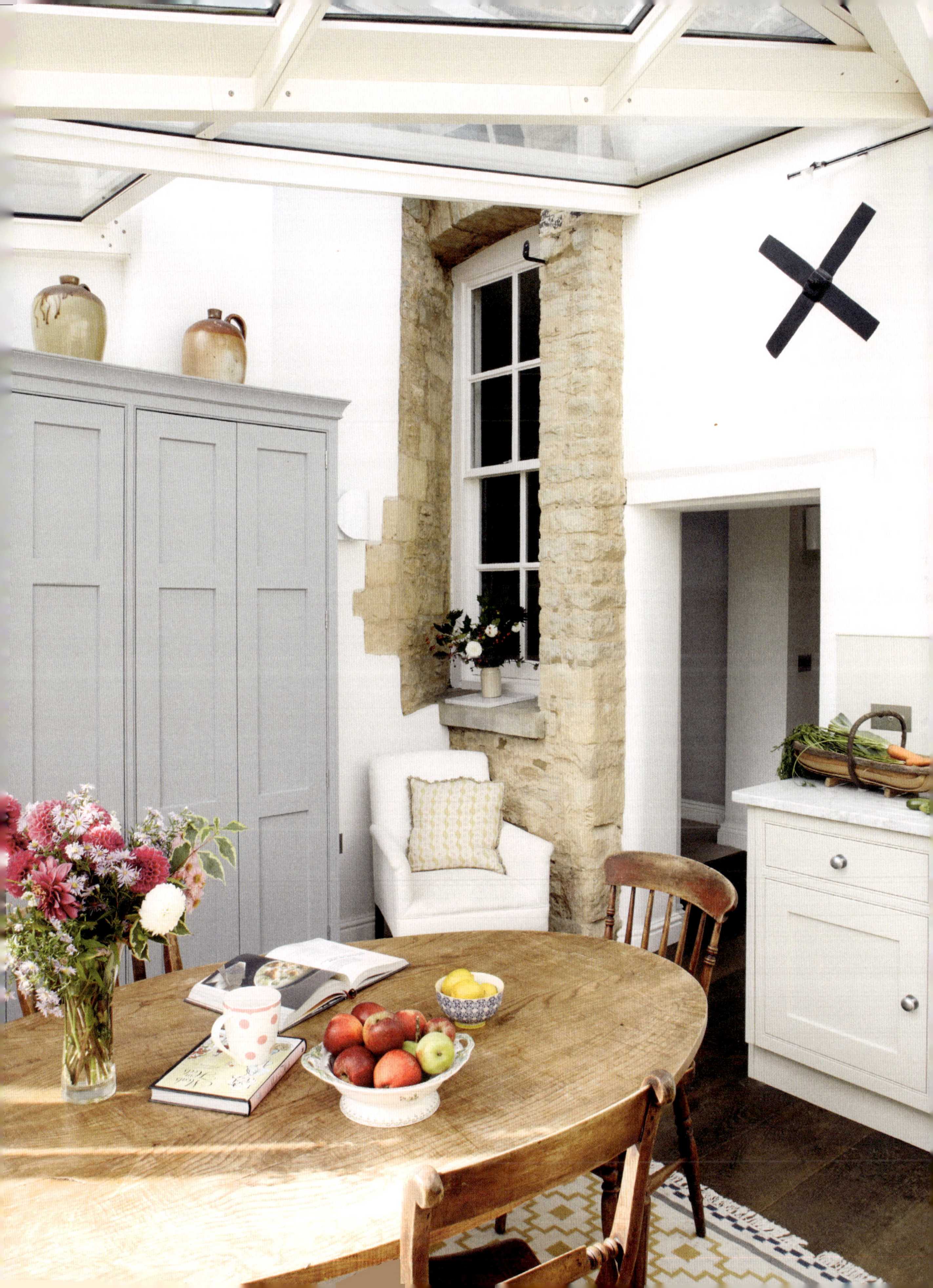

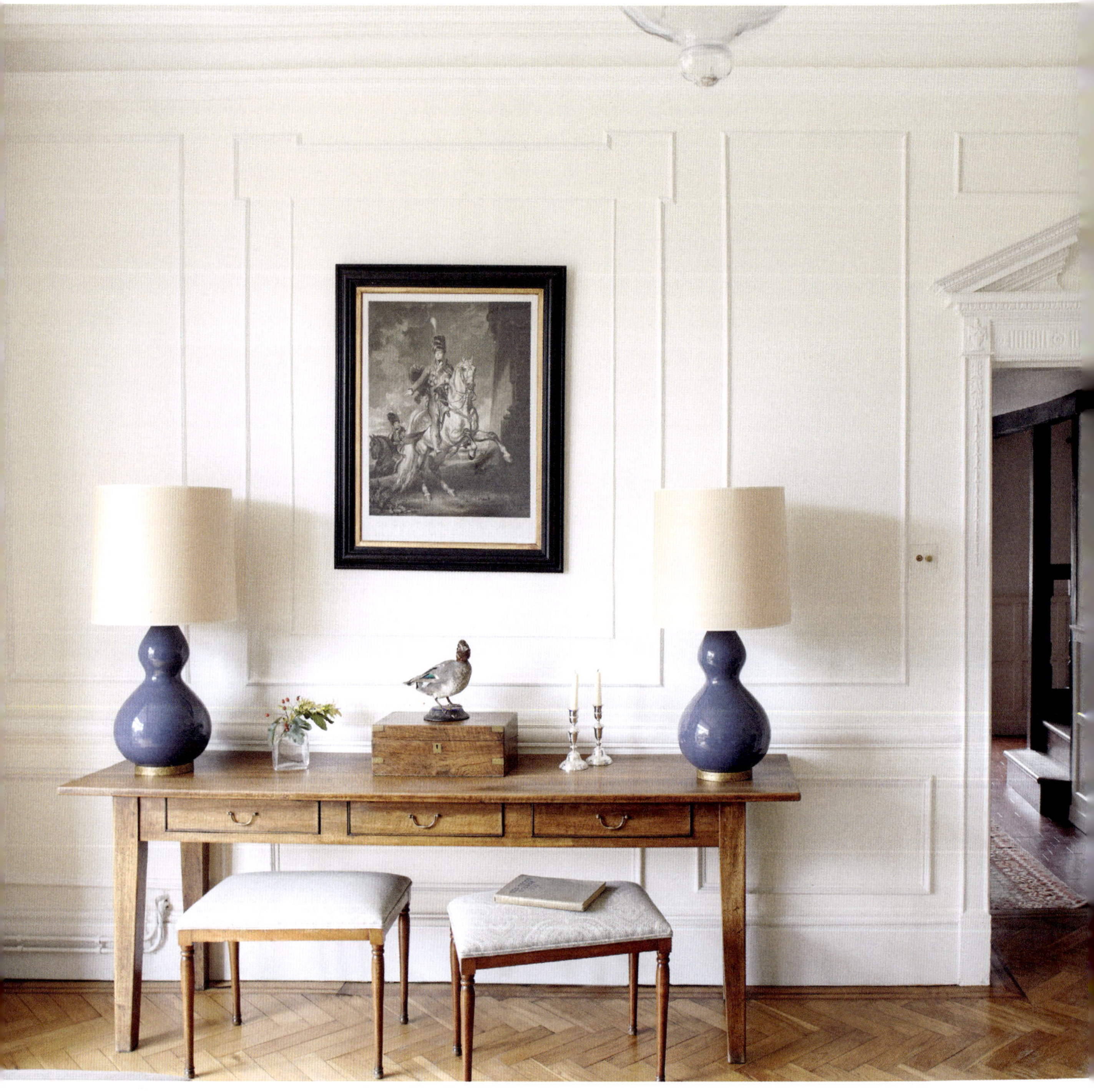

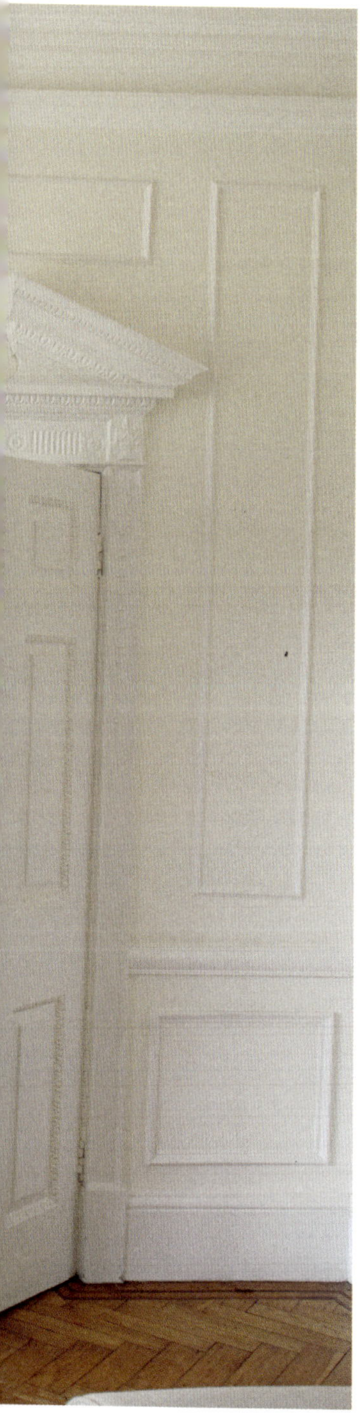

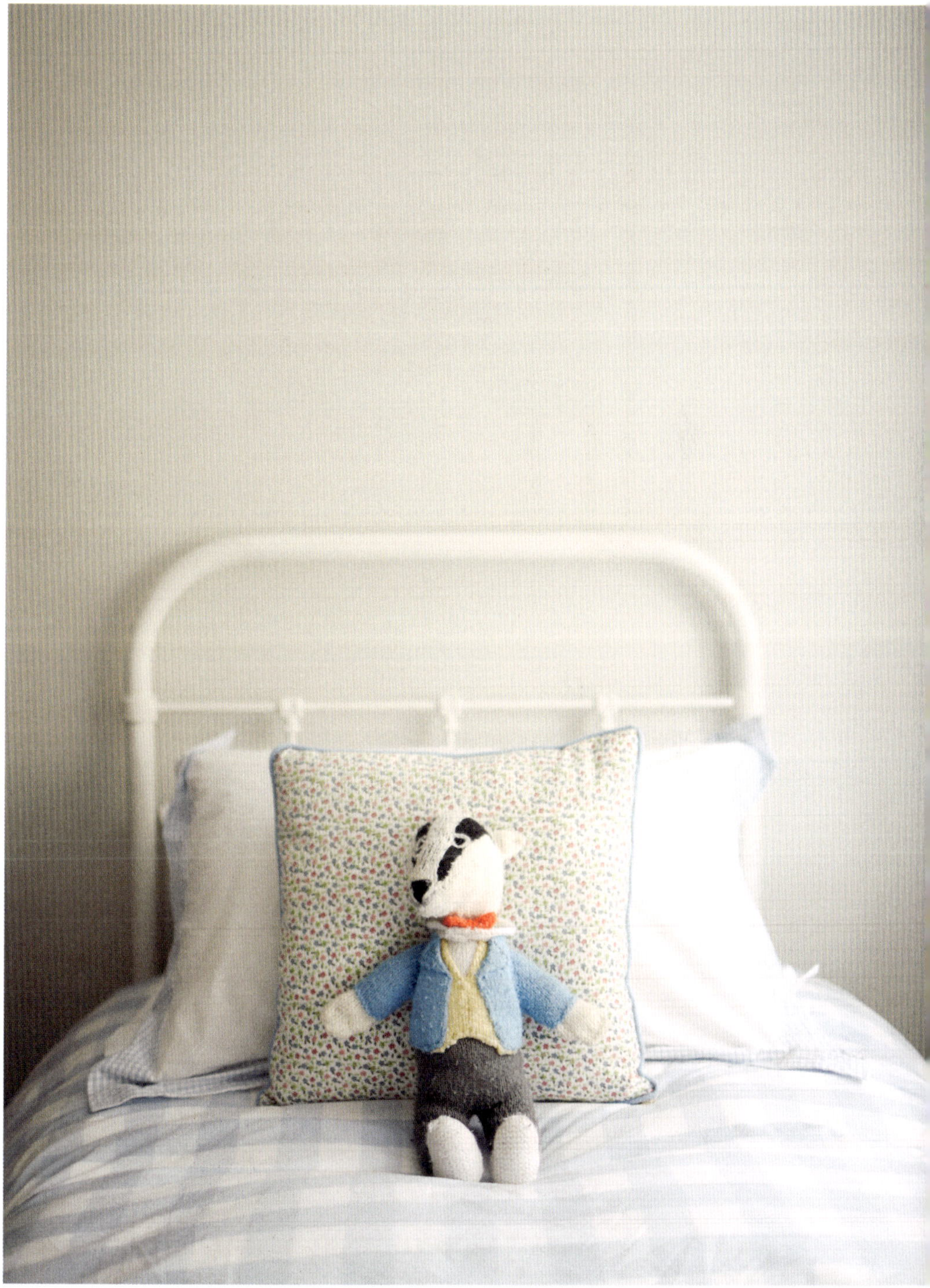

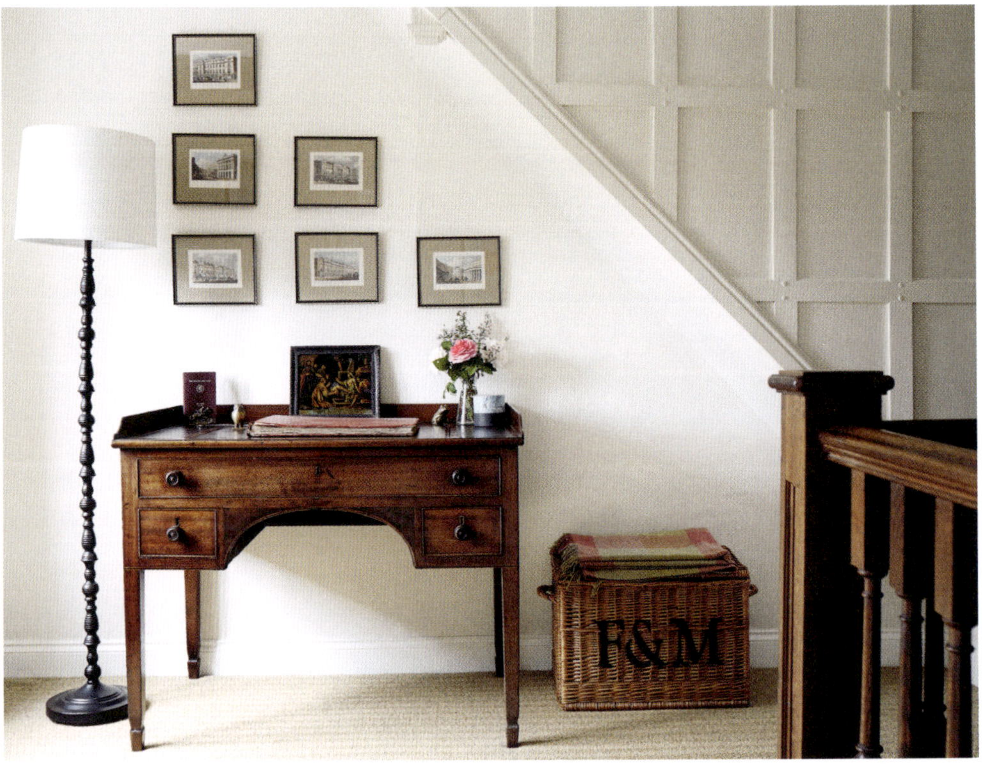
F&M

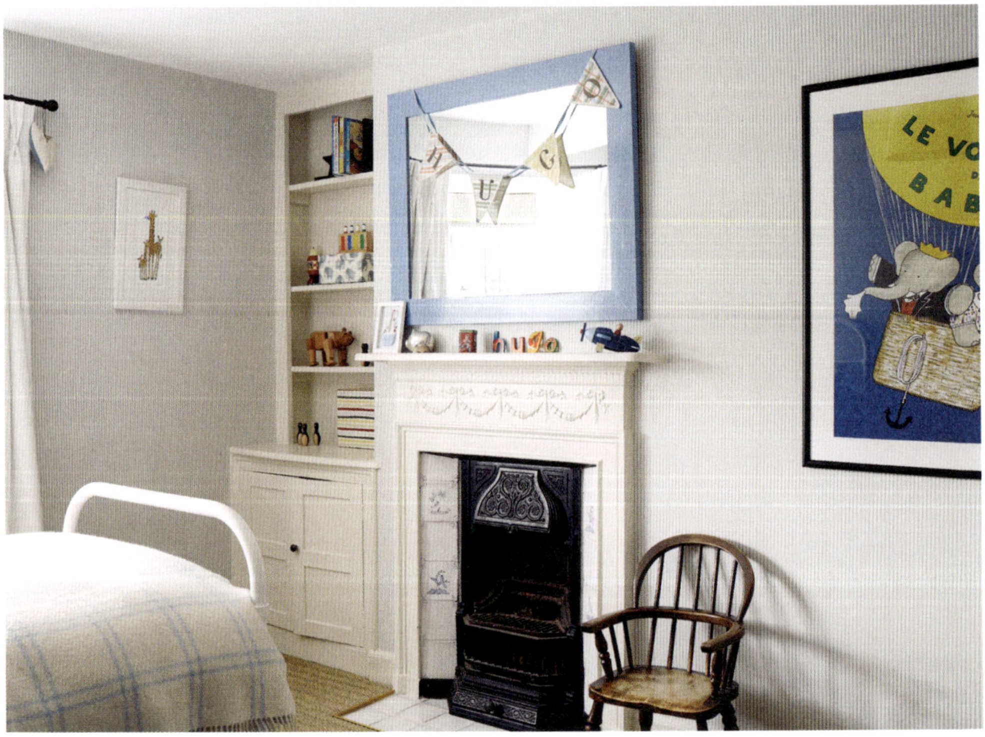

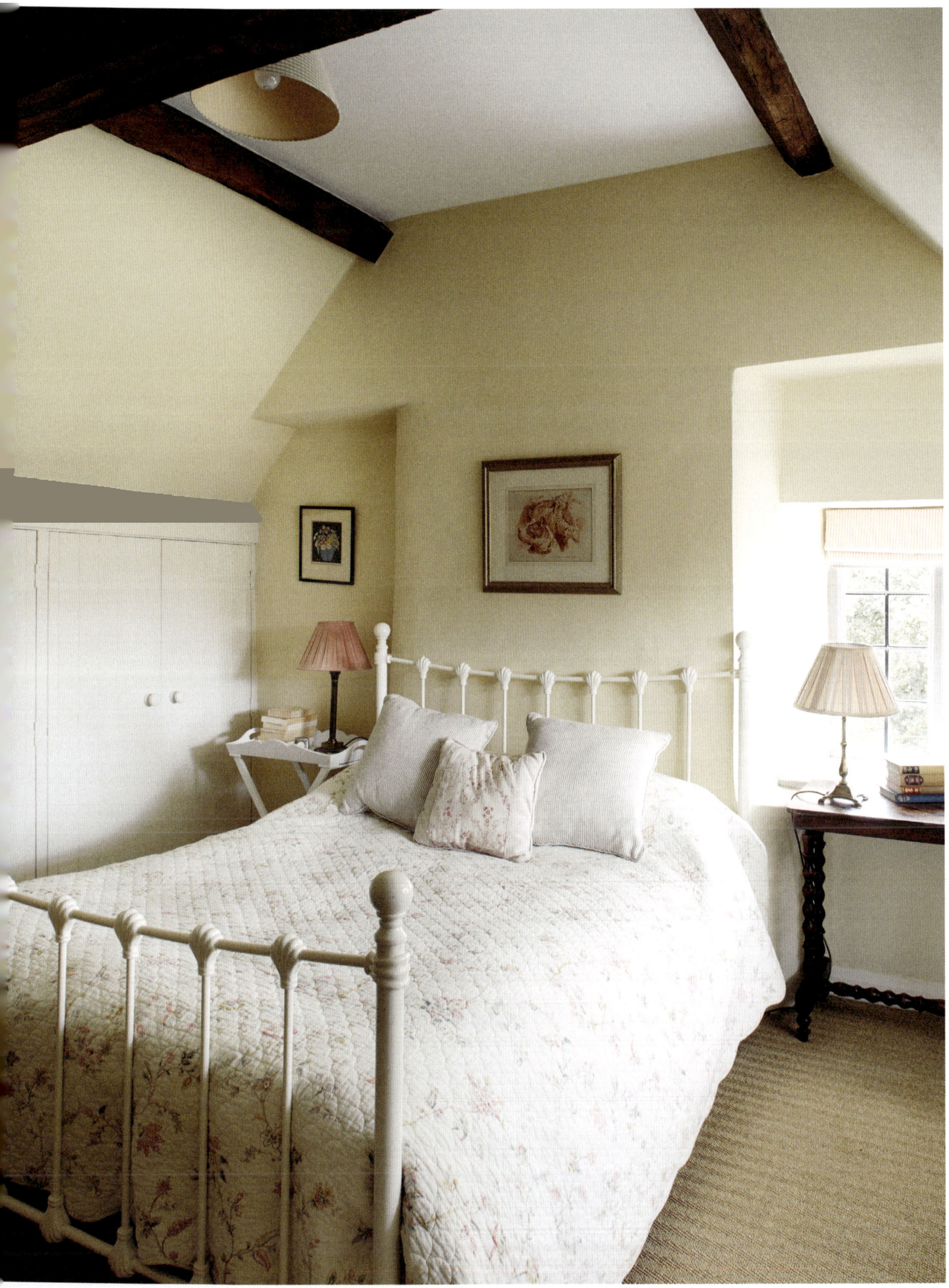

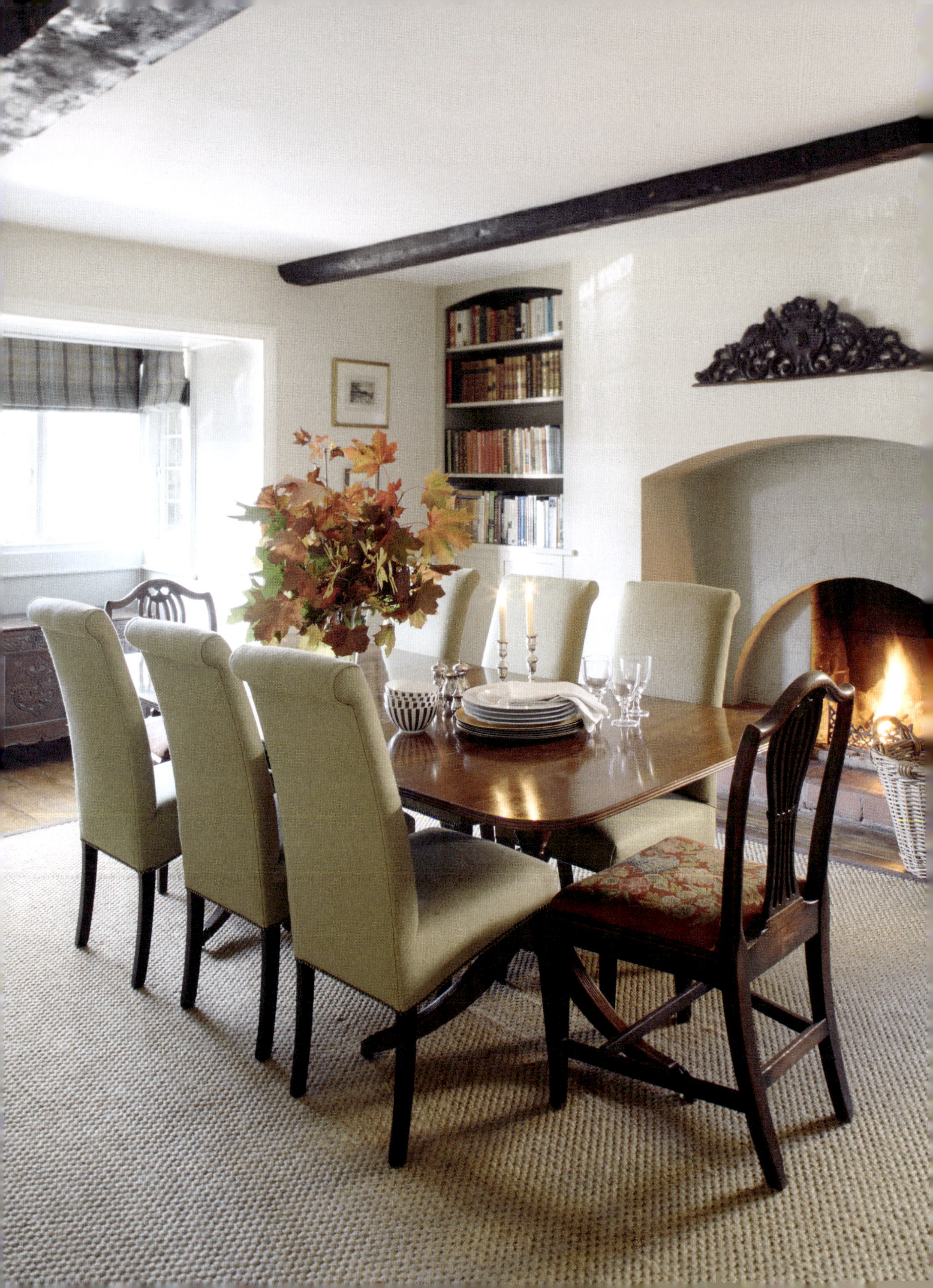

Time passed and the family were for the most part delighted with their new home, bar one remaining niggle for professional caterer Louisa: the kitchen. She longed for a larger and more practical kitchen for catering jobs and family meals. The kitchen was small, poky and dark, with little surface space and seating. It had a decent utility room/pantry attached, but neither room was quite big enough.

Work on the kitchen started in August and their second baby, Hugo, was born one month later. Louisa watched as calmly as she could, babe in arms, while part of her home was demolished. The project involved turning the former kitchen into a cosy family sitting room and gutting the ancient utility room next door to transform it into the working side of the kitchen. This space had an oppressive low ceiling with a small room above, so they had the ceiling knocked out to raise the roof to the rafters. The building's Grade-2 listing prevented Louisa and Charlie from knocking through the outside wall of this room to expand the space for a family kitchen, so the couple opened up all the windows and doors and had the family part of the kitchen built alongside. With its glass lantern roof and floor-to-ceiling windows, it has a lighter character than the other half, but with their lofty ceilings the two blend and offer a perfect work-life balance.

Bringing their home back to life has awakened an interest in the house's history. Louisa and Charlie always knew that the oldest part dated back to the 1800s, but they have since learnt that there has been a dwelling here since the 1600s that was originally a smallholding farmed by monks. After that it was the site of a royal equerry's hunting lodge. History abounds here, and the house's calm character implies a peaceful past. The greeting on the plaque above the front door seems particularly fitting: 'This house, though small, doth welcome all.'

'WE WANTED TO KEEP

a sense of calm flowing through the house, so we chose a pale and neutral colour scheme and added shots of strong colour to spruce it up.'

'AS THE HOUSE WAS LISTED
we made sure that all internal changes were sympathetic to the age and character of the house.'

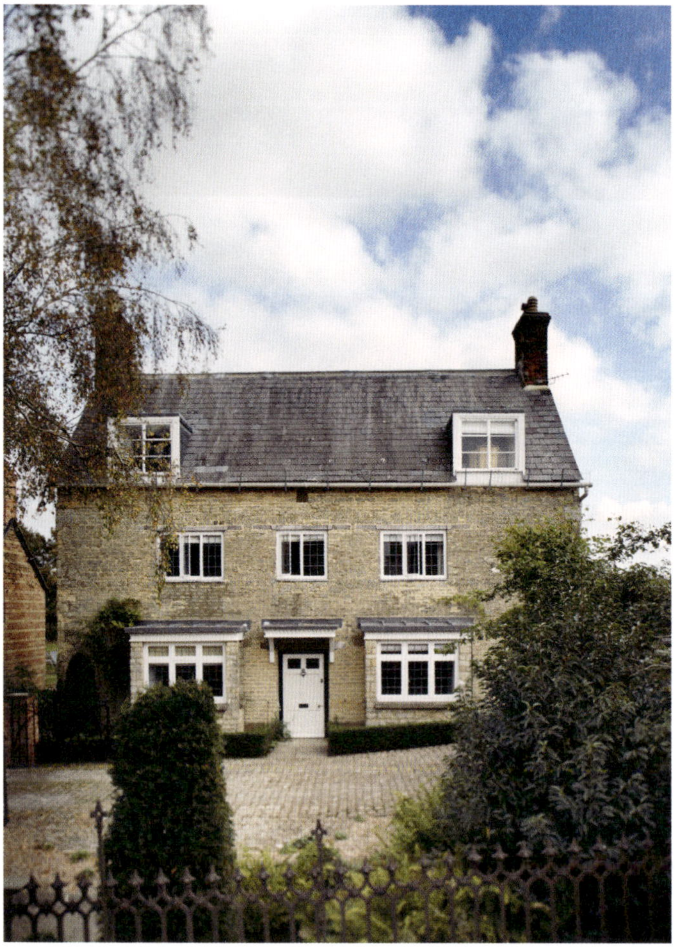

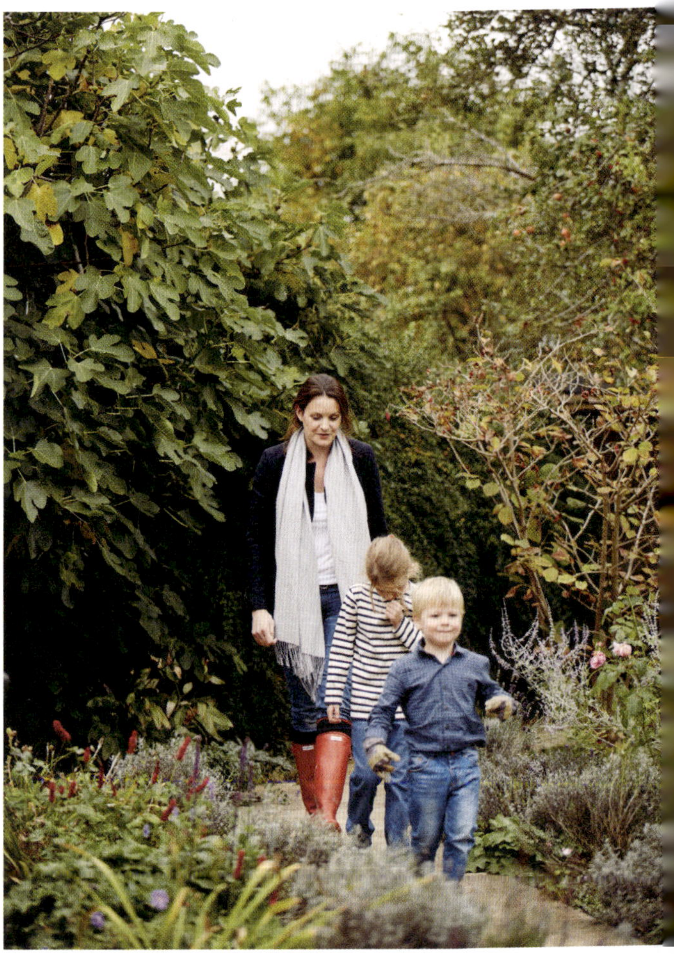

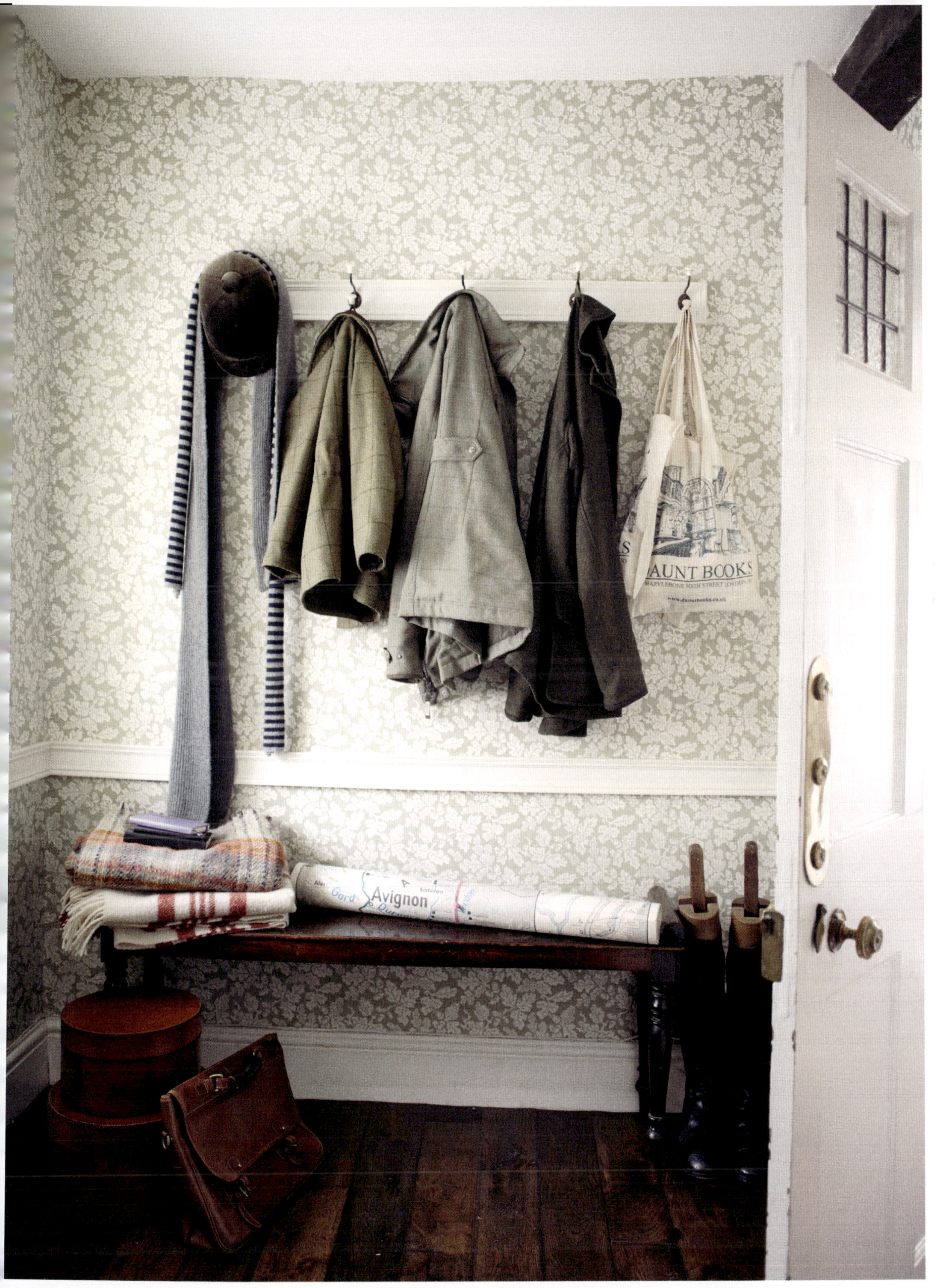
DAUNT BOOKS
Avignon

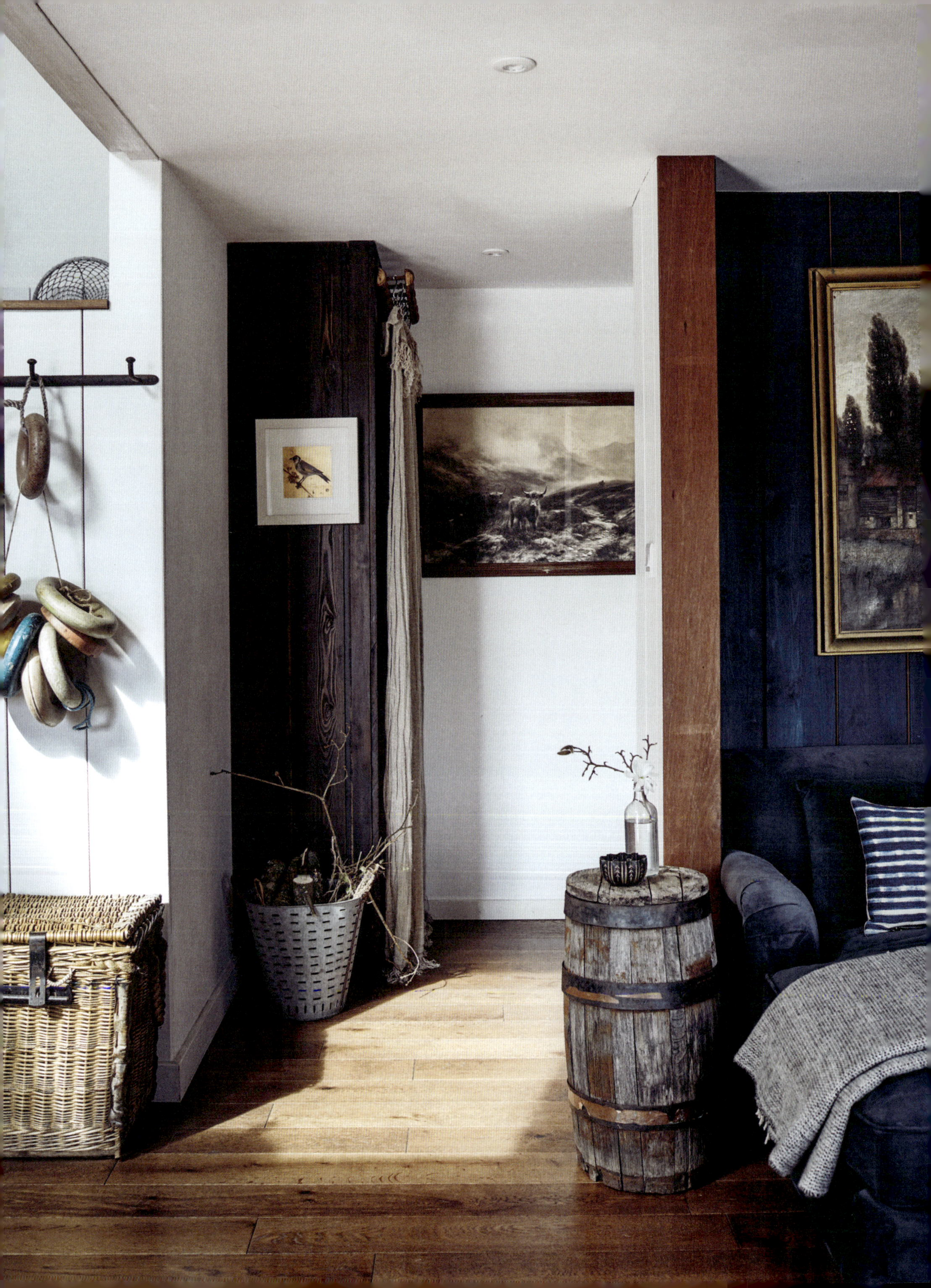

BOATHOUSE BOLTHOLE

Highly acclaimed artist Miranda Gardiner has carved a prominent position in the West Country's art scene with her exquisite landscapes, and her paintings are popular far and wide. Her converted boathouse is evidence that interior design too can be a true work of art.

As the shadows lengthen on the banks of the Kingsbridge Estuary on a February afternoon, one lone figure is left crouched by the water's edge inspecting what the tide has brought in during the day. The figure is Miranda Gardiner, and she's found a small crab shell, almost the exact replica in miniature of one she has displayed in her boathouse, which is perched just above the beach. It is a dream of a place, overlooking perhaps England's most perfect stretch of water.

Not any old flotsam and jetsam passes muster in Miranda's boathouse. She isn't one for stuffing her surroundings to bursting with nauticalia. Her artist's eye picks out one-off treasures and these she allows a place. Arranged casually among other unique finds from ... 'Well, everywhere really,' Miranda says. 'Flea markets, salvage yards, family heirlooms and things we've found on our travels.'

Ten years ago, the family returned to their Devon home after a year's travelling the world. They had all fallen in love with New Zealand, and Miranda had lost a small part of her heart to the wild coastline of Auckland. 'I longed to refind that rugged peace,' she remembers. Almost obsessively she started searching for a waterside bolthole. She never imagined that the place would be fifteen minutes from her home.

'On first impression it was pretty lacklustre,' she admits. Comprised of a breeze-block shell almost invisible under massed decaying undergrowth, it was a rather damp and slimy home to a surprisingly beautiful Salcombe yawl. 'My friend, who'd come to advise me, thought I was mad,' laughs Miranda, who thrashed through the undergrowth to get a true feel for the place. 'Once I saw the incredible views and the hidden beach, I knew it was the right place.'

Miranda and her husband Diggory were no strangers to property development, having moved and improved several times, and a new building project presented an exciting challenge. They recognised that this high-raftered boatshed could become an open-plan space downstairs with a double-height ceiling to incorporate a bedroom and bathroom upstairs.

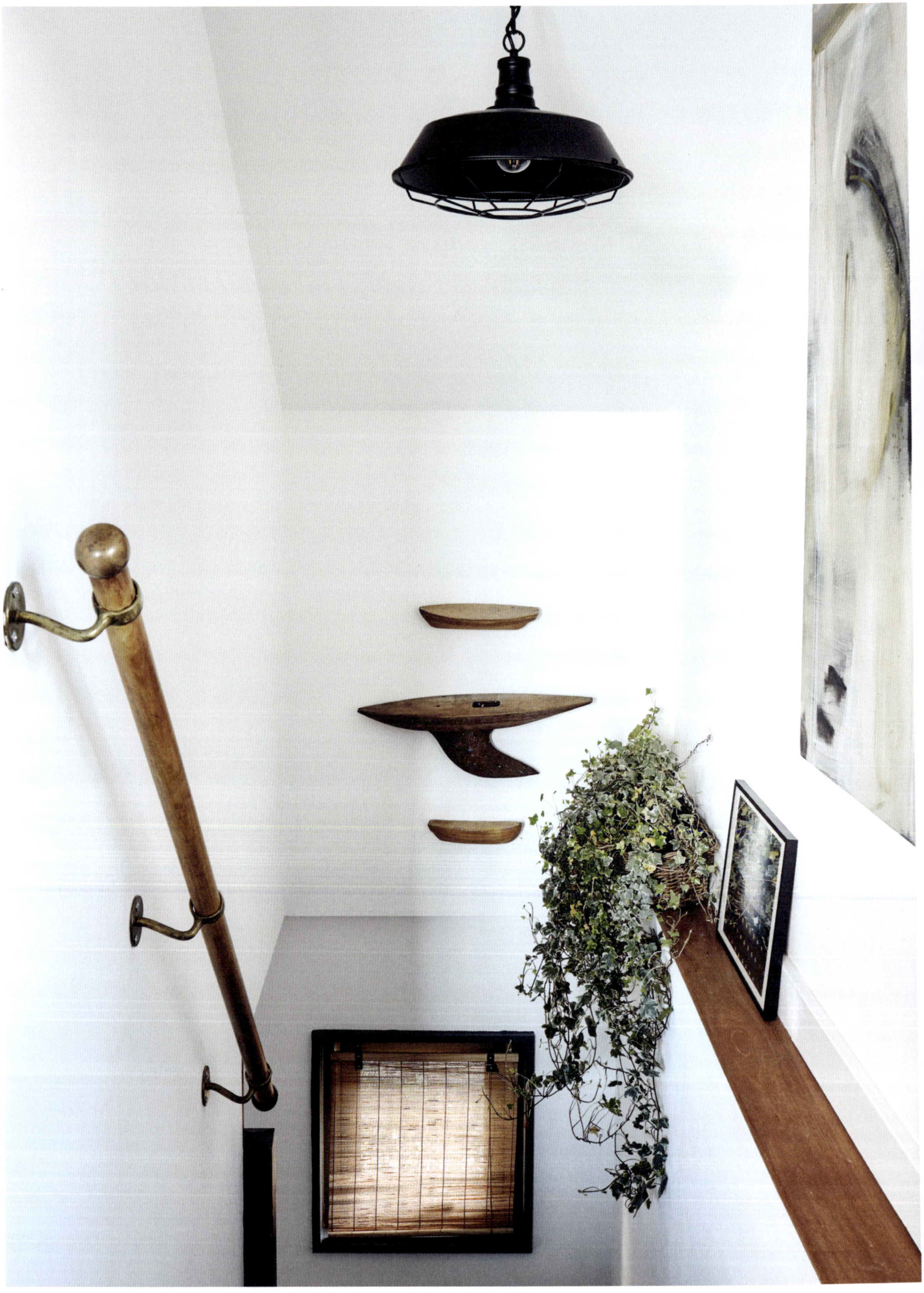

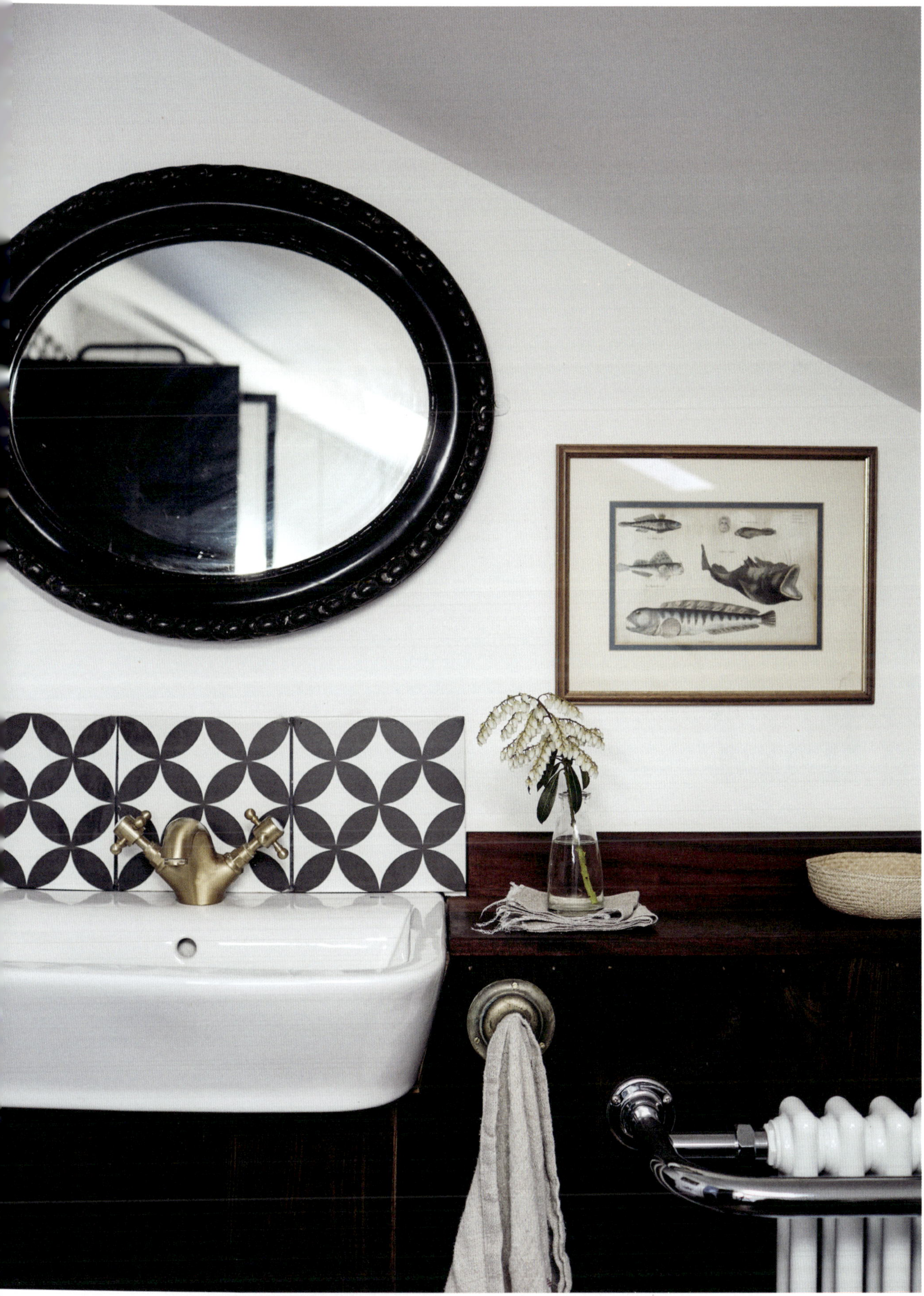

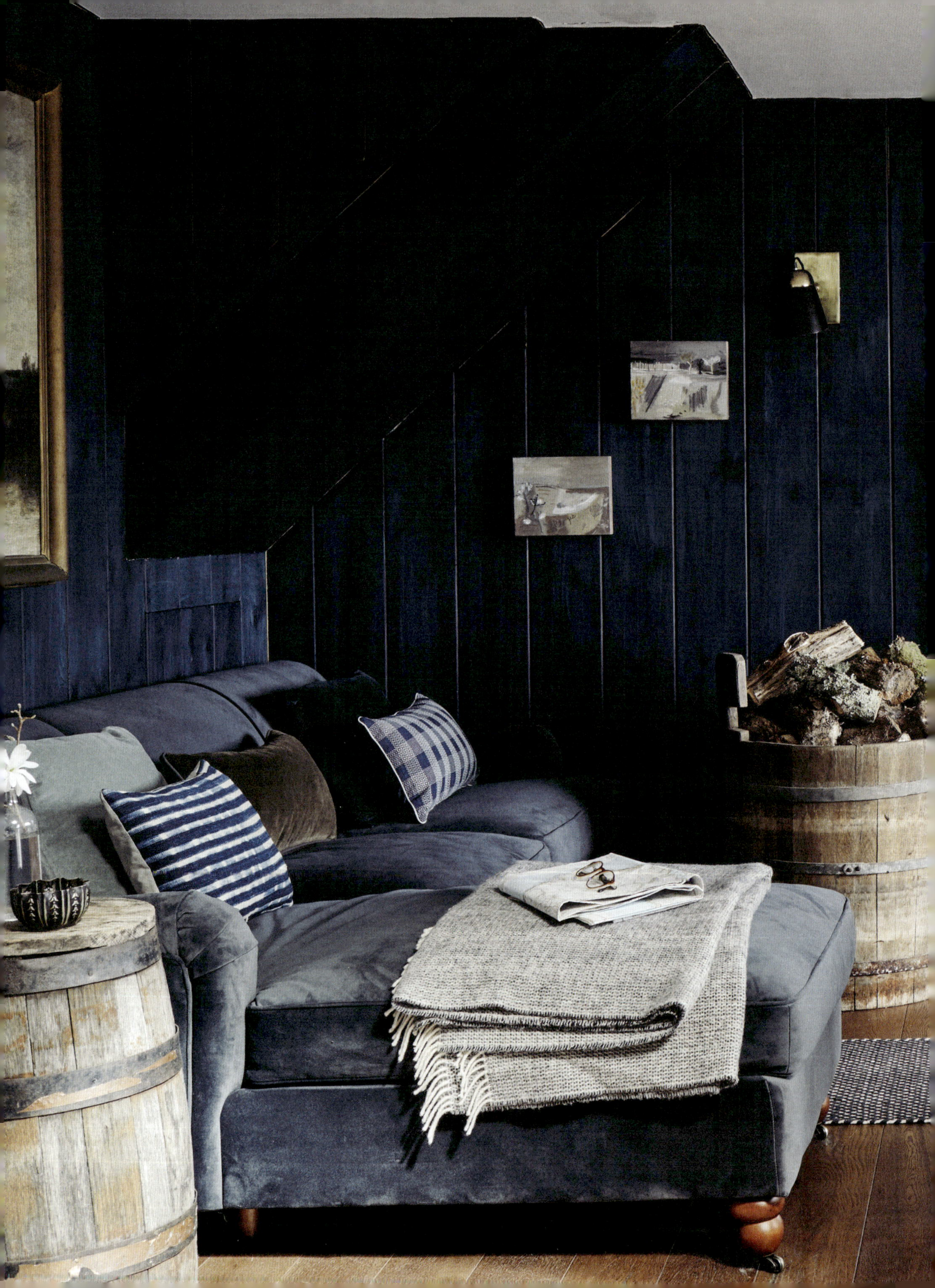

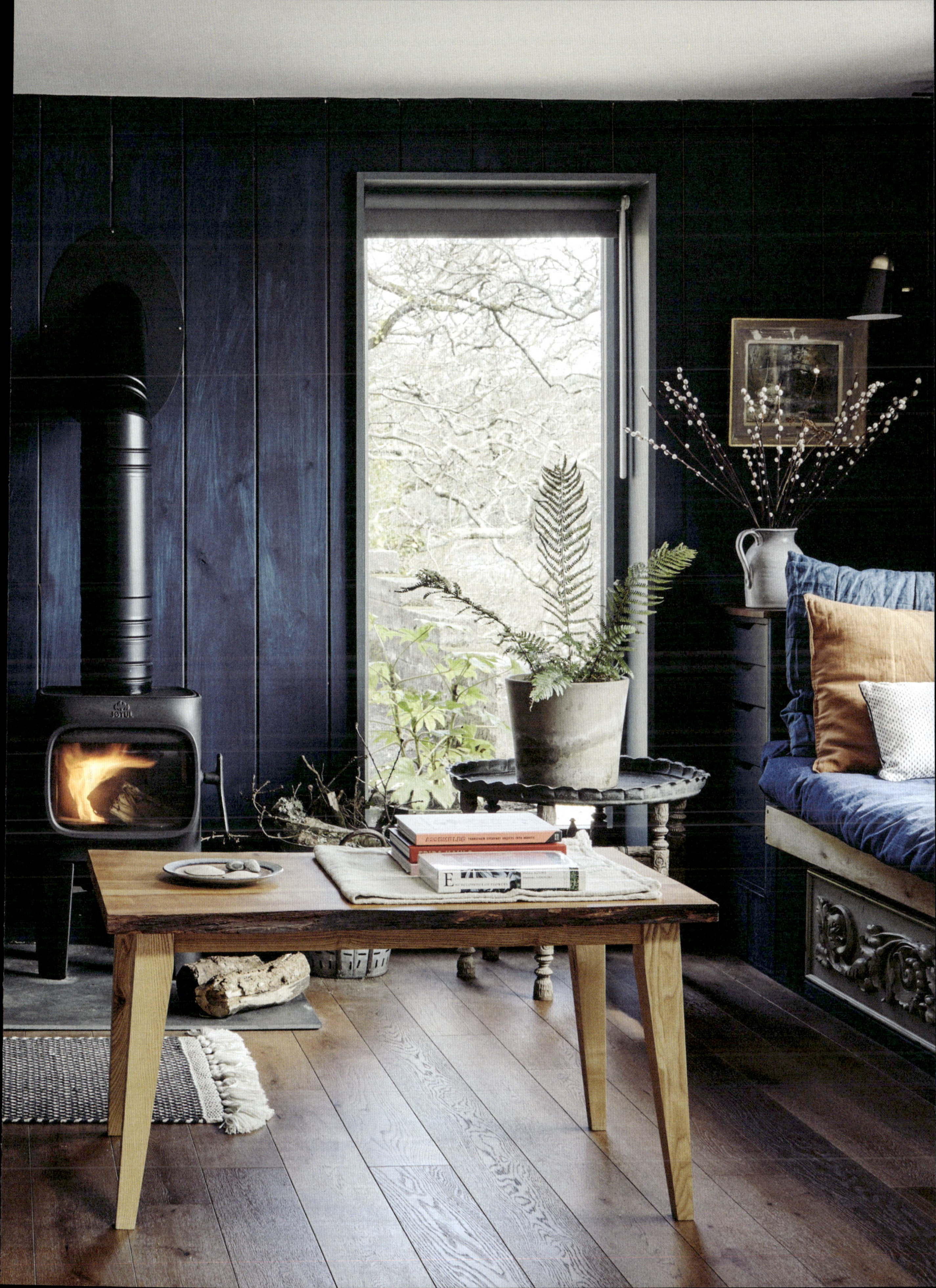

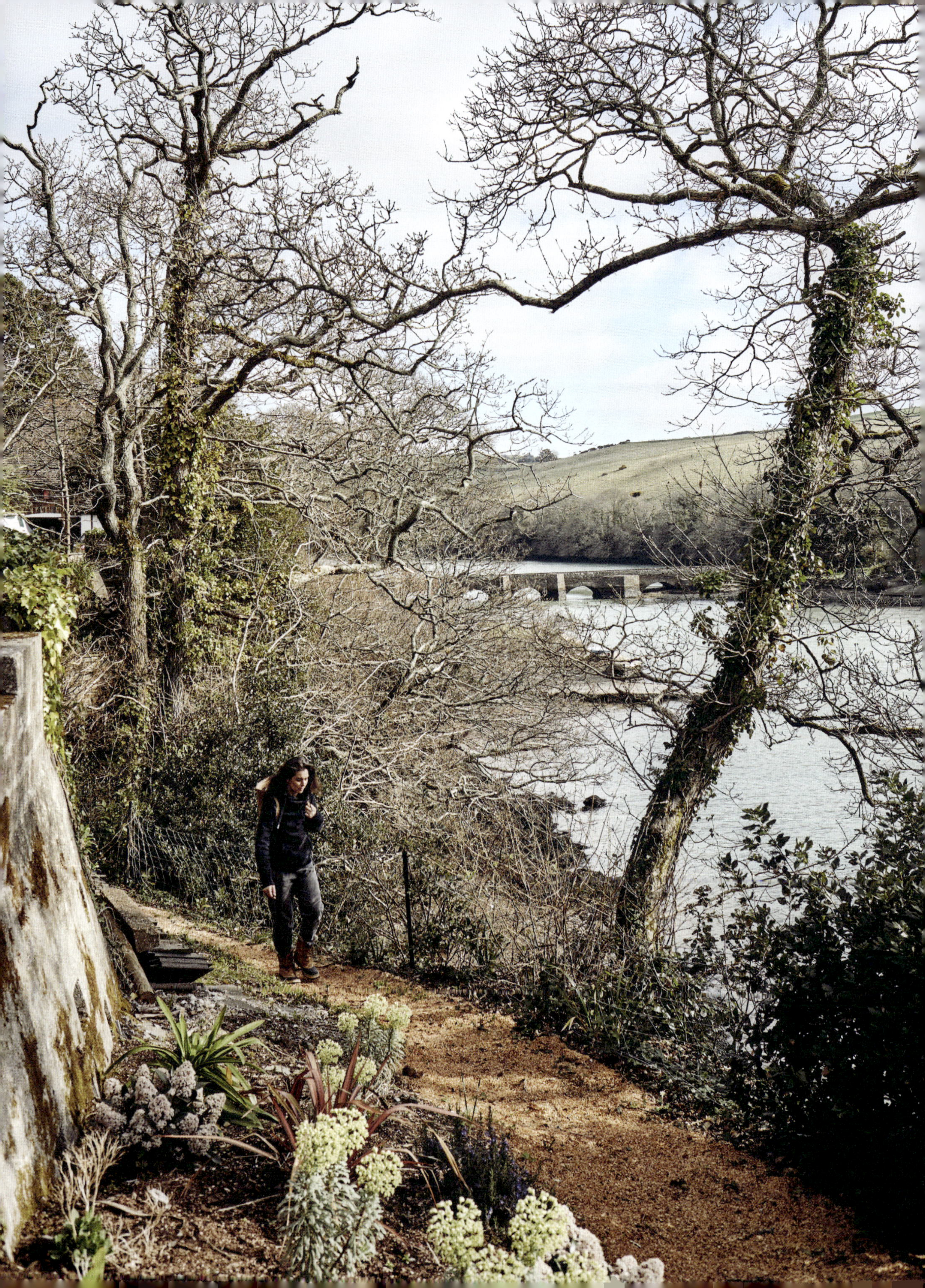

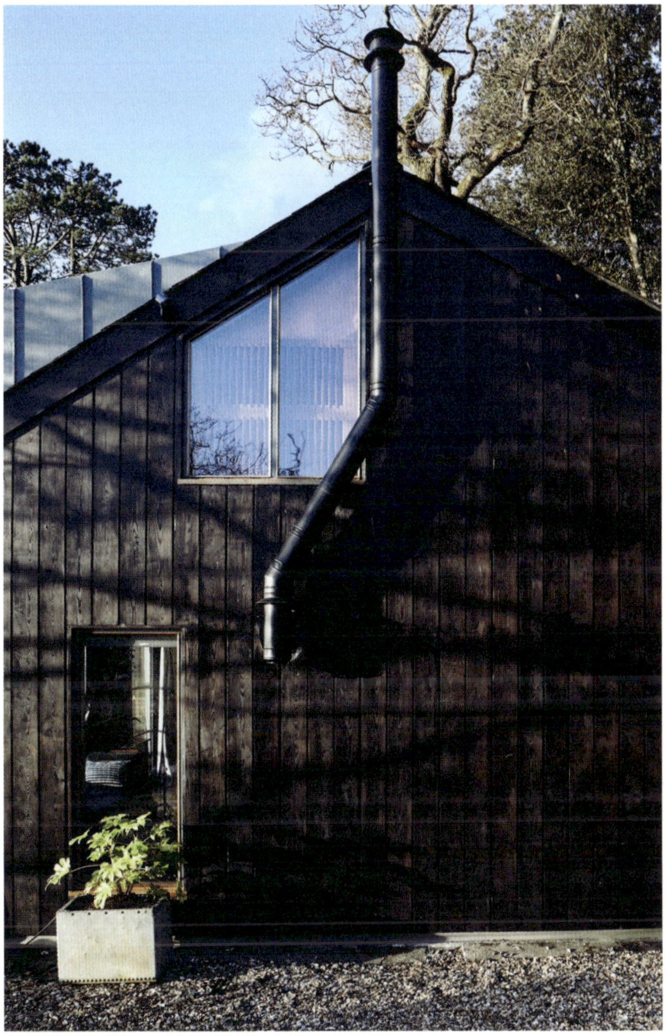

'THE WARM COLOURS OF WINTER

by the estuary inspire me. I have chosen many colours for my home as well as for my own paintings based on these gentle natural hues: olive greens, midnight blues, rusty browns and mustard yellows.'

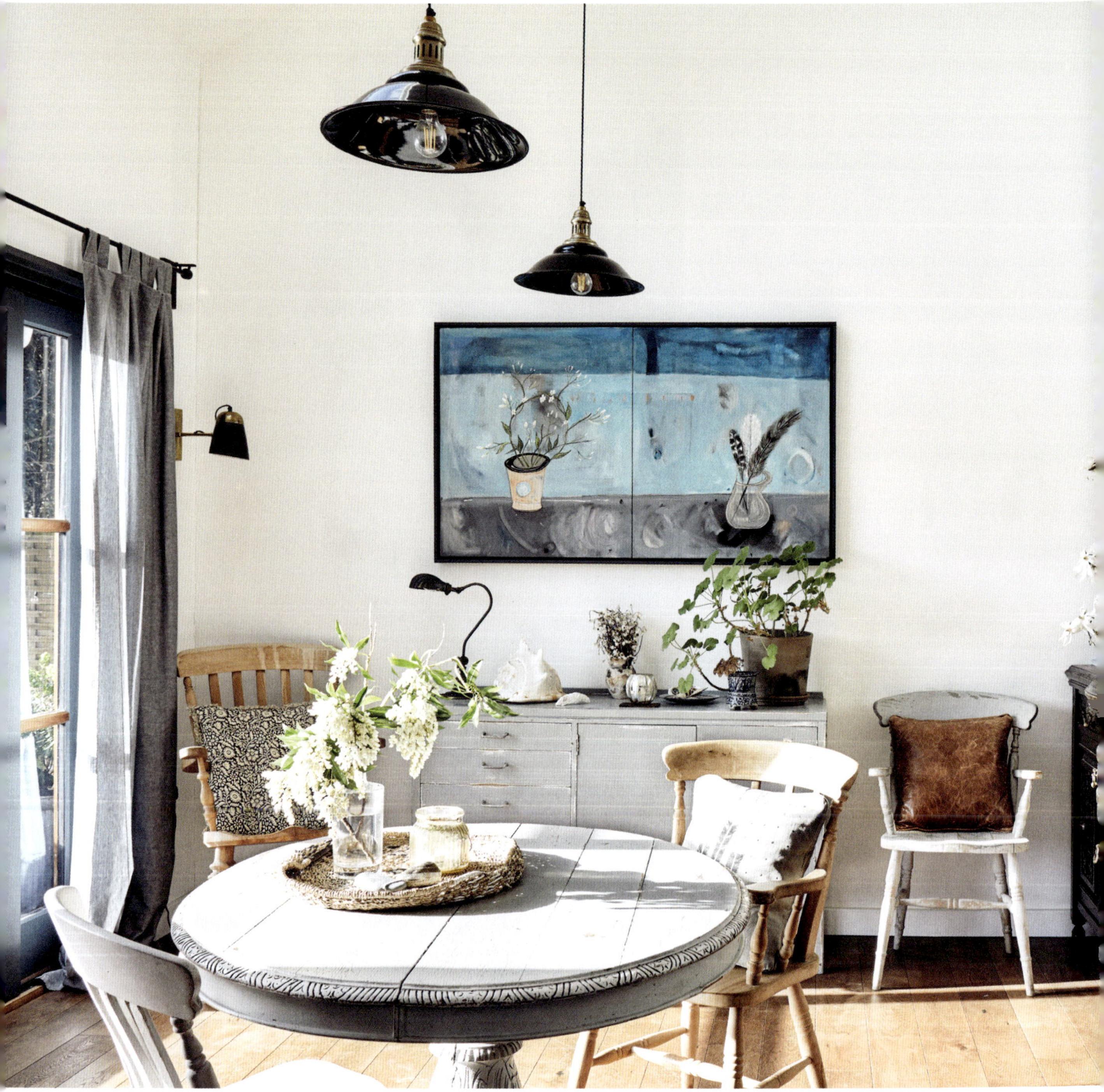

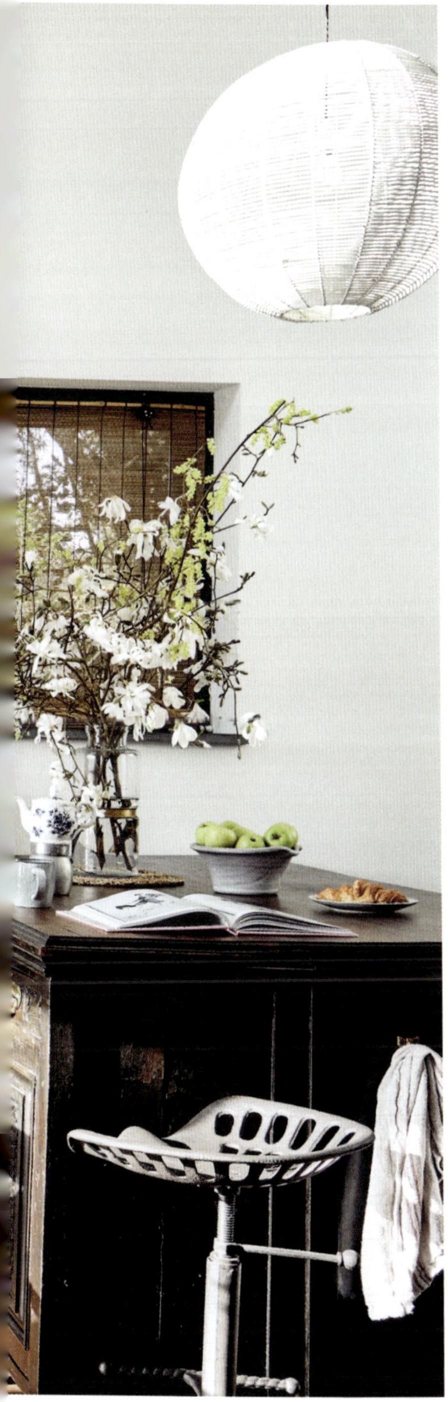

A plan was devised to turn the high-ceilinged side of the downstairs into the kitchen and dining area. This would be plastered and painted white to make the most of the light and space. The other half-height space could incorporate a relaxing sitting area with a wood burner. By contrast, this cosier space was to be wood panelled and painted in moodier tones. They decided that upstairs should be a blend of both - white-painted walls and wood panelling in the bedroom would keep it as light as possible and darker wood would suit a bathroom better.

What Miranda and Diggory have done, apparently effortlessly, is not only to find the way to use the space itself to best advantage, but to furnish it in an intriguing and unique style. Nothing here is customised or repeated elsewhere in the house. They have chosen muted colours - strong but natural tones. Miranda's paintings, some huge, some tiny, likewise reflect this unostentatious appreciation of colour. Textures are varied - there is varnished wood, bare wood, driftwood, earthenware pieces and even a piece of antique carved plaster. There's a copper worktop in the bathroom that came from a Torquay hotel bar ('Very *Faulty Towers*,' laughs Miranda), mismatched bronze hooks and handles, wrought-iron coat hooks. Likewise soft furnishings come in a wealth of textures: a blue velvet sofa, some leather, some woven cushions and bed sheets in charcoal and brown linen.

Their finds and choices speak volumes about their own creativity and these items sit so comfortably in this space that it seems that they were always intended for it. Dividing the kitchen and dining areas, for instance, is a sturdy and ornate chest of drawers which Diggory has seamlessly twinned, back to back, with a kitchen storage unit, more utilitarian but in similar wood. Together the two serve as a beautiful breakfast bar / workstation. There are countless unusual pieces: an old seed chest serves as a kitchen cupboard, milk churns stand in for bins, a farmyard animal feeder makes a towel basket. 'I can't help this urge to surprise,' admits Miranda.

Among her favourite finds are a ship's pole for a banister, a seemingly random choice, although in fact something that she'd hoped to find for months. She also loves the shutter upstairs. 'It was determined not to fit in its intended portrait position, so I turned it on its side and sanded a few stubborn edges off,' recalls Miranda. ' It's even better from this angle because the slats give the perfect line of sight out to the estuary.'

As for the estuary itself, Miranda and her family will never tire of it. The light, flora and fauna change constantly throughout the year, and the peace they have found here has satisfied even Miranda's wanderlust. Bowcombe Boathouse is available to rent.

'THE RUGGED BEAUTY

of coastal New Zealand has had huge appeal for me, as has the rustic warmth of Scandinavian waterside homes. The Boathouse gave me a chance to explore these styles.'

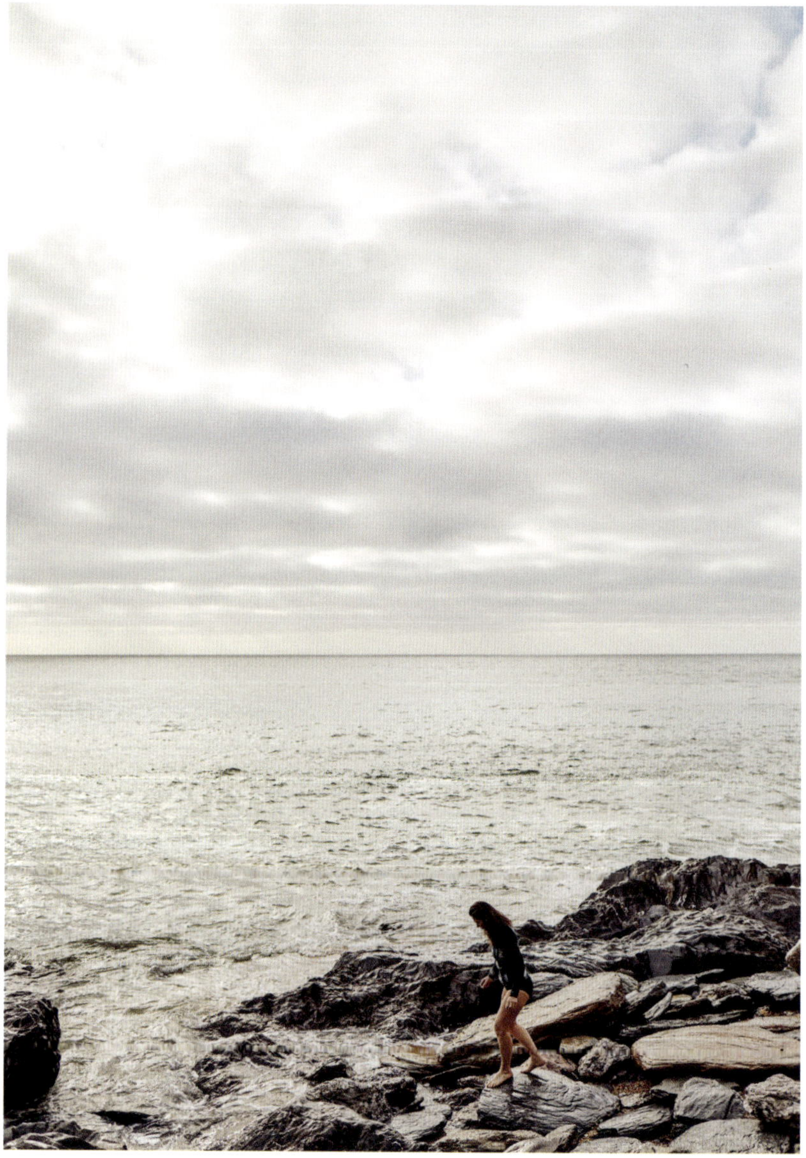

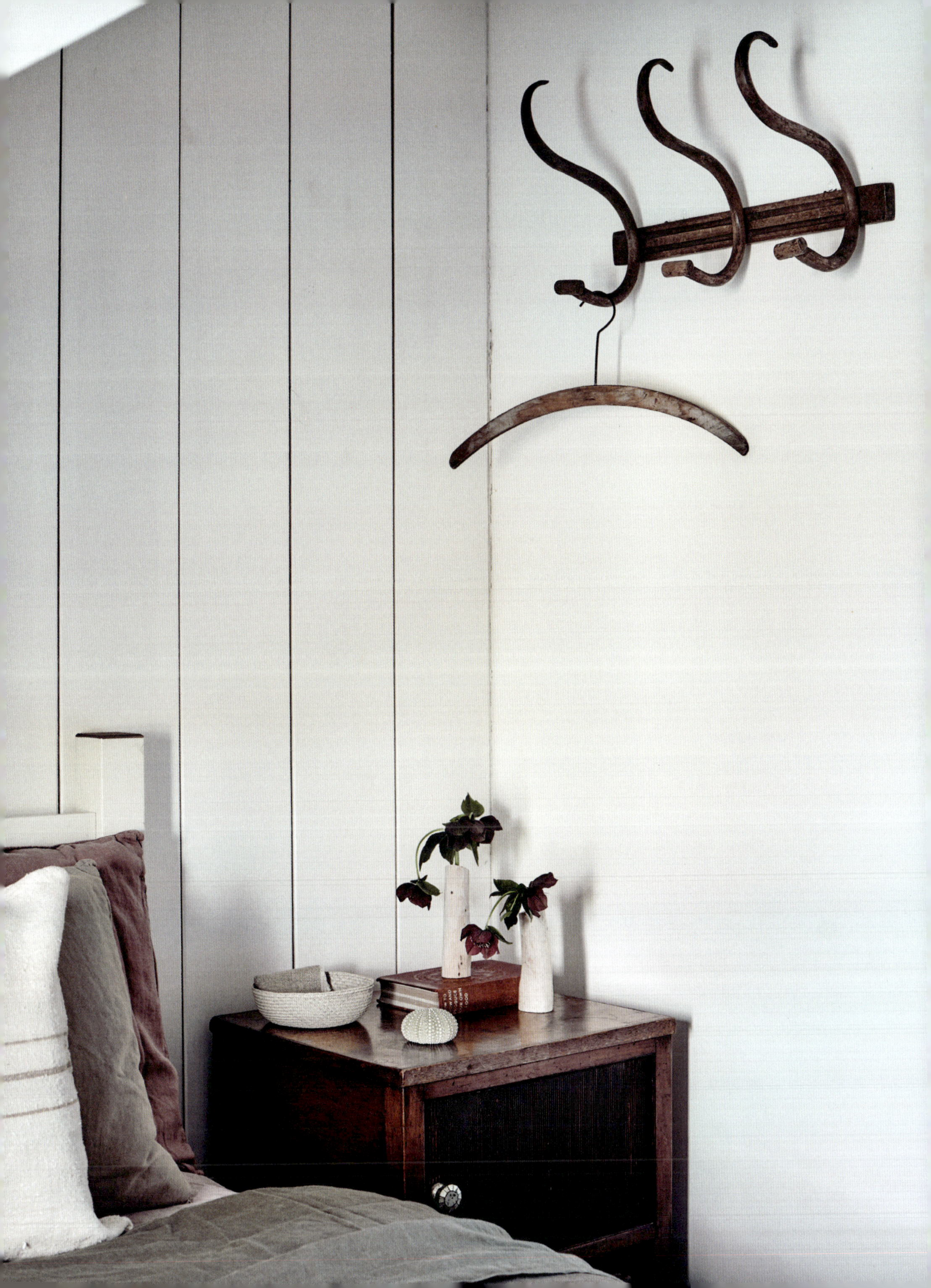

FIRST IMPRESSIONS

After a negative first impression, it took a fortuitous twist of fate for the Colvilles to see their future home in an entirely different light.

There is a time of early evening in mid-summer when the sun turns the Colvilles' home to gold. 'These are the moments when we love this place the most,' reveals Charlotte. 'But it's the opposite of what we saw when first we viewed the house!'

The Colvilles had great expectations of the 18th-century cottage in their favourite north Oxfordshire village. Yet their first impression of it, sitting empty on a chilly January afternoon, was not favourable. A long, thin house huddled in front of a hillside and, facing east, it had very few windows at the back to catch the afternoon sun. It had some redeeming features, including a huge inglenook fireplace and an Aga in the kitchen, but both were unlit and the overwhelming impression was of a long, dark railway carriage. They left feeling crestfallen.

That evening Charlotte realised that she had left her scarf at the cottage. 'Some mistakes are meant to be,' she says, because on returning the next morning they saw the same house in literally a quite different light. Sunshine poured in through the windows and the rooms with their quirky period features came to life.

'We felt pretty fickle but put in an offer then and there!' says Ned. There were compromises, of course, but it felt right, and had recently been renovated in the style that Ned and Charlotte love: modern country with respect for the house's 18th-century origins. Freshly painted pale walls, a farmhouse-style kitchen and classically designed bathrooms appealed to the couple. New seagrass carpets, along with slate and wooden floors, complemented quirky cottage features such as exposed beams, arched doorways and wonky walls. It had three bedrooms, but one was up its own staircase. The main part of 'upstairs' consisted of two double bedrooms, each with an en-suite bathroom, and a large open landing in between. The couple had one child, Lily, at the time, but with a larger family in mind they knew they would need to reconfigure. They couldn't imagine how immediately.

Two months later they were in, and the need for an extra bedroom became pressing when they found out that no. 2 was on the way. 'We hadn't really planned where a second child would sleep,' recalls Ned, 'but after a lot of measuring and head scratching, we came up with a scheme.' By taking out the second bathroom and pushing one of its walls into the landing, they could make a bedroom for baby Arthur. They could then create a smaller bathroom in the remaining space on the other side of the landing.

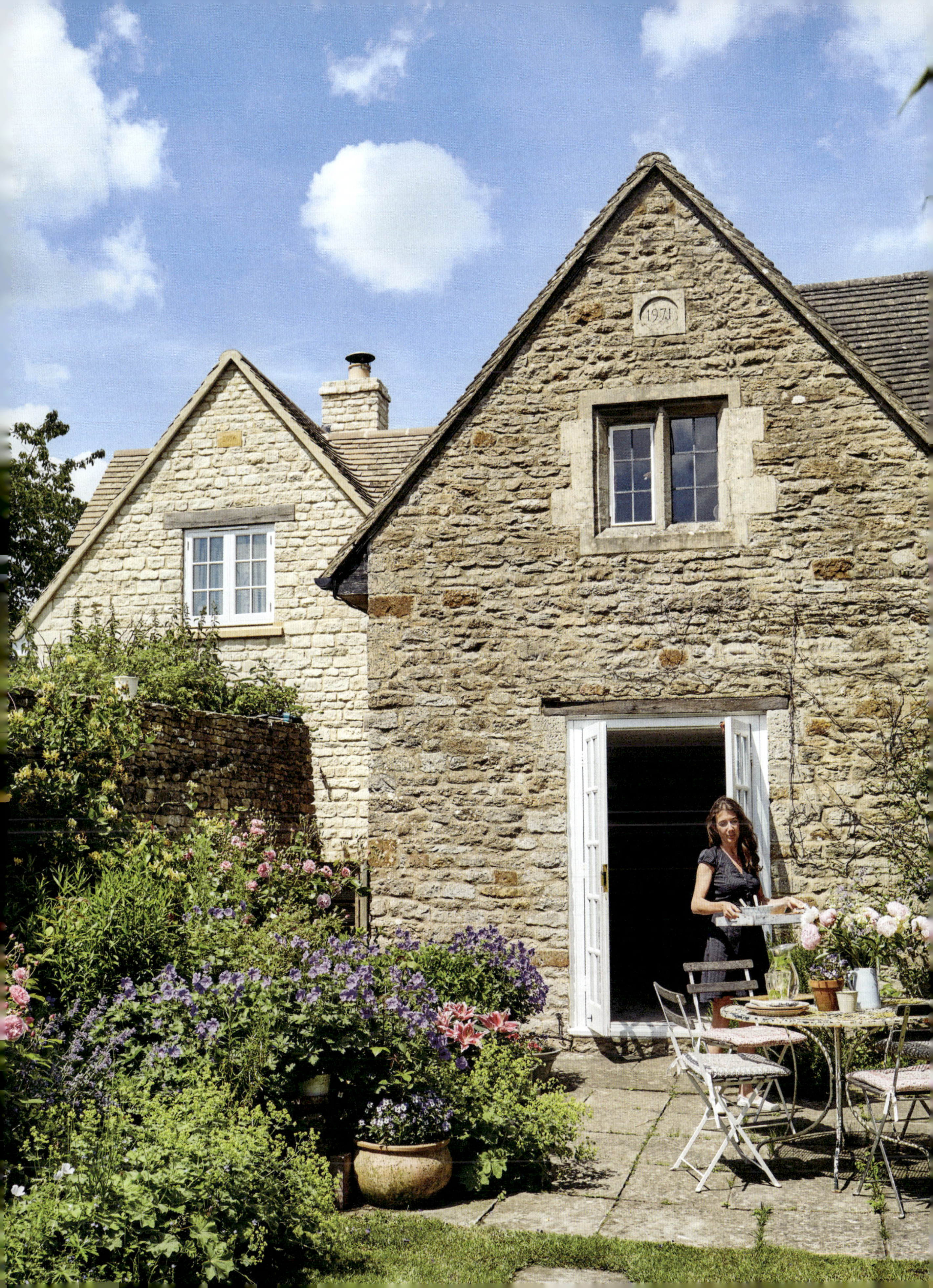

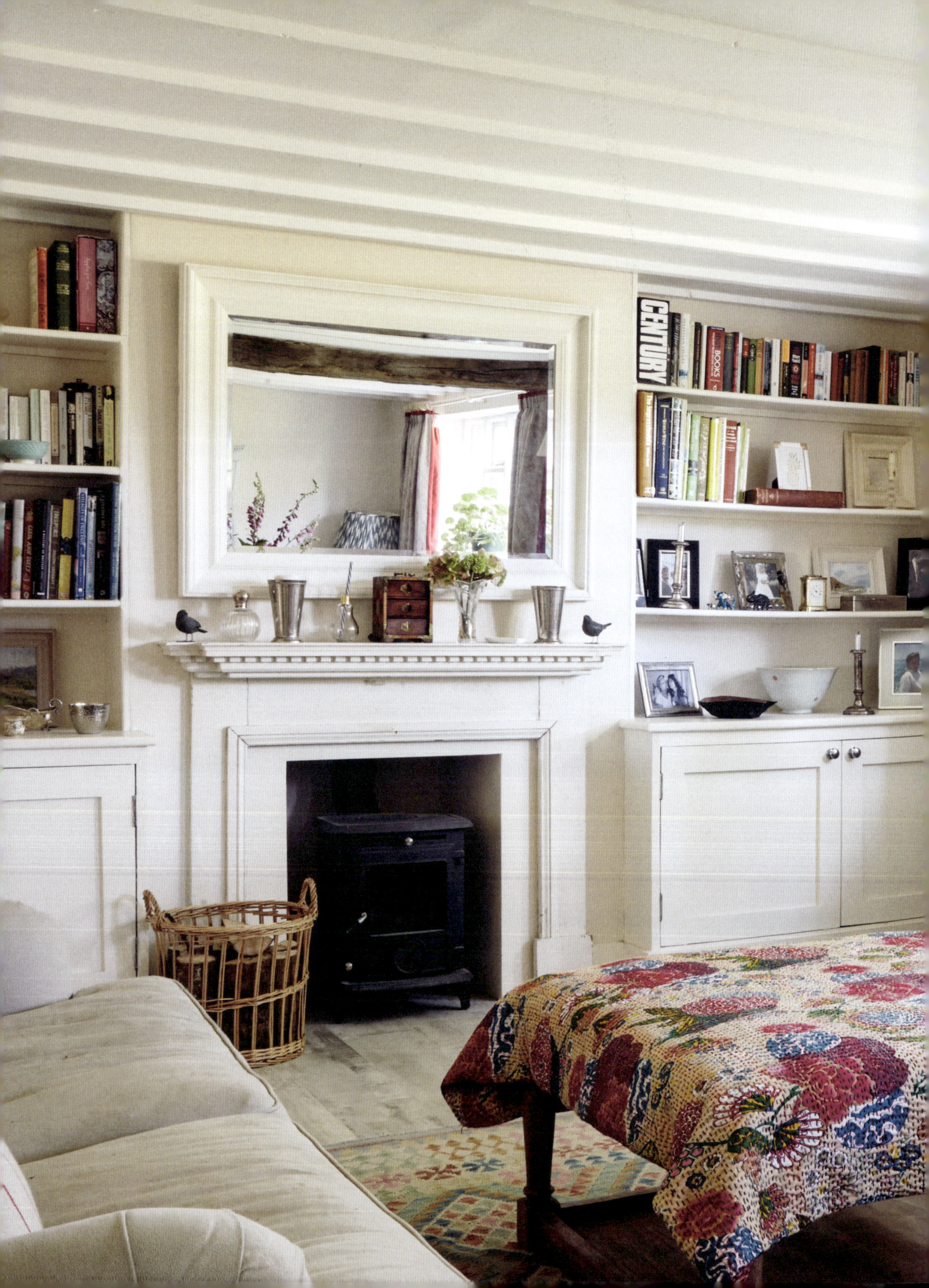
CENTURY

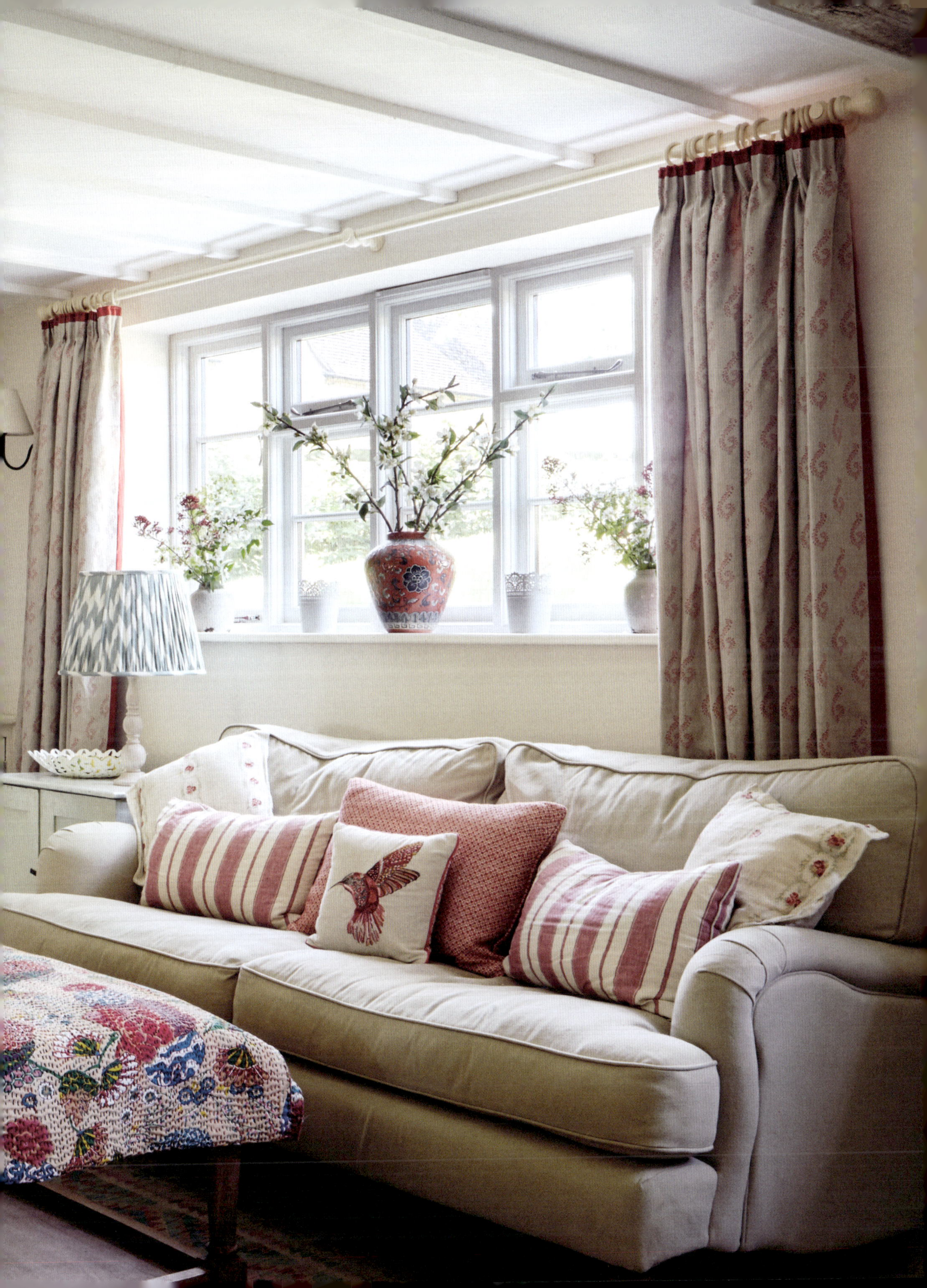

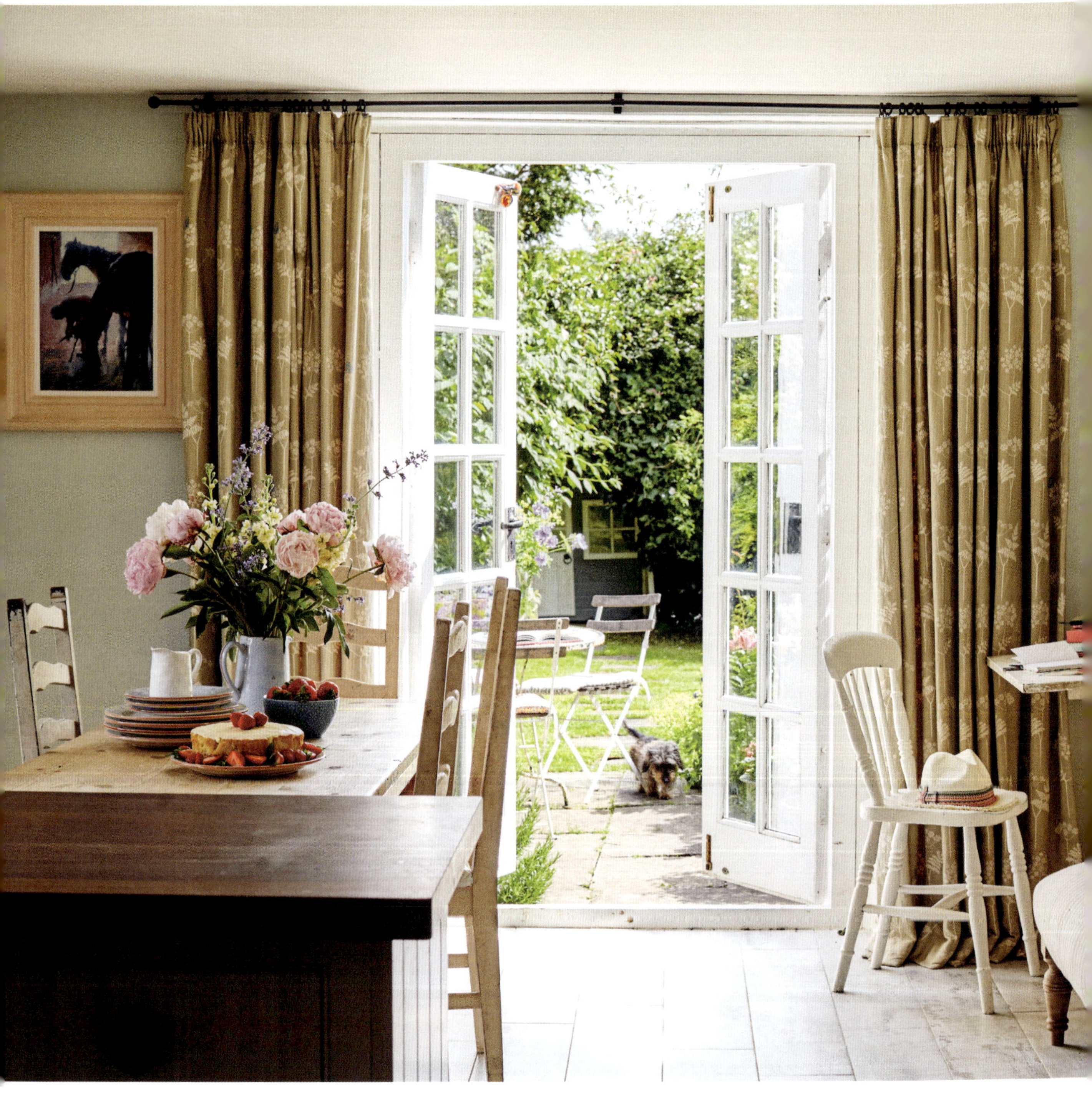

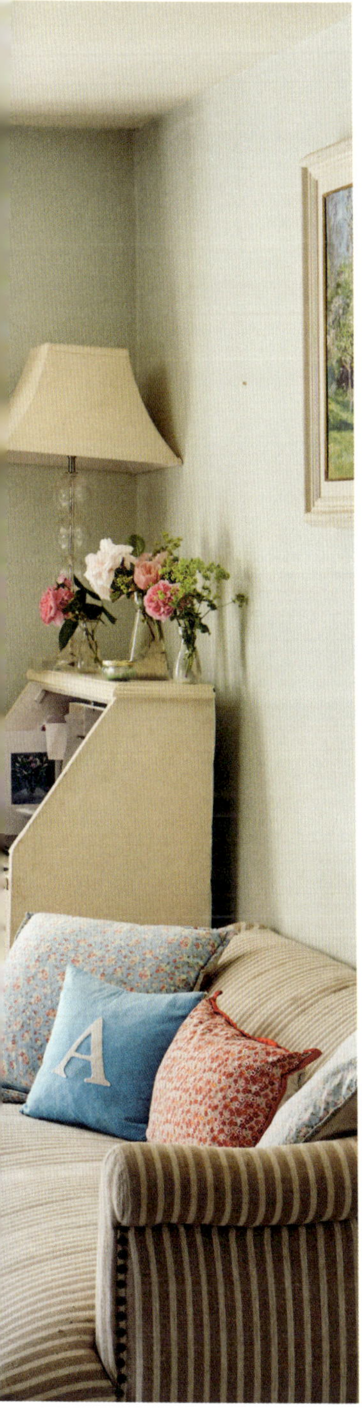

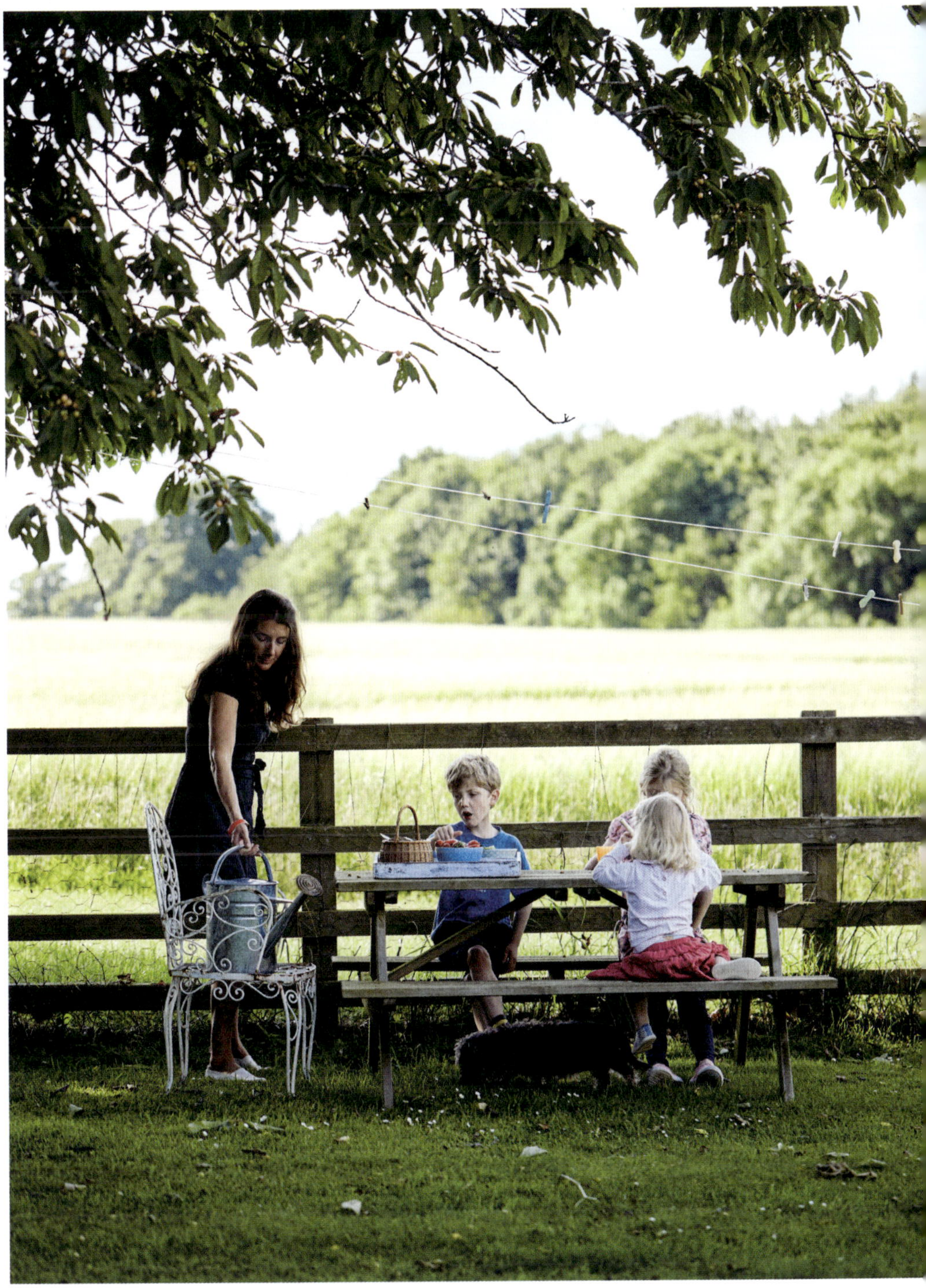

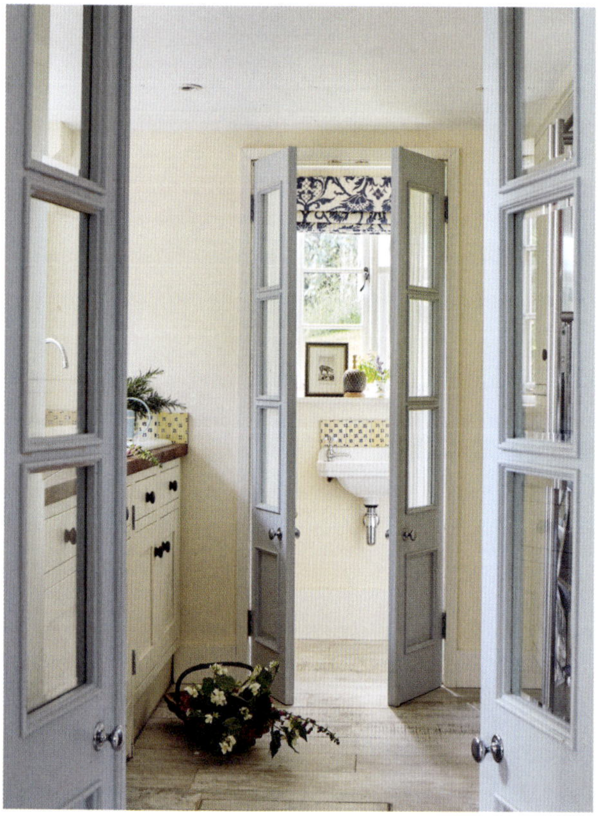
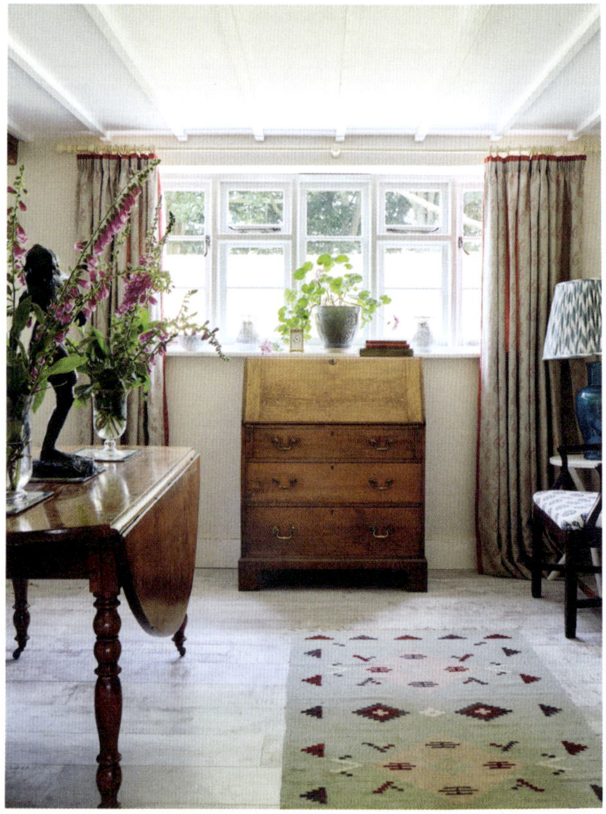

'WOULD WE LIVE THROUGH

another building project?' asks Charlotte. 'Possibly not with a baby getting into every nook and cranny. But when that wonderful golden evening light now floods not just over the garden but in through the windows too, even on a chilly winter day, we realise how much we have gained.'

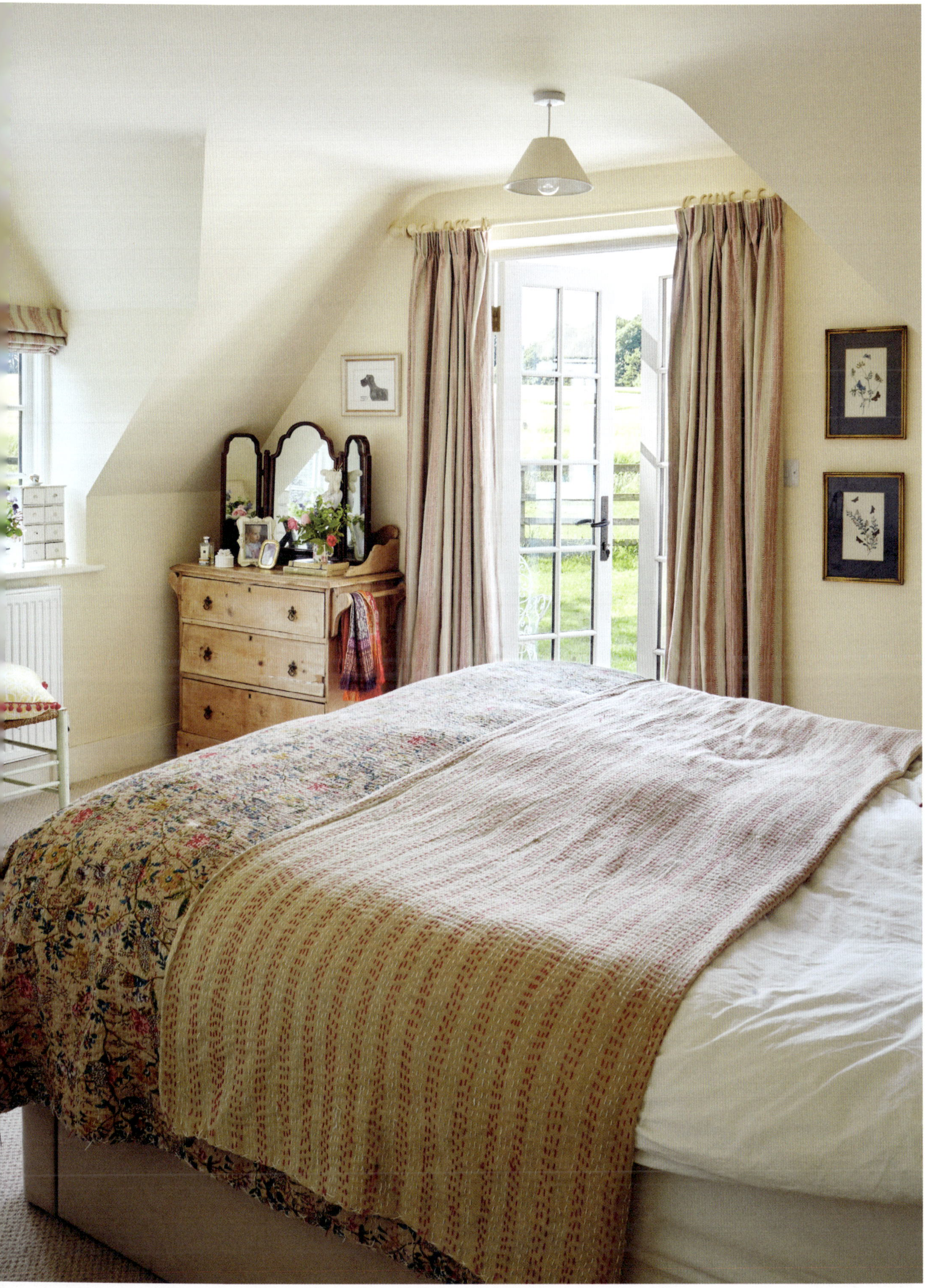

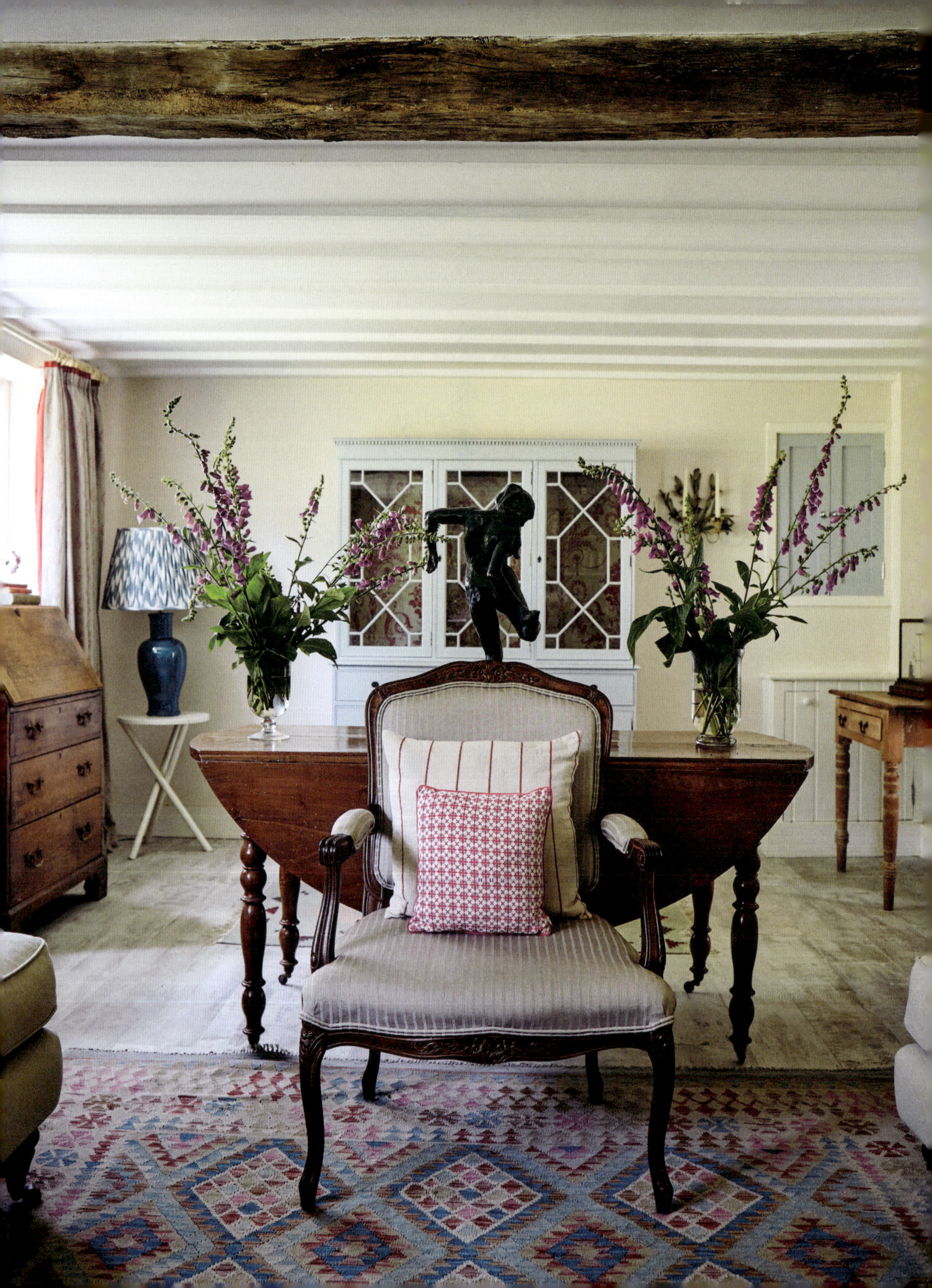

Although the Colvilles loved their home, two niggles persisted: the long, narrow layout and the lack of west-facing windows. Only from Arthur's bedroom could the countryside views be seen. 'We began scribbling plans for a west-facing two-storey extension,' says Ned. 'Just as we started muttering to architects, we realised that no. 3 was on the way.'

This was to be a far more challenging project, coinciding with Lara's first eighteen months. They had decided to add a spacious family room opening from both the sitting room and the kitchen, and a utility room and loo accessed from the other end of the kitchen. Upstairs a bedroom for Lara and a new master bedroom and bathroom were to be added. Bringing light to the cottage was a priority and blending the extension naturally with the 200-year-old part of the house was paramount.

'The building project almost cost us our sanity!' admits Charlotte. Firstly, to extend at the back involved a major dig-out, and the Colvilles watched an ever-deeper, muddier hole appear in their back garden. 'That was the easy bit,' remembers Charlotte, who had not fully anticipated life with a new baby, a constant stream of tradesmen, walls being demolished, dust settling everywhere and tarpaulin standing in for walls. There were constant changes to sleeping arrangements as rooms were knocked about, often with all five sleeping in one room. 'It felt a bit like living on a ship at sea,' remembers Charlotte. 'Tarpaulin flapping, rain hammering upon the makeshift roof and wind whistling throughout.'

'We could hardly believe it when eventually the job was done, so familiar had the team of workmen become,' she continued. Predictably the budget ran out before they came to decorating. Ned and Charlotte got down to painting their new rooms themselves when Lara was in bed. It was a tough, long haul, but finally - by Christmas 2016 - Lara had a bedroom and the family had every reason to celebrate in their new/old house.

'OUR GOAL WITH BOTH

building projects was to keep the country style flowing and to bring character to the new parts of the house,' says Ned. 'Our builders looked at us in amazement when we told them we wanted to put a reclaimed fireplace and a gnarled old oak beam into the newly-built family room!'

FULL FAMILY CIRCLE

Architectural historian Tim Whittaker had always felt drawn to a particular longhouse that had once been home to his seventh-great grandparents.

Tim Whittaker mocks his teenage self for his passion for historical buildings and for the time he spent cycling the tangled lanes of Cumbria exploring its ancient villages. He grew up in the Eden Valley – a gentle lowland flanked on the east by the Pennines and on the west by the Lake District. He loved the local landscape from a young age, and he developed a fascination with heritage buildings and architecture, history and antiques. He often followed his father – a conservation architect and antique collector – round heritage sites and antique markets.

It was on one of his cycle jaunts that 16-year-old Tim weaved his way to a particular house that had for its first two hundred years belonged to his family. A 17th-century longhouse – a farmhouse that would originally have had a stable and granary attached – built in the local red sandstone and with a slate roof, it was originally known as Parke's Farm (Tim's ancestor's name). In the mid-19th century it was sold to the nearby Newbiggin Hall as its home farm.

Tim struck up conversation with tenant farmer Alan Thornborough, who lived at the longhouse at that time. Upon learning that Tim's family had owned this house, Alan offered to show him round. Young Tim was wide eyed, soaking up the history and atmosphere, and he learnt the original uses of each room. The living room, complete with 300-year-old wood panelling, was named the firehouse, the master bedroom (then downstairs) the parlour, and the two bedrooms upstairs the parlour chamber and the kitchen chamber – these referred to the rooms below them. Tim was struck when John pointed out the letters T & A P and the date 1695 carved into an ancient cupboard; these are the initials of his seventh-great grandparents Thomas and Anne Parke.

The house never left Tim's heart. He returned in 2008 to see it again, and in 2018 he found himself there once more. On this occasion, as if the house had summoned him back, he discovered that it was on the market. 'Of course, we had to bring it back into the family,' explains Tim, referring to himself and his partner Harvey Cabaniss. Together with Tim's mother they made the move from east London to the Cumbrian lowlands.

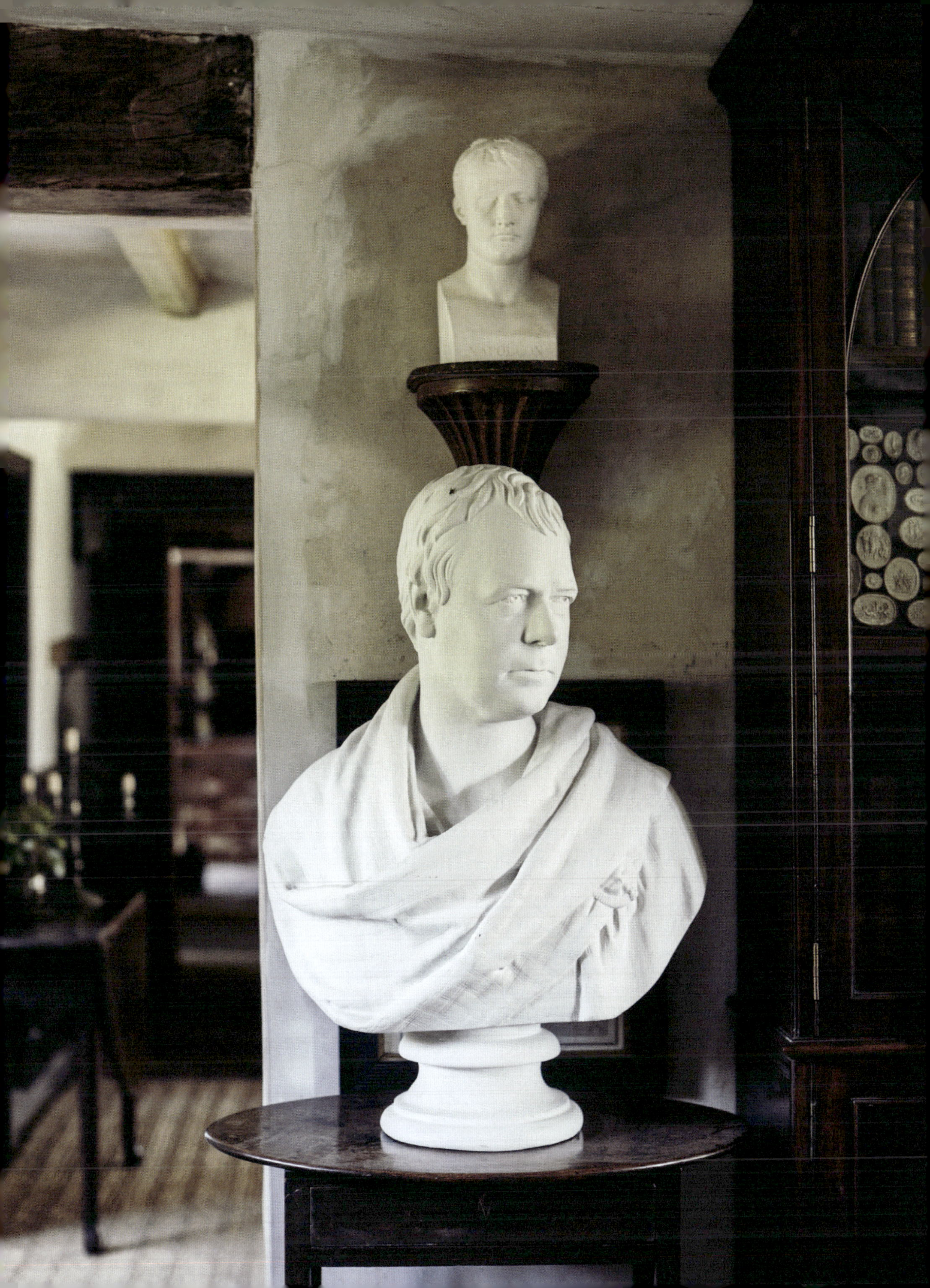

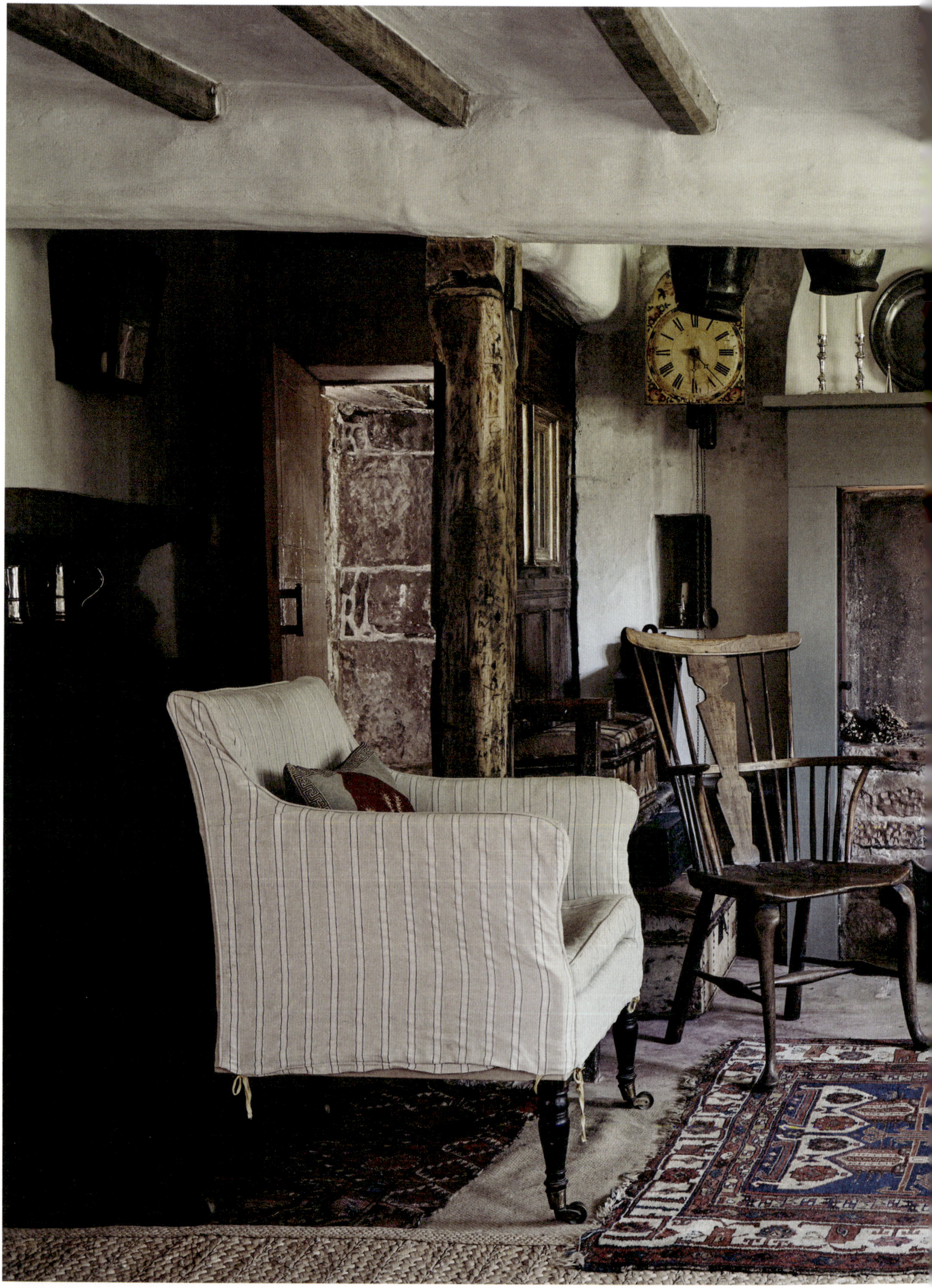

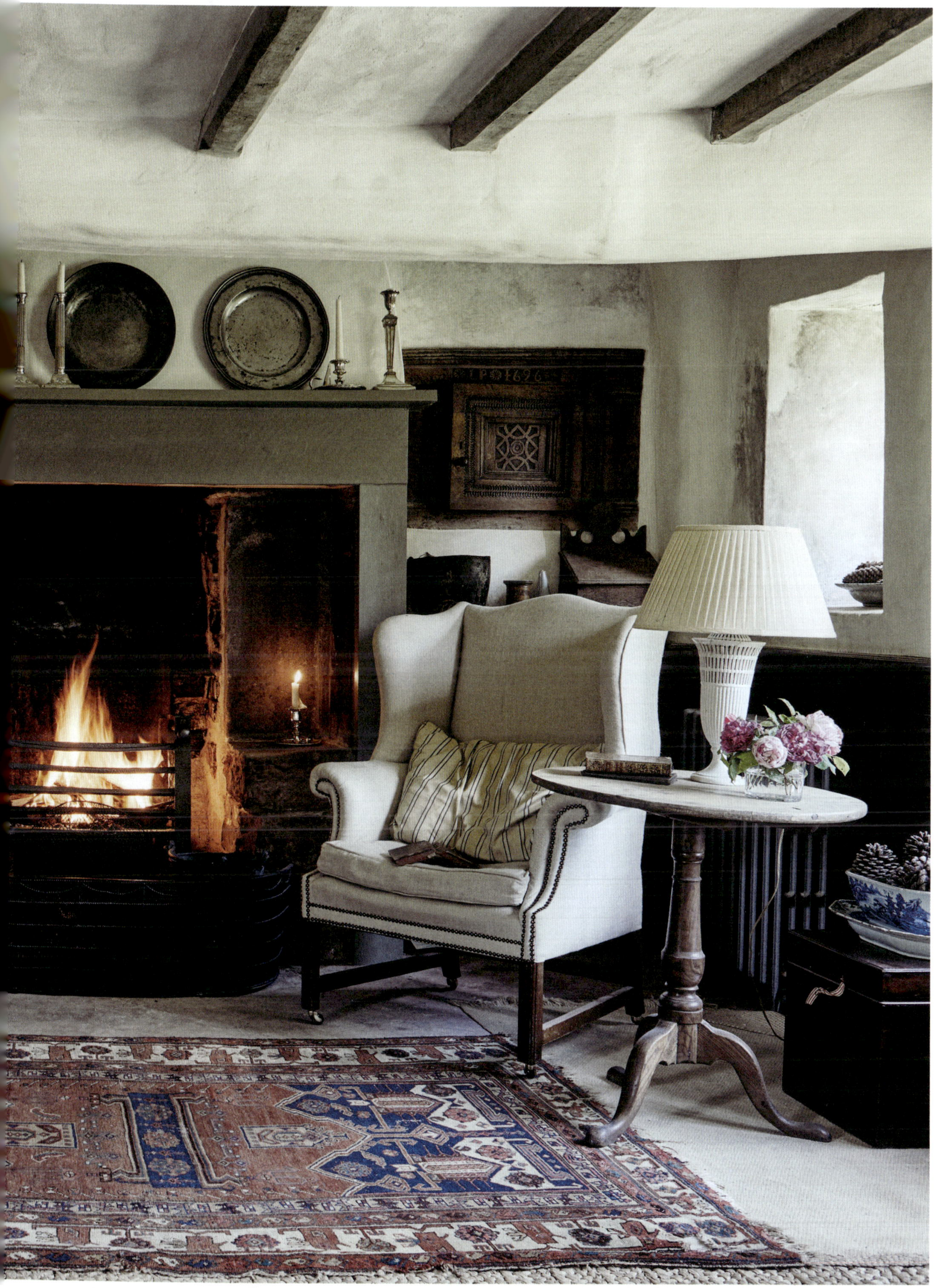
I P 1696

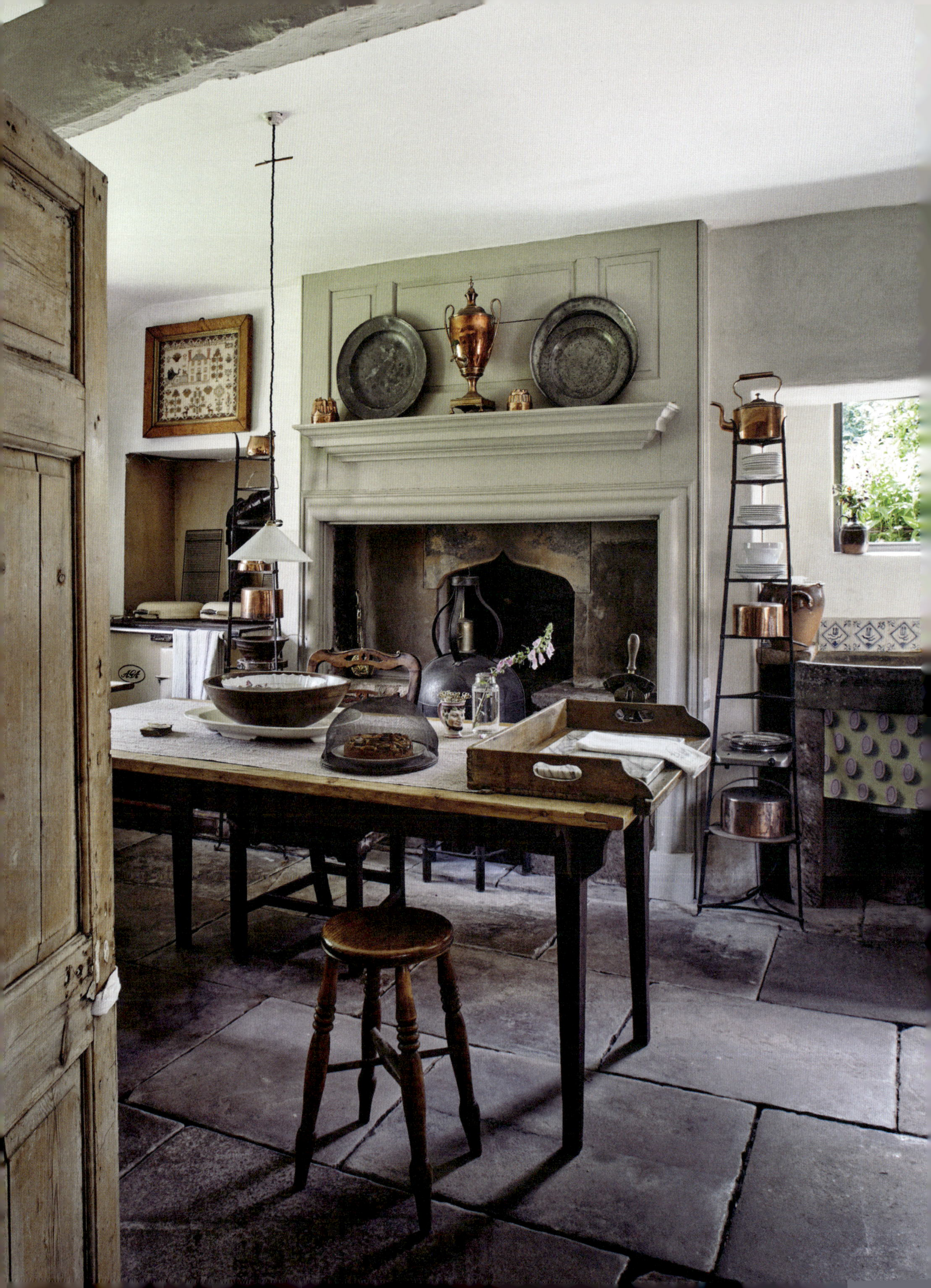

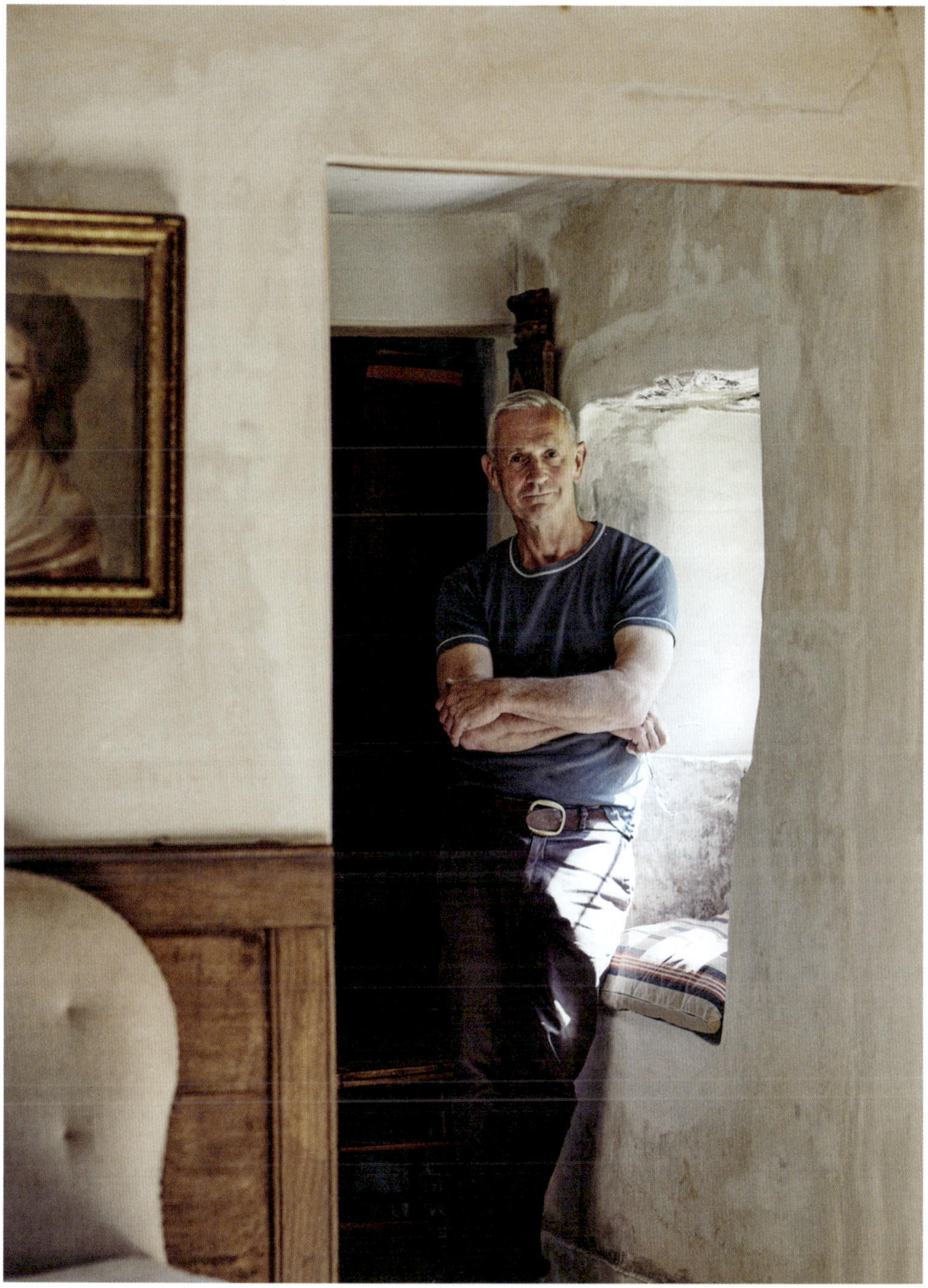

'WE RECENTLY DISCOVERED

my seventh-great grandmother's will, in which she writes in great detail about furniture, fabrics and ornaments that she was bequeathing to her children. The fact that these very possessions would once have lived within these walls moved us greatly.'

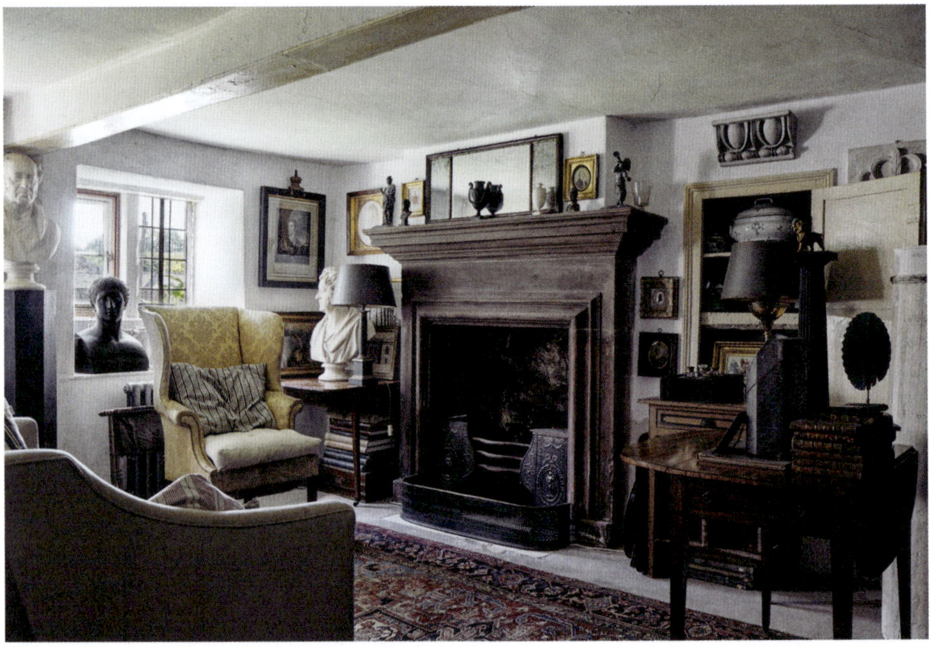

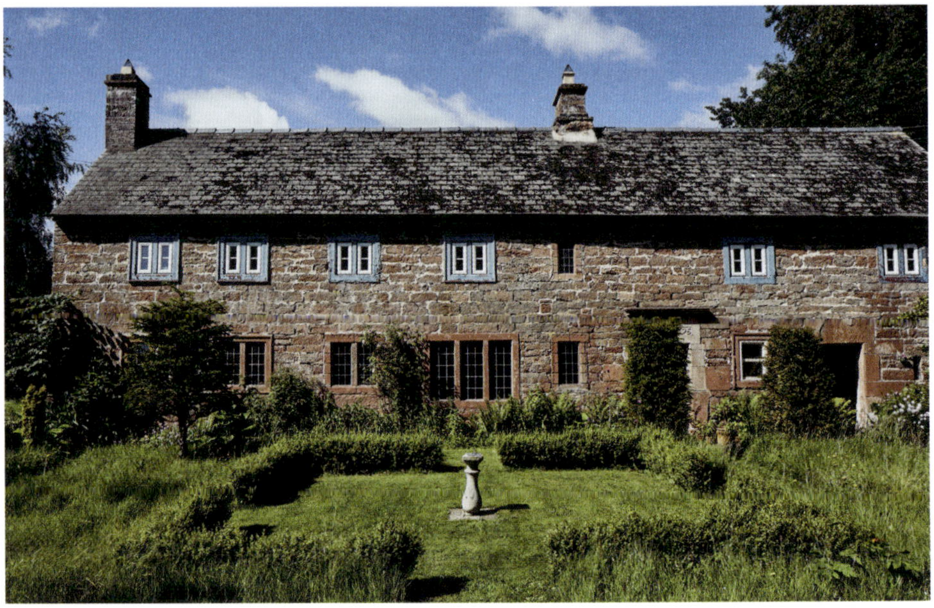

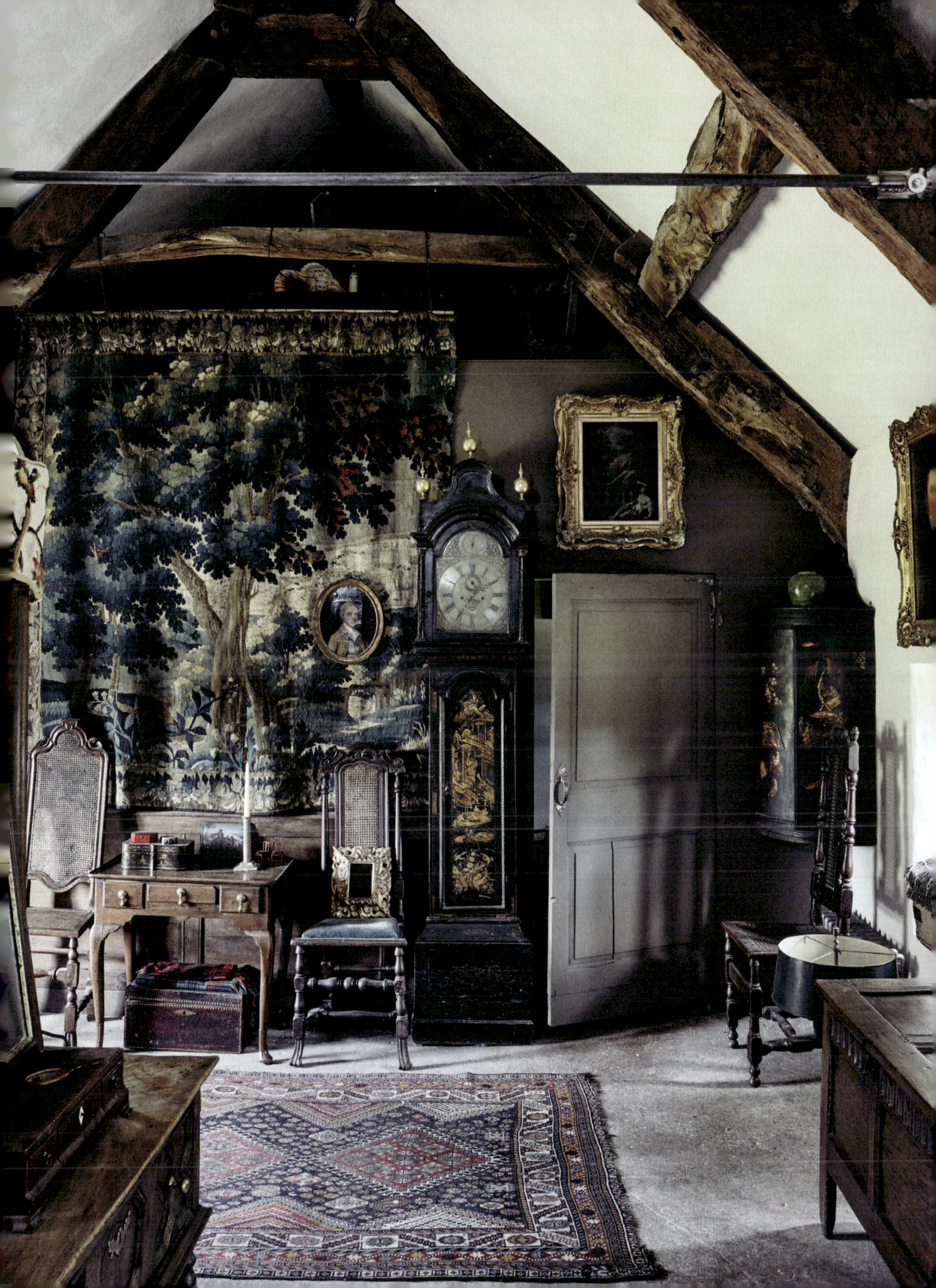

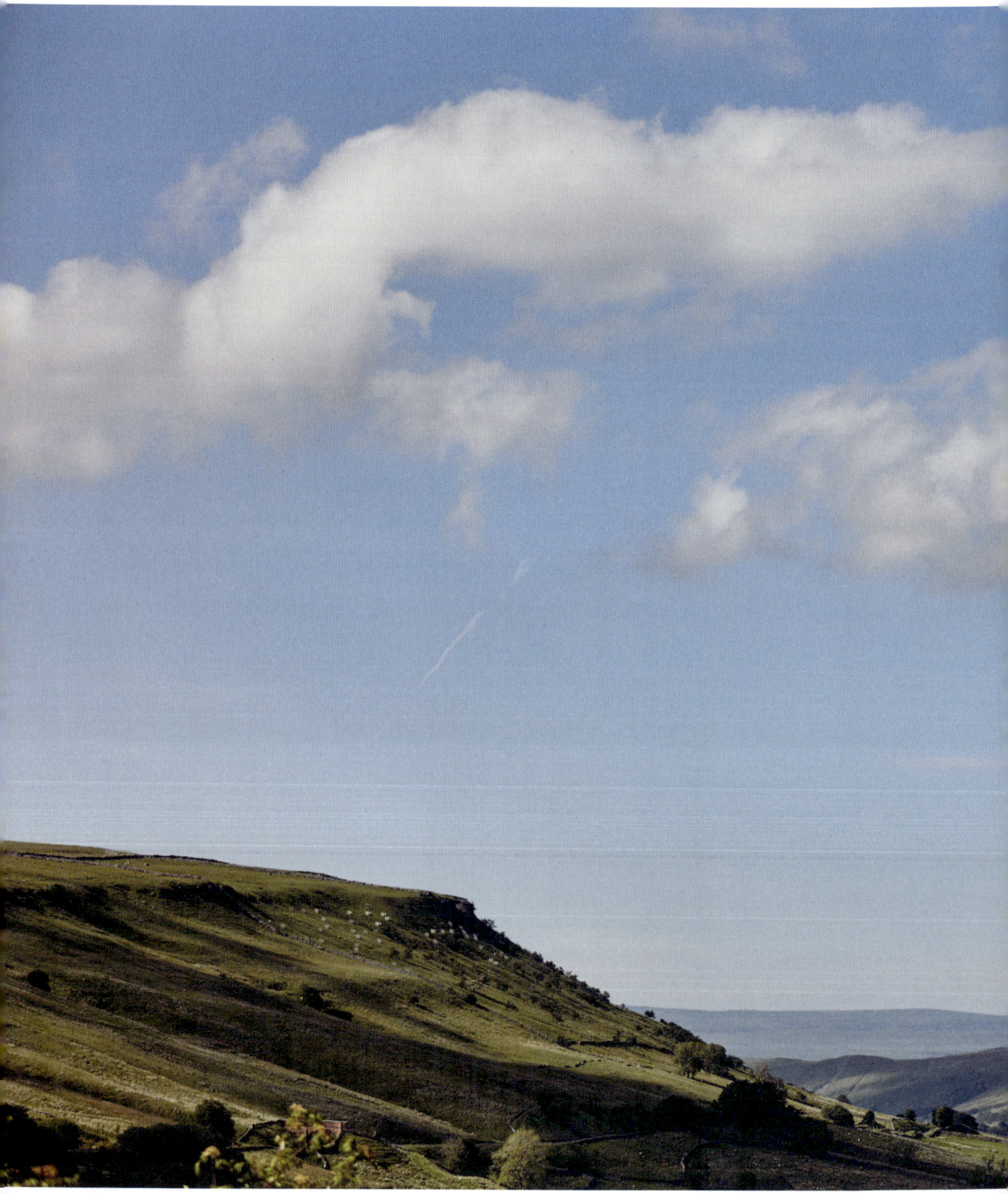

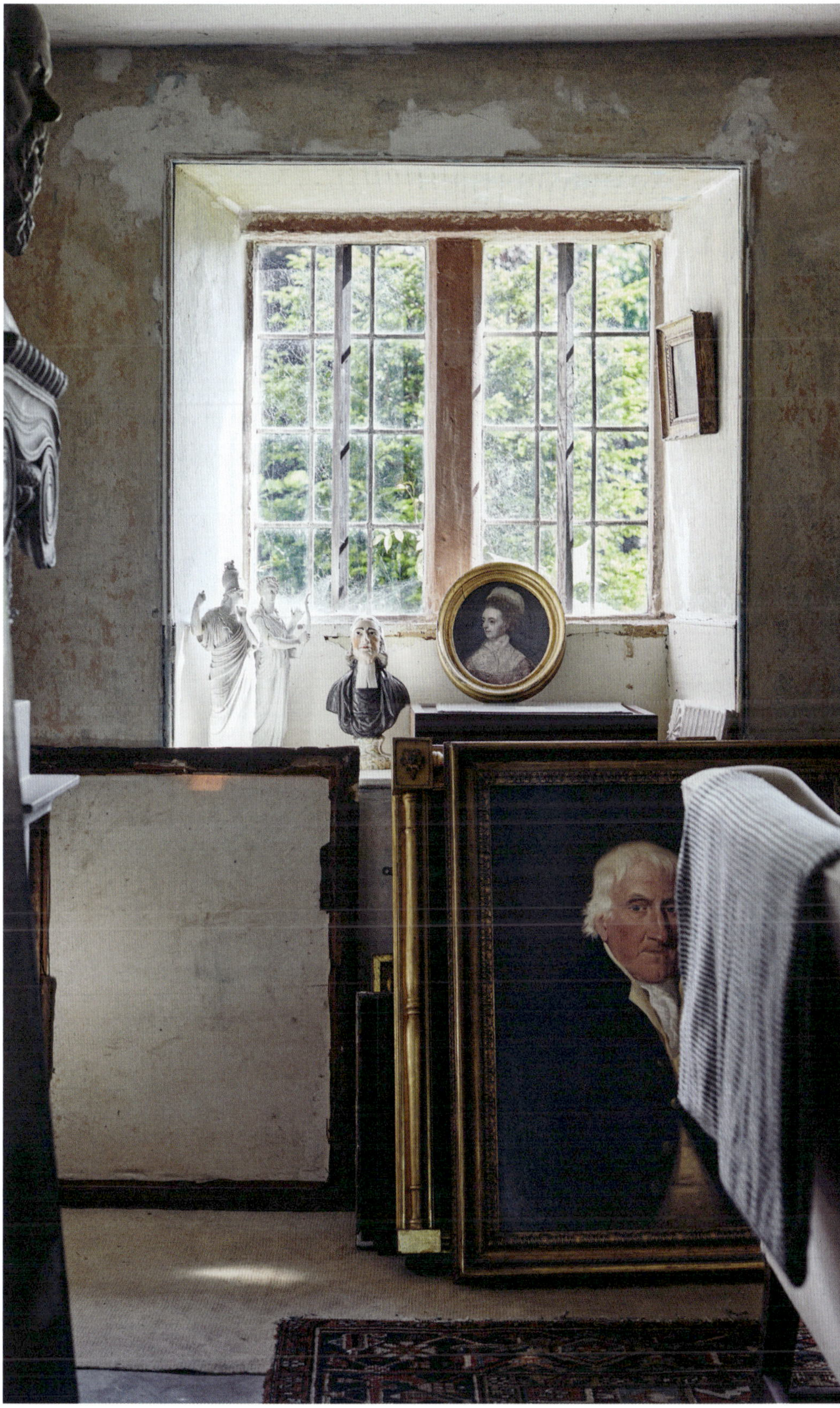

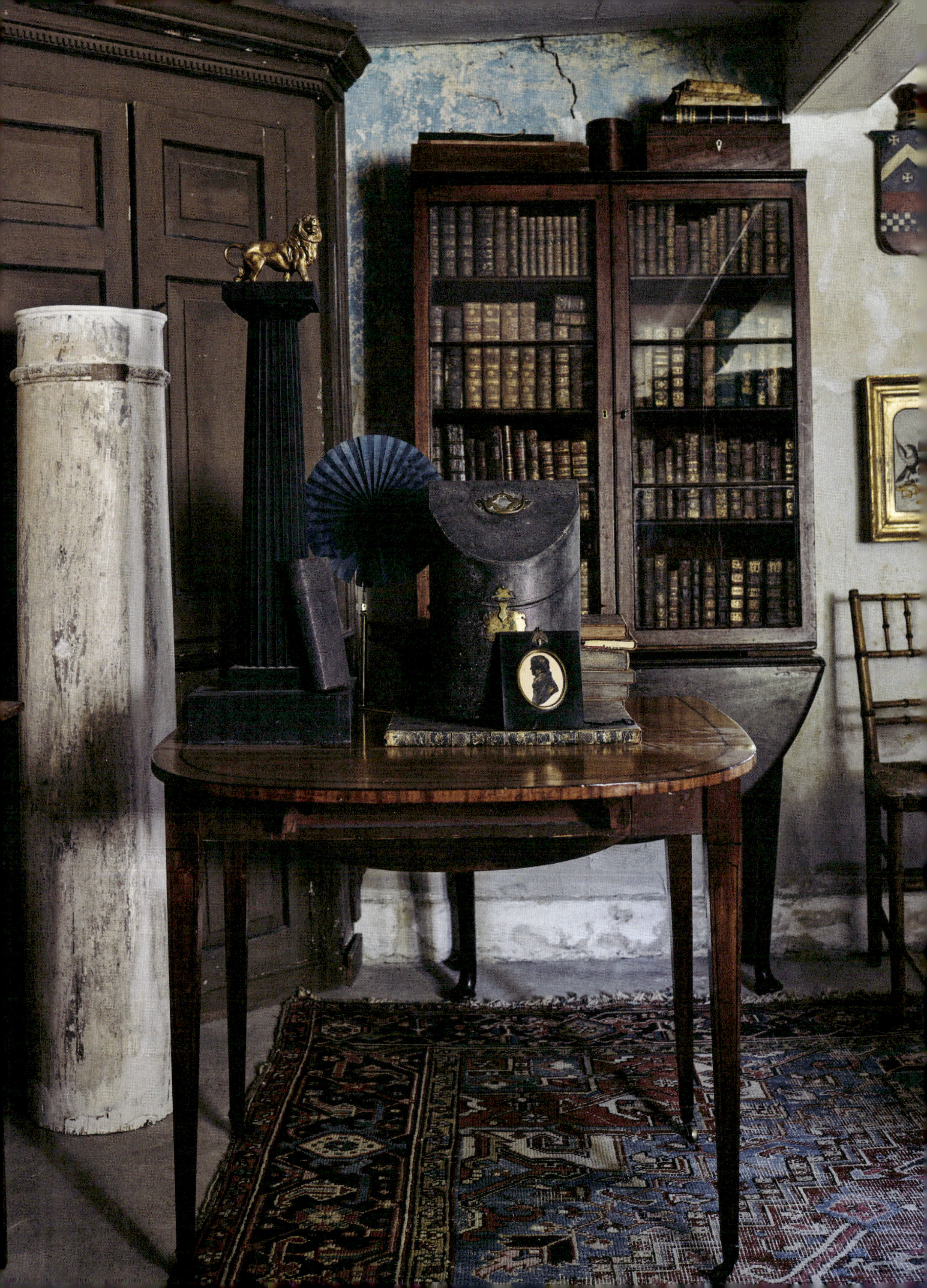

'I couldn't believe my luck, that I could restore it myself.' The house simply groaned with history - regardless of the changes it had undergone over the years. He knew exactly what was needed: a sympathetic restoration rather than drastic renovation to return the longhouse as closely as possible to its former state. Despite being a farm building, it had been handsomely built with some features - such as gypsum floors and high A-frames in the roof - typical at the time in more prestigious buildings. Of course, Tim wanted to preserve those features, uncover as much character as he could and get to the bones of the place.

With delight Tim and Harvey discovered stone inglenooks boxed in behind 1980s fireplaces, flagstones and wooden floorboards beneath threadbare carpets, and gnarled oak beams under plaster. Possibly the best discovery was a flight of stone steps bowed with age and worn to a shine from three centuries of footfall, covered up beneath wooden steps. Upstairs the space had been divided with partition walls into four small bedrooms and two bathrooms, but Tim and Harvey returned it to the original layout of two large bedrooms and gave each an en-suite. 'We insulated the roof and added cast-iron radiators to keep the Cumbrian chill at bay,' he explains, 'and even in winter this thick-walled, well-built house keeps out the cold.'

Once they had worked their magic on the restoration, they were able to introduce their flawlessly timeless style. A lifetime working with heritage buildings and joyous trawling of antiques fairs stood Tim in good stead. 'We had amassed many treasures,' he says, adding with relish, 'and with the extra space here we had a free rein to hunt for more.' Gradually the house filled up with stately antique oak furniture, sumptuous yet unostentatious fabrics, portraits, sculptures, busts and ornaments, all set against a quiet colour scheme. The result is an utterly appropriate blend of grace and humility sitting with ease in the farmhouse.

Winding the clock back thirty years to Tim's first teenage visit, it seems that fate had a plan for this man and this house to unite. There is no doubt that his seventh-great grandparents would have approved.

'IN TERMS OF DECORATING STYLE,

we wanted to reflect the house's age and character and bring only items that would complement the house and sit comfortably in its 300-year-old walls.'

A PEACEFUL PAST

A village house with a rich history makes a characterful yet cosy home for the Sandford family.

It was completely by chance that Wendy and Ian Sandford stumbled upon the village where they subsequently found their home. They had decided to take a scenic route when driving round rural Warwickshire one day. When Ian asked 'Left or right?' Wendy picked right and they found themselves weaving through the narrowest, prettiest of lanes and into a village that felt as if it had been frozen in time. Charming stone houses huddled round a large village green, and nothing other than the odd tractor or dog roaming the lane disturbed the timeless peace of the place.

Wendy and Ian - who at the time lived only a few miles away - at first couldn't believe this well-kept secret was real. They began to come here regularly with their little boy Harry and dog Taggie for walks, or for a drink in the local pub. It wasn't long before they got to know the locals, and Wendy happened to befriend Nadia, a lady who lived in a particularly lovely village house. Wendy would often sit in Nadia's kitchen gossiping, and Nadia promised to keep an eye out for property on sale in the village. One day, to Wendy's surprise, Nadia asked her if she would be interested in buying the house they were sitting in. Wendy, who was pregnant with no. 2 at the time, remembers thinking 'That's a no brainer!' She explained, 'I already loved the place and wanted more space for the family.' And a couple of months later, just before Freddie's arrival, they found themselves the happy owners of this wonderful family home.

Dating back to 1760, the house was once made up of three separate dwellings: a bakery, a post office and a butcher's shop. It is full of quirky period features: crooked doorways, age-worn flagstones, creaky floorboards and wonky beams, all contributing to an atmosphere of calmness and history. It was easily spacious enough to accommodate their family of four, a generous size for entertaining friends comfortably, but still very cosy when the family were at home by themselves. It also has an extensive, exciting garden 'with lots of hidden nooks and crannies for the boys to explore' plus a converted barn that could be rented out for extra income. It ticked every box.

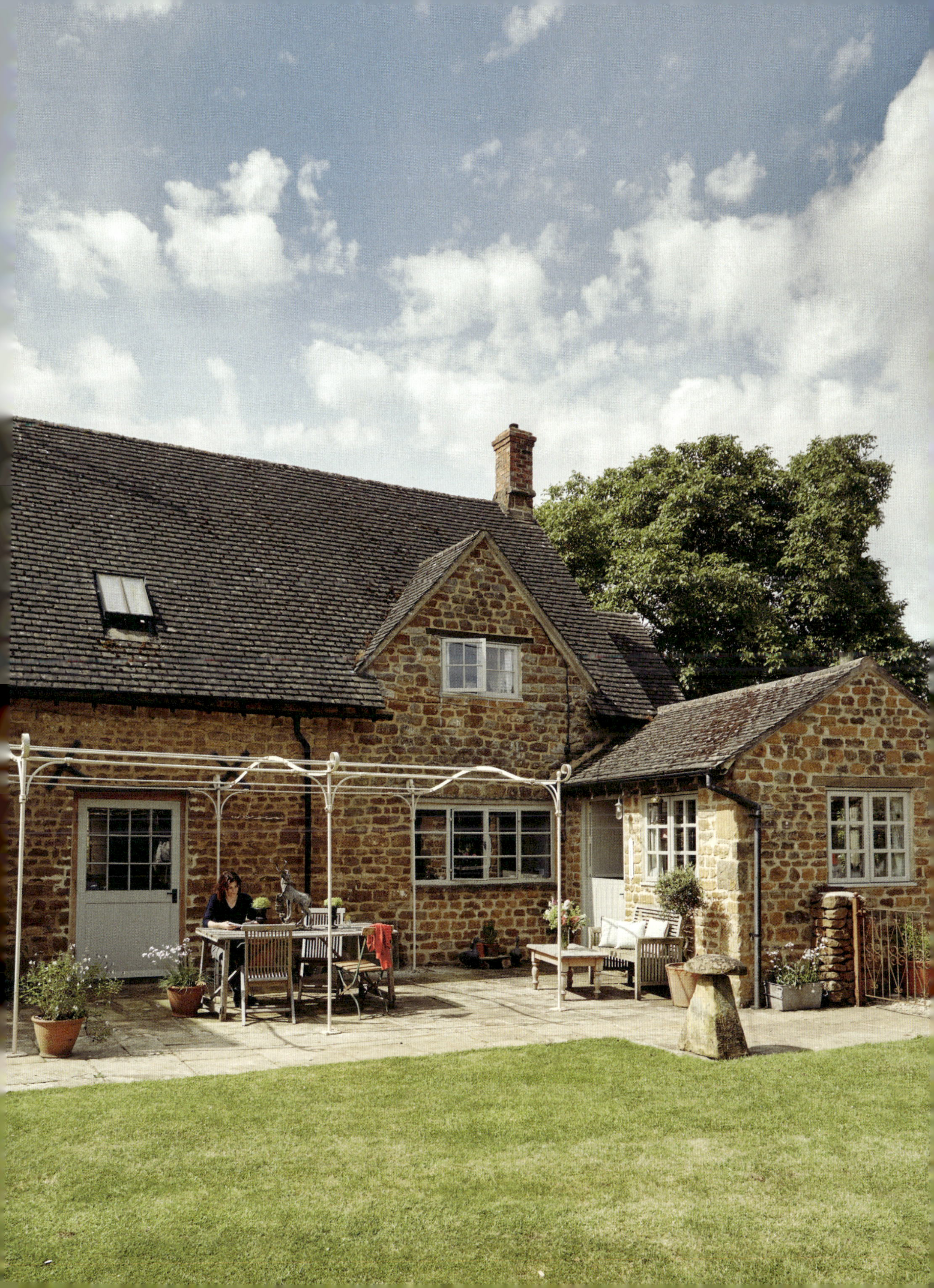

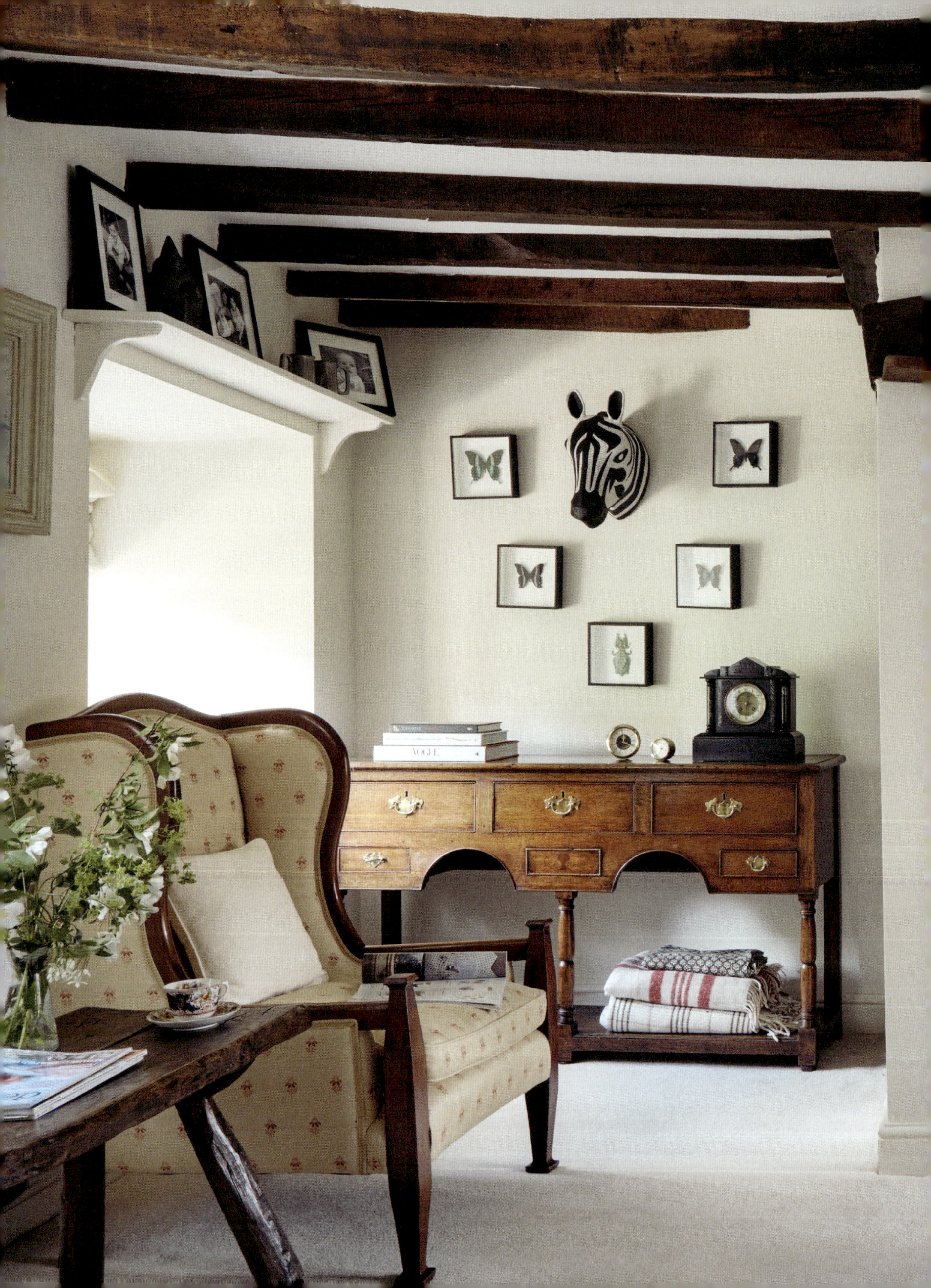
VOGUE

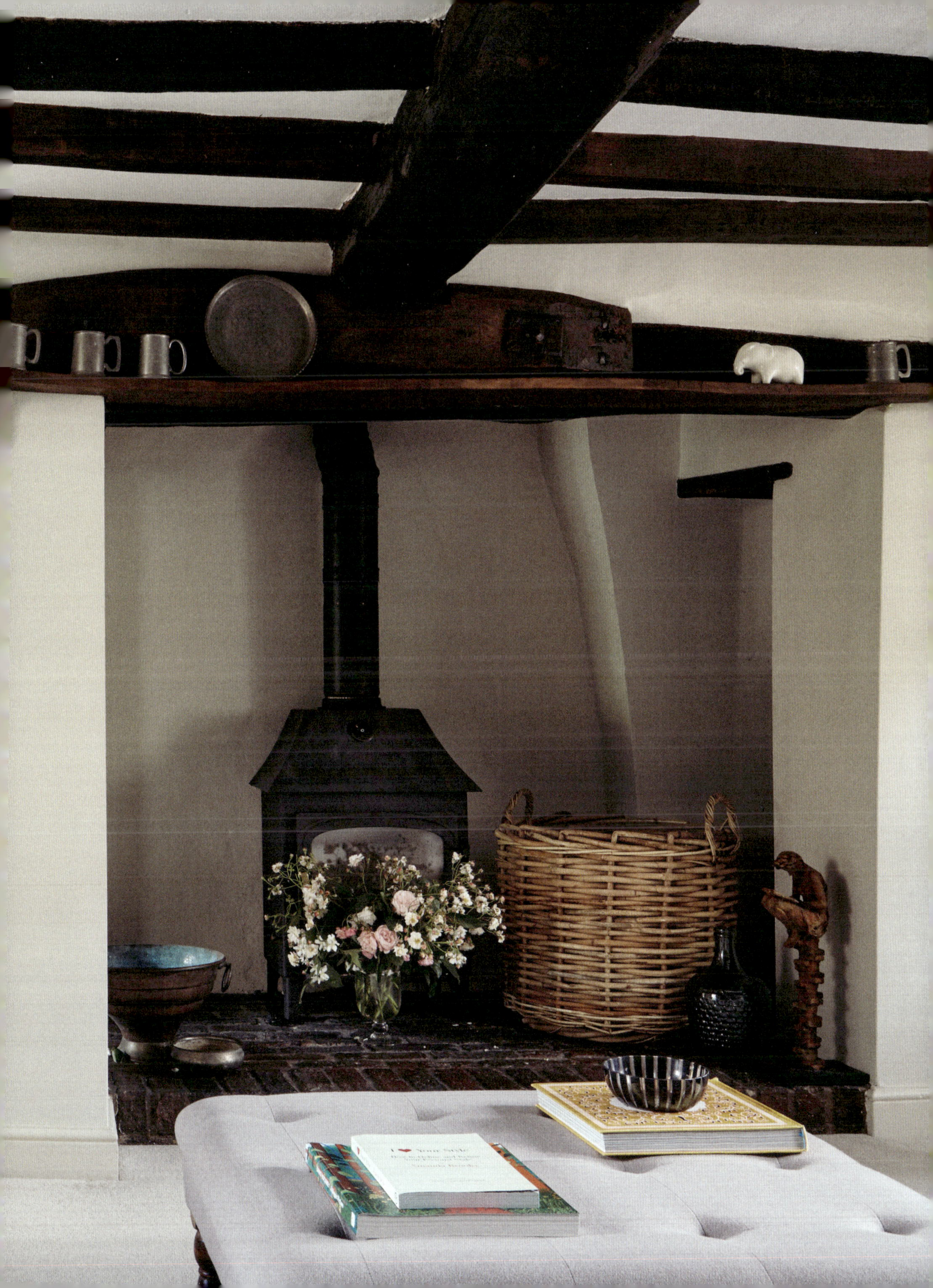

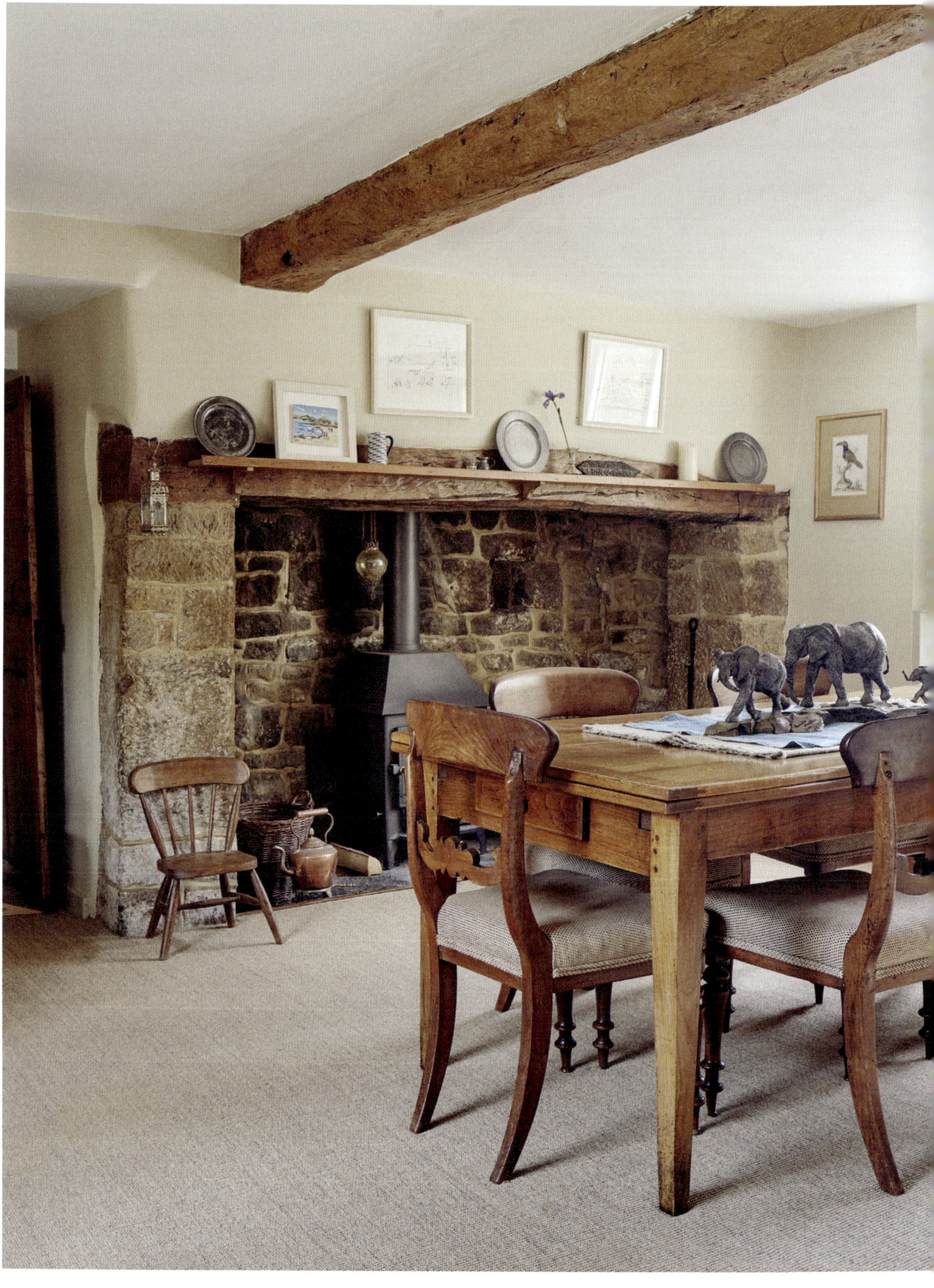

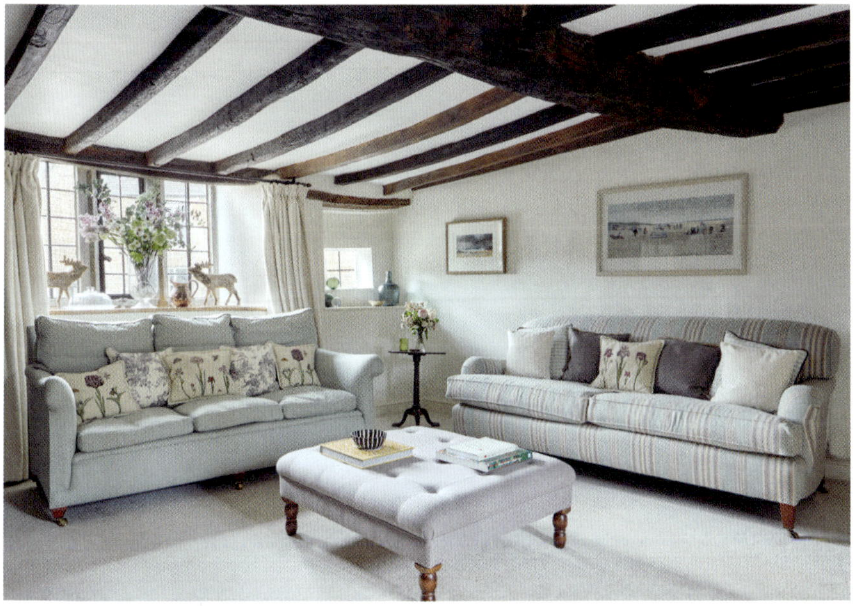

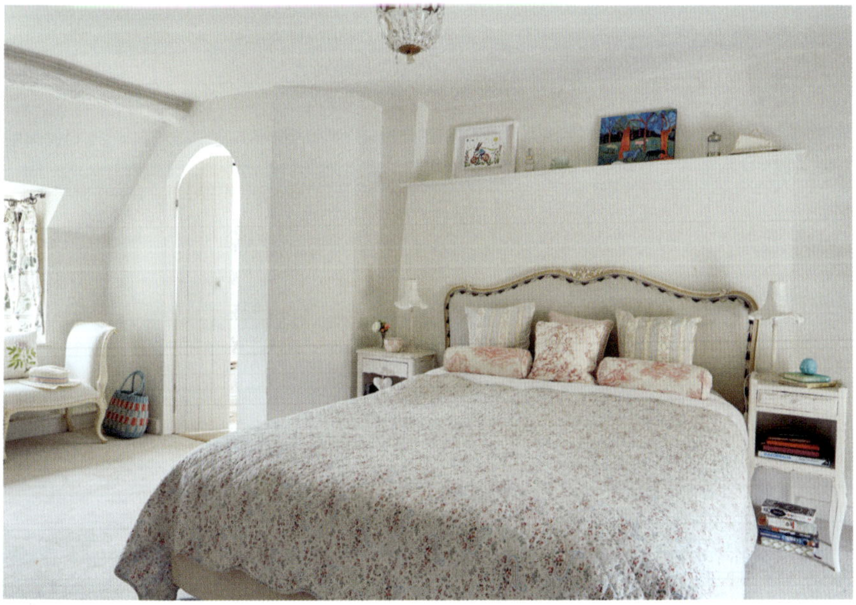

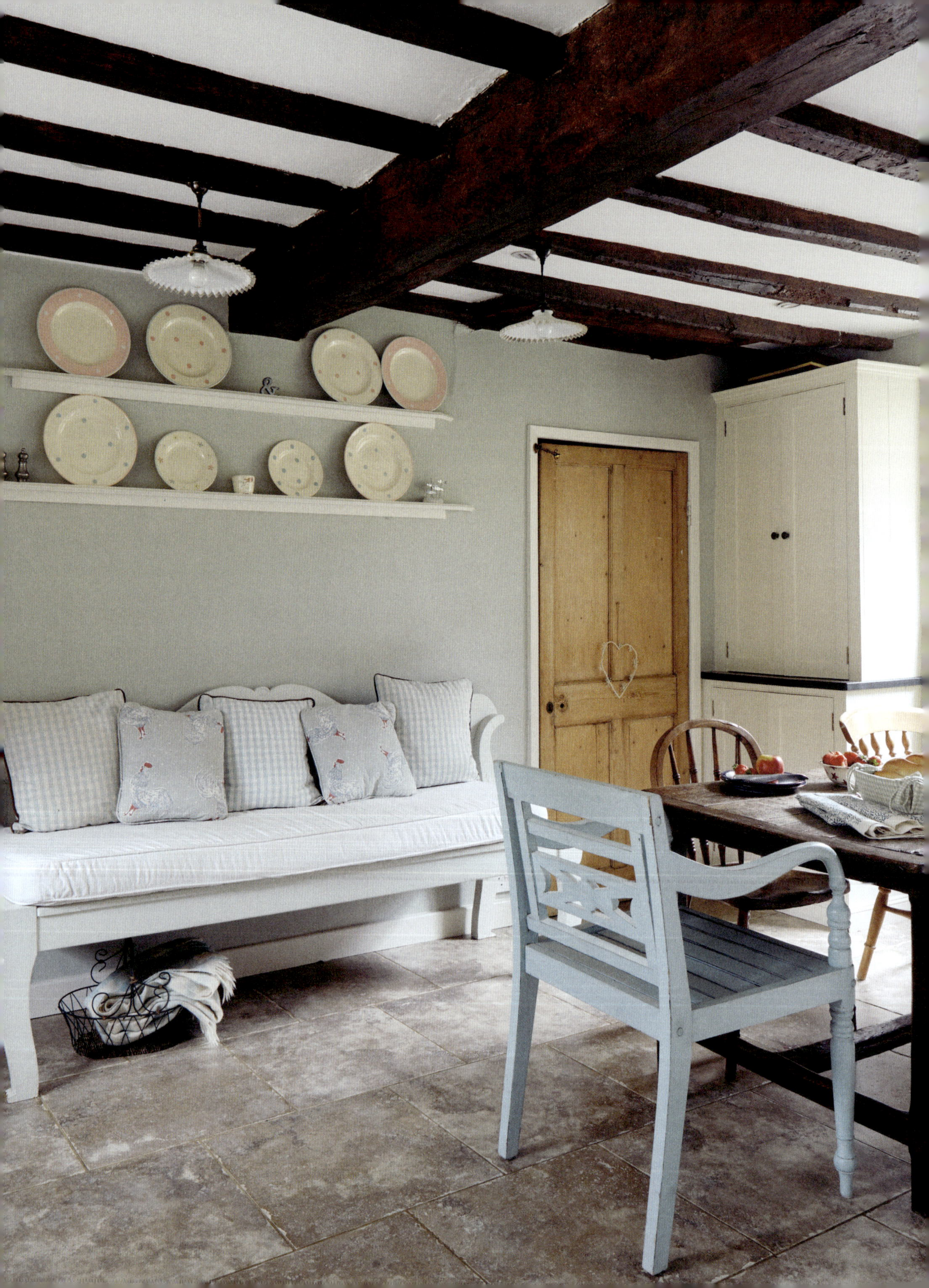

Life was busy with two very little boys, and so - other than repainting the house from top to bottom - Wendy and Ian just got to know their home before making any major changes. When Freddie was 2, they took action and embarked on bringing their lovely but jaded home up to date. Time had taken its toll on the three chimneys, which after standing proud for over three hundred years had begun to crumble alarmingly. They had all three rebuilt in keeping with the period of the house. They then had the two tired bathrooms gutted and replaced with fresh modern fittings. Next, they refloored the kitchen in light grey flagstones and had the old units replaced with a fitted Shaker-style kitchen, again in pale, light-enhancing colours. Then they recarpeted throughout in pale colours to give the whole house a feeling of light. Wendy loves a traditional English country style with French and Scandinavian influences. She feels great affinity with the character of this old country house and relishes the chance to buy it fitting gifts, usually the result of a visit to the local auction room for an unusual antique or interesting work of art.

When life had calmed down and their home was complete, the family took a well-earned holiday. Their peace was shattered when their cleaning lady called them in a panic with news that the bathroom had flooded into the sitting room beneath. The family rushed home to find the newly painted and carpeted room in chaos, with damp plaster and pools of water all over the floor. In their true calm style, they took it their stride and it wasn't long before the 260-year-old house had recovered. It was just one more story to add to its history, and Wendy says, 'That's what we love about the house. It must have so many secrets, but somehow they are absorbed into its ancient walls, and each one adds character.' And no doubt it has a great future ahead of it too because this family is not going anywhere, 'It's our home for life,' declares Wendy proudly.

'MY STYLE EVOLVES

as I get older, and trips abroad have inspired and influenced me.
I love to add a fabric, painting or ornament found on a trip away
to remind me of another place. It's all part of our life story.'

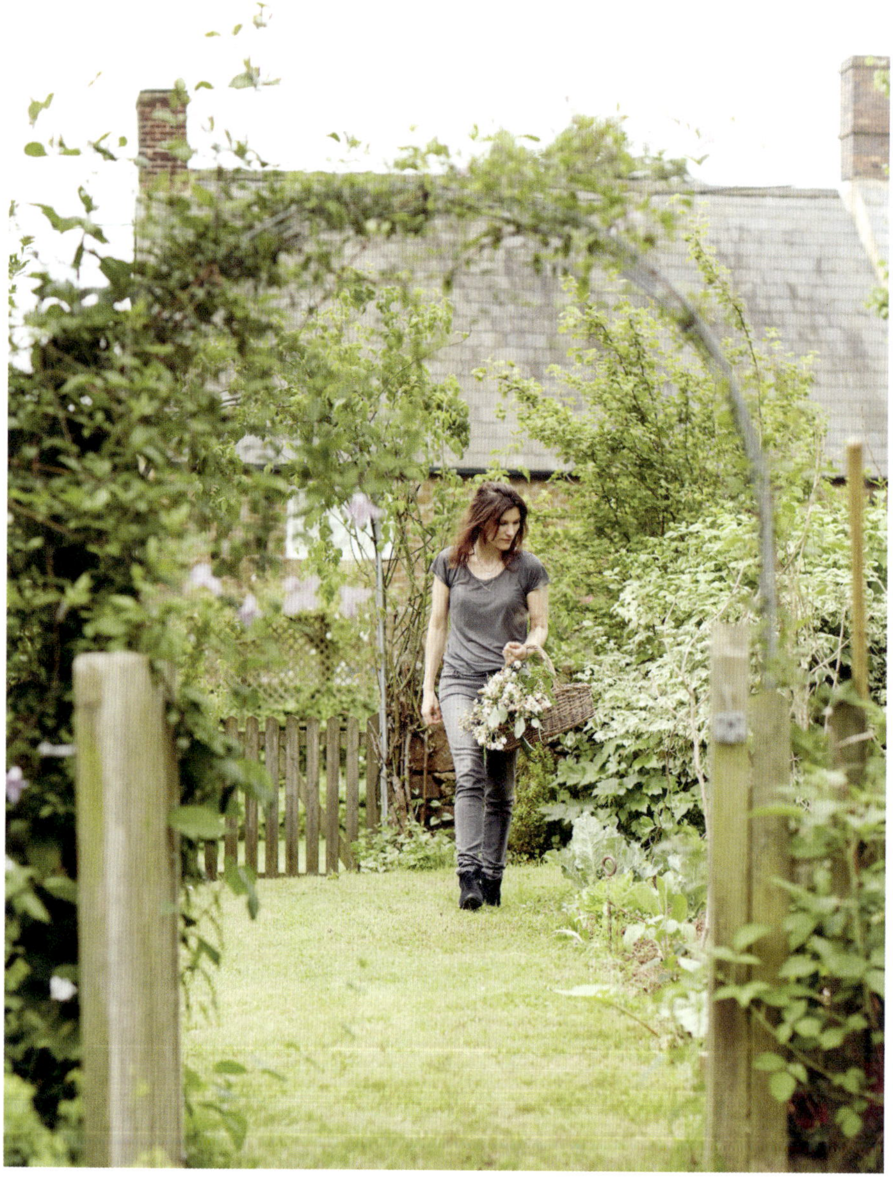

'THE HOUSE WORKS SO WELL

throughout the seasons – I open all the doors and windows in summer and the house is filled with the sound of birdsong and the scents of summer, but in winter we batten down the hatches, light the fires and enjoy the cosiness of this sturdily built stone house.'

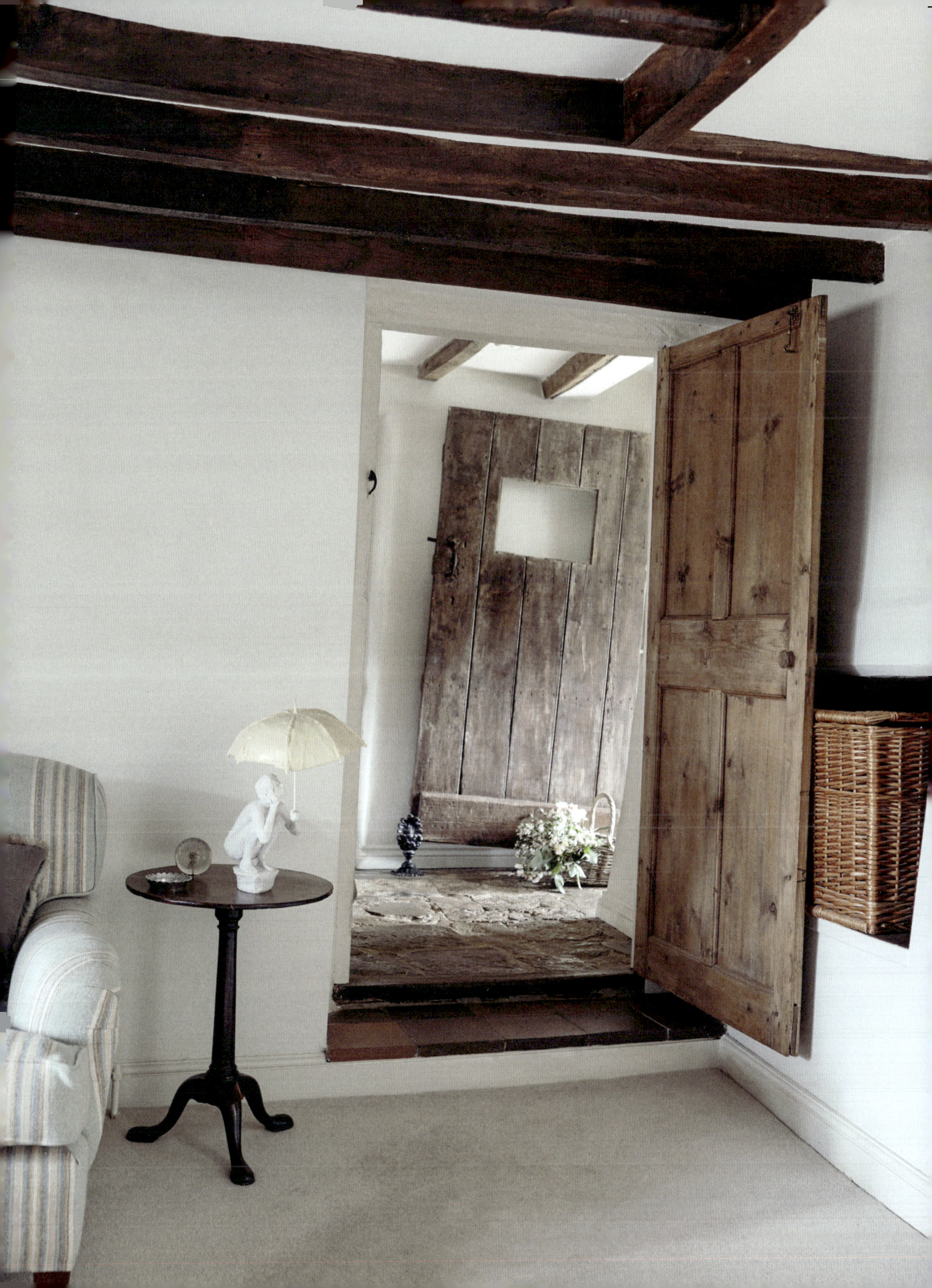

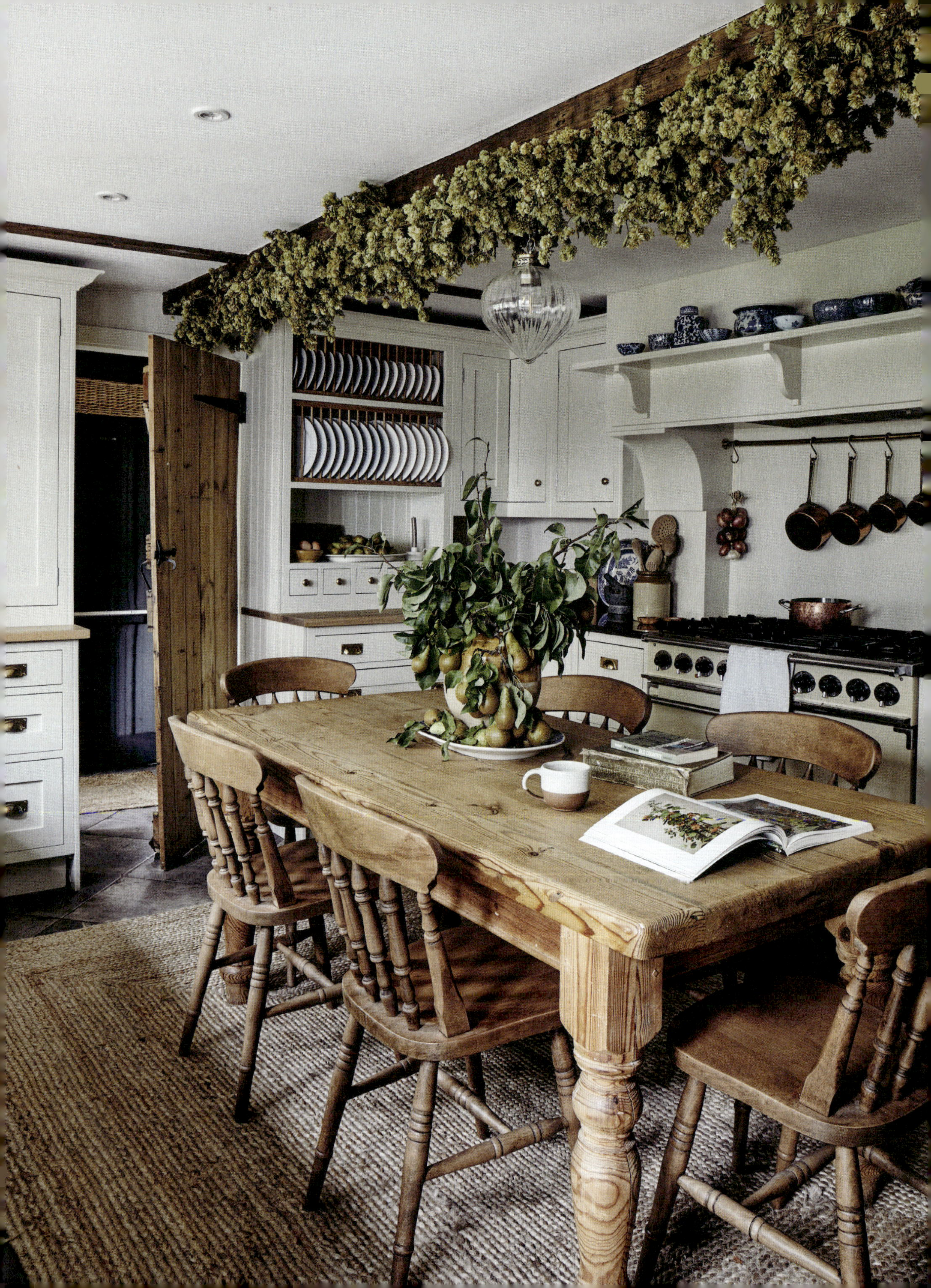

ROOM AT THE INN

A glimpse of the biggest fireplace she'd ever seen was enough to convince Kate Pinnock that this converted coaching inn was the place for her.

There's a little-known town in rural Hertfordshire that was once a hub of activity, as the main coaching stop between London and Cambridge. Back then it boasted twenty-two coaching inns, of which all bar one have been converted into homes. When Kate Pinnock learnt that one of these – a 400-year-old timber-framed property – had been on the market for some time and not yet been snapped up, she raced to see it. Kate works in Cambridge as a consultant for a historic building regeneration company, and had for some time wanted to move out of the city. The chance to live in a period property such as this was irresistible.

One look inside and Kate realised instantly why the house had not received a single offer. The stench of cats (evidently lacking litter trays) was unmistakeable. The carpets were thick with filth, the walls were stained and greasy, windows were rotten with broken panes, light fittings had been wrenched from their sockets, and the garden was hidden beneath piles of rubbish. 'The tenants did a midnight dash,' was all the agent could offer in explanation. Closer investigation revealed that for the past decade the owners – who lived abroad – had rented it out. No-one ever knew quite what had gone on in the poor house or why the tenants had vanished under the cloak of darkness.

While most viewers declined the full tour, Kate was undaunted. 'I'd caught sight of the most beautiful, huge ancient brick fireplace,' she explains. 'I didn't need to see beyond that.' Kate's profession had exposed to her to a great many near-derelict period properties and she knew there was always a future for a building that had stood the test of time. 'It had incredible bones,' she recalls. 'Beams running wonkily down the walls, exposed brickwork and wonderful creaky oak doors.' To this day she is almost grateful that the house was in disrepair because the price was within her budget.

Kate moved in April 2019, the month in which the Beast from the East paid its unwelcome visit. The east of England was hit particularly hard, and the temperature dropped to -8. 'The wind comes straight from the Urals,' locals sagely explain. And Kate could quite believe it. Her new home had no electricity or heating for her first six weeks. 'Where a tile had come off the roof, I had a small waterfall pouring in,' laughs Kate. 'In those very first weeks it became an icicle.'

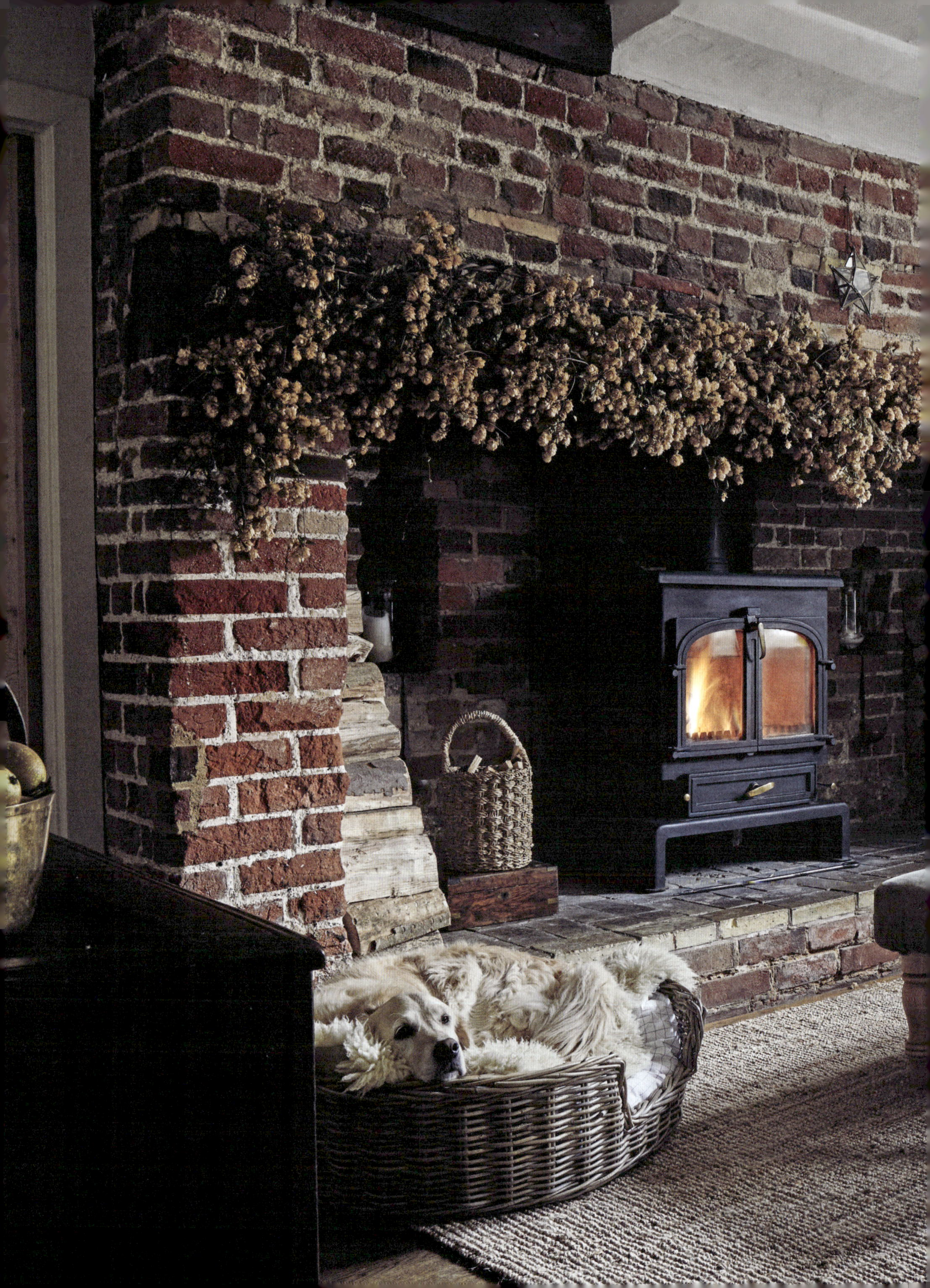

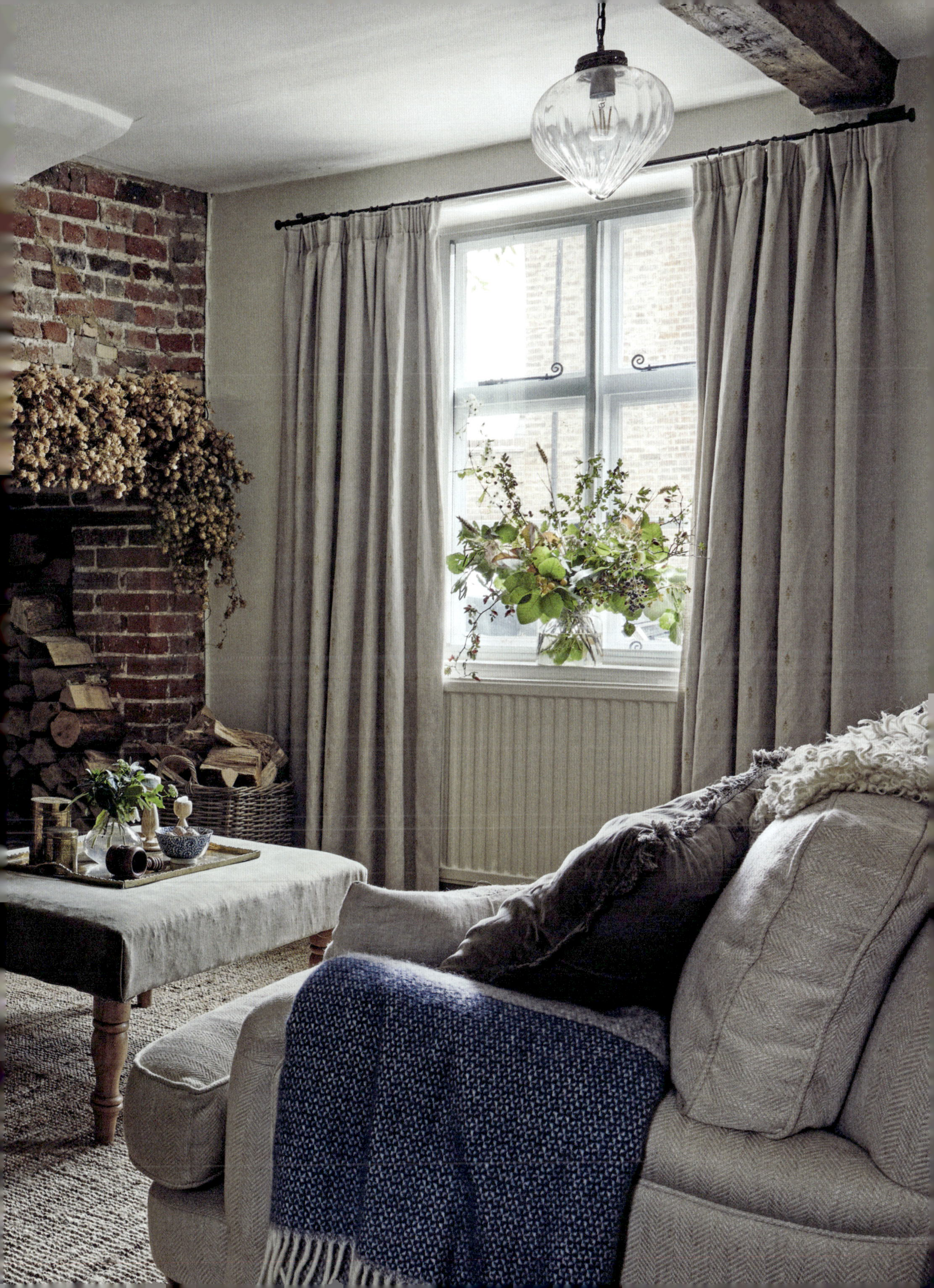

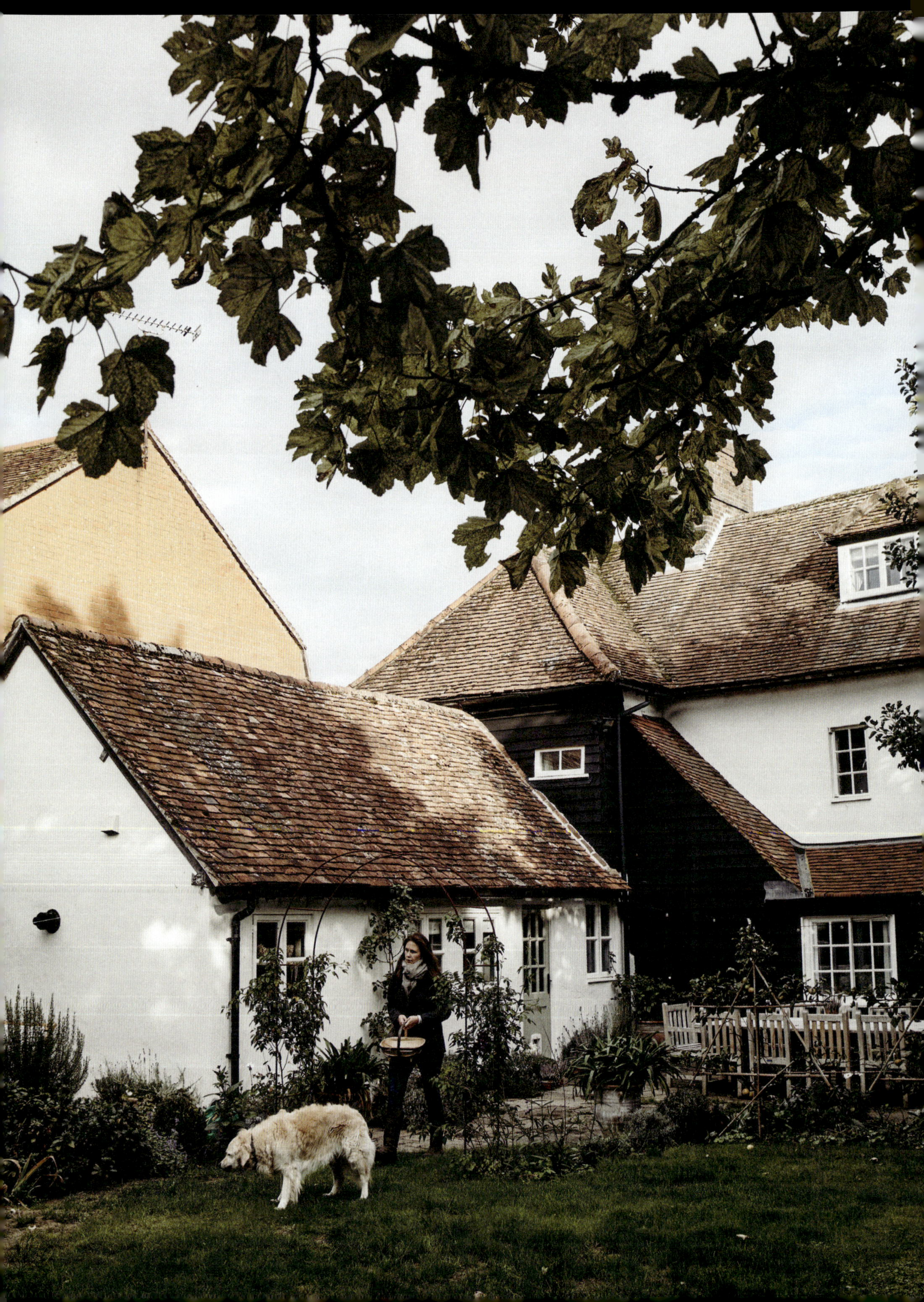

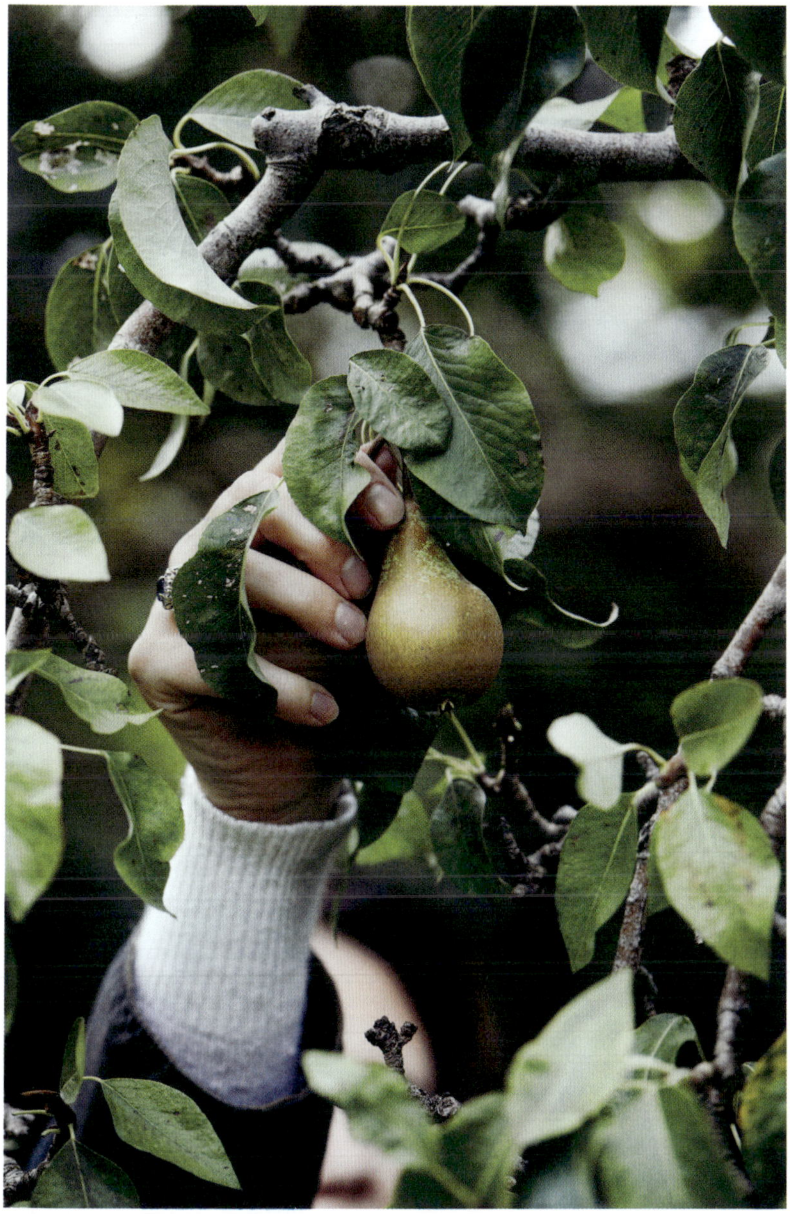

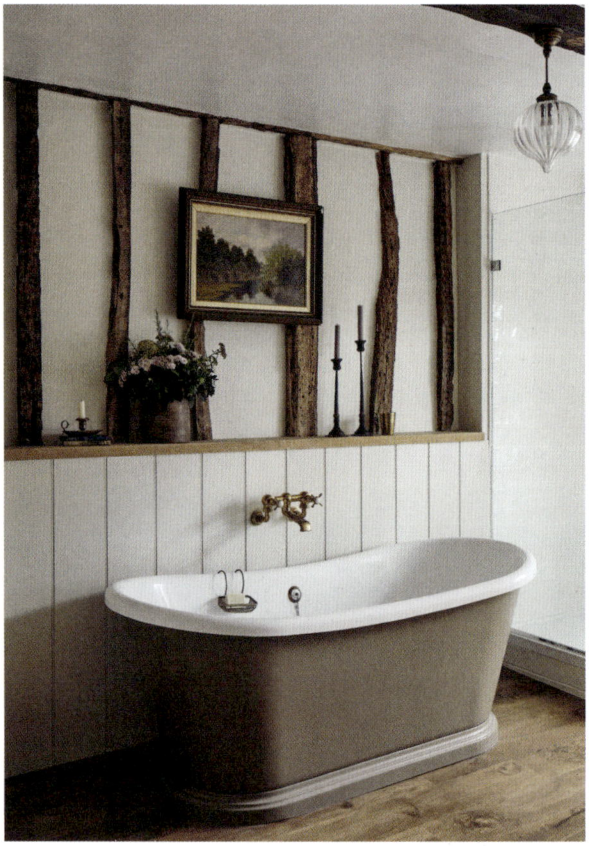

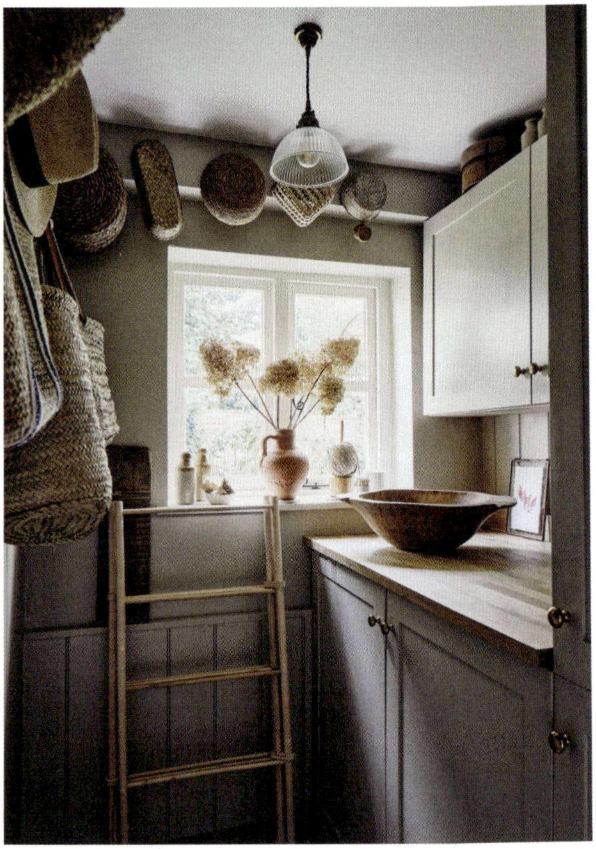

'THE HOUSE STEERED ME AWAY

from displaying much artwork,' says Kate. 'Instead, I picked architectural drawings, etchings of old castles and a fair few antique maps. These seem appropriate in a former coaching inn, a building that played host to many travellers.'

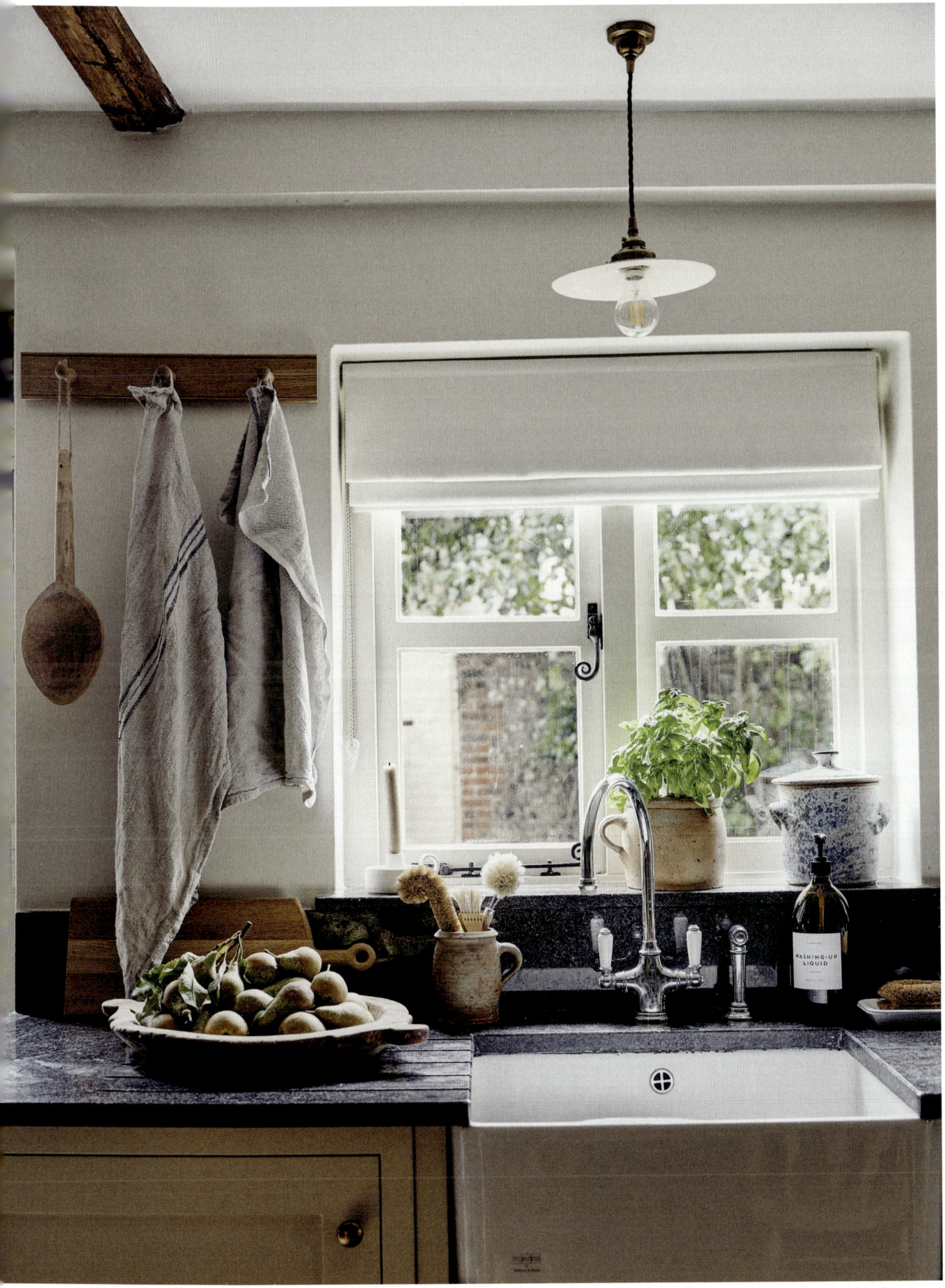
WASHING-UP
LIQUID

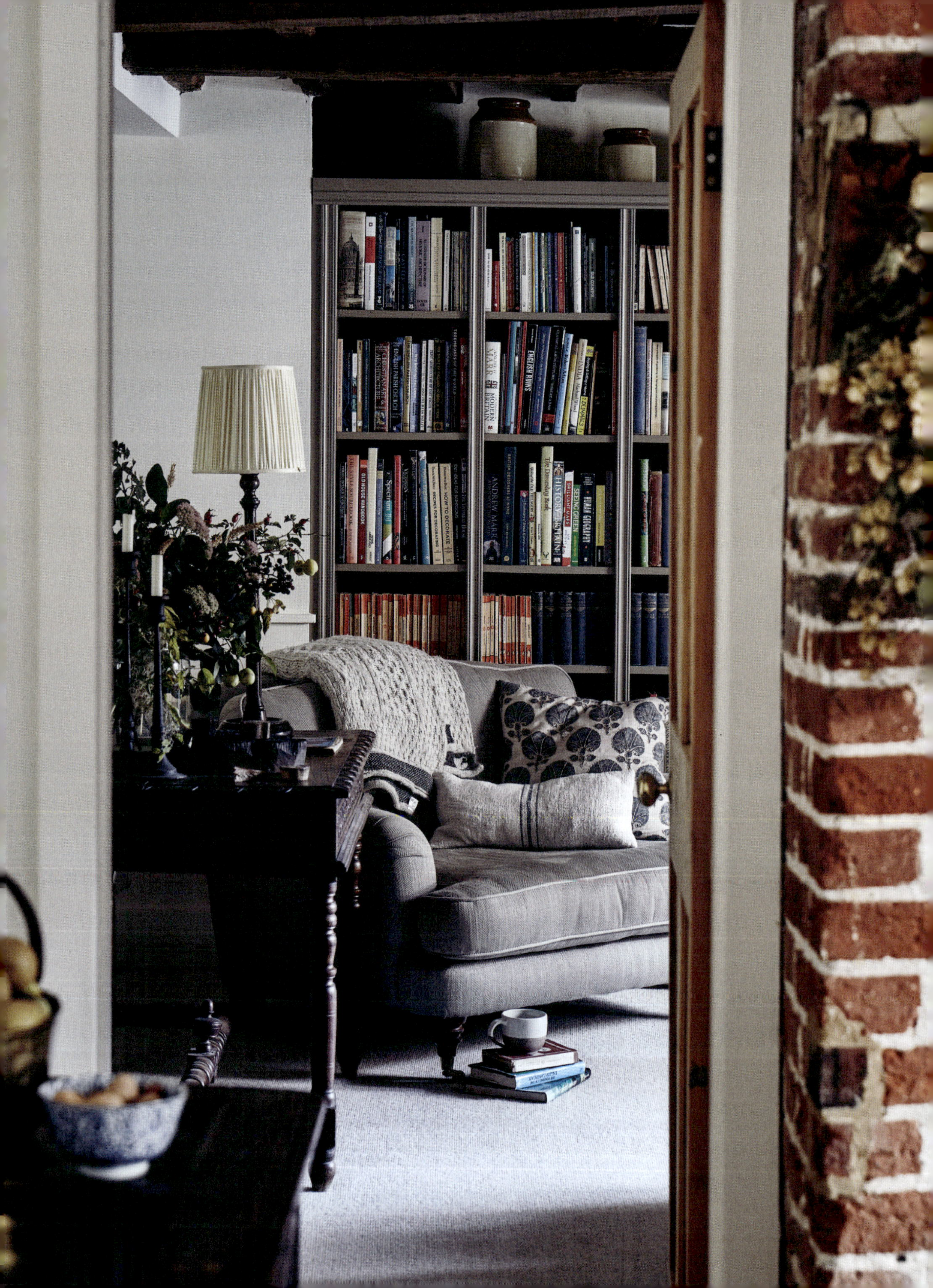
ENGLISH RUINS
HUMAN GEOGRAPHY
ANDREW MARR

Kate lived to tell the tale, and by June the house began to warm up. She lived with scaffolding up for six months while the roof and windows were repaired. Meanwhile she got to work on whatever she could do herself, starting with the top floor and working downwards, sanding the bathroom floors, scrubbing the tiles and doing much of the repainting herself. 'In a house with so much history, you have to take away layers added over time to reveal its true character.' Slowly but methodically the house took shape - and Kate found unusual ways to show off its best features. In the master bathroom, for instance, she left a frame of uncovered beams set back into a wall of panelling to lay bare the original bones of the room.

'It sounds far fetched, but I had to listen to the house,' explains Kate. 'While I had thought I would bring bright colours and bold furnishings in, the house had other ideas. Before long I realised that the look I was creating was very muted. I was choosing very natural colours: pale sage greens, off-whites, shades of brown. Probably a similar colour scheme to that of the original coaching inn.' The result is calm and harmonious. Nothing clashes, and the eye is not distracted by loud furnishings but instead drawn to the original features.

When it came to furniture, Kate again worked with the house and chose mostly items that fitted its history: oak farmhouse tables and chairs, antique dressers, reclaimed cabinets. She has added appropriate ornaments and accessories, choosing only vintage-style items which complement the timeless scheme. Her choice of natural linens, weaves and textiles likewise blends effortlessly. She opted for aged brass fittings and handles, finding one-off pieces in reclamation yards and on eBay.Her kitchen is a particular pièce de résistance and starkly reminiscent of the pub's heritage. A swathe of hops hangs above the kitchen table, and copper pans, earthenware pots, wicker baskets and hanging wooden breadboards recall the past life of this old coaching inn.

'What I've learnt from my professional job as well as the project on my old pub,' reveals Kate, 'is to let the building lead the way. If you keep quiet, and patient, it will guide you.'

'MY COLOUR CHOICES

were straightforward. I had never done this before, but I chose one column of a paint chart and painted in the different shades throughout.'

RISEN FROM THE ASHES

A thatched cottage that five years ago almost burnt to the ground has had new life breathed into it by its resourceful and creative new owner.

'A garden and character,' were Harriet Orr-Ewing's two stipulations when house hunting in west Oxfordshire. Having lived in London for twenty years ('Ten years too long, I now realise,' she says), she was more than ready for a change. Since trading in her office job for her true love, garden design, she had grown out of pavement pounding and the confines of small city-garden jobs and wanted to broaden her canvas. 'I loved the diversity of London but I'm a country girl at heart,' she confesses.

'The penny finally dropped when I got a puppy,' Harriet reveals. Dandie Dinmont terrier Elfie changed everything. 'Loading a reluctant dog, a load of plants and gardening equipment off the pavement each day into a hot car seemed totally wrong,' says Harriet. Within a few months of Elfie's arrival, she had sold her west London flat.

Harriet had a narrow search area, and it took over a year of hunting and a lot of disappointment before she found 'the one'. Just as she was losing hope, a cottage came up for sale, strangely next door to a cottage she had hoped to buy a year before. A thatched cottage, sturdily built in stone, with a sunny south facing façade, its pavement appeal was huge. Harriet hardly dared hope that its promise would continue inside. But the interior had great potential too. With two reception rooms downstairs with south- and north-facing windows and a double aspect master bedroom above, the three main rooms of the house were generously sized and flooded with light.

An elderly lady had lived here for many years and unsurprisingly the interior decor was somewhat old fashioned, with green carpets throughout and quite a lot of heavy, dark wood. However, it had wonderful features too: a sash window, gnarled beams, old scrubbed pine shutters, deep window seats and a vast inglenook fireplace. And it was in good structural shape, with new timber windows and, importantly, a recently replaced thatched roof.

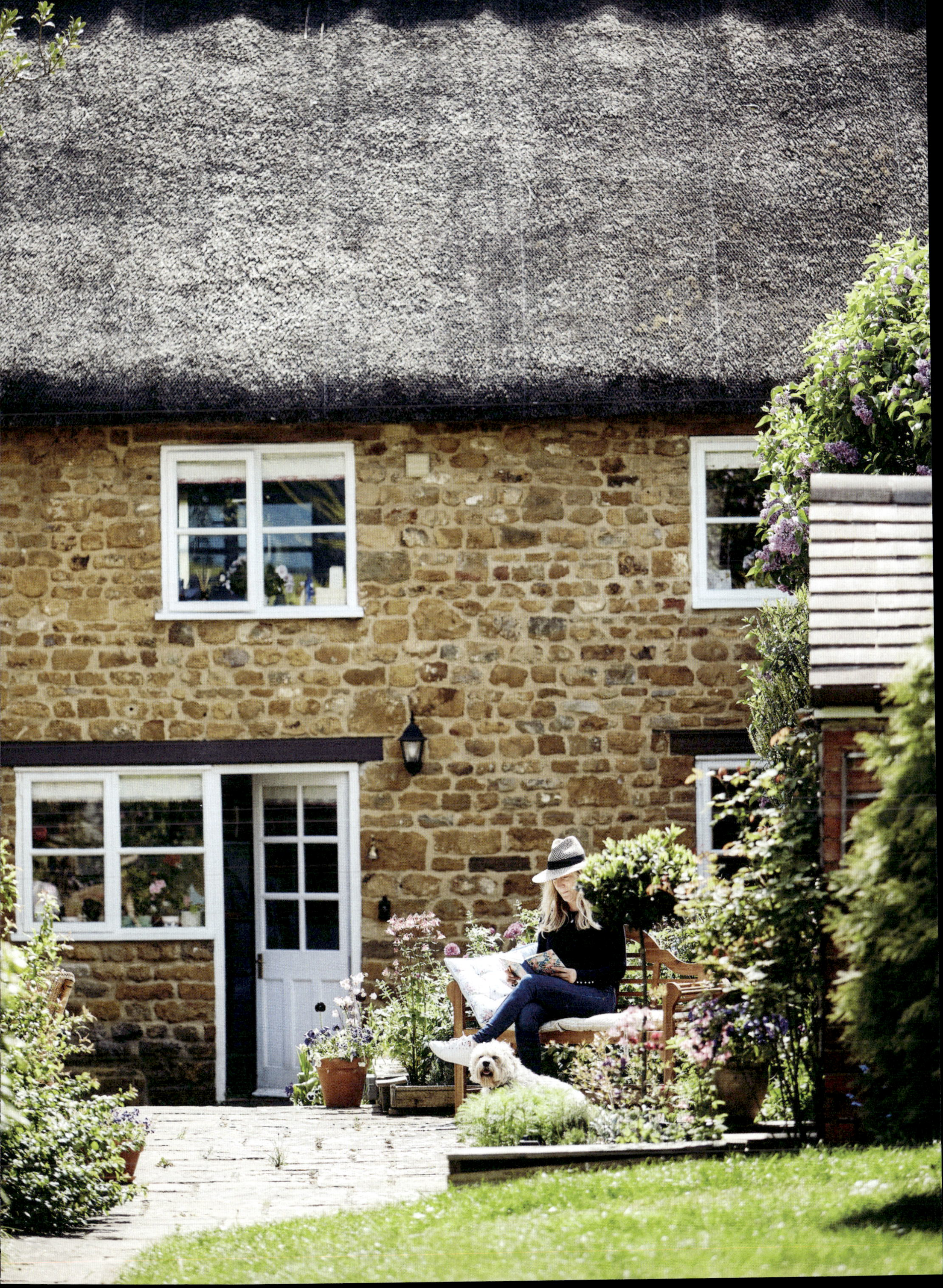

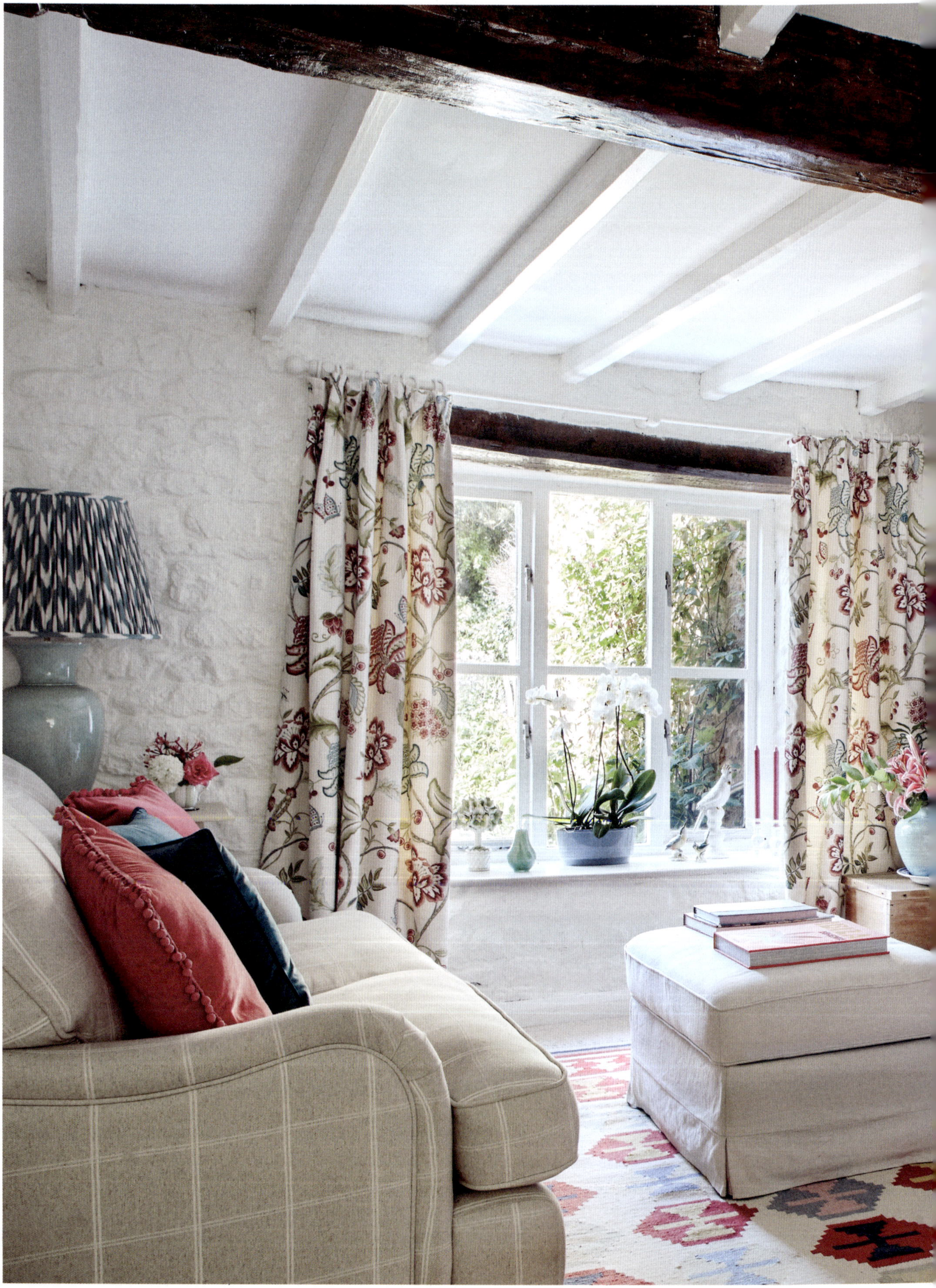

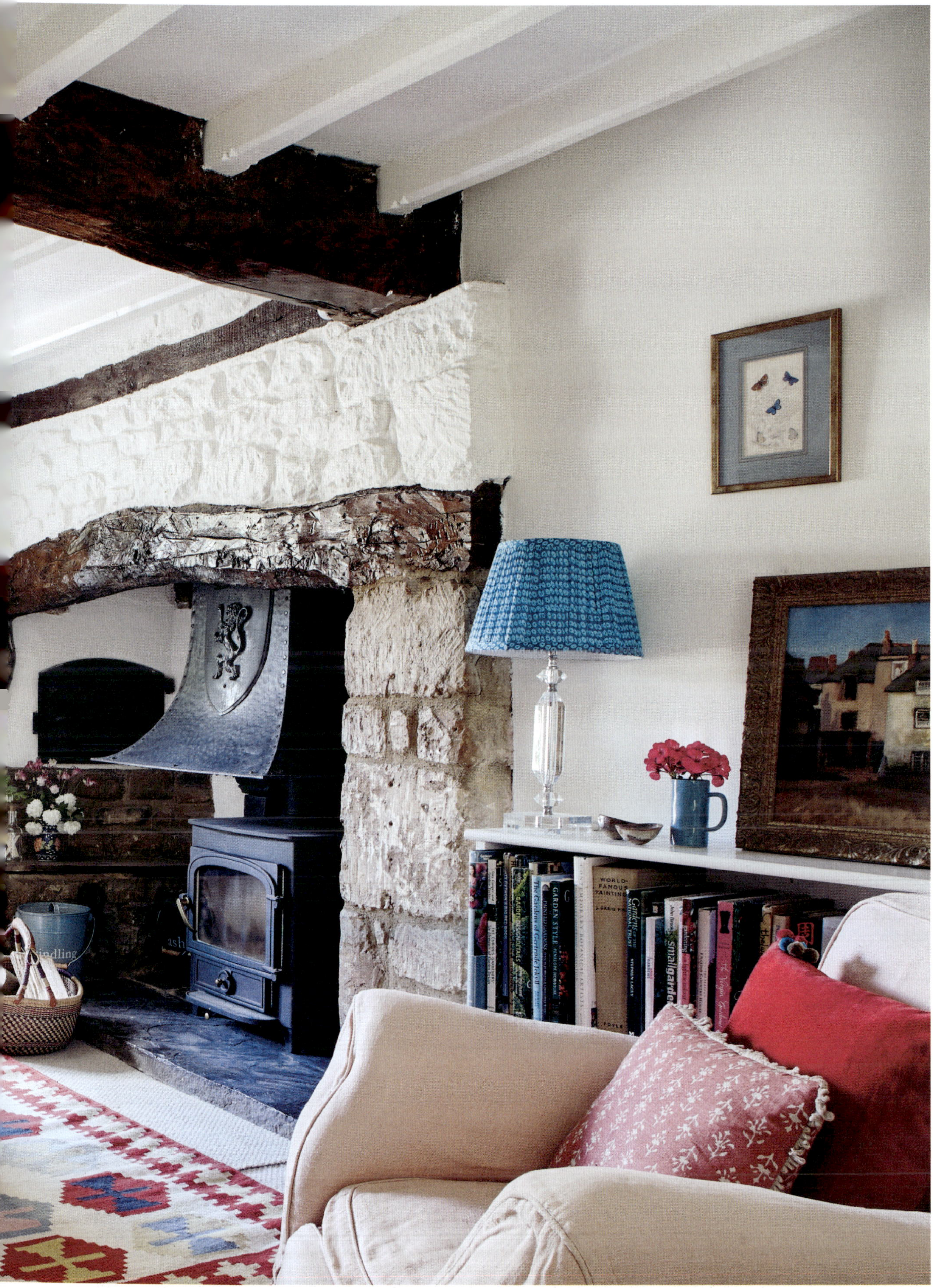

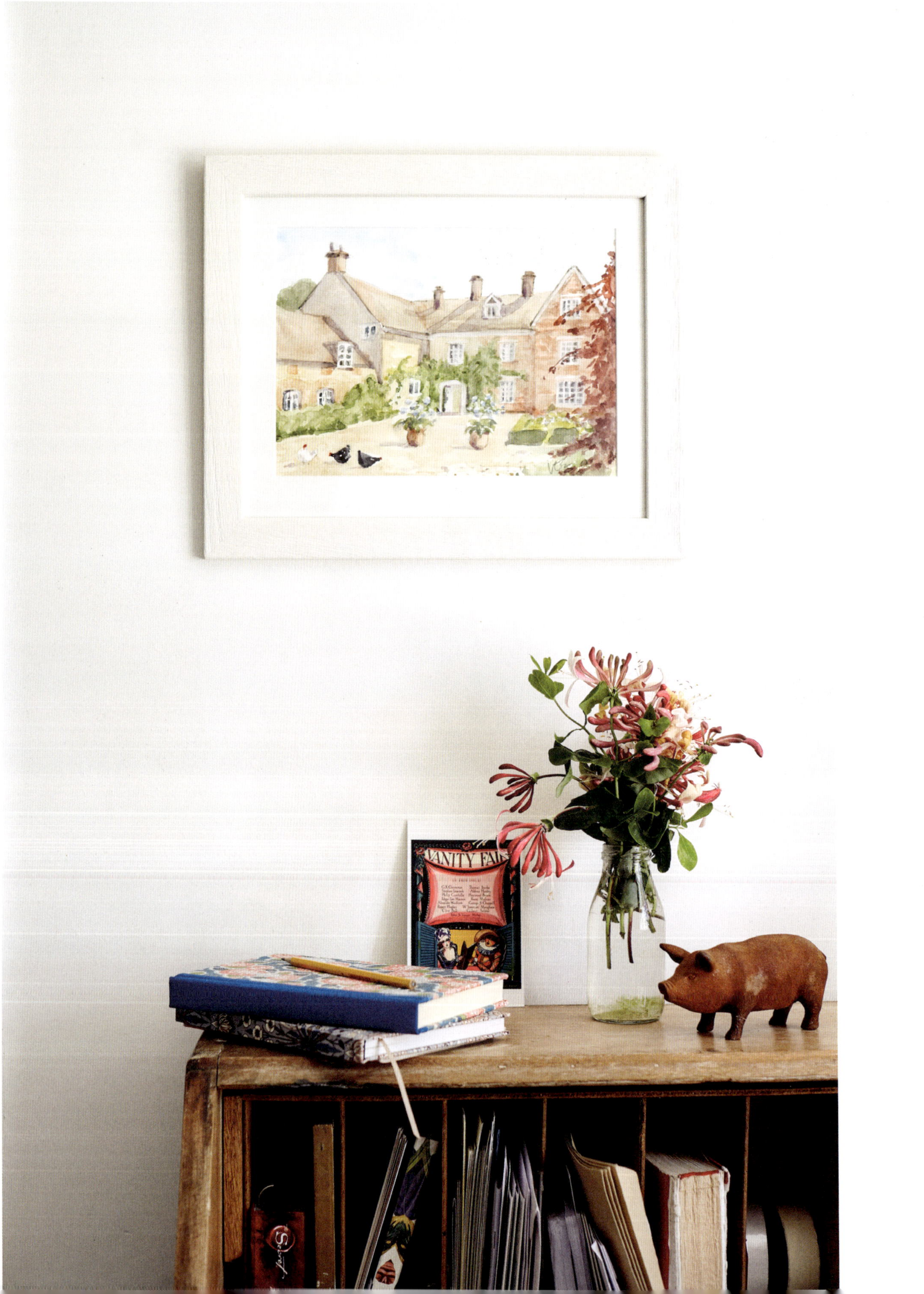
VANITY FAI

'MODEST, DATED AND CHILLY,

it was – having sat empty for three winter months,' recalls Harriet. 'Yet it had a warmth of character that really stood out.'

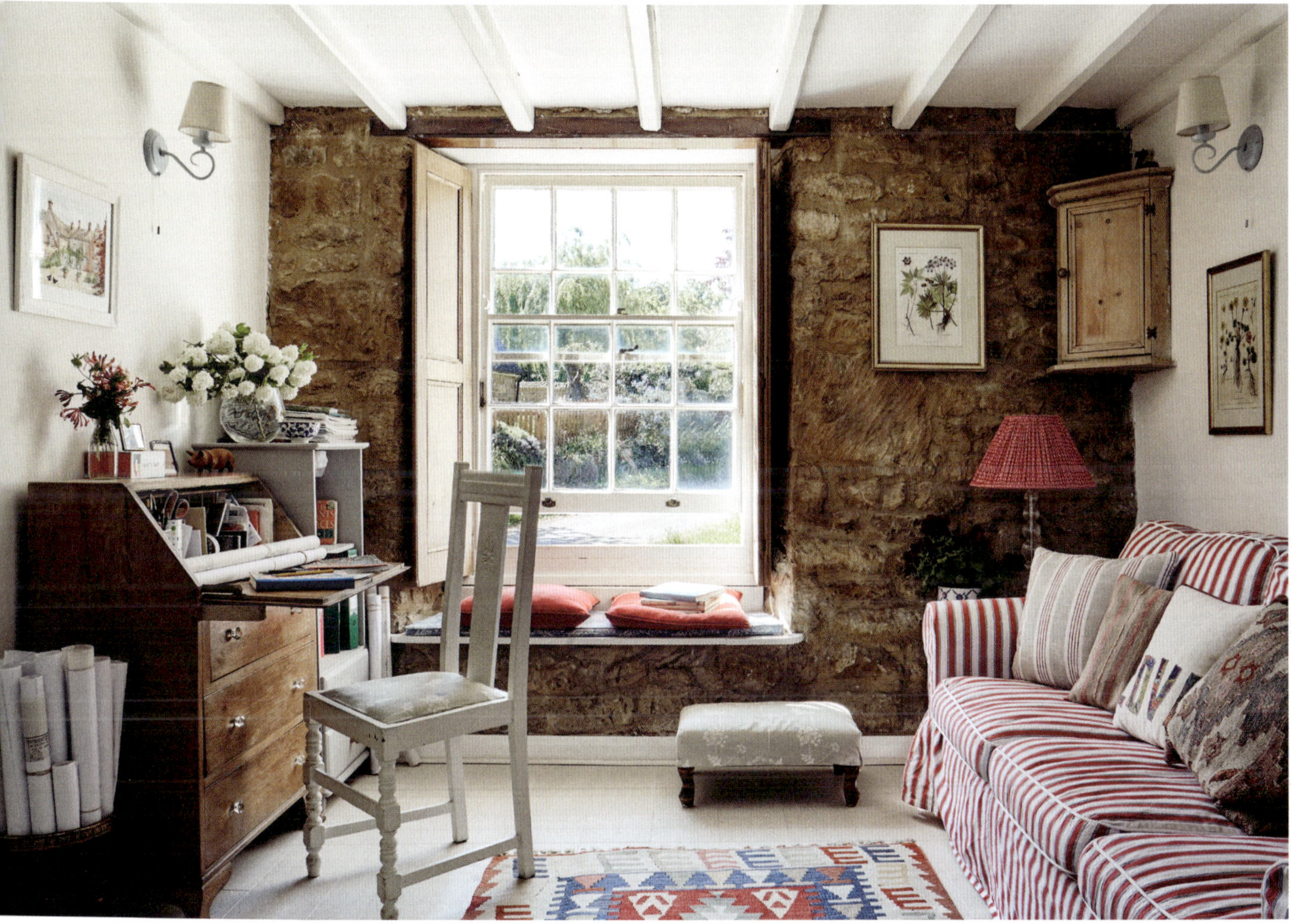

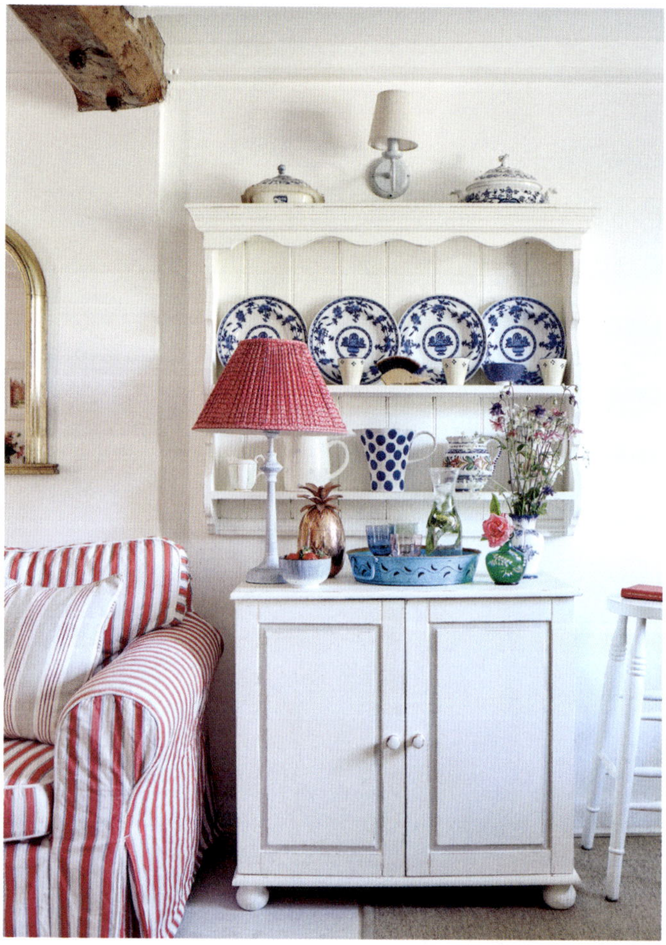

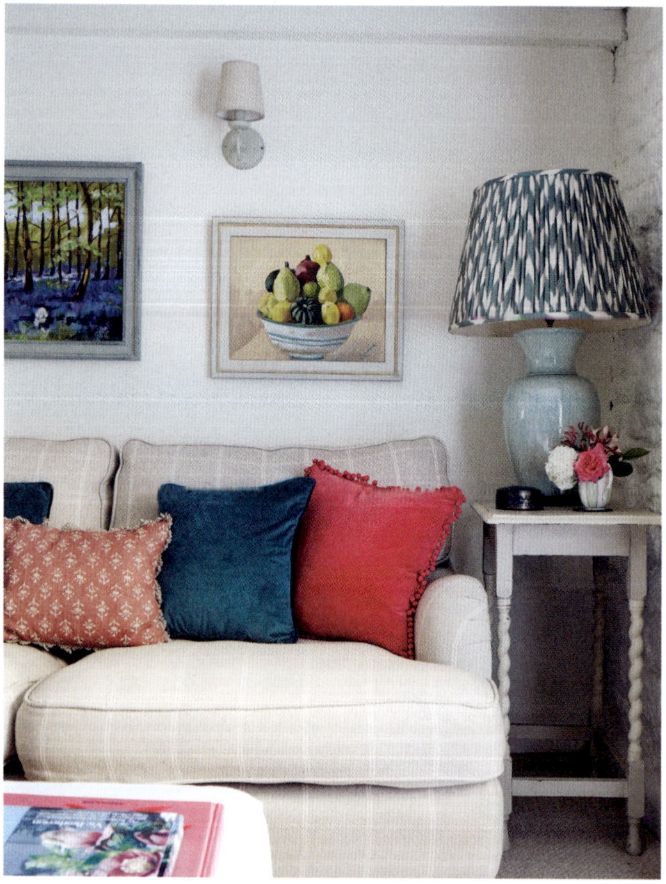

'I FEEL I HAVE

picked up where the previous owner left off,' Harriet says. 'Old houses are worthy of respect and I wanted to honour its history. Any changes I made were mindful of times and of residents gone by.'

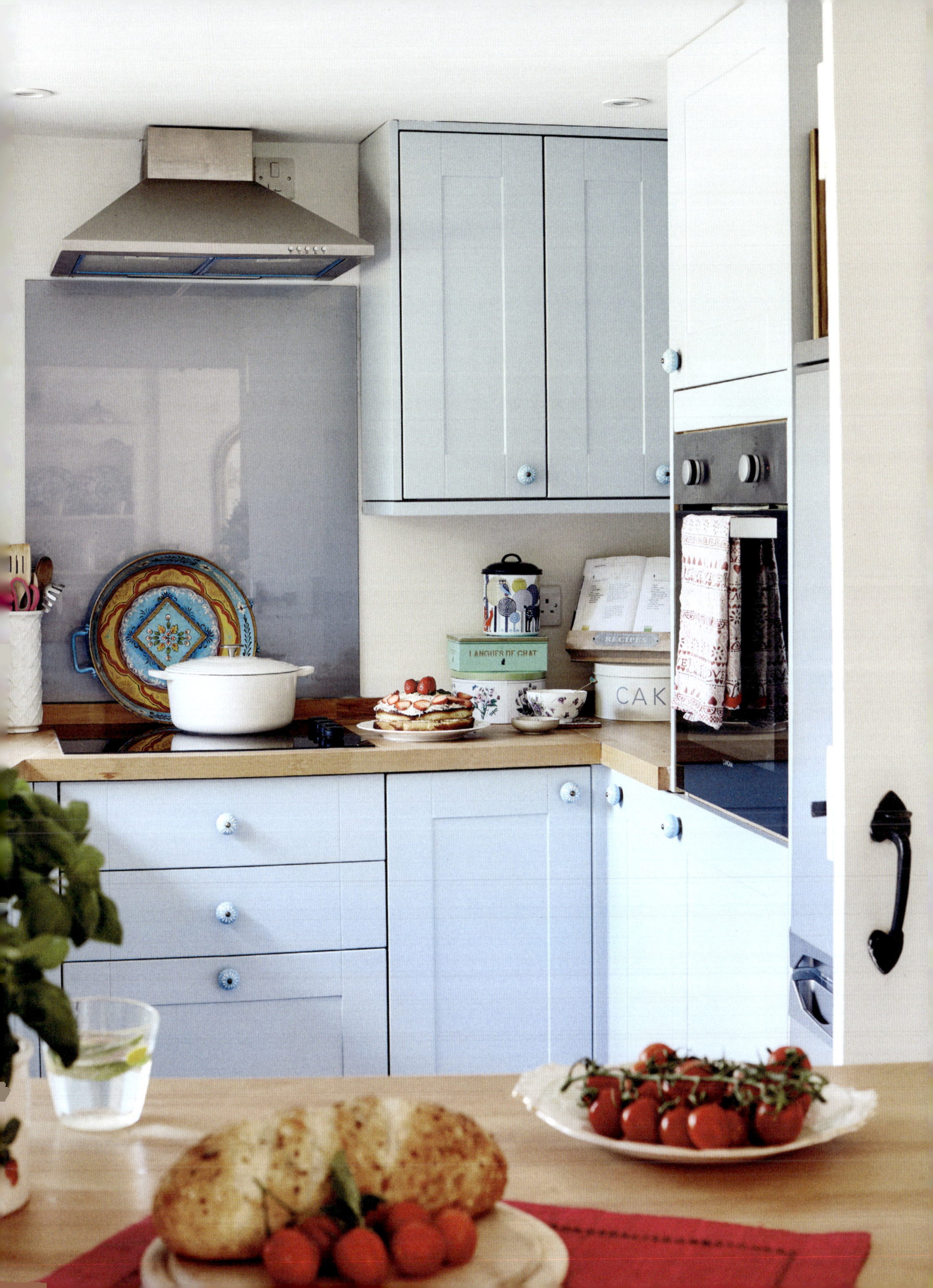
LANGUES DE CHAT
RECIPES
CAK

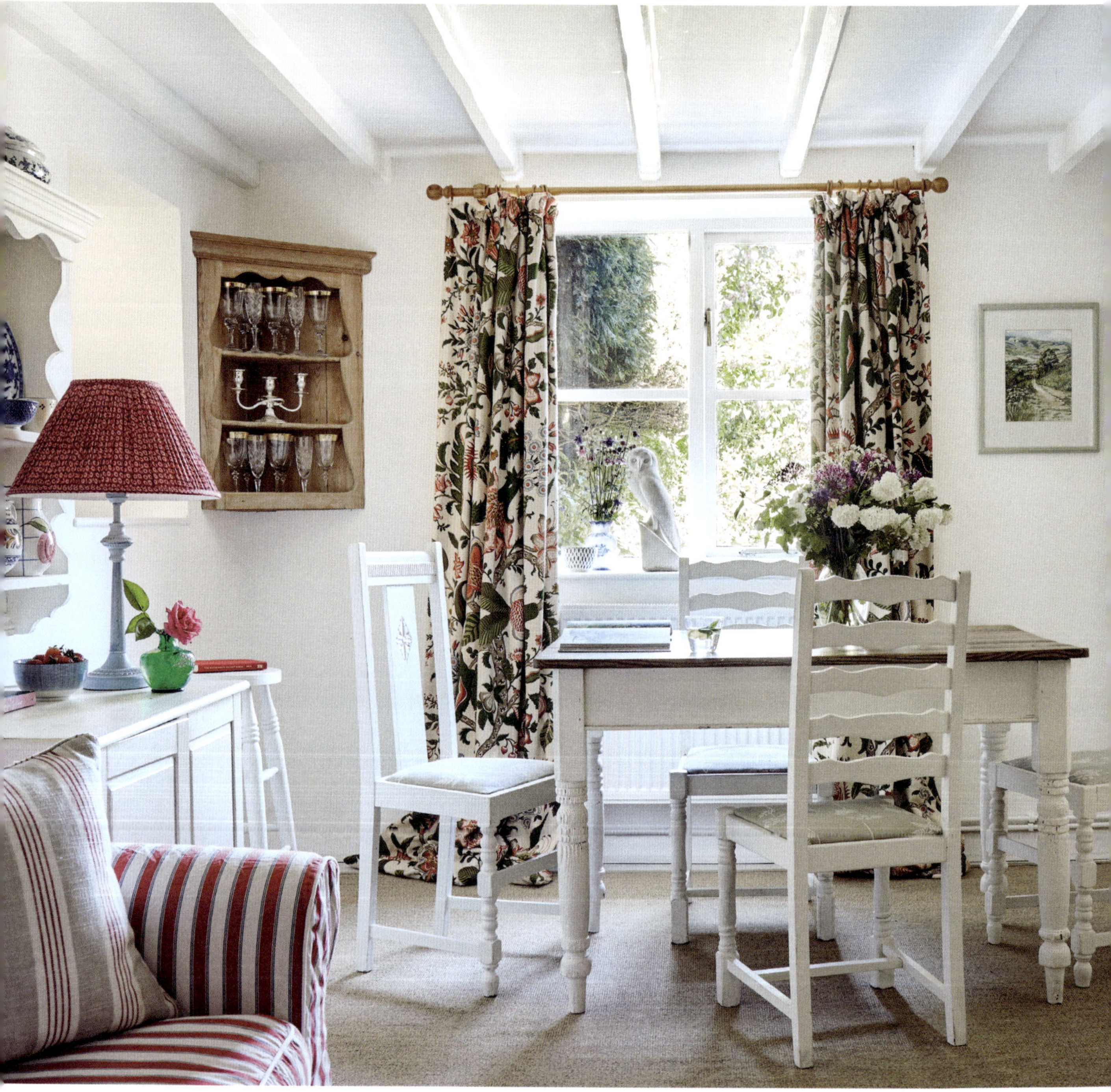

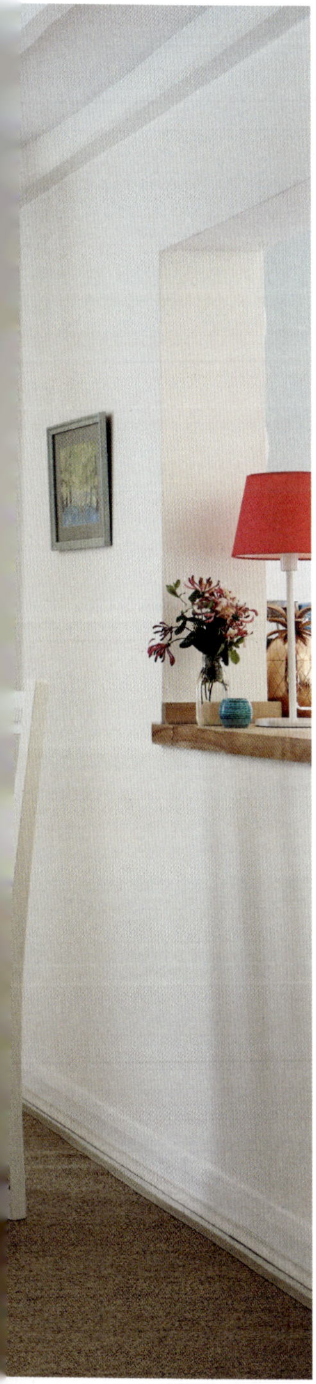

The agent explained that five years previously the cottage had suffered near disaster. It had almost burnt to the ground after a spark from next door's barbecue had set light to the thatch. The fire brigade put out the initial blaze, but the thatch had smouldered on for weeks. The house lived to tell the tale, but most of the windows had to be replaced and smoke and ash damage meant that it had needed completely gutting to be made habitable again. Old houses always have a story of their own, and somehow Harriet felt great respect for this one that had literally risen from the ashes and for its owner. It's a happy place now, with Elfie's little face peering out of the front window. 'She's a nosy neighbour,' laughs Harriet, but clearly owner and dog are quite at home. Over their five years here they have really made it their own.

She wanted to make the most of the natural light that floods into the house by lightening the interior as much as she could. She spent her first winter repainting; wall colours are now paler and some of the beams and exposed stonework were painted in lighter tones. She also painted over the brown kitchen cupboards in a fresh, French blue. The green carpets upstairs and in the sitting room have been replaced with a neutral cream carpet and off-white floorboards have been laid in the dining room. 'Since then, it's been very much "Make do and mend,"' says Harriet, who has trawled salvage yards, second-hand shops and markets - and not least a local recycling centre frequented by locals and fondly known as The Dump. Family heirlooms, eBay finds, upcycled one-off pieces of furniture and a great deal of work and imagination have come slowly together, and from them a home of great calm, character and creativity has evolved.

Harriet spent her first winter working her magic on the house, and a long and chilly winter it was. 'I got snowed in twice,' says the former Londoner proudly. When the winter finally retreated, she took great joy in seeing her garden come to life. The previous owner had clearly been a keen gardener, and Harriet watched with joy as some of her favourite plants and flowers sprang up. She is constantly adding plants and updating and is never happier than when pottering in her flowerbeds, with Elfie snuffling nearby. 'A garden and character,' were the two things Harriet had hoped for. This place has both - in bucketloads.

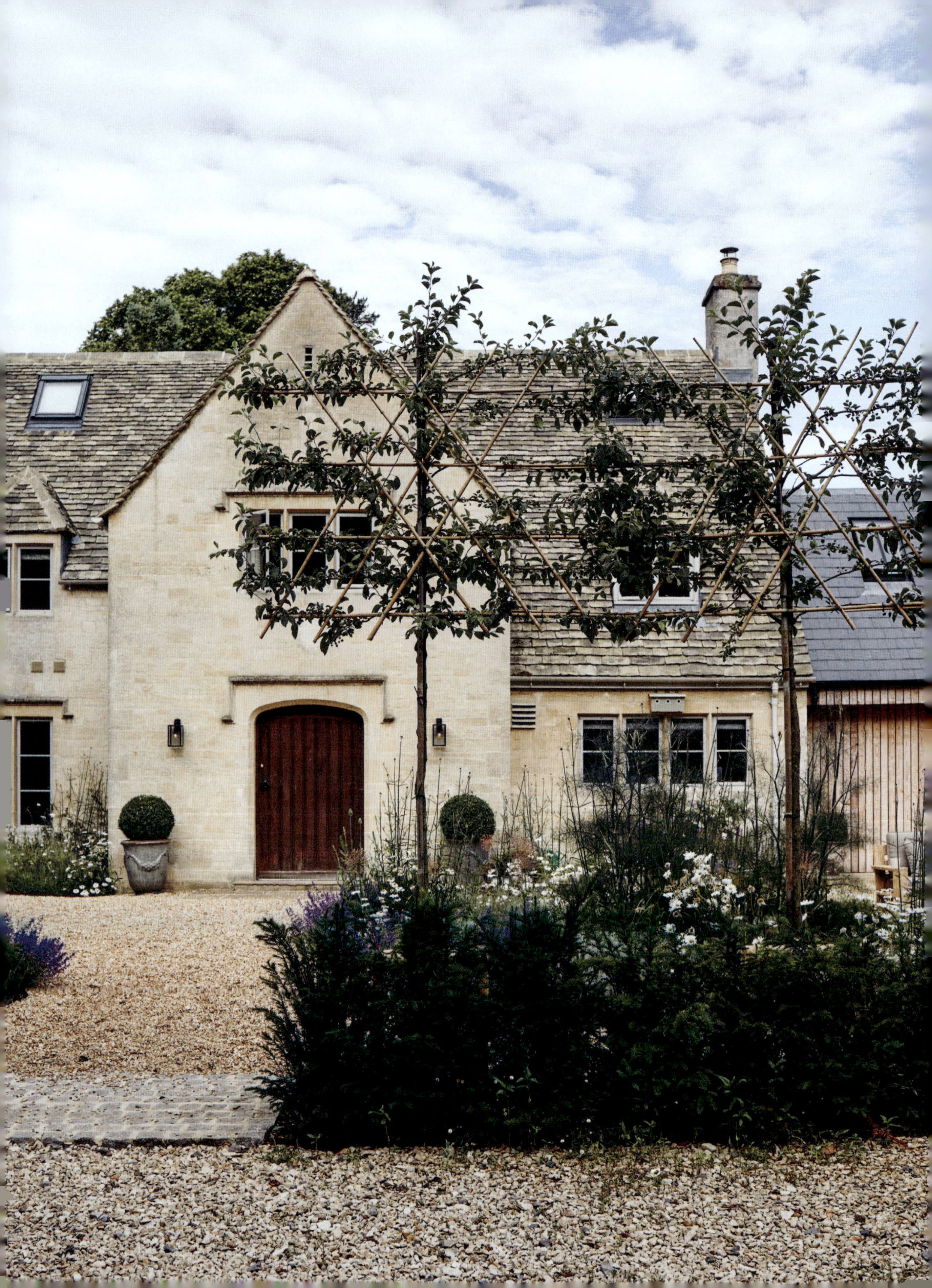

A FINE MENAGE

A family house and exquisite garden have been designed with space and companionship in mind to suit a family and their four-legged and feathered friends.

Chickens scratch up dust in the gravel parterre, two guinea pigs squeak companionably in their run, a pair of whippets swirl round each other in abandoned excitement at the arrival of a guest, and a fat grey cat flicks her tail and turns away bored, as if she's seen it all before. 'She's pregnant again,' scoffs Henny. 'It's down to her bad family planning that we had to upsize!'

Joking aside, the family's need for more space was pressing. Henny and Rupert's three sons were hurtling towards their teenage years. 'We'd lived in a village cottage with a small garden for ten years and were beginning to burst at the seams.' A place that had the right balance of house and garden took some finding. Wiltshire wasn't really in their immediate stamping ground, but Quentin House just over the border piqued their interest. Stone built and handsome, it stood in a garden of a little under half a hectare, had five bedrooms, and even featured a timber-clad annexe.

'I could instantly picture us here,' recalls Henny. 'I hardly needed to see beyond the entrance hall, and Rupert disappeared into the garden, pacing out potential football pitches. He was sold too.' That said, the house wasn't exactly the perfect layout for their sprawling household. The inside space was divided into several smallish rooms and neither the kitchen nor the living room had a view of the garden. 'As it wasn't listed, we knew we would be able to shuffle the layout and extend the kitchen to maximise the space,' says Henny, 'but we knew that we'd need to live in the space for a while to find out exactly how to improve it.'

‘WE CHOSE LARGE
double doors downstairs to open the space and help with the flow from room to room. We didn't want anywhere to feel excluded.’

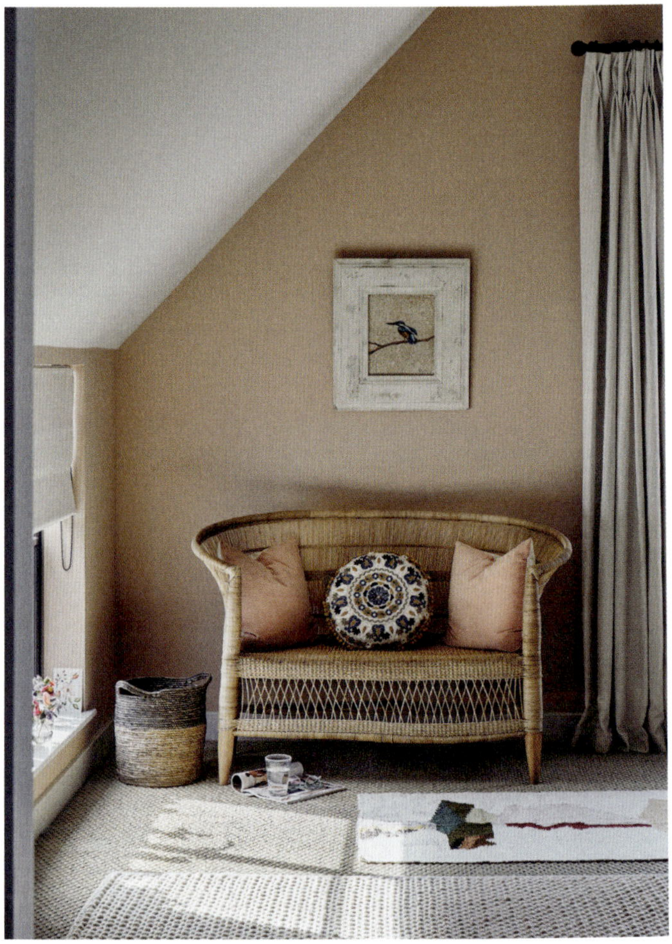

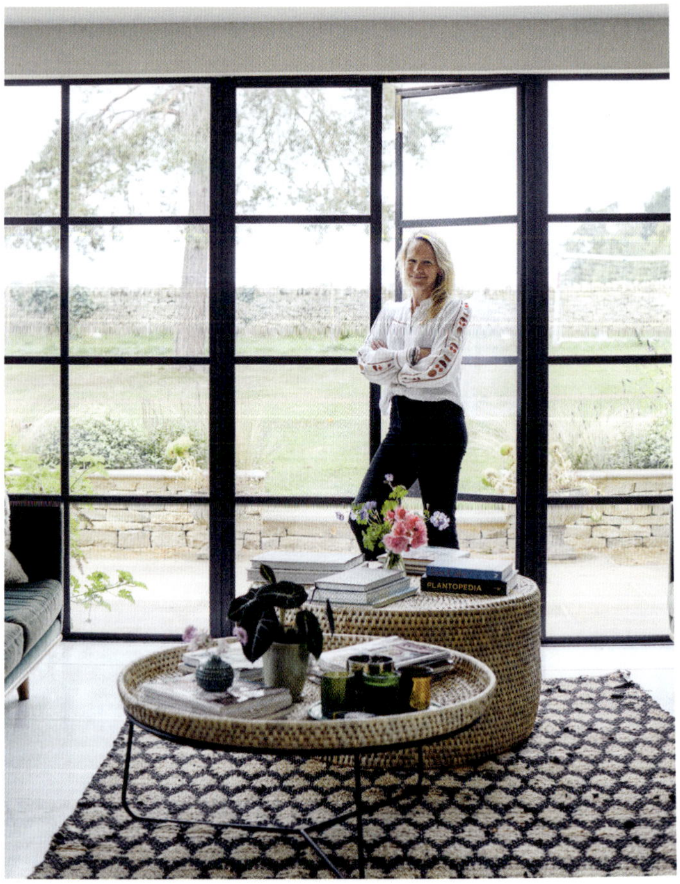

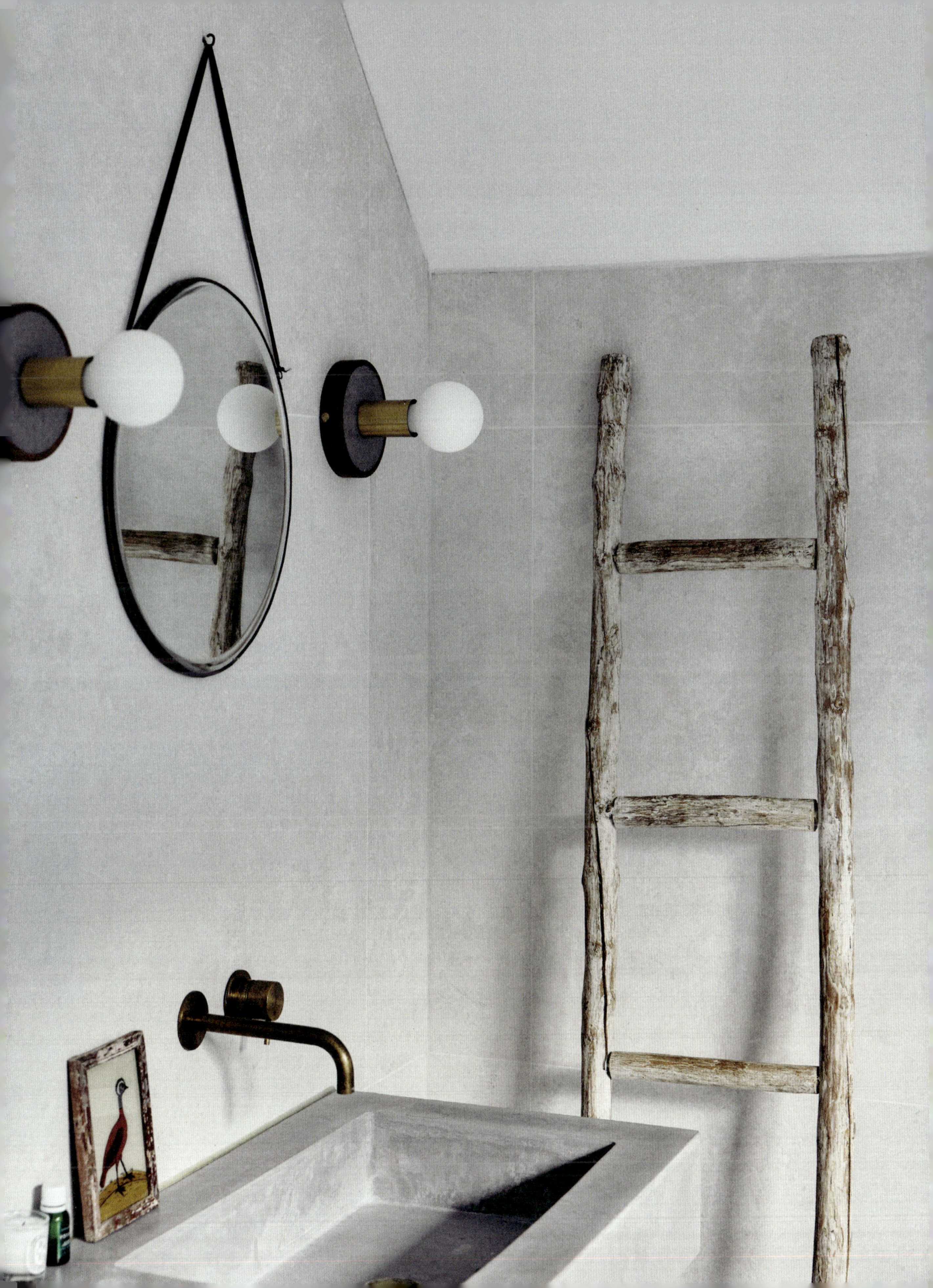

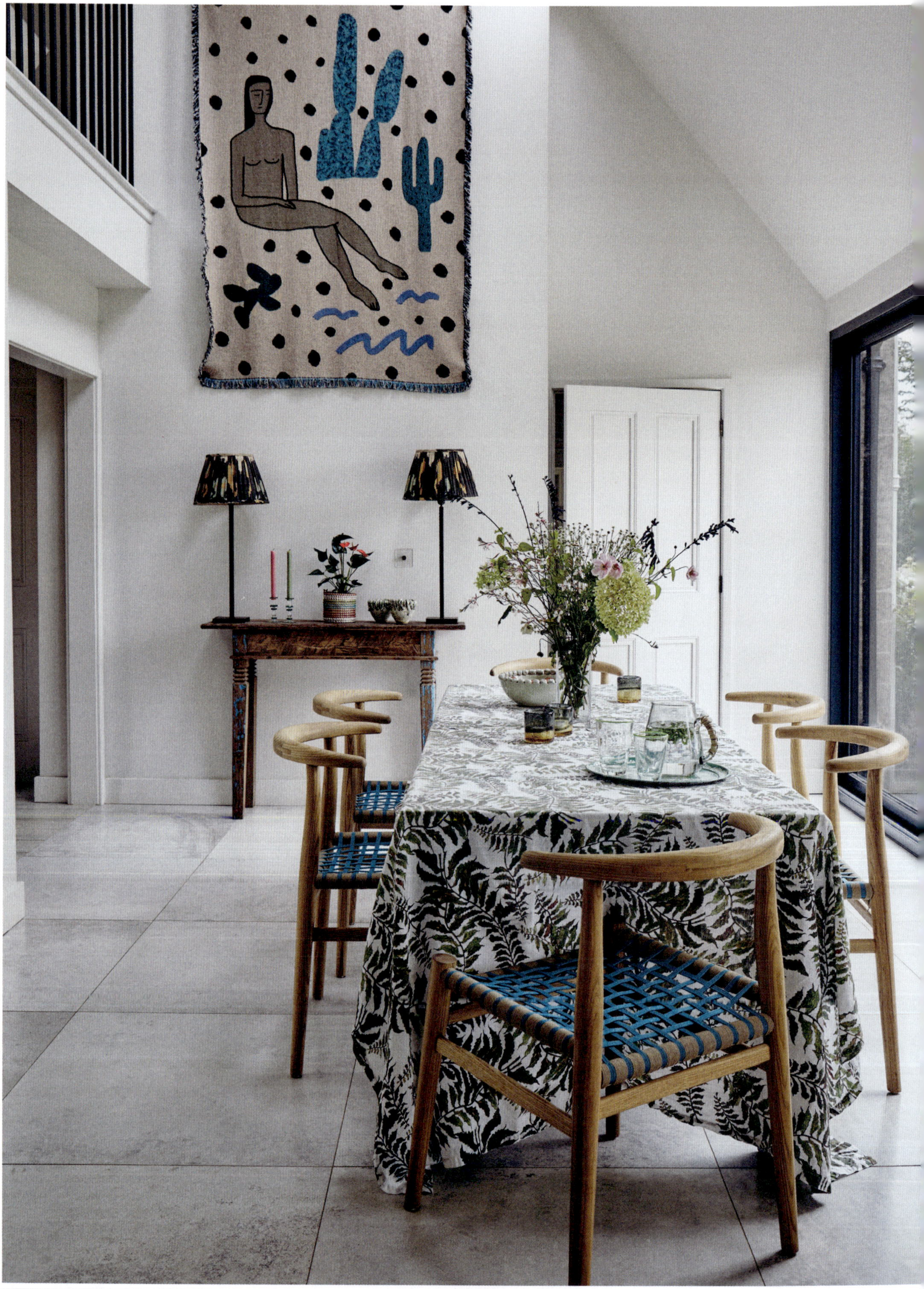

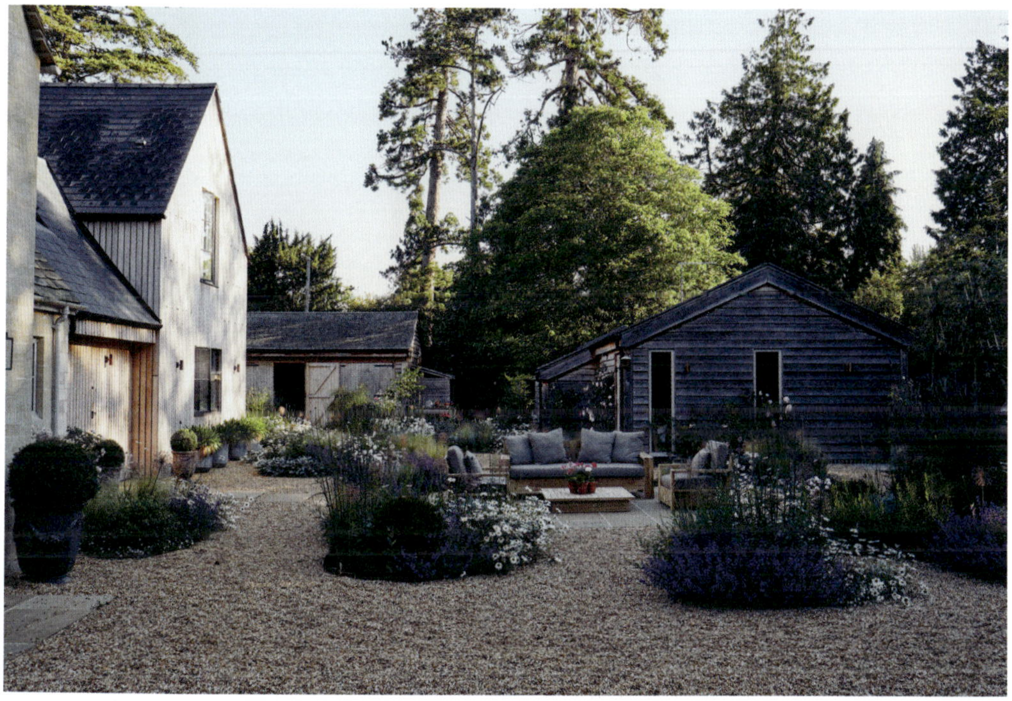

'HAVING LIVED IN COTTAGES
until now, I craved high ceilings. This house had more generous dimensions anyway, but we kept the ceiling above the dining area double height to stretch up to the rafters.'

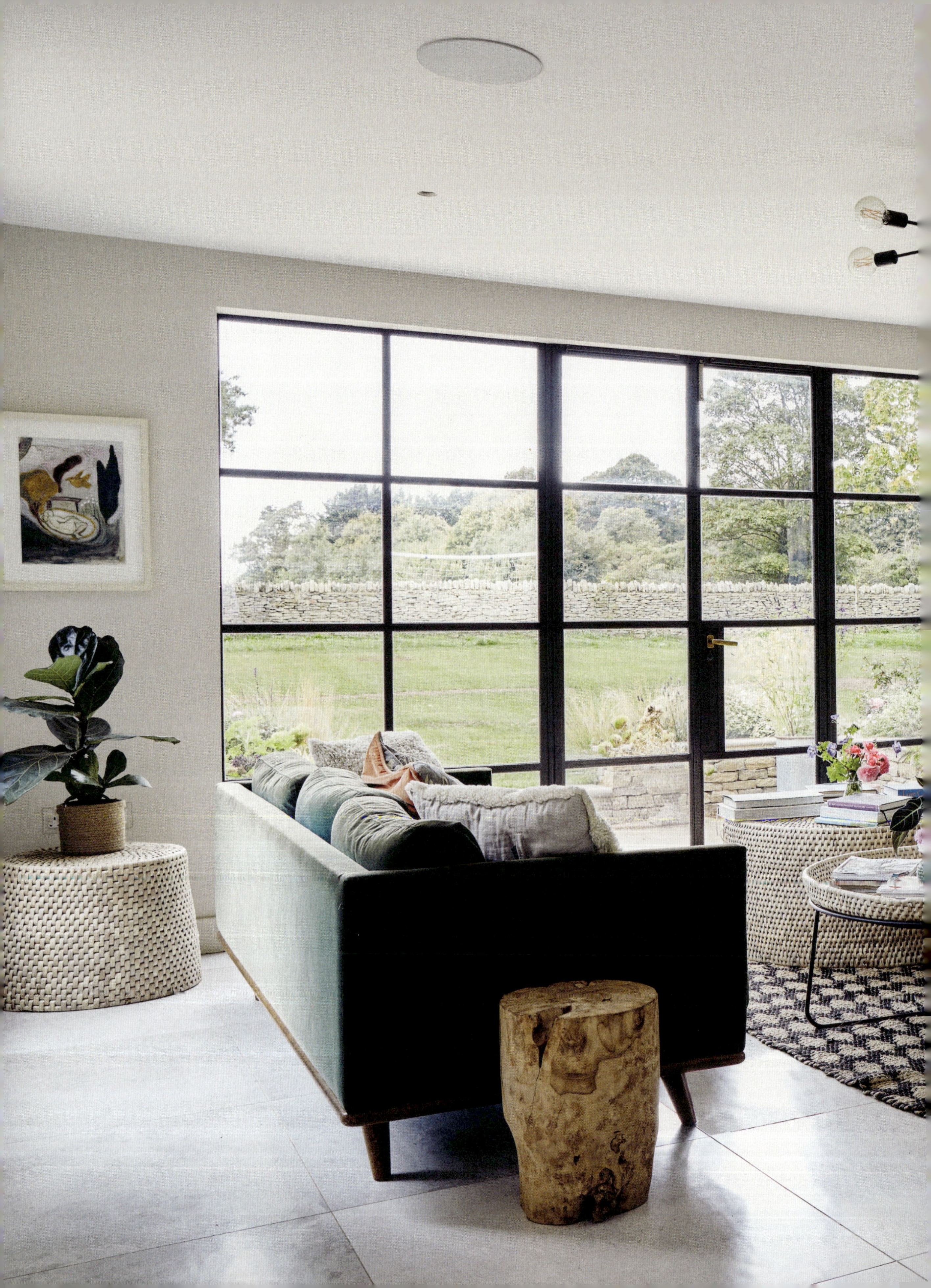

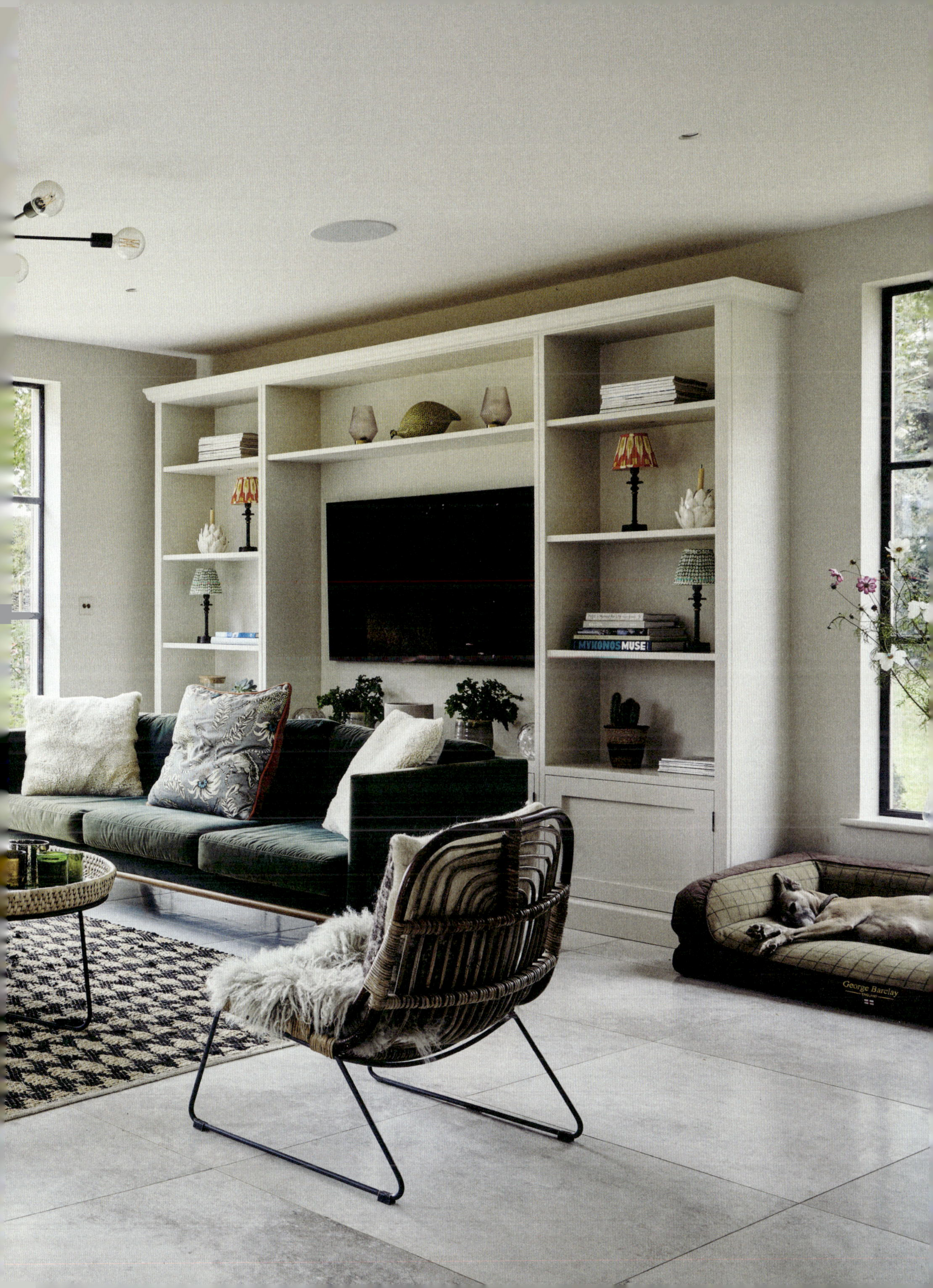
MYKONOS MUSE
George Barclay

Three months later they were in and spending their evenings feverishly scribbling plans. They designed the extension to retain the original façade of the house and add a similar-looking - but timber-framed - gabled extension to the right-hand side of the house. The old and the new would blend naturally and marry the main house more closely to the timber-framed annexe. Internally they would do away with many of the walls and maximise the space. They wanted to remove cottagey doors, replace them with french-style glazed double doors, and open up the hall to create an entrance space with external doors front and back. They would turn the poky living room into a utility room and extend the kitchen and breakfast room, adding huge Crittall doors and windows opening onto Rupert's dream garden, a fusion of traditional English country garden and modern design. Upstairs they would add a master bedroom and bathroom above the new kitchen and reconfigure the attic space, adding a bathroom and Velux windows to make the space teenager fit.

'We didn't time it well,' Henny laughs. 'Just as the demolition work began we went into lockdown!' All five family members - and a fair few pets - moved into the one-bedroom annexe. It wasn't until a year later that they emerged, slightly shell-shocked, to move into a home of entirely different proportions.

The house today is the antithesis of poky. Although it has fewer actual rooms than previously, the new layout is all about space and light. 'Our vision was to create a house with no wasted areas, where the whole space would be lived in,' explains Henny. The kitchen/garden room/dining room was always intended to be the main hub. Most days, the family and pets are to be found filling up this generous space. Small wonder that they do: it is so inviting, surrounded by the ever-changing colours of the garden outside; and so warm, thanks to underfloor heating in winter and the sun streaming in during the summer. 'When they've had enough of us, the boys can trickle off to the smaller sitting room to escape.'

Henny and Rupert consciously moved away from traditional cottage style, yet their more refined style still has a cosy and inviting appeal. This is enhanced by the plethora of natural textiles and fibres that they have chosen. Wood, cane, linen and wool add depth and texture; and Henny's colour choices have been natural and pale apart from surprise shots of colour - bright turquoise seat covers and a sunny yellow console table, for example, stand out in an otherwise mellow dining area.

Every house has a character of its own, and Quentin House today is welcoming, unfussy and calm - somewhat surprisingly considering the wealth of pets that call it home. 'I do whip the Dyson round quite often,' admits Henny, 'but somehow the bigger space seems more relaxed. The mess has more places to hide!' Her pride in the house is well deserved; what she and Rupert have created is truly a home for all.

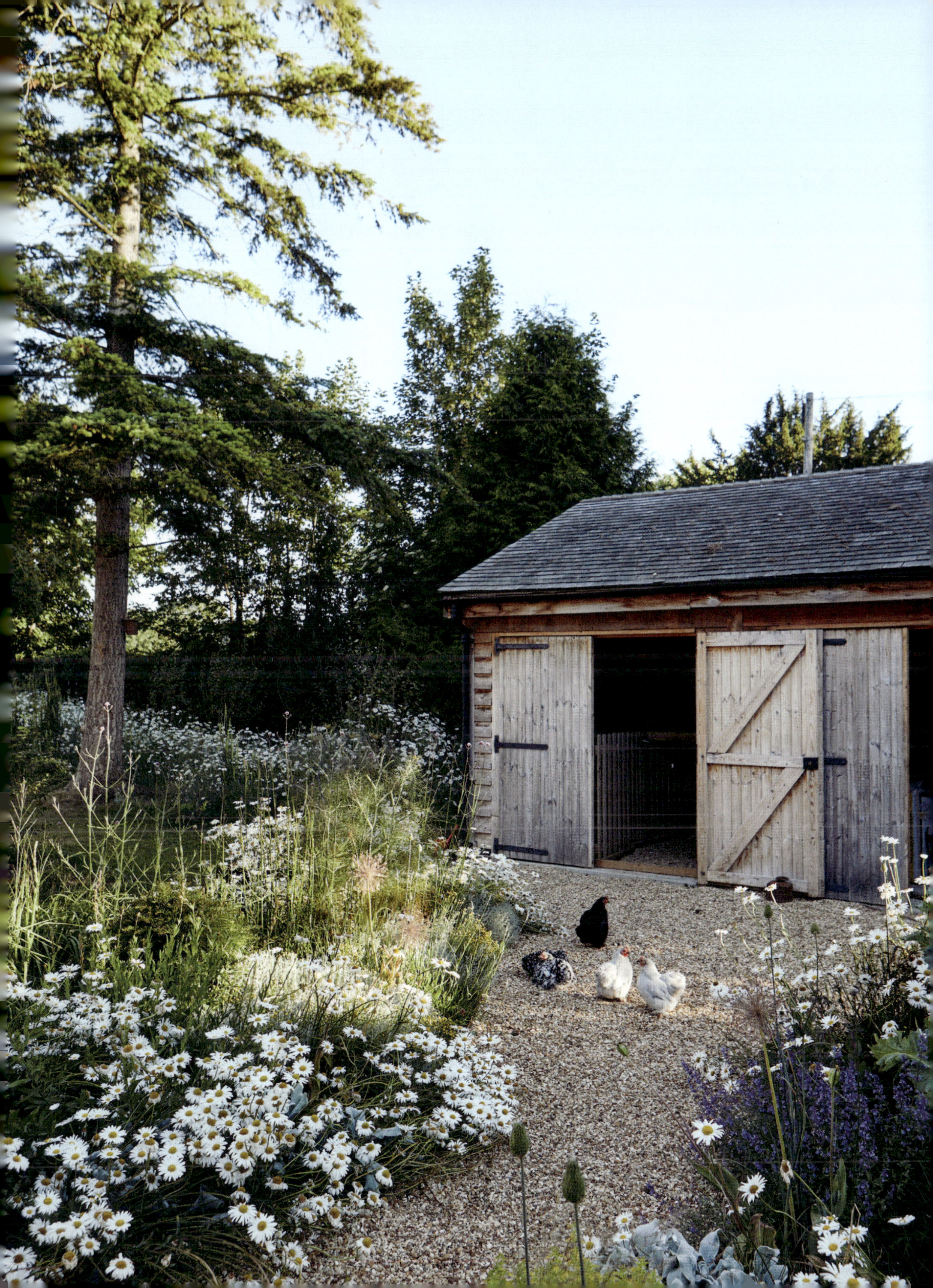

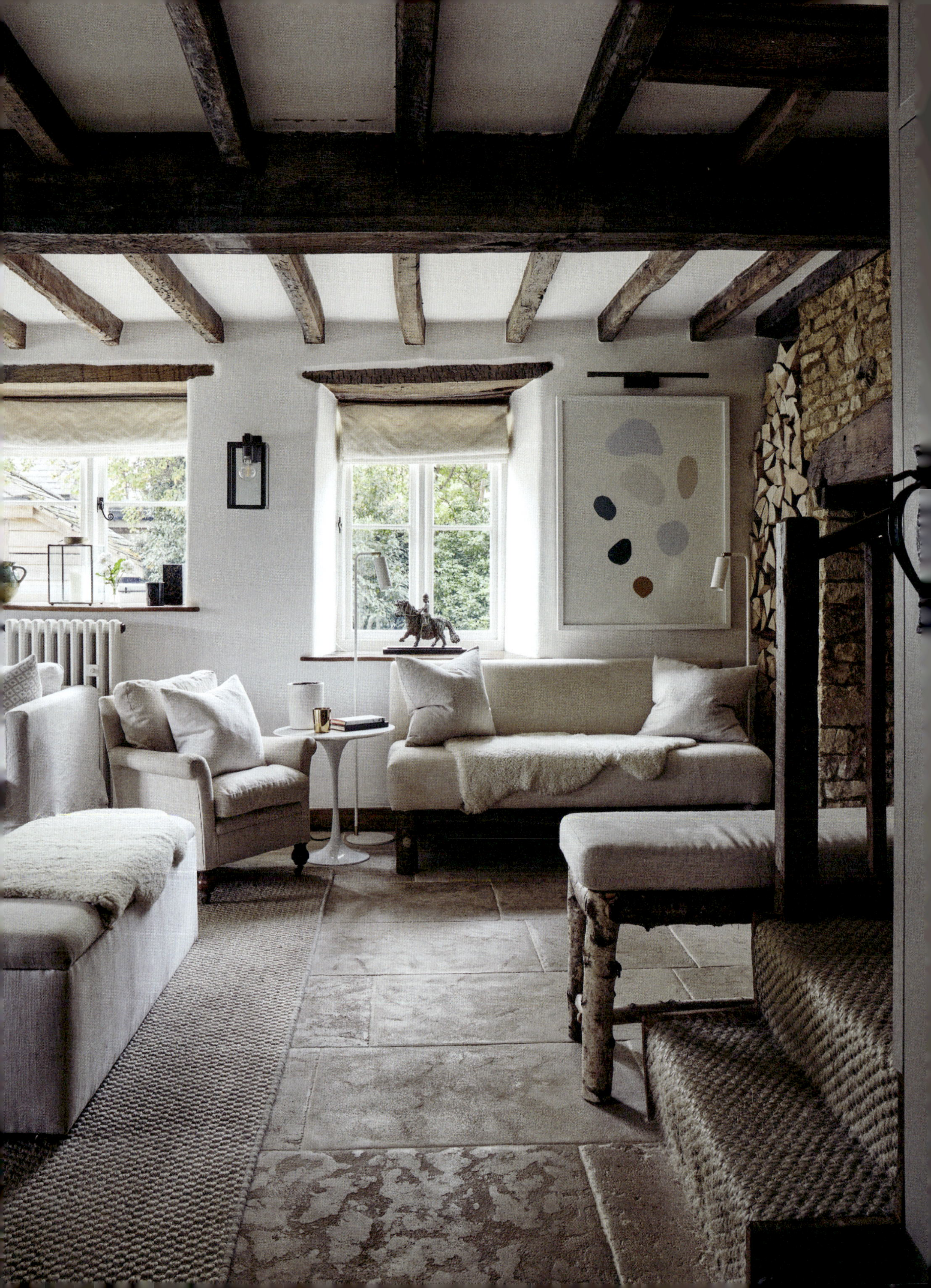

A BRIGHTER SHADE OF PALE

Max and Isabelle Alton moved from London to 300-year-old Cotswold House and have embraced all that is calm, timeless and simple about country life.

Tucked away in a popular Gloucestershire village is a well-kept secret. Rose Cottage sits hidden behind not just one, but two stone walls, entirely invisible from the road. The two walls border a gravel driveway, and the house is set far back behind the second one at the end of a beautiful cottage garden. 'It was the seclusion that drew us to it,' says Isabelle. 'Total privacy and yet only two minutes' walk from the village amenities, including a fabulous village pub.'

The children were tiny when the family moved in 2016, and the house and garden had the added benefit of being child-friendly. The garden and ground floor were all on one level, so tiny Kit and Evie could safely toddle and scoot round the house and garden without tumbling down any dangerous steps. Upstairs was a little more hazardous, but the children were enchanted with the nooks and crannies of this wonky old house.

While the bones of the house were strong, the interior needed modernisation. The Altons had recently visited The Wild Rabbit inn nearby and were inspired by its sumptuous yet understated interior style and calm, warm atmosphere. The inn is built in Cotswold stone similar to that of their house, with oak beams, exposed stonework and roaring fires. 'We loved all the natural fabrics and textiles as well as the different uses of simple rustic wood and knew that a similar look would work in Rose Cottage,' explains Isabelle. 'We also felt that a pale colour scheme would be complemented by the south-facing windows that flooded light into the house.'

They set to work, painting over the dark wood window-frames - in dove grey outside and white inside - and sanding down the varnished chestnut kitchen units before repainting them in white. They painted over dark kitchen tiles and removed upper-level cupboards in the kitchen to open the space, adding a handful of simple open shelves. They then got to work on the flooring in the rest of the house - removing tired, dark carpets to reveal floorboards beneath which they painted white, all the while enhancing the feeling of light and space. They laid mandarin stone tiles in the sitting room and added sisal rugs to make the seating areas warmer underfoot. Upstairs they laid sisal carpet in the corridors and bedrooms and stripped back and laid white oiled oak floorboards in the bathrooms. 'Slightly to the children's dismay we took out a Jacuzzi in the family bathroom,' laughs Isabelle. They replaced it with a more traditional bath, adding painted wooden panelling. 'Every change we made was to make the best use of space and light, and we wanted to keep all of the cottagey character but to show it in - literally - its best light.'

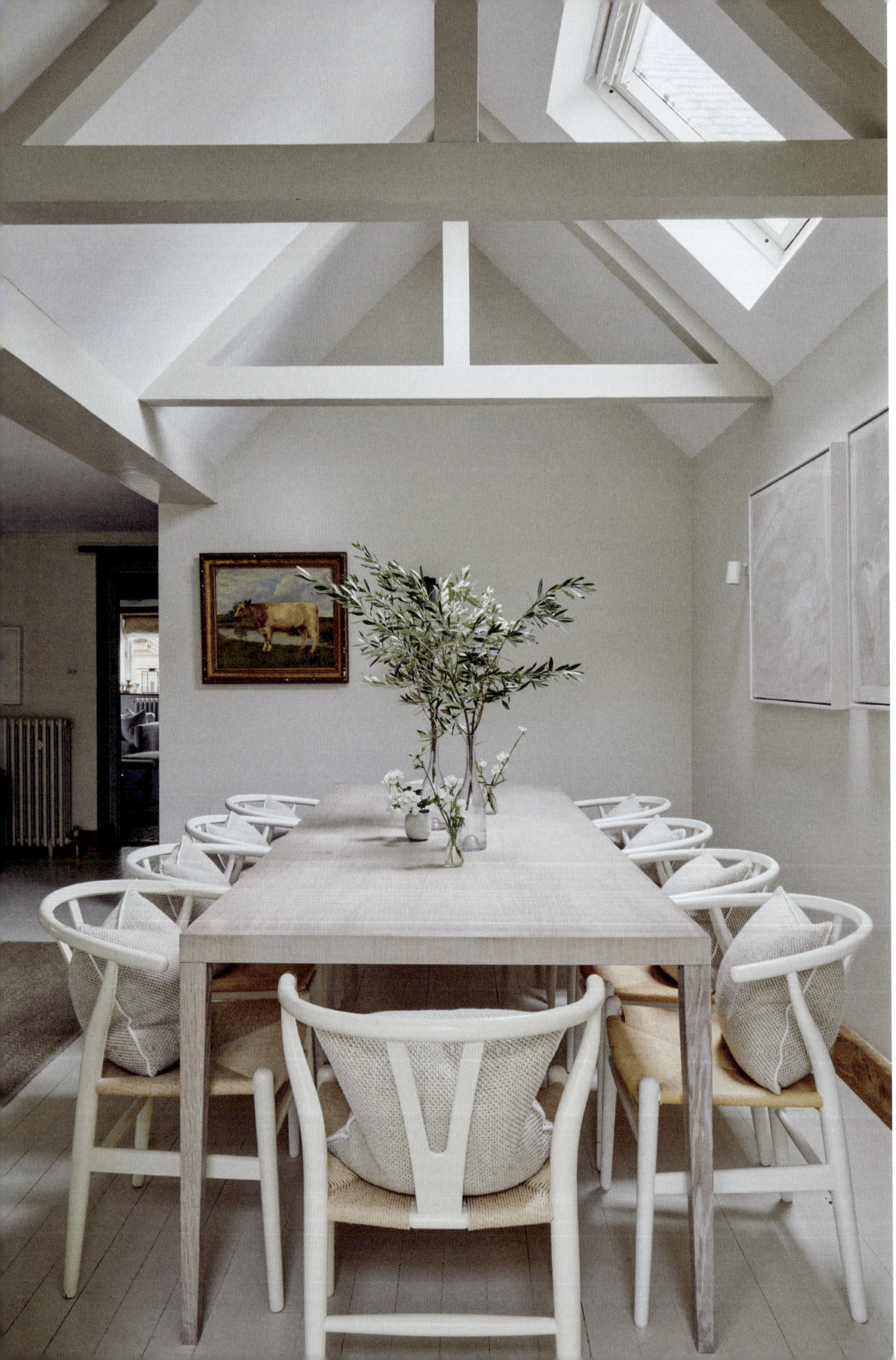

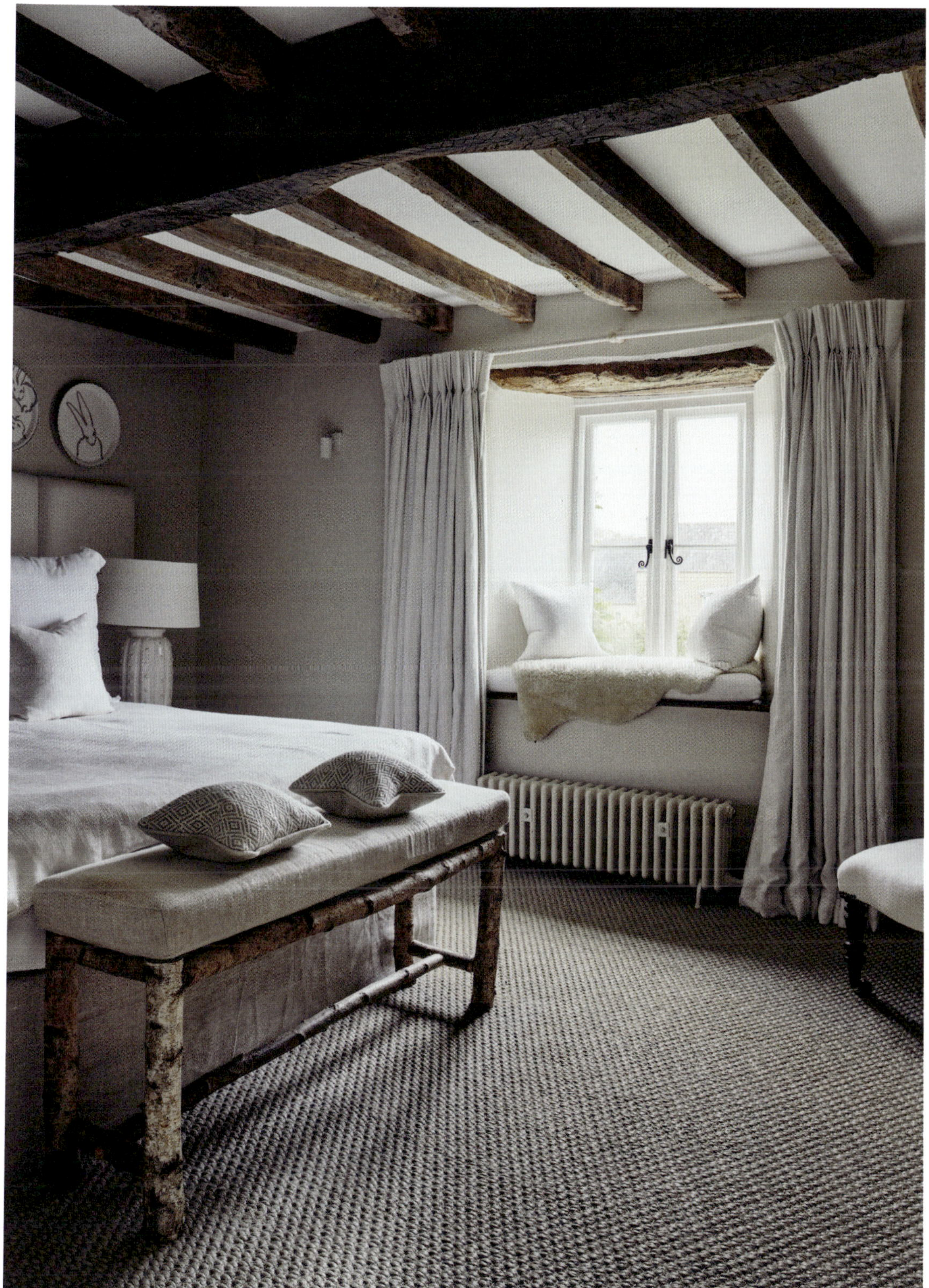

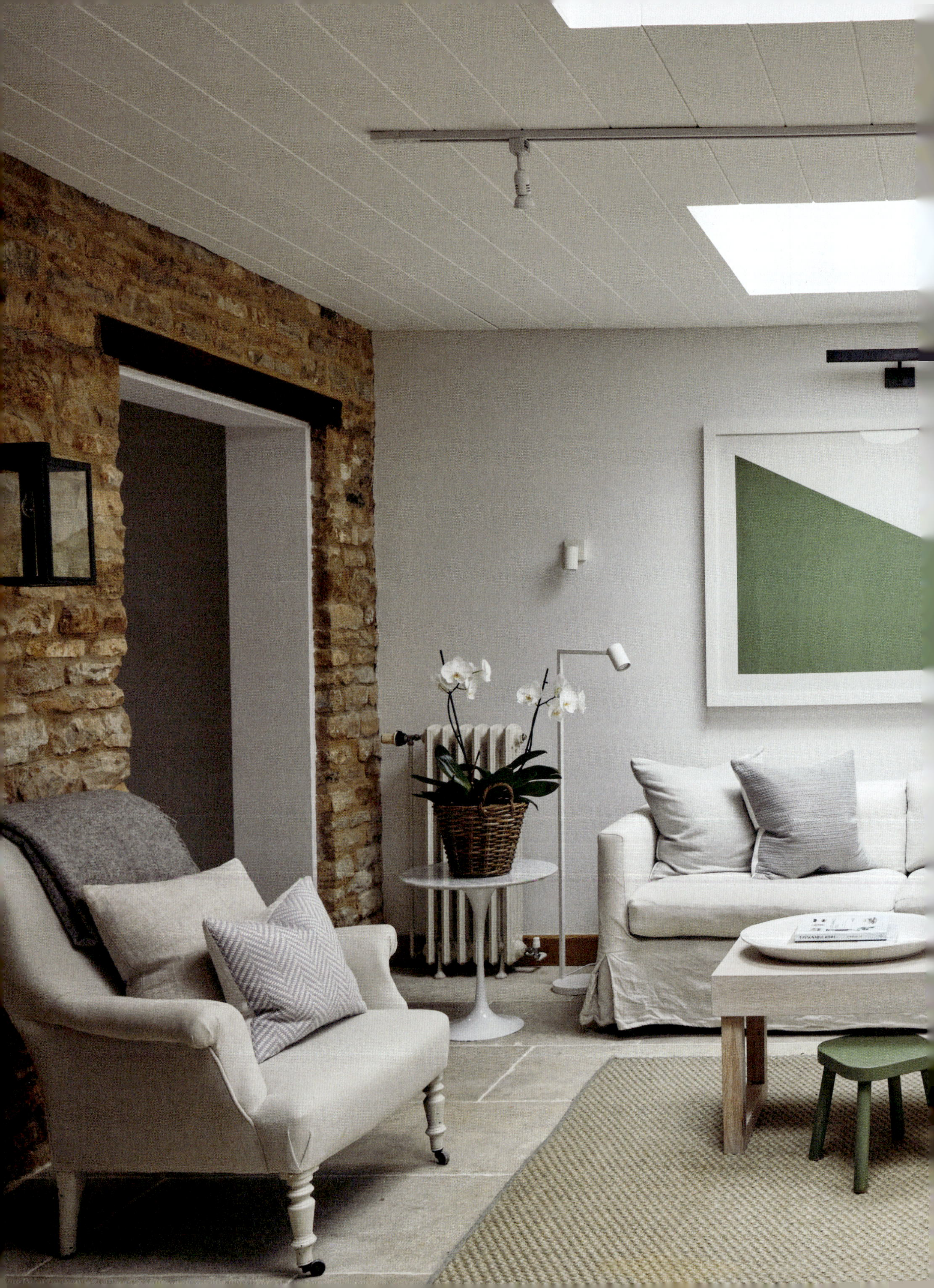
SUSTAINABLE HOME

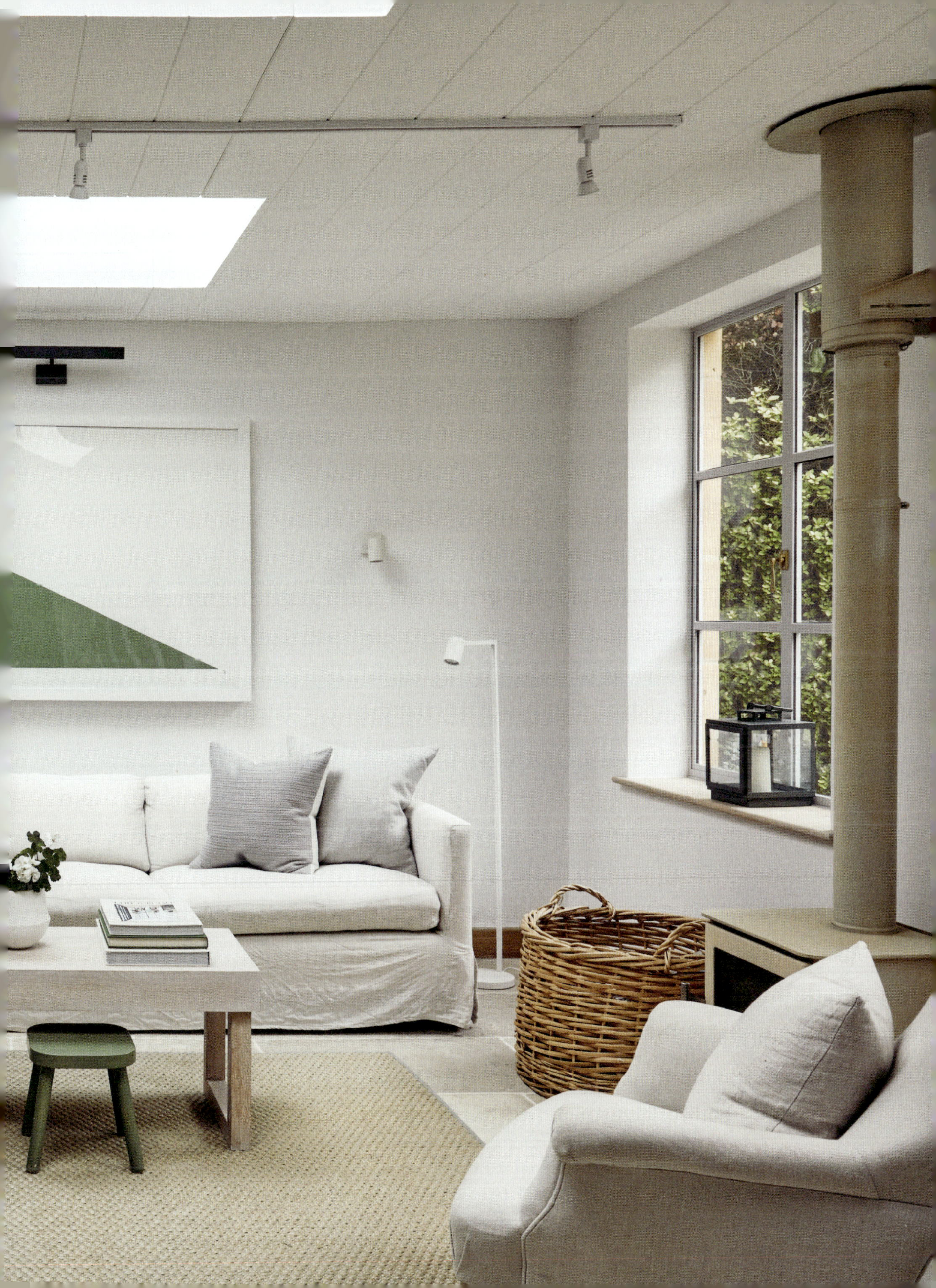

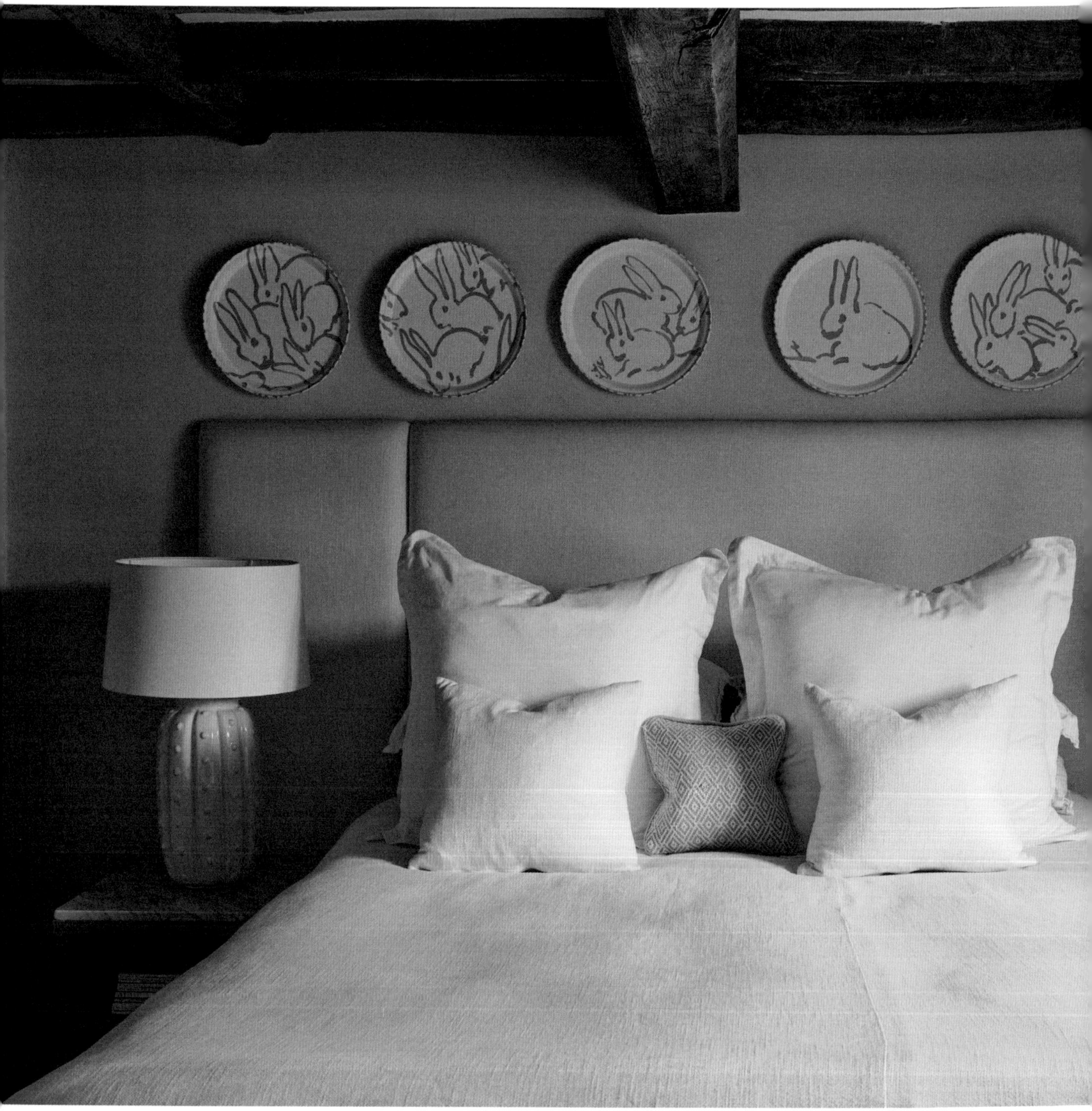

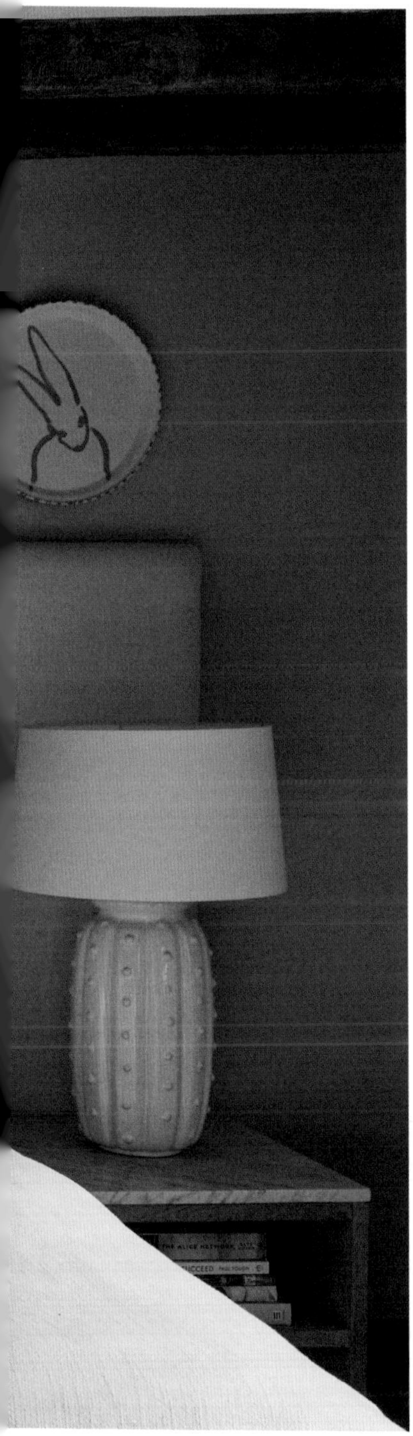

While the Altons saw the house taking shape as the unfussy space they had envisaged, they had one persistent niggle. At some point in the last half-century a conservatory had been added. While it was a useful space ('mostly as a dumping ground!' recalls Isabelle), it was neither particularly attractive nor very well insulated. 'We loved the idea of having somewhere sunny to sit on winter's days, but in reality the conservatory was baking hot in summer and chilly and comfortless in winter.' As they came out of the first Covid lockdown, they embarked on a rewarding project to create the conservatory they wanted. A simple, stylish and light-flooded room, with two roof lights and windows on two sides, now sits at the eastern end of the house. Built in Cotswold stone to blend with the older side of the house, its modern look contrasts beautifully inside and out with the 300-year-old sitting room at the opposite end. 'And then we heaved a sigh of relief because we could feel instinctively that the house was complete.'

In terms of style, Isabelle and Max followed their instincts and kept their decorating and colour scheme as understated – yet warm – as they had first intended. The colours are mostly pale or white, and occasional slate blues and shades of grey creep in. What stands out here, and adds depth and tone, is the wealth of textures that the Altons have introduced. Natural linens and cottons layered with cosy lambswool and the occasional sheepskin, set against the original stonework, exposed woodwork and beams, all give warmth and simple sumptuousness. Rustic wood has been charmingly used – hooks and handles made from branches and mirrors framed in wonky wood are quirky, yet natural. Artwork, ornaments and ceramics are unostentatious and mostly modern. Look closely and the rabbit seems to be a recurring emblem. 'Well, of course,' admits Isabelle. 'It was The Wild Rabbit that inspired the entire place. We had to pay it homage!'

'PEOPLE OFTEN EXPECT *to take their shoes off and tiptoe with caution round the house because, I think, it seems like a spotless place. It isn't. We just chose hard floors and sisal carpets because they are so easy to clean. We don't mind at all if the kids bring a bit of the outdoors in.'*

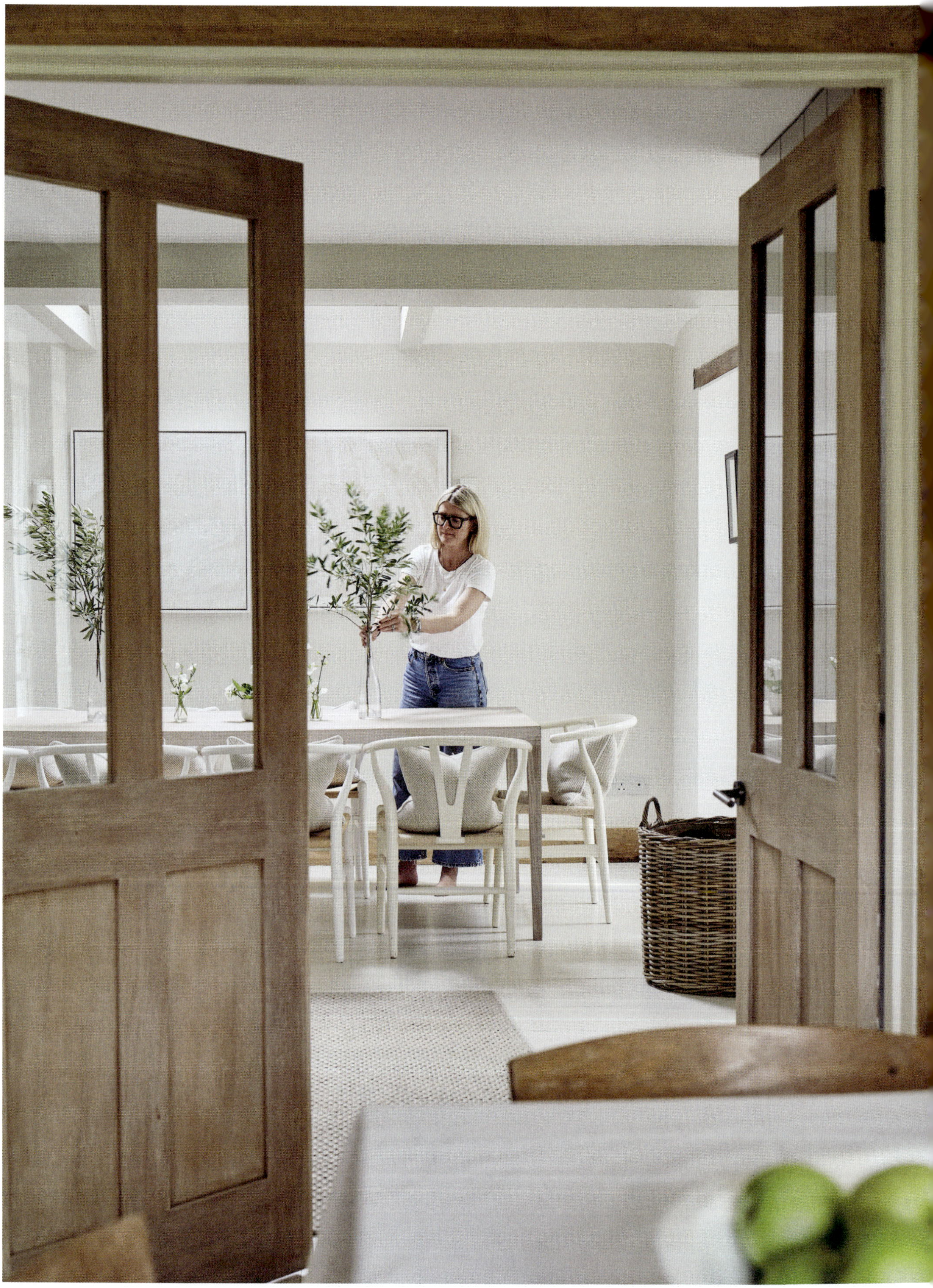

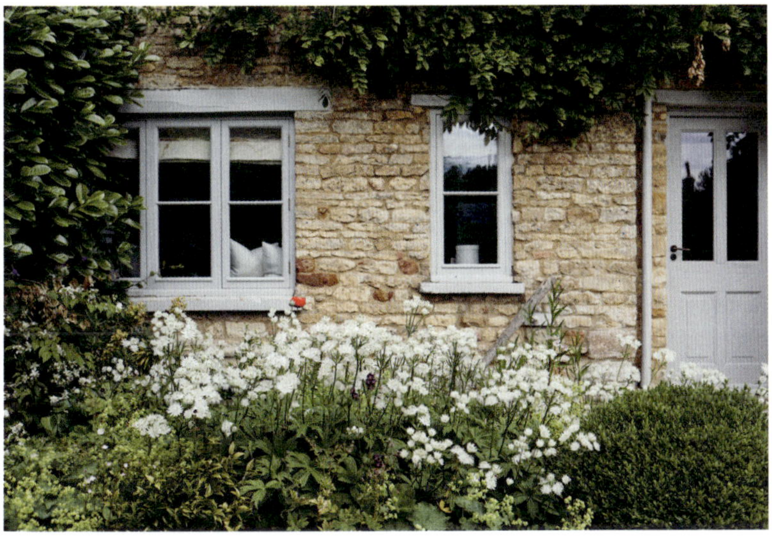

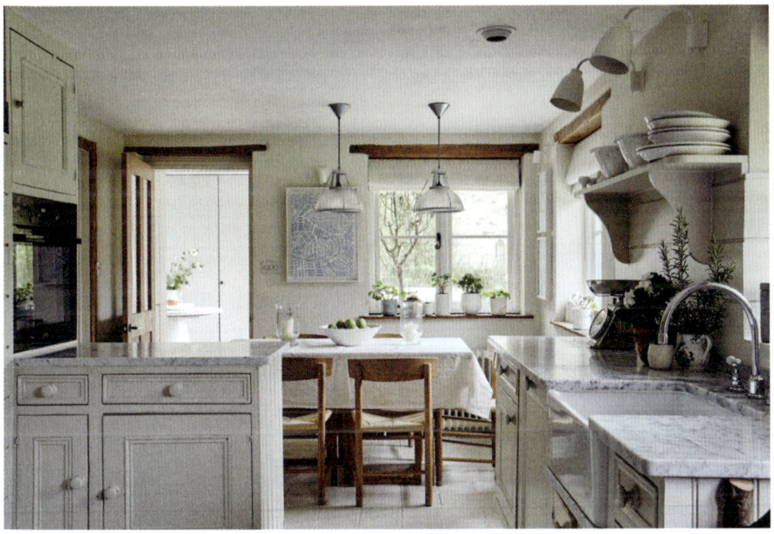

'AS WITH ALL HOUSE PROJECTS,

you always think one thing will bother you forever. The structural pole bang in the middle of our sitting room was a major sticking point for us, but we knew that the house would collapse without it. Of course, seven years on, we barely notice it, and sort of love its stubborn insistence on taking centre stage!'

THE SHAPE OF THINGS TO COME

The O'Hagan family took on a monumental building project to turn an outdated and awkward converted octagonal chapel into a liveable, beautiful space for their young family.

When it comes to awkward spaces,' says Heloise, 'an octagon-shaped, three-storey chapel really takes the biscuit.' Yet, within seconds of entering this unusual space, it is clear how well it works.

Rewind the clock twenty years, to when Heloise and her husband moved to this Cotswold town. They bought a cottage neighbouring an imposing chapel that was home to two elderly sisters. Set on three huge levels, it was dingy with a faintly damp smell, varnished wood panelled walls, a dark stained ceiling, and dark green carpets that sprouted occasional weeds. It also had a bizarre layout, with two staircases, one heading up, one down, set at opposite sides of the building. The lower ground and top floors were rabbit warrens of rooms. A friendship developed between the owners and the young couple. When nine years later they died, within weeks of each other, the ladies' cousin approached the O'Hagans. She saw a future there for this this couple, who had begun looking for a larger home to start a family.

'No way,' is what Heloise remembers thinking. 'I couldn't imagine a family home in that inconvenient space.' But she was urged to take a second, and then a third, look and she began to see the chapel's potential. With some major reshaping it might be a versatile space. 'We decided to put in an offer.' It was accepted on the day that Heloise found out she was pregnant.

Baby Johnny, and then two years later Lara, joined the family. While far from perfect interior-wise, the house worked - temporarily - for the young family. 'We spent months, if not years, planning and eventually came up with our masterplan.'

When Lara turned two, they began work on the chapel. They gaped as doors, walls and eventually floors disappeared and the space became a cavernous tower. At this early stage disaster struck. The builders, having given a fixed price for the job, suddenly downed tools, demanding more money. The O'Hagans simply couldn't meet the new price and had to dismiss the builders, leaving the house in an unliveable state. Three months of despair followed until an unlikely lifeline materialised. A kitchen company which they knew from previous projects offered to take on the job. 'They specialise exclusively in kitchens but craved a bigger project. Their craftsmanship is fantastic, so we decided to give it a go,' explains Heloise.

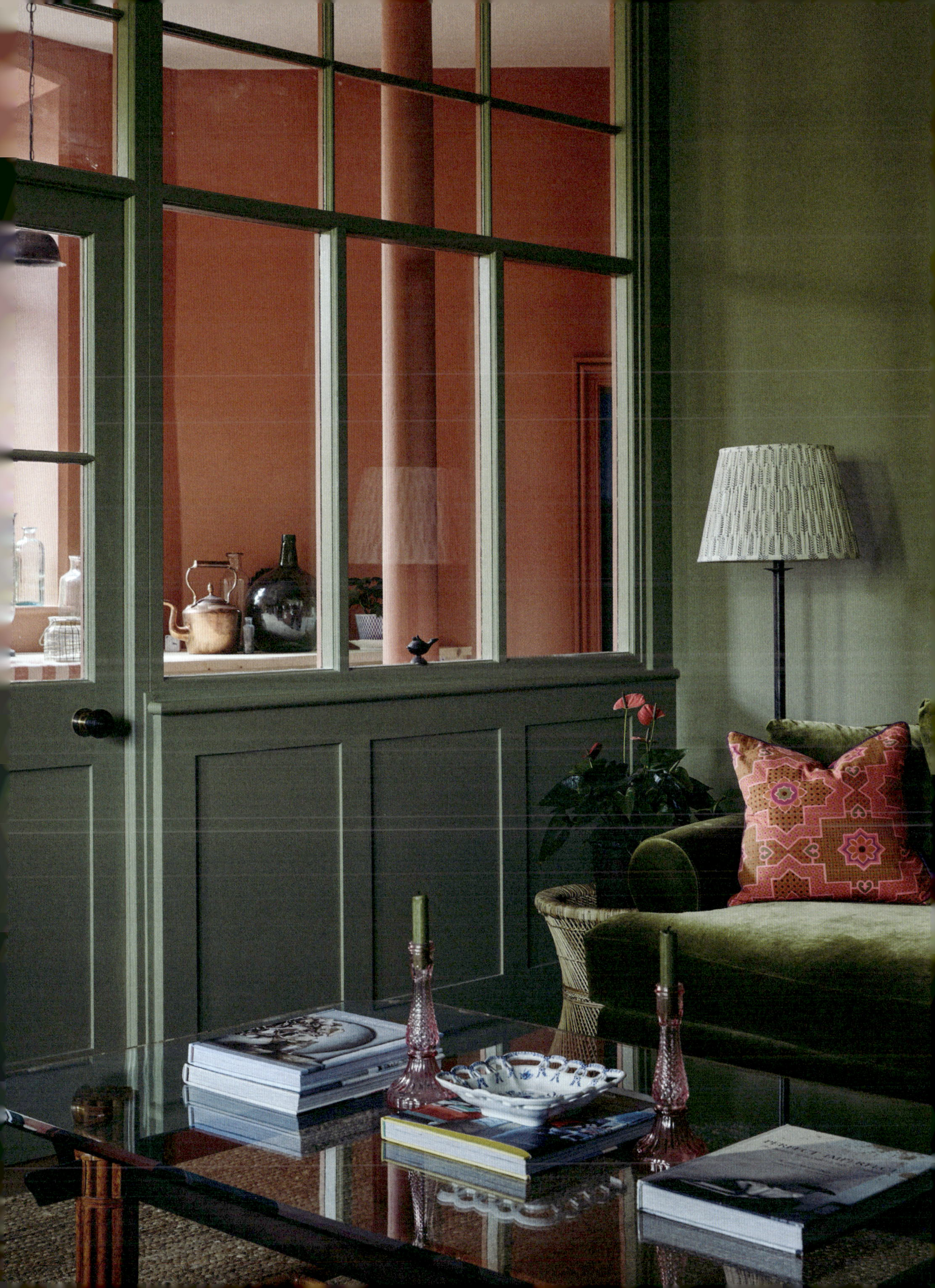

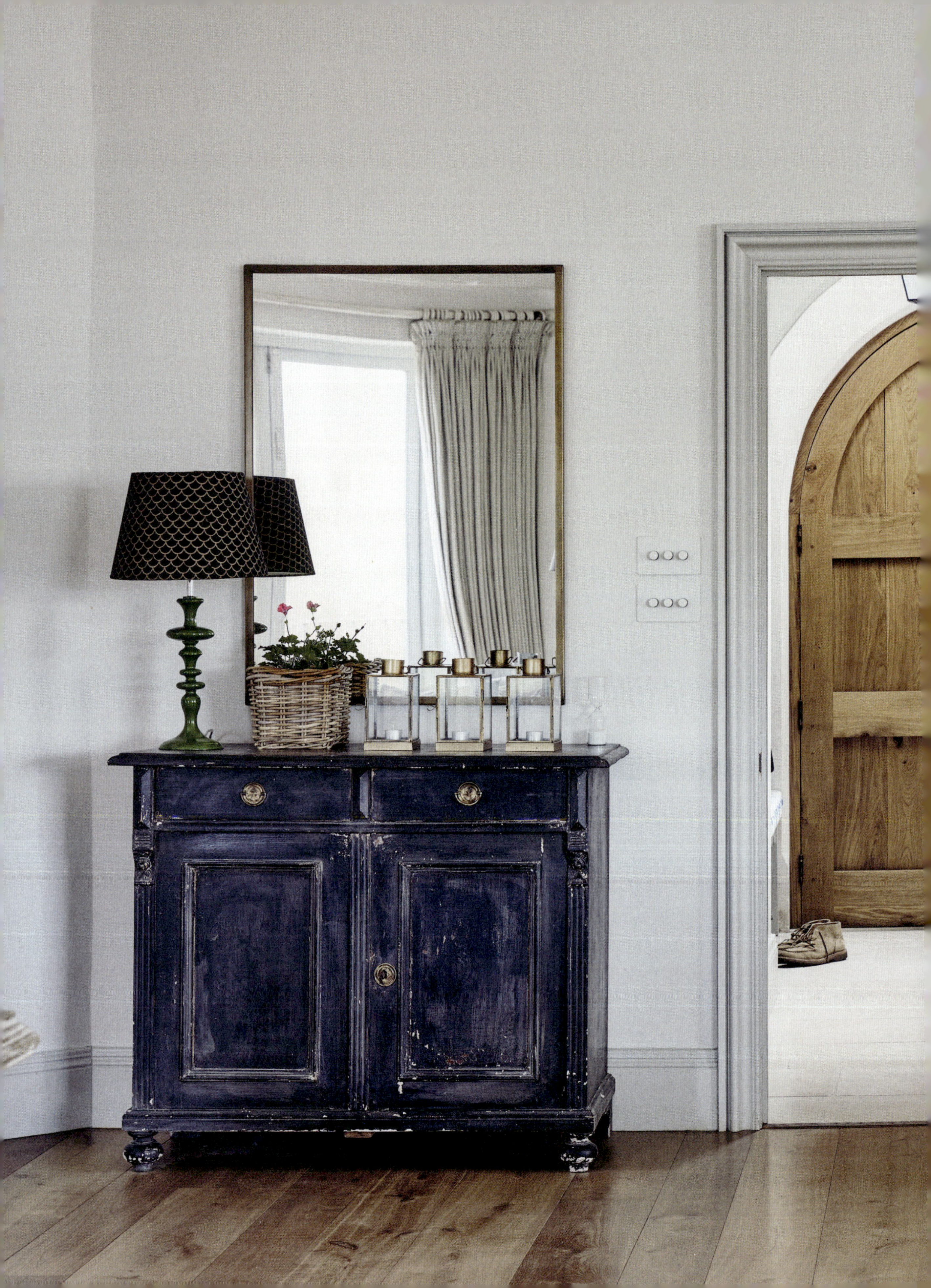

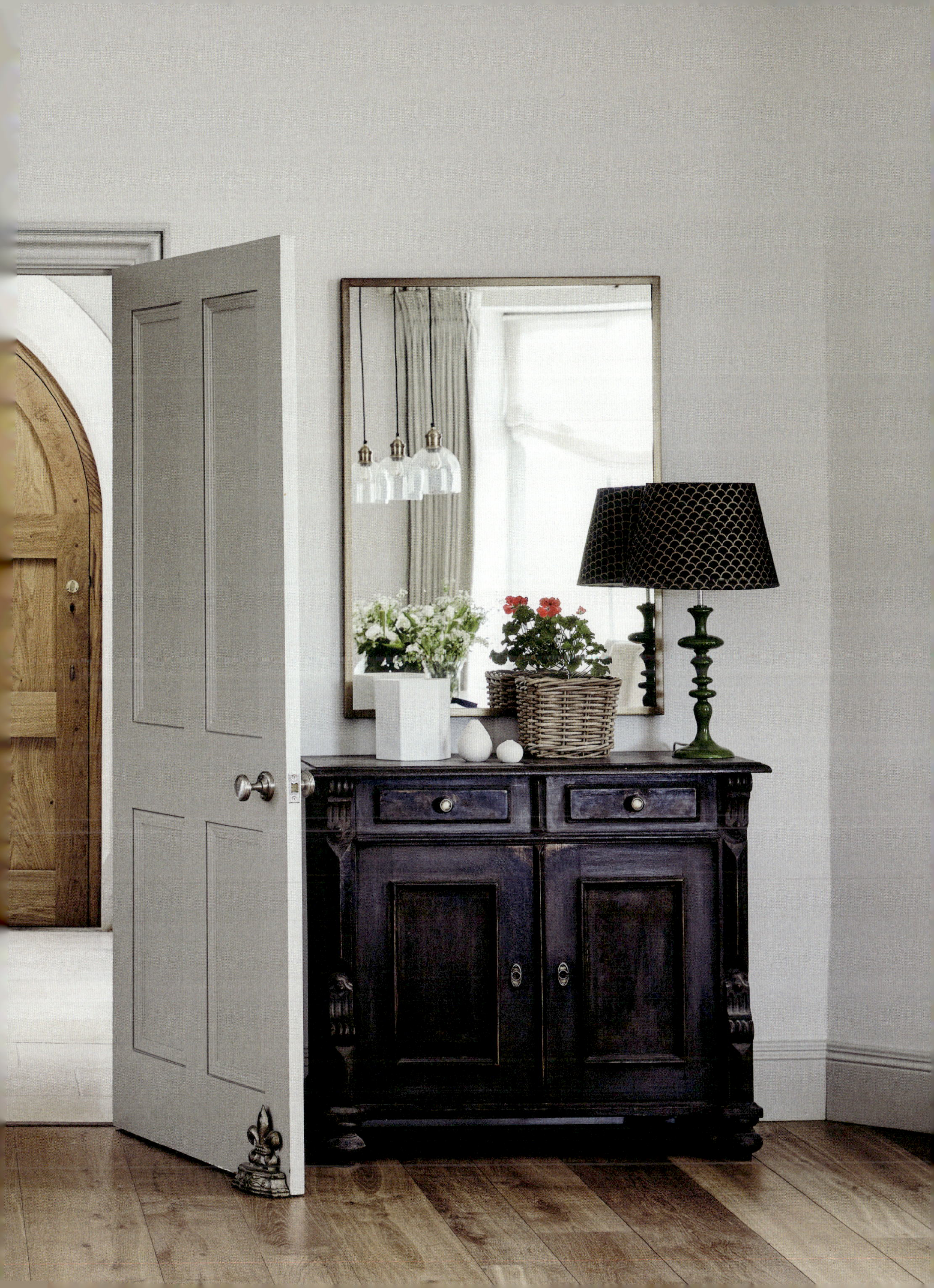

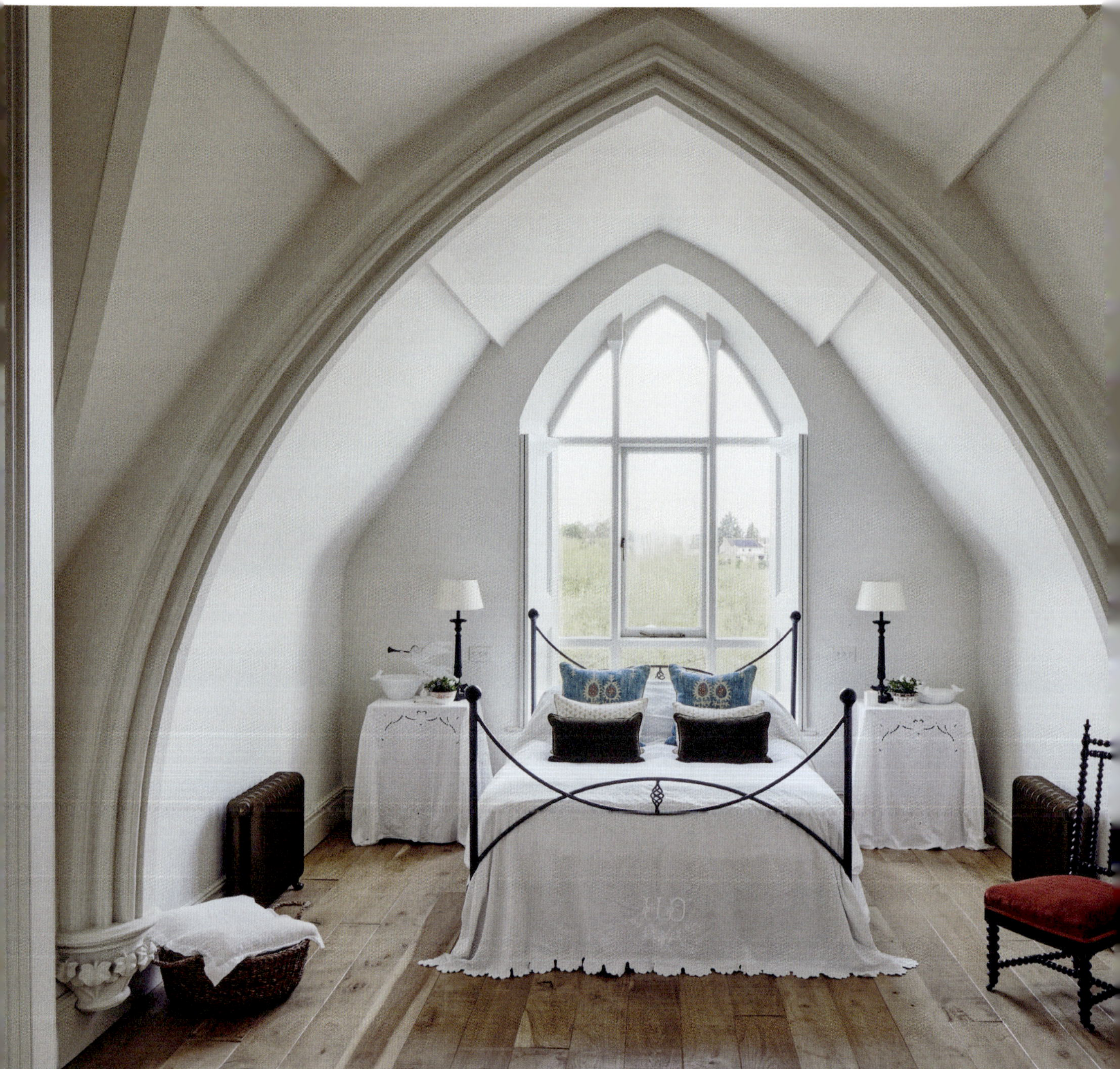

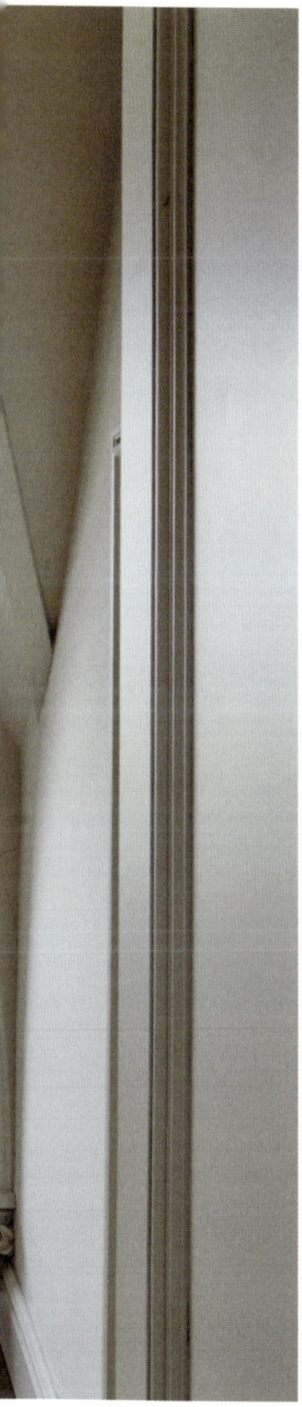

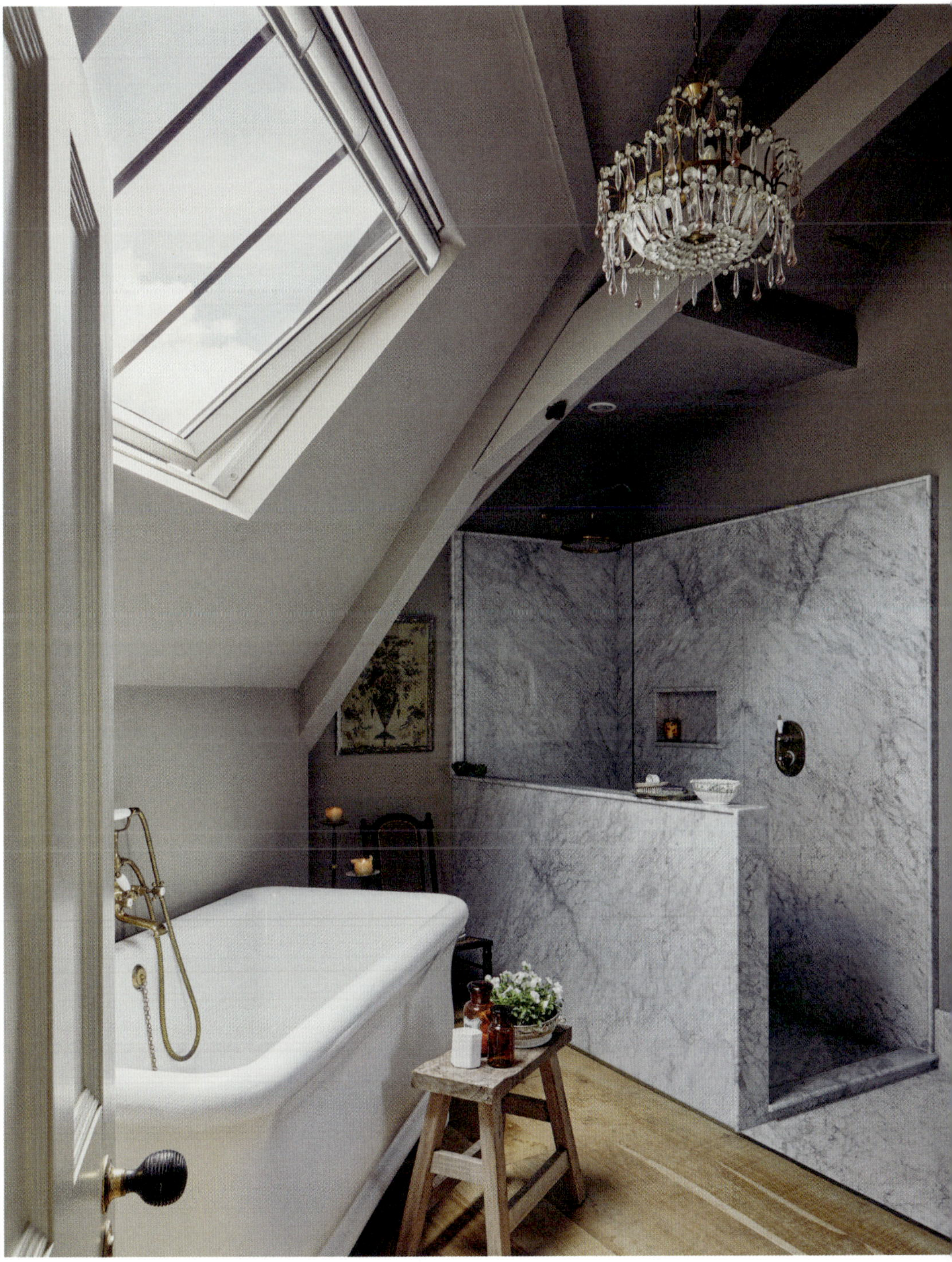

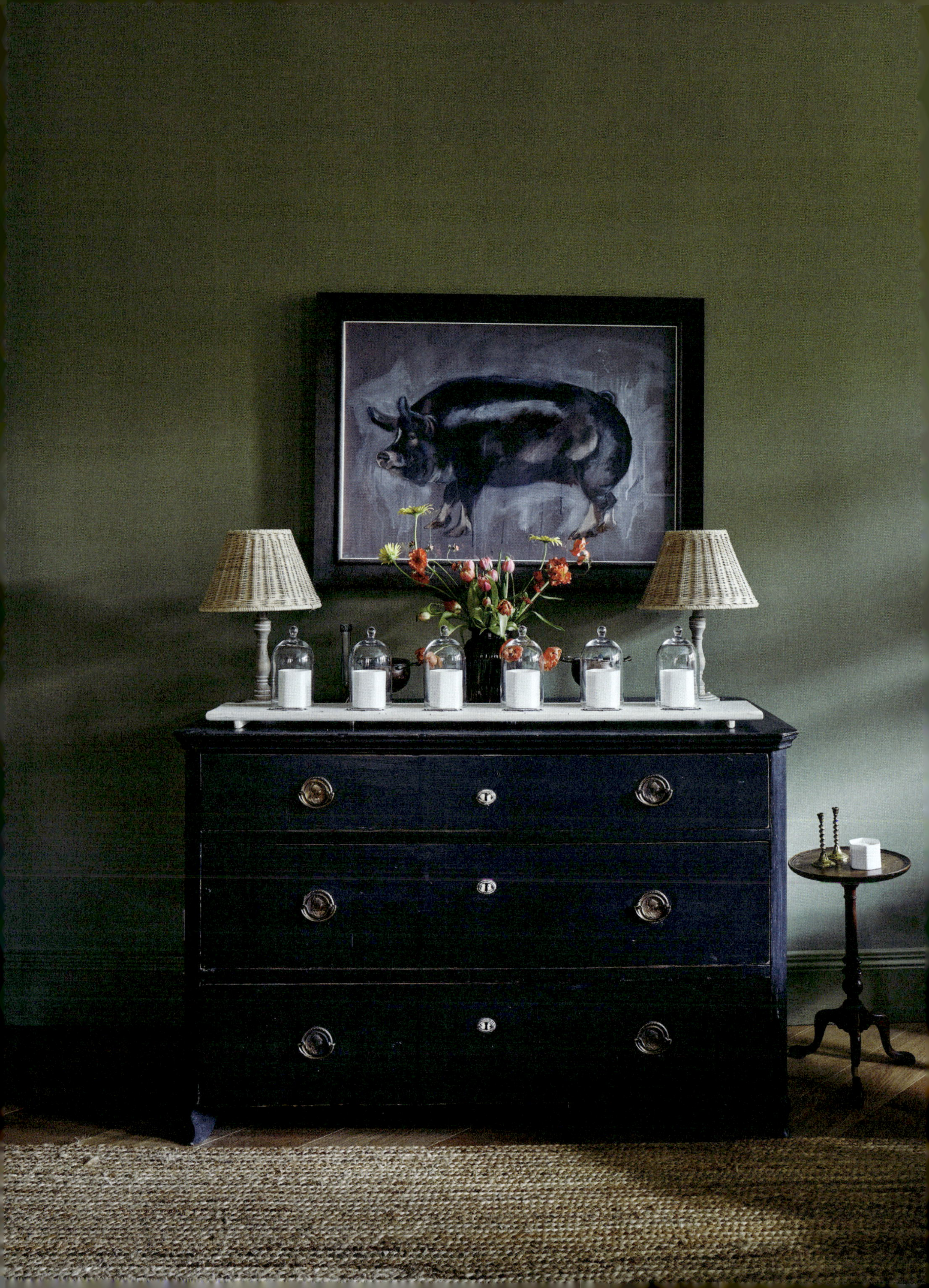

A huge birdcage of scaffolding was built within the hollow space, and work started from the top. Rafters came first, and then a top floor and a more convenient single staircase to improve the flow of the house. The middle floor presented a major challenge. Built as a Methodist chapel, the floor was originally built at a 17-degree angle to afford the congregation a view of the minister. The elderly sisters had stepped across the floor on three inconvenient levels. The O'Hagans decided to lower the kitchen by one step and section off a playroom one step up behind a partition wall. They incorporated a step down to the french doors and balcony. This means that the rest of the living area is on one level: dining to the left and seating to the right.

The previously dingy lower level has been transformed into an intimate sitting room, an office and a laundry room. They raised the entire lower floor by nearly 8 centimetres to reduce the 'basement' feel. The top floor is a flowing space with three family bedrooms, two bathrooms and a large reception area in the middle.

The O'Hagans have brought great style and comfort to their home. They have taken inspiration from gracious English and French historic houses and added contemporary twists of their own. The large space requires some impressively sized pieces and a certain amount of formality. Inspired touches such as a chandelier twinkling over their classic-style kitchen and the antique dining table and chairs bring sophistication. However, there is great comfort here too – sofas and beds are layered with throws and cushions which ensure that these areas are warm and welcoming. These days the whole house also has a remarkable aroma – a subtle flowery, citrusy herby treat of a scent emanates from somewhere ... Those who look (or sniff) closely usually come upon a candle from Heloise's own natural range, named after her and shaped to reflect her unusually shaped home. The delicious scent adds to the sense of comfort and well-being in this exceptional house.

It took extraordinary vision to turn this daunting space into the beautiful, deeply relaxing place it is today. When it comes to inspiring spaces and ways of living, the O'Hagans' octagonal chapel has hit the jackpot.

'BECAUSE OF THE SCALE

and shape of the rooms, I had to find large items of furniture but tried really hard to make areas cosy and intimate. Positioning sofas and armchairs at precise angles is crucial.'

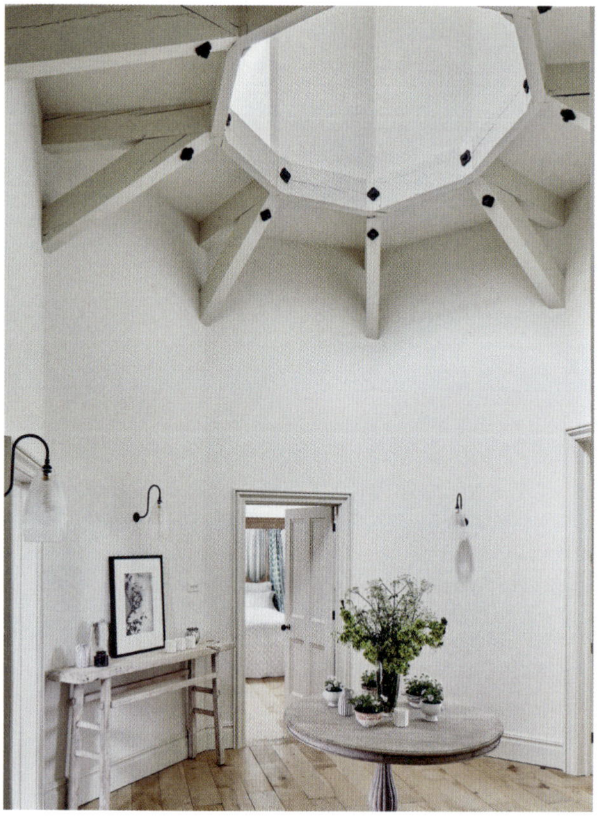

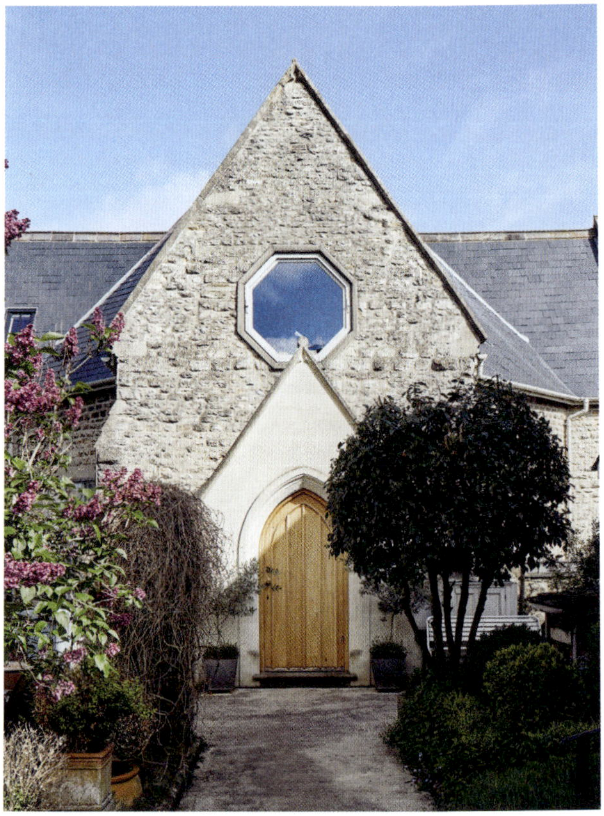

'EVEN THOUGH

I don't like clutter, I love a new interiors discovery and am constantly inspired to update areas in my house. The result is a constantly evolving home, and cupboards stuffed to bursting!'

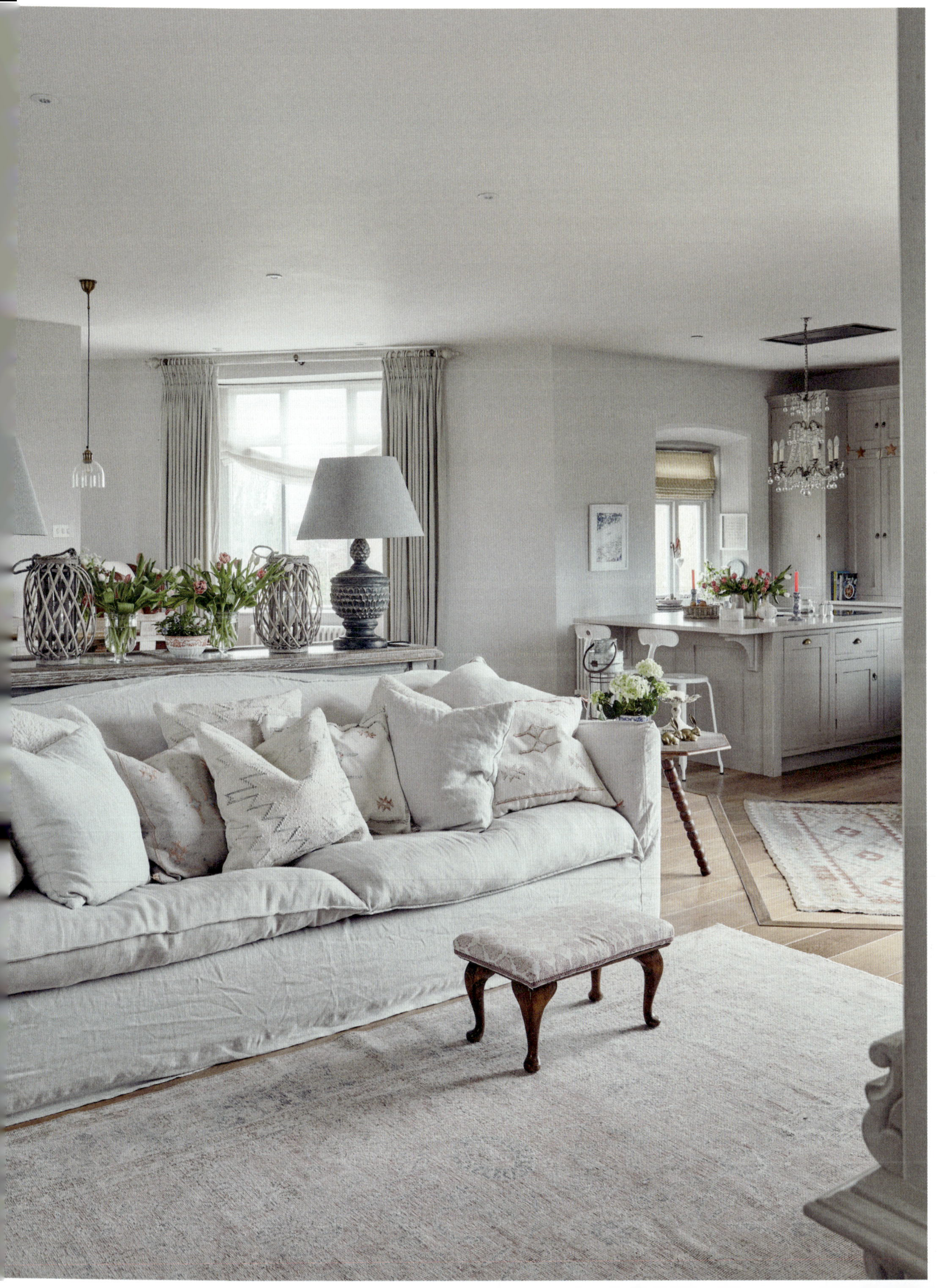

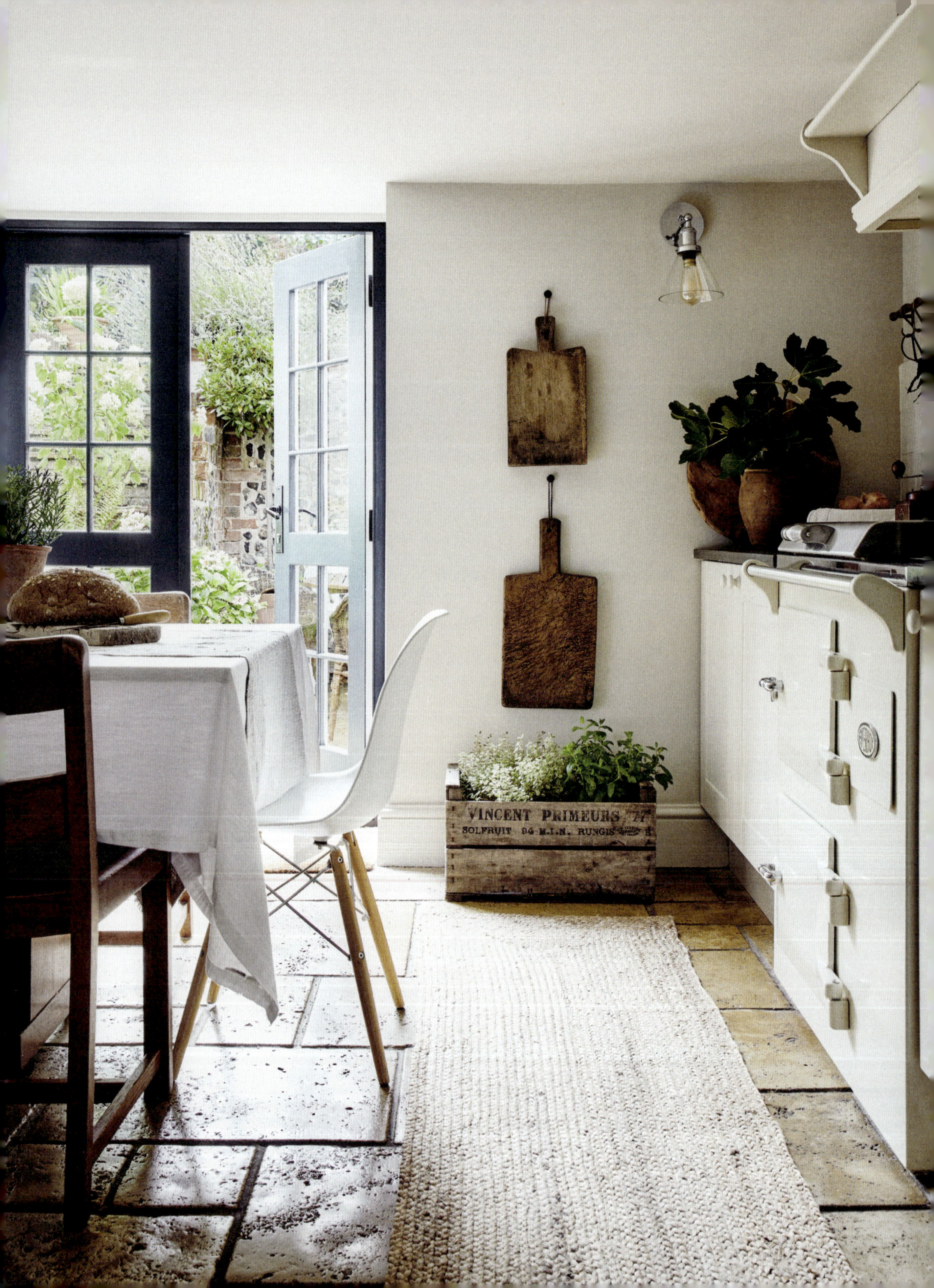
VINCENT PRIMEURS 77
SOLFRUIT 94 M.I.N. RUNGIS

THE TRUE TEST OF TIME

Holly Clements has always felt a powerful affinity with historical houses and felt an instinctive draw to a Georgian cottage named St Agatha.

One winter's night in 1713 a fire swept down the high street of Hambledon village, leaving devastation in its wake. One house, a valiant little thatched cottage named St Agatha, lived to tell the tale; while its thatch was burnt to a cinder, the bones of the place survived. Only the uppermost beams today provide the charred evidence that the house withstood the fire. These blackened marks are also the only clue that St Agatha gives to her true age - somewhat over 310 years old. Beyond that she keeps her age a secret.

It was her mysterious history, and indeed her immense character, that had Holly and Matt Clements signing on the dotted line within minutes of entering St Agatha. 'Buildings are intuitive,' says Holly. 'On an instinctive level I felt the house speak to me and I was at peace here.' It is a peaceful place indeed, the panelled entrance hall opening into the prettiest sitting room with a bay window lighting up the Georgian proportions. Behind the stairs was a sunny farmhouse kitchen, with french doors onto the garden. Upstairs the layout became gloriously unpredictable. Corridors twisted this way and that, walls sloped and floorboards creaked, and eventually Holly counted four bedrooms and two bathrooms - all of varying size and wonkiness.

'People had clearly loved the house over the years, and it was structurally in good shape,' she explains. 'However, like all old houses it had obviously withstood many fashions and fortunes.' She and Matt wanted to take it back to its most authentic, original state. External walls had been rendered in pebbledash and internal walls in cement, some of the sash windows had been painted shut, beams had been boxed in and floorboards were carpeted over.

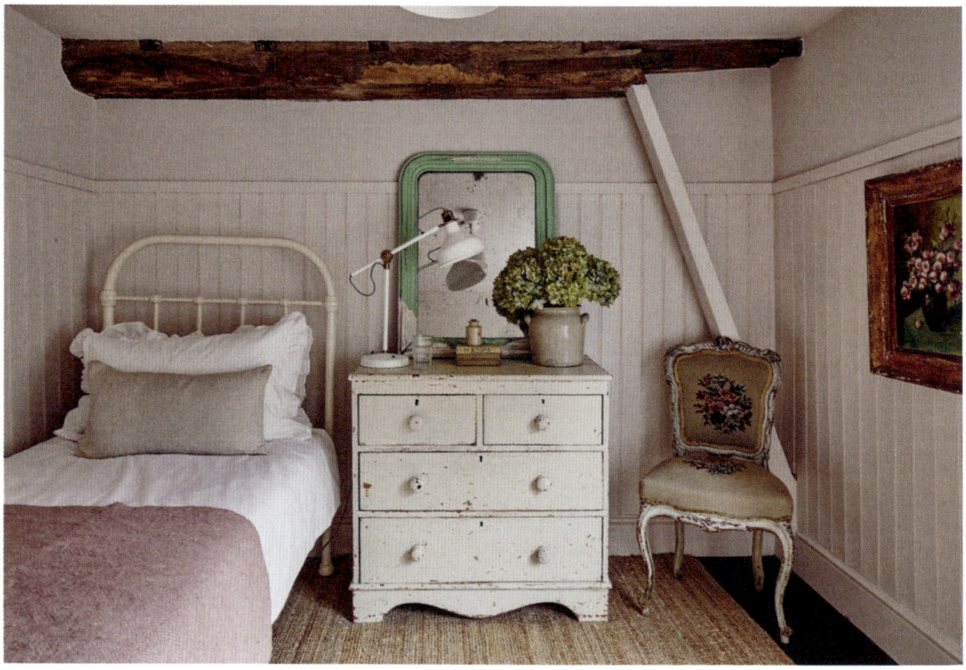

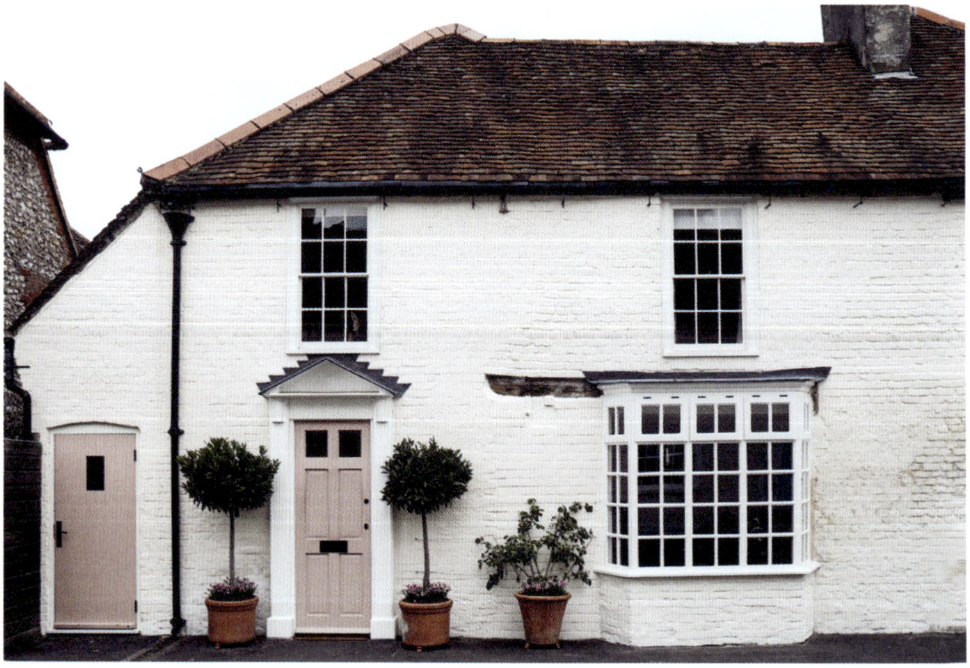

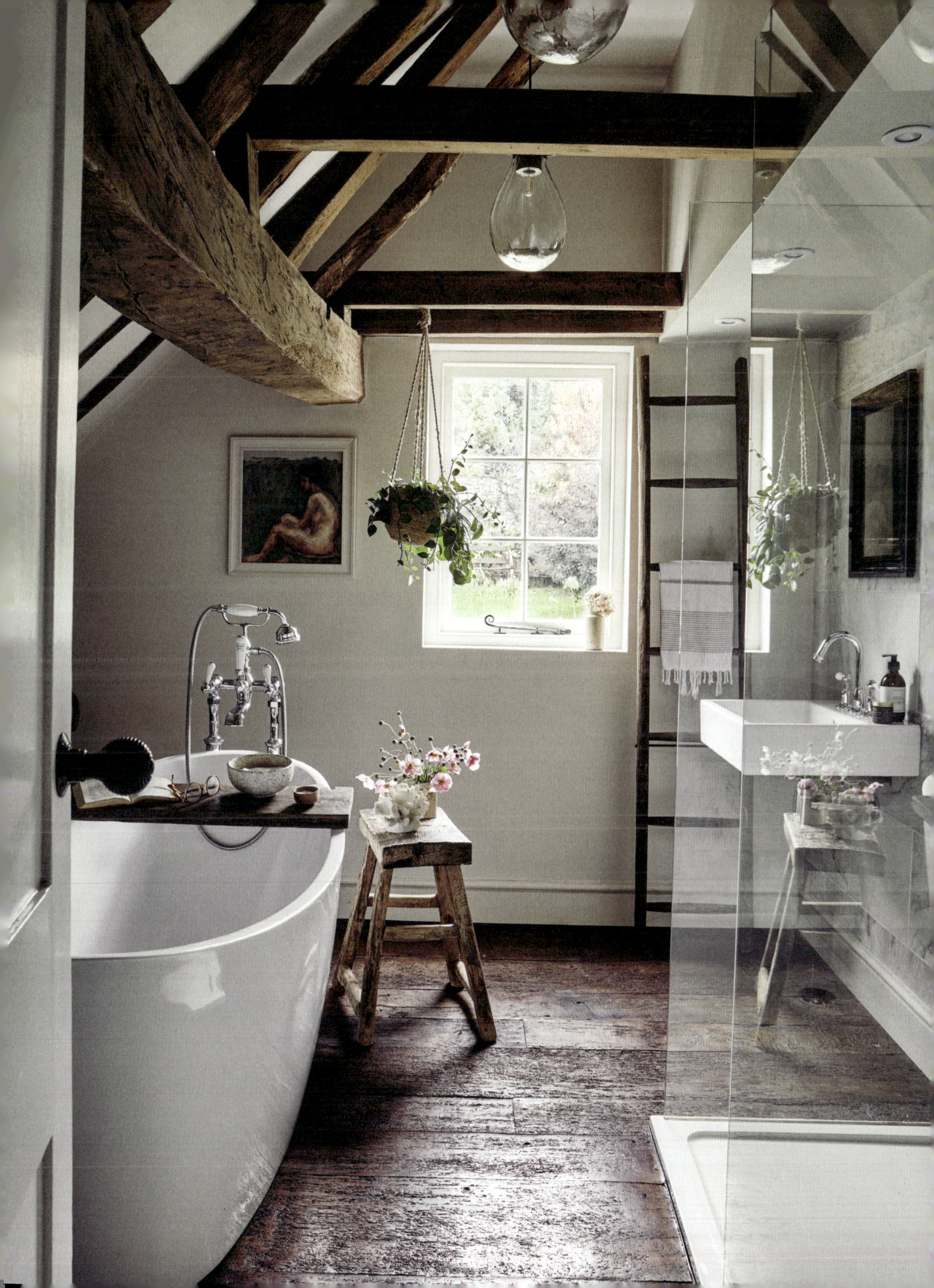

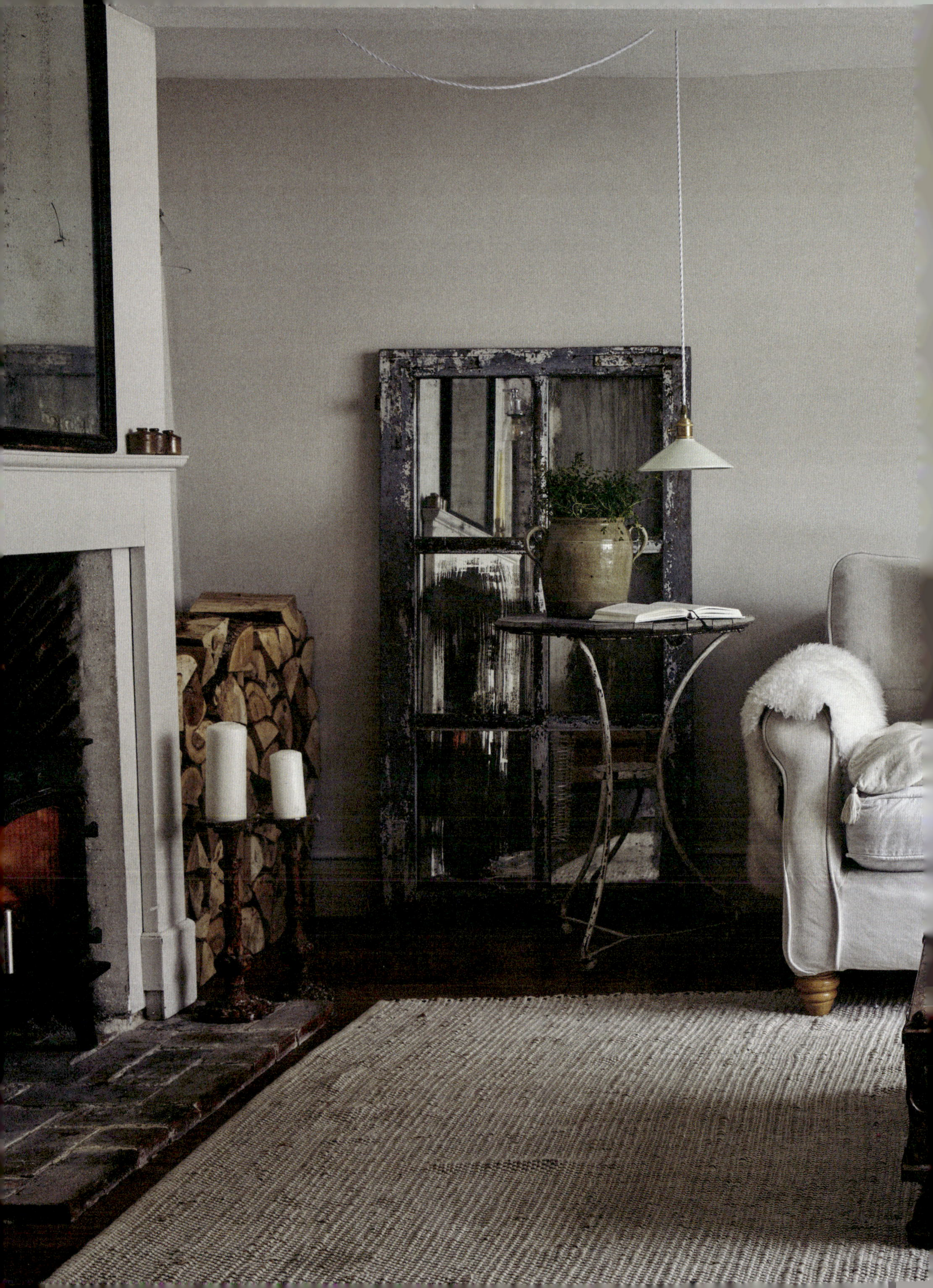

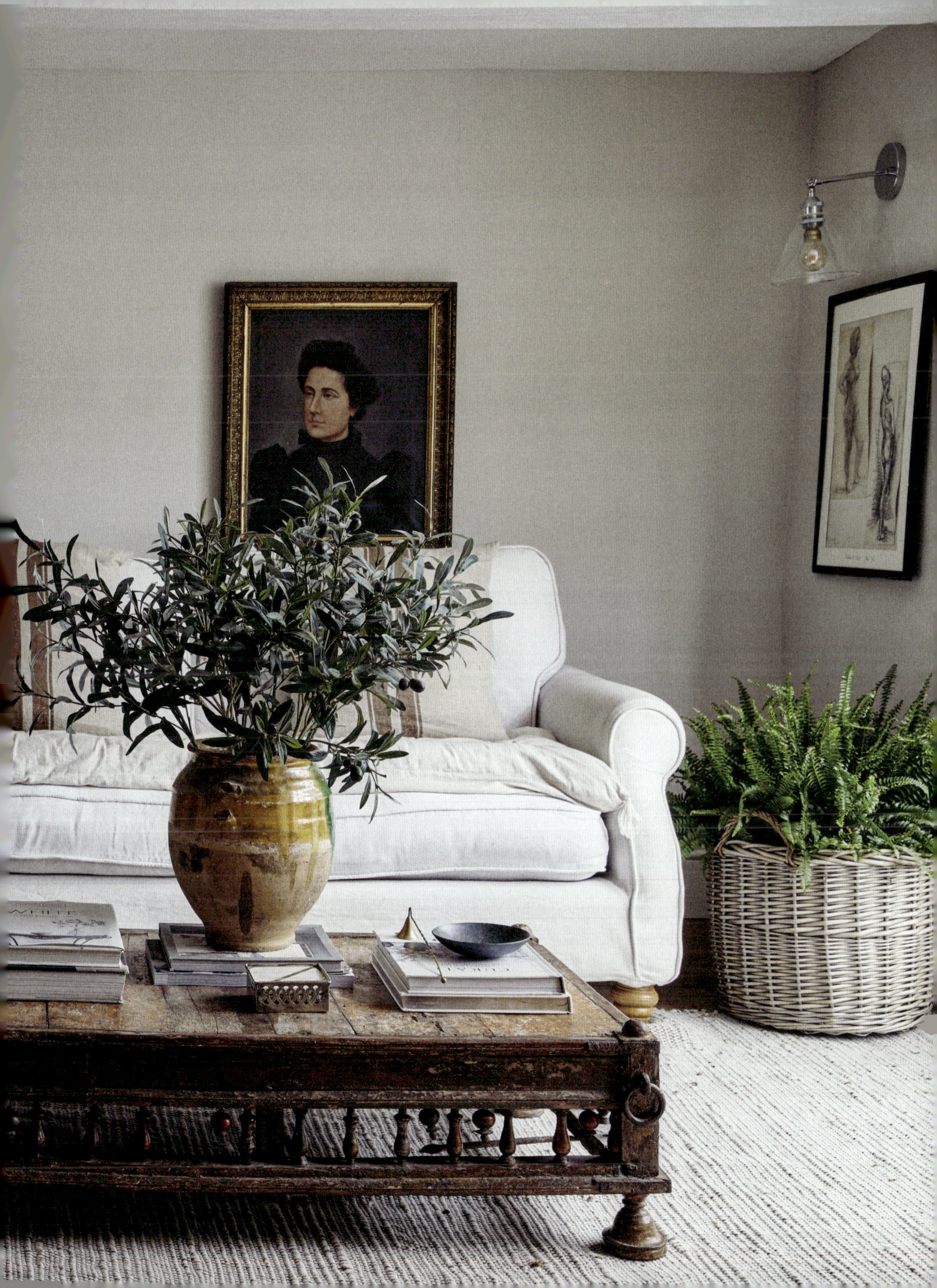
WHITE

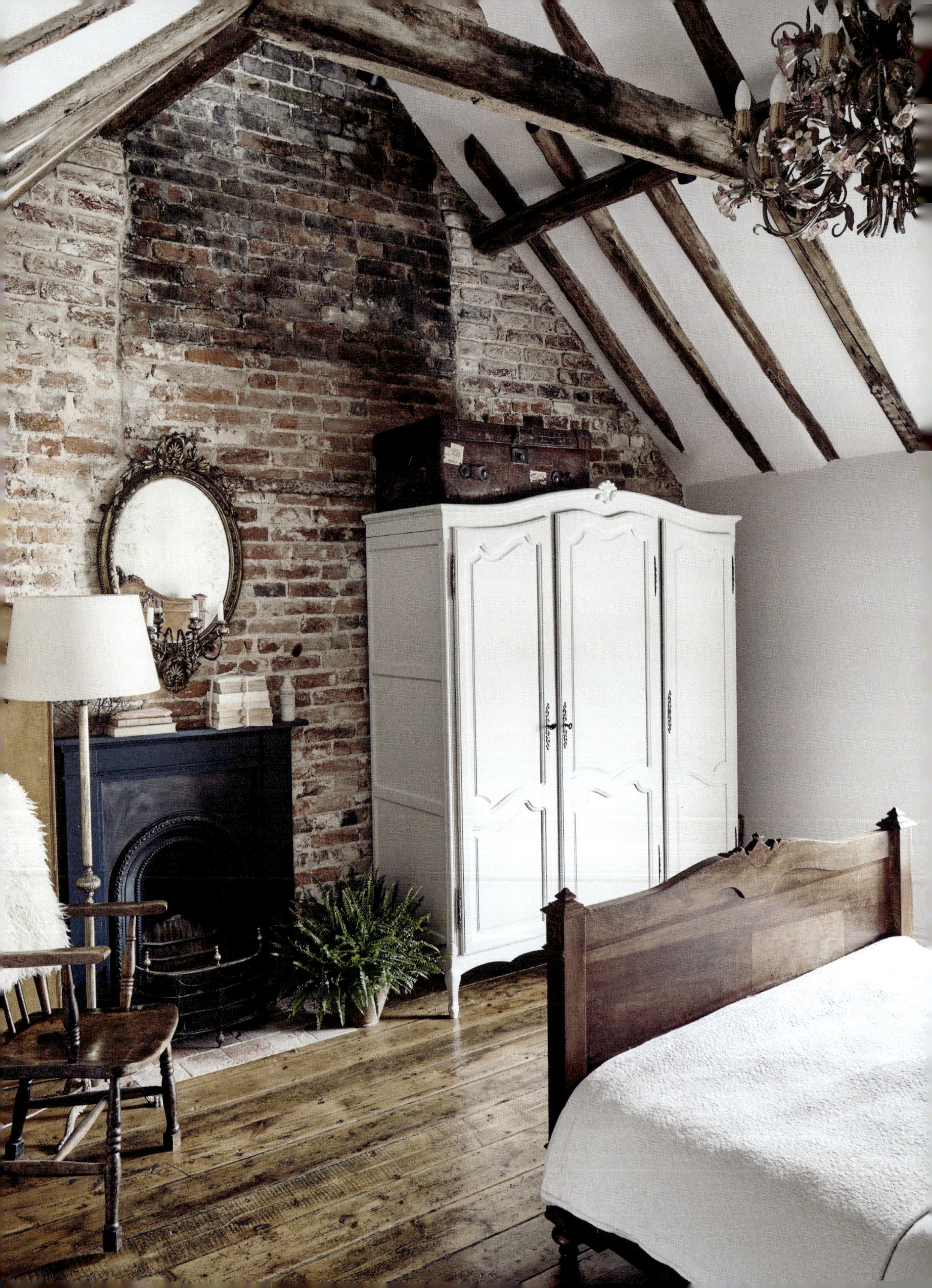

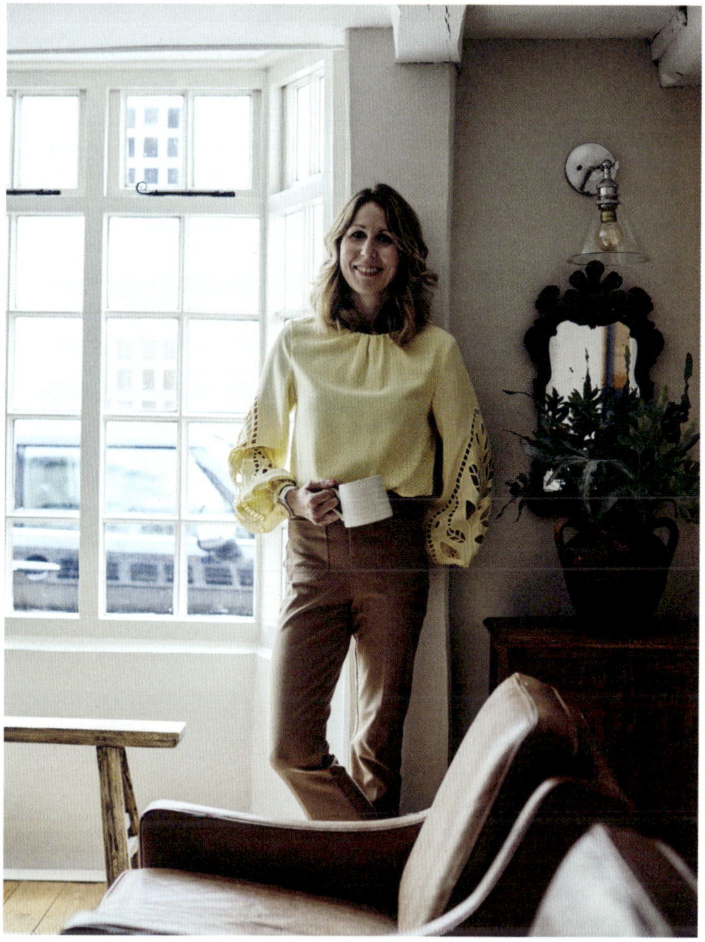

'IT POSITIVELY RESONATED
with character, and had that integrity and dignity of old houses – we could feel its long history emanating from its very walls.'

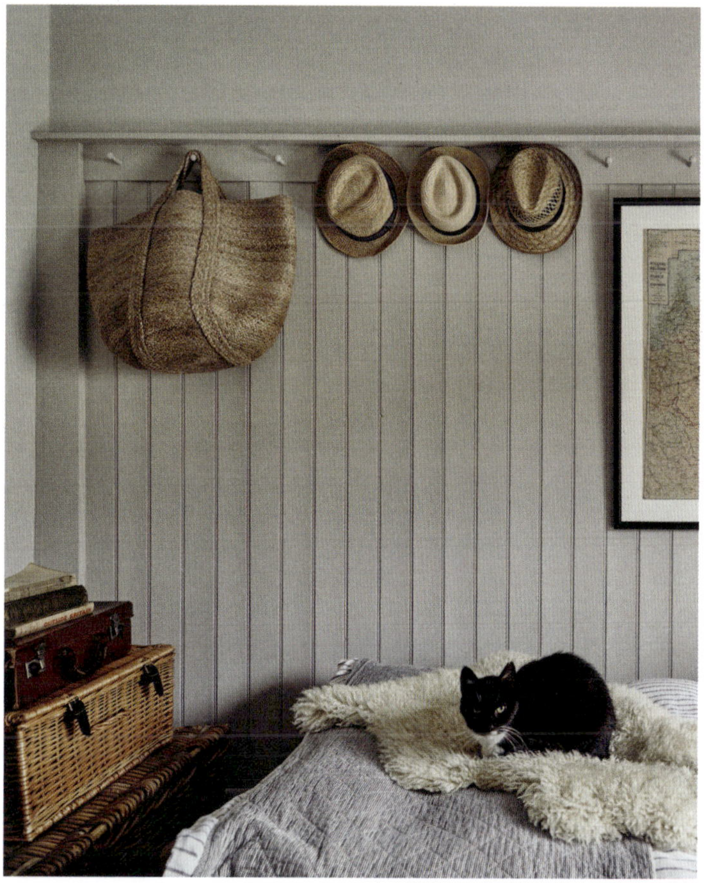

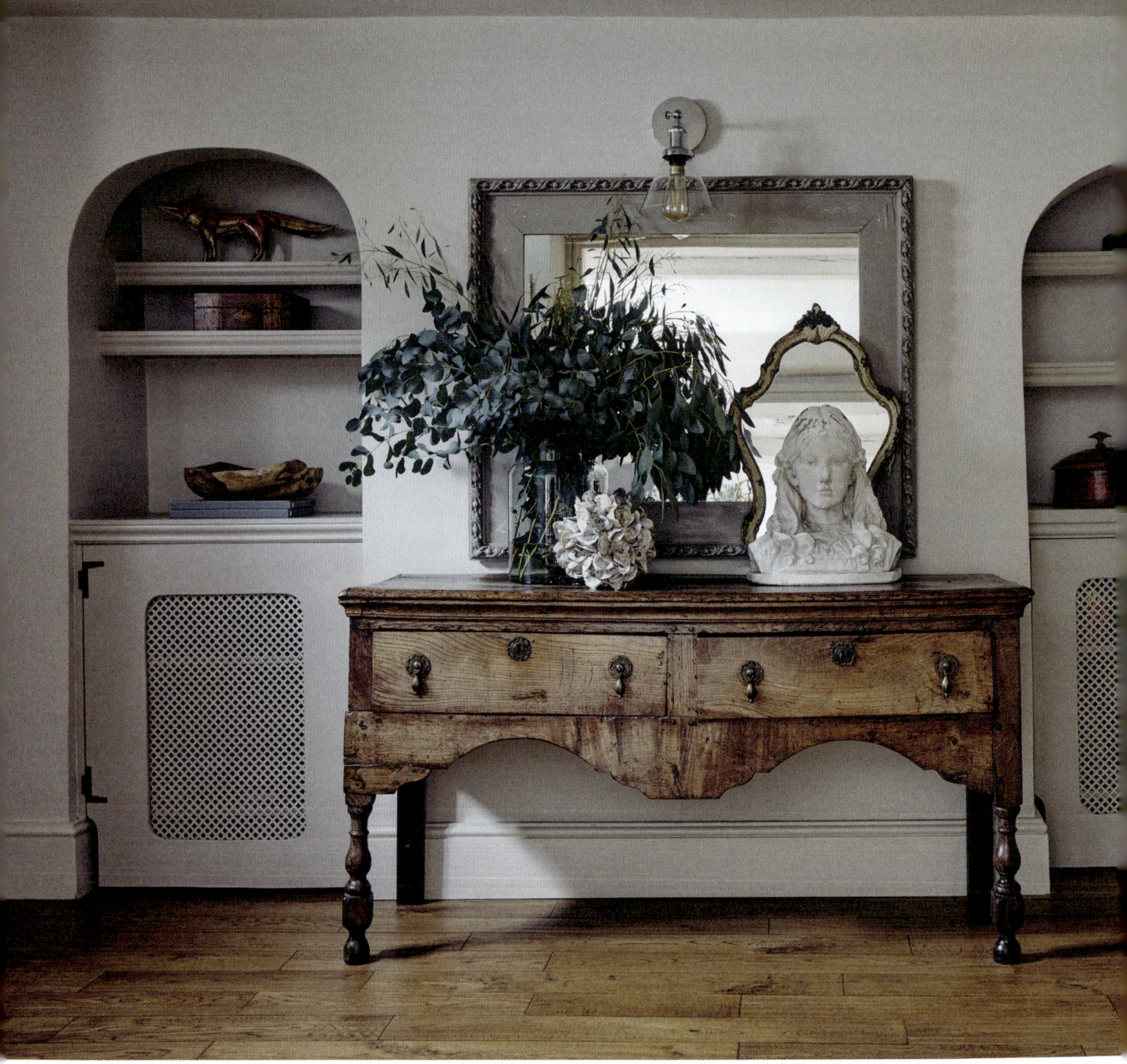

'ITS ATMOSPHERE

worked its magic on the children too. On their very first night here, toddler Oliver and baby Harry both slept soundly, not a bit unsettled by their new surroundings.'

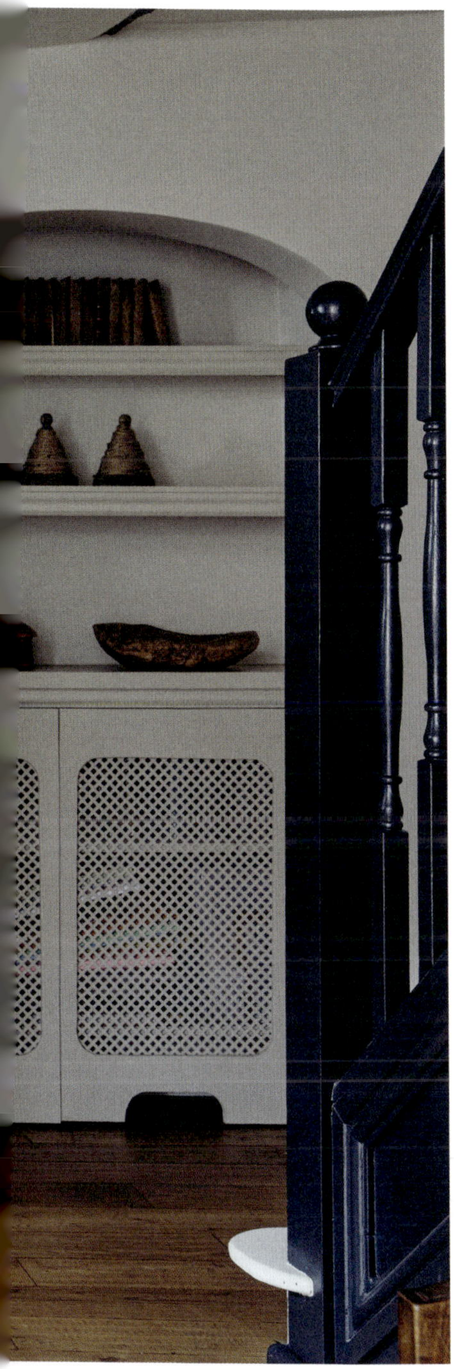

'We aren't the types to be daunted by a project,' admits Holly. Their resilience paid off over the next few months while tarpaulin stood in for windows and dust clouded the place. 'It would have been cheaper to replace the lot, but we decided to repair each window individually, replacing the damaged panes with hand-blown glass.' As for the walls, they found a wonderful lime plasterer who removed the external pebbledash, revealing original limewash beneath. He matched the colour and re-limewashed the exterior walls, one coat at a time. Likewise he painstakingly removed the cement inside and replaced it with horsehair and lime render. 'The house needed to breathe,' she continues. 'We noticed that the faint mushroomy smell disappeared once the walls had been returned to their original lime.'

Meanwhile Holly and Matt made some wonderful discoveries. Peeling up carpets, they found original floorboards, worn smooth with years of footfall. And later, knocking on their bedroom walls and ceiling - which they had found surprisingly smooth and uniform for this wonky old house - they heard a hollow echo and chipped a hole into the plasterboard. Beneath was an ancient brick wall and a tiny fireplace. The wall went up and up, right into the A-frame of the house. 'We had to completely reorientate our bedroom, having originally had our headboard where we found the fireplace.' On the wall which is now behind their bed, they found fragments of centuries-old floral wallpaper. 'Sadly, it wasn't in a fit state to keep, but we matched it with the most similar look we could find.' The bathroom had a lowish smooth ceiling that was beginning to curve down in places. The Clements again braved the situation and pulled down the plasterboard to find original rafters soaring above.

'Wherever we've been able to, we have taken the house back to its original appearance,' explains Holly. On that historical backdrop they have furnished it in a timeless, sympathetic style. She has trawled the flea markets, collectors' fairs and reclamation yards of England, as well as the brocantes of France, to find antiques and vintage pieces worthy of a place in St Agatha. Her favourite items are of course those whose history she knows - the kitchen table, for instance, that has been in her family for three generations and the dolls' house made by her father. Every corner of this house has a story to tell, and even the stories they don't know have a peaceful resonance. 'We marvel that a house that has suffered something as dramatic as a fire can feel so calm,' says Holly. 'But we recently learnt that the real St Agatha was known for her feminine healing powers, among which was her power to cure those who had suffered burns. Perhaps this explains the house's extraordinary atmosphere of contentment.'

TWISTS OF FATE

Do people choose houses, or do houses lie in wait for the right owners? The Evans-Pollard family searched for months for the right house, but ultimately the one on their doorstep that they had long coveted seemed to choose them.

Chris and Susie Evans-Pollard have lived in various Victorian and Georgian flats and houses in London and love light, high-ceilinged homes. Artist and writer Susie particularly craves a light, airy working environment. 'While we love a country cottage, we were hoping to find a place with higher ceilings and big windows,' says Susie. Back in 2009 they had recently moved from London with their two young children and were renting a cottage, treading water until they found a place to buy. The village where they rented was rural – with country walks from the doorstep and a thatched pub over the road – yet it was only fifteen minutes from the Chiltern Turbo railway line so they could both commute to London. The location struck the perfect balance.

Every day they would walk past a square red building, pausing to imagine living in this elegant house built some 150 years ago in Georgian style with a perfectly symmetrical façade. Tantalisingly, it came onto the market soon after the family started renting in the village but was beyond their budget. They watched from across the road as potential buyers streamed through and had to accept that the house was not for them. They knuckled down to finding somewhere else.

Months later, wilful fate played her hand. The family were finally half-heartedly on the brink of putting in an offer on a house in the neighbouring village. The square red house had, astonishingly, received no offers and the asking price was being lowered. Of course, they had to have a look, and predictably they loved it. 'The houses we had viewed were quite pokey, but here you could breathe,' remembers Susie. It had a reception room on either side of the front hall and a generous and light kitchen at the back; upstairs were four bedrooms with soaring vaulted ceilings and exposed rafters.

A dream house for the Evans-Pollards, and suddenly within a whisker of their reach. They didn't waste a moment before putting in their offer. 'We could barely breathe as we waited for an answer,' remembers Susie. 'You should have heard the hollers when it came back YES!'

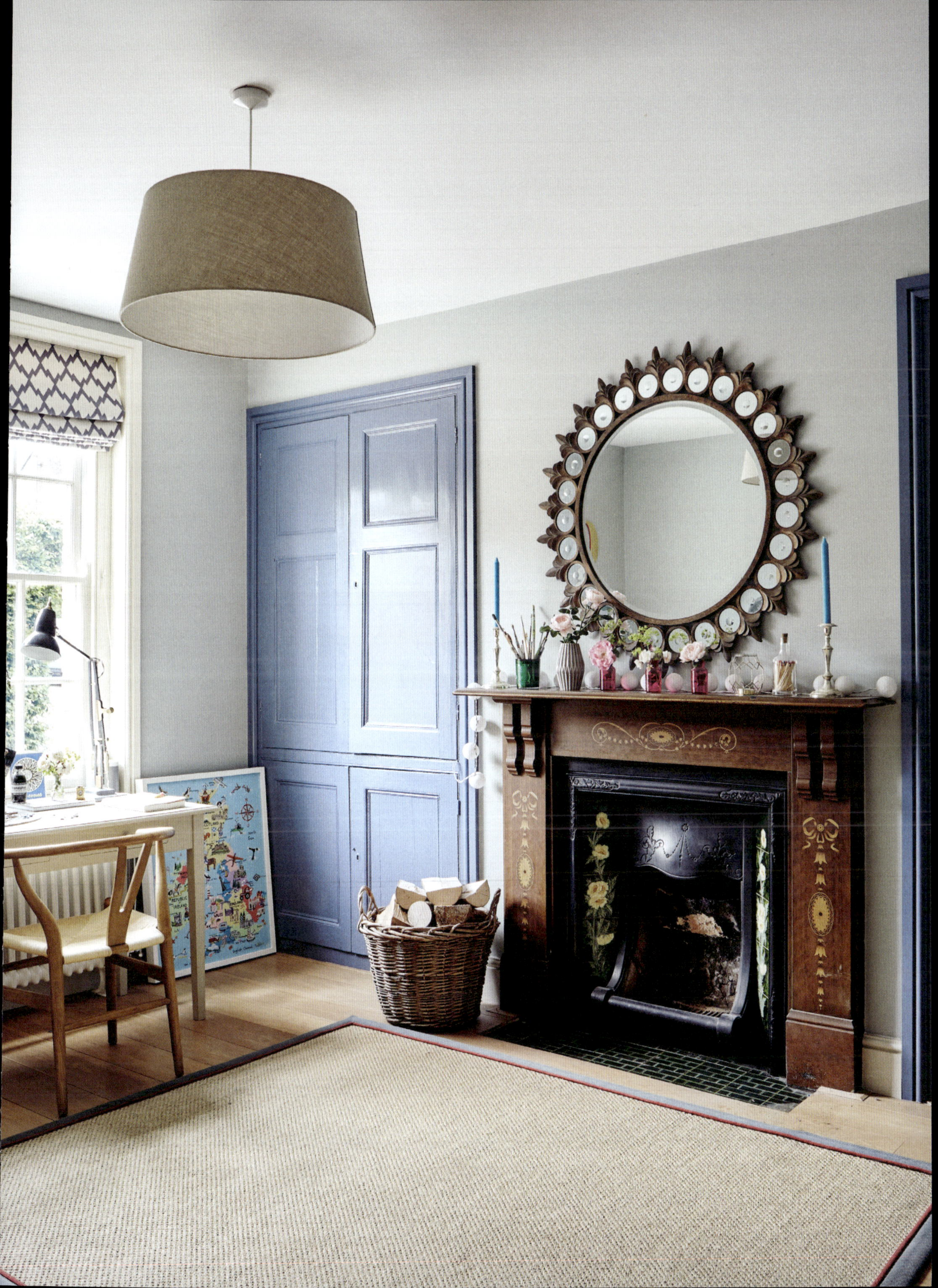

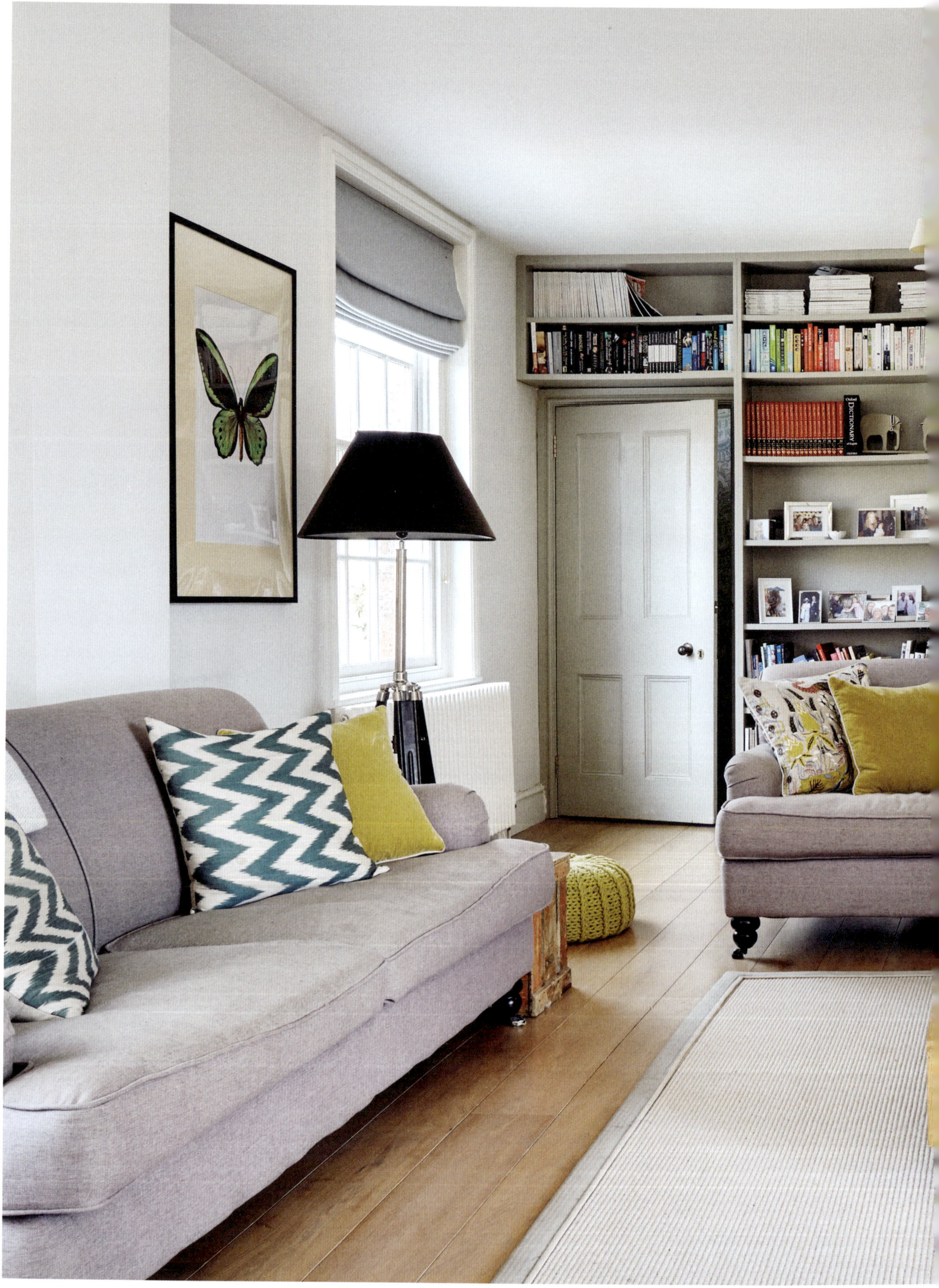

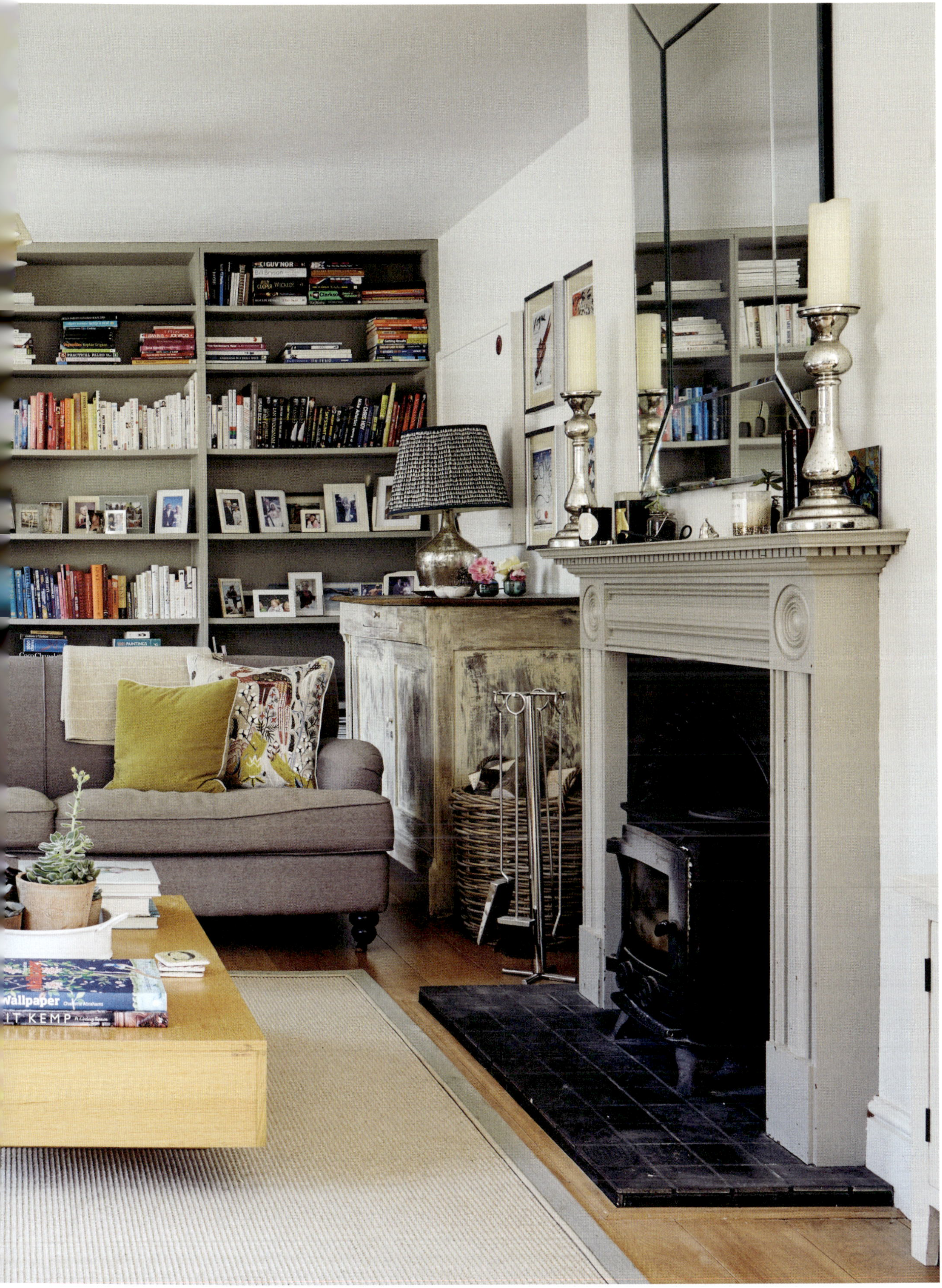
Wallpaper

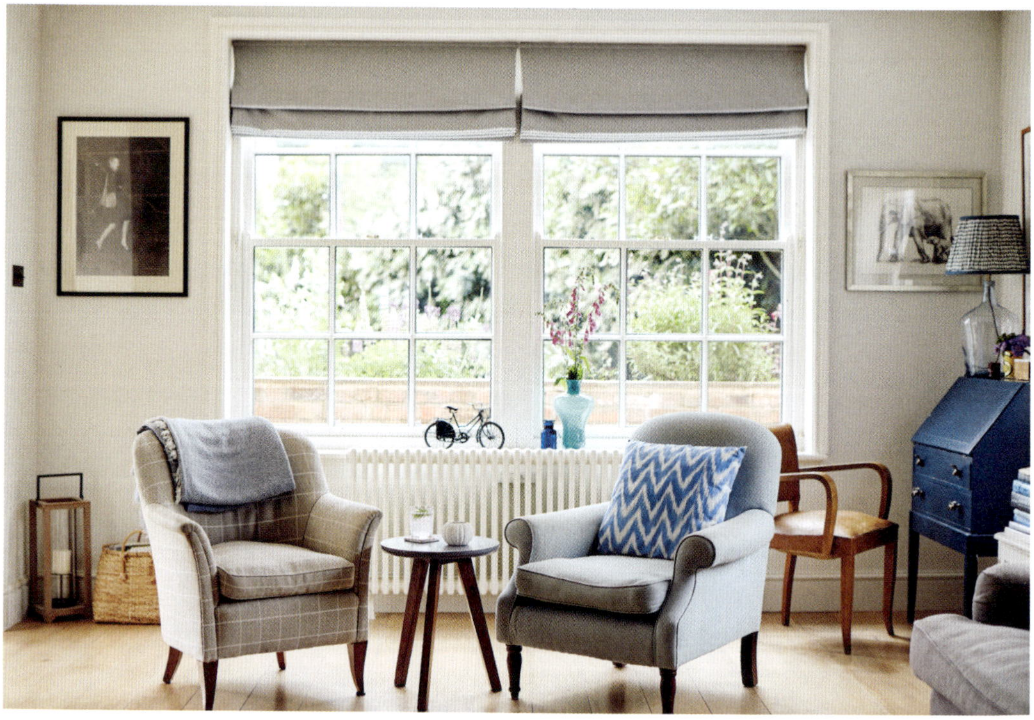

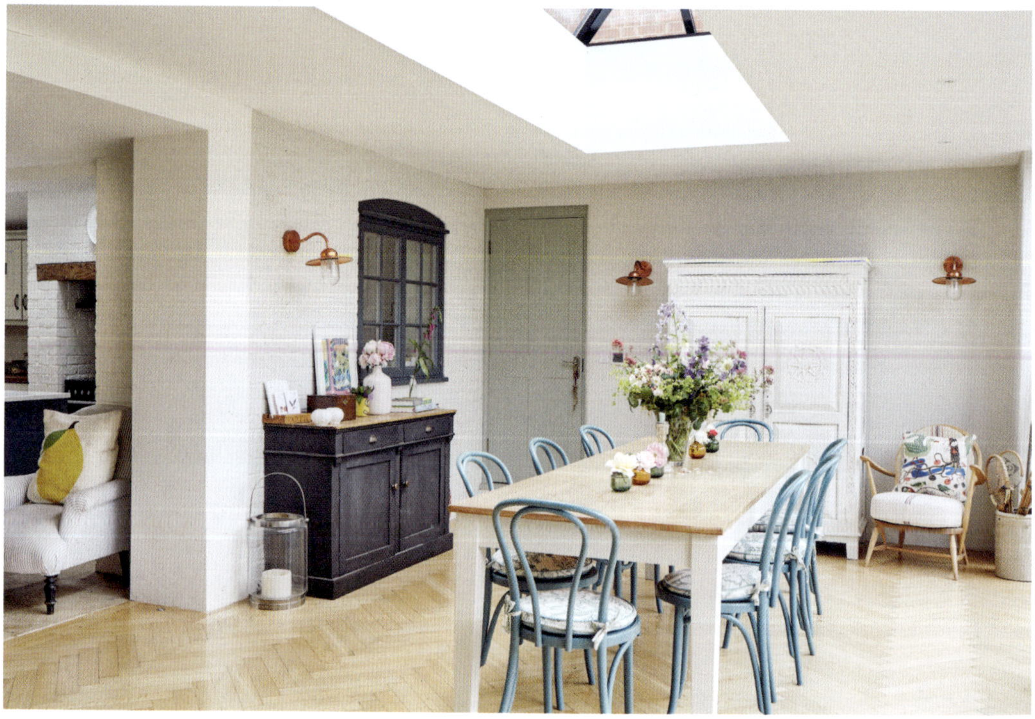

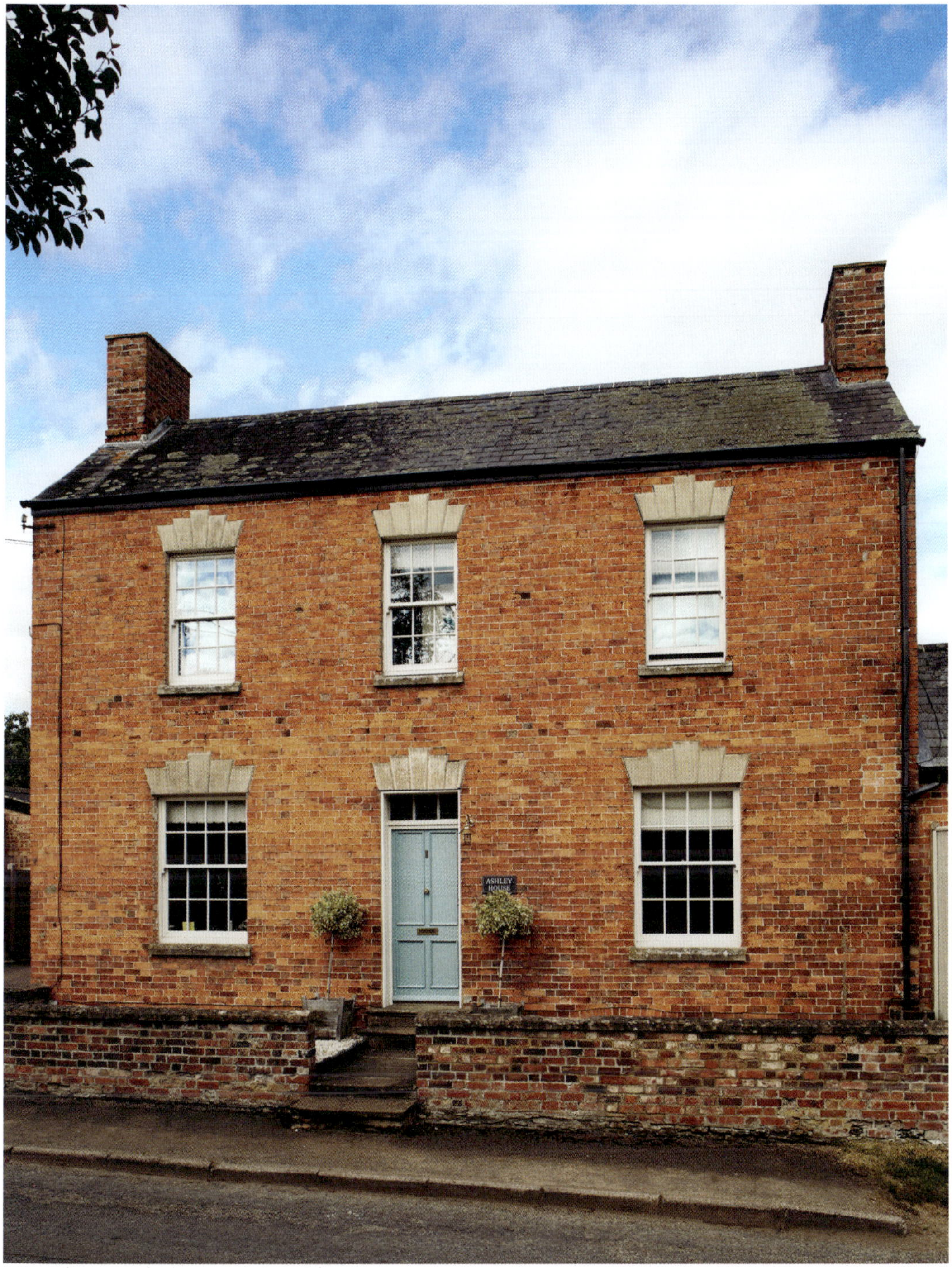

'WHILE I LOVE BRIGHT COLOUR,

I really try to bring only colours that naturally occur in nature to my home. Slate blues, rose pinks, autumn yellows. Nothing I wouldn't see in the outside world.'

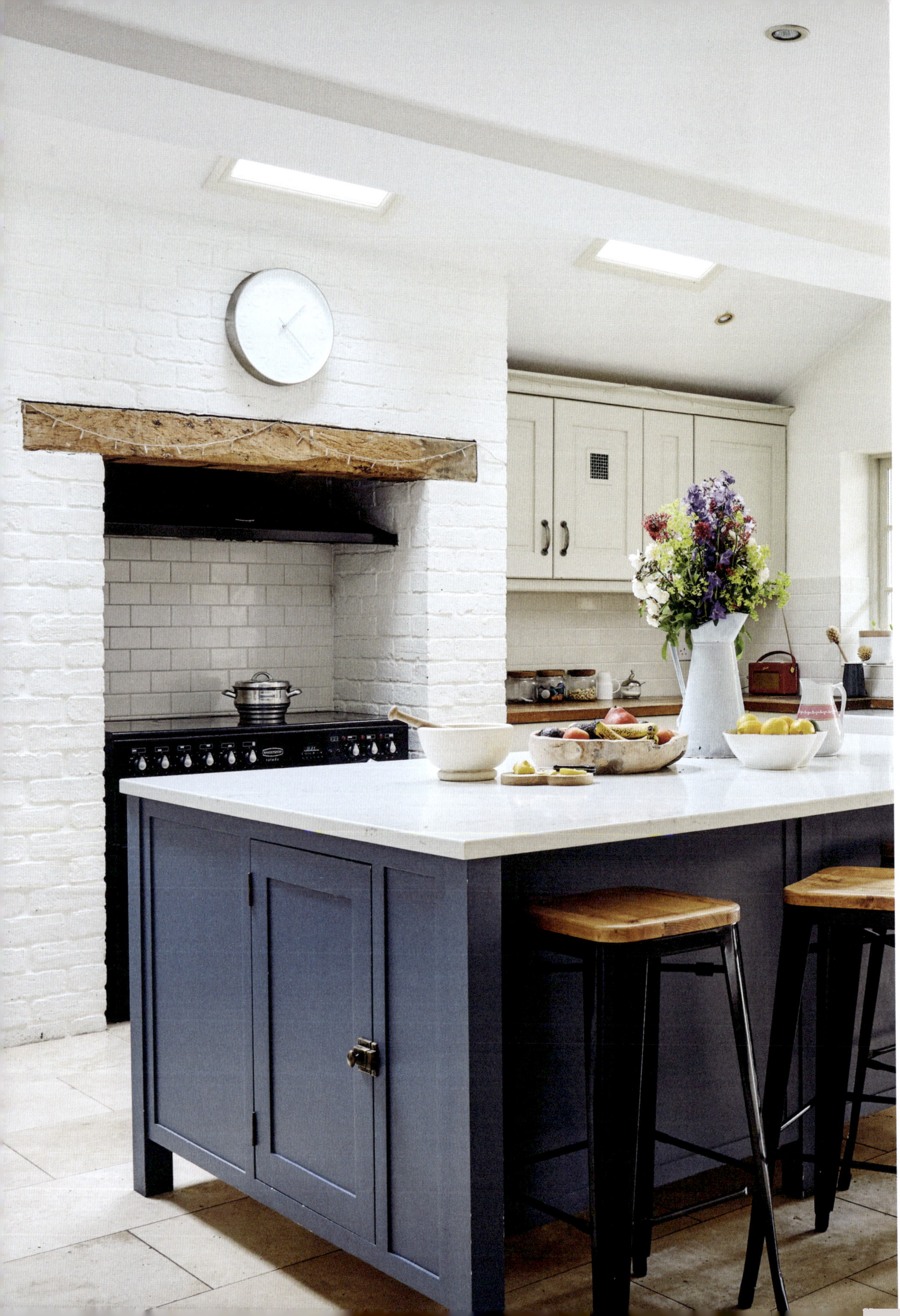

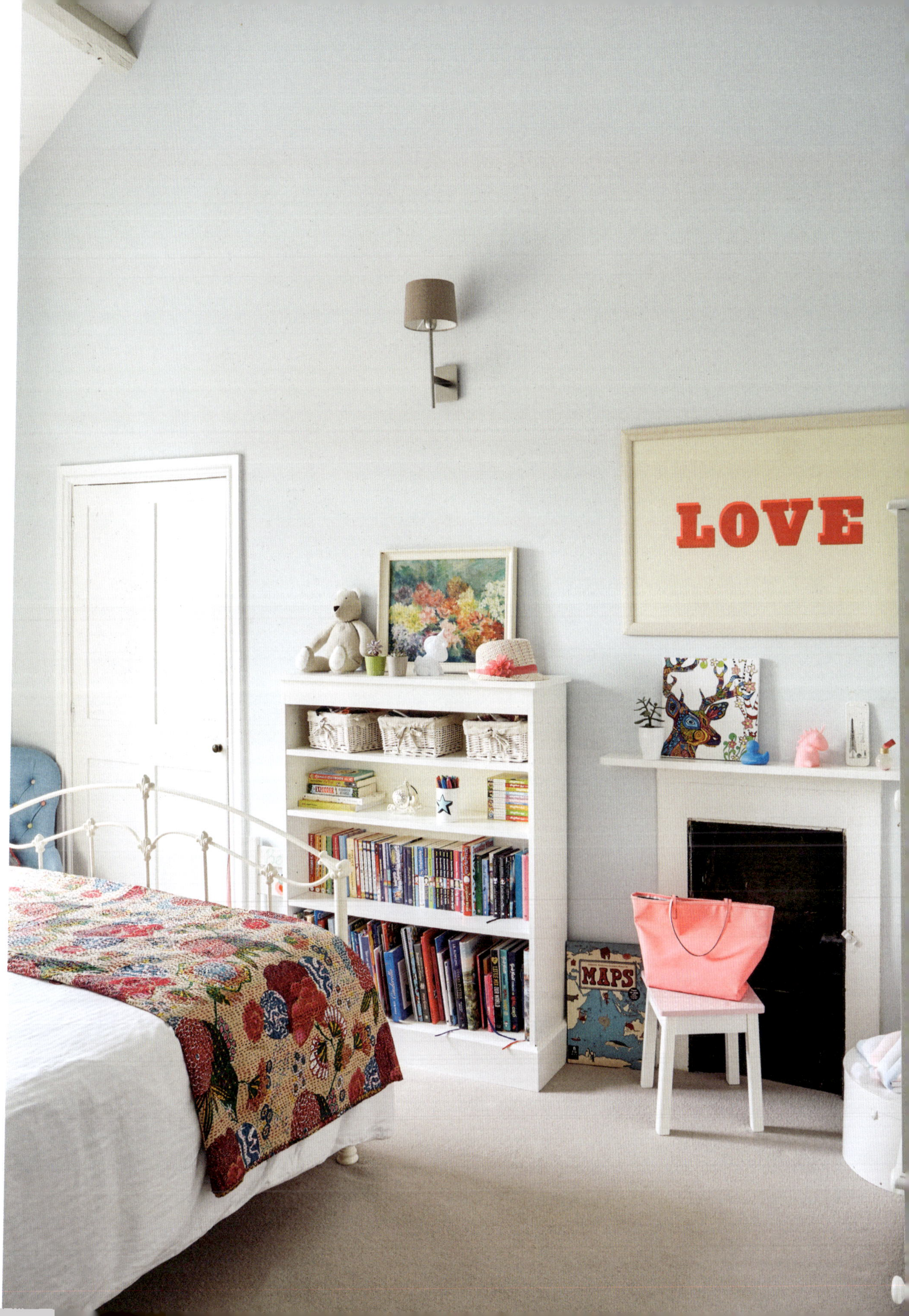
LOVE
MAPS

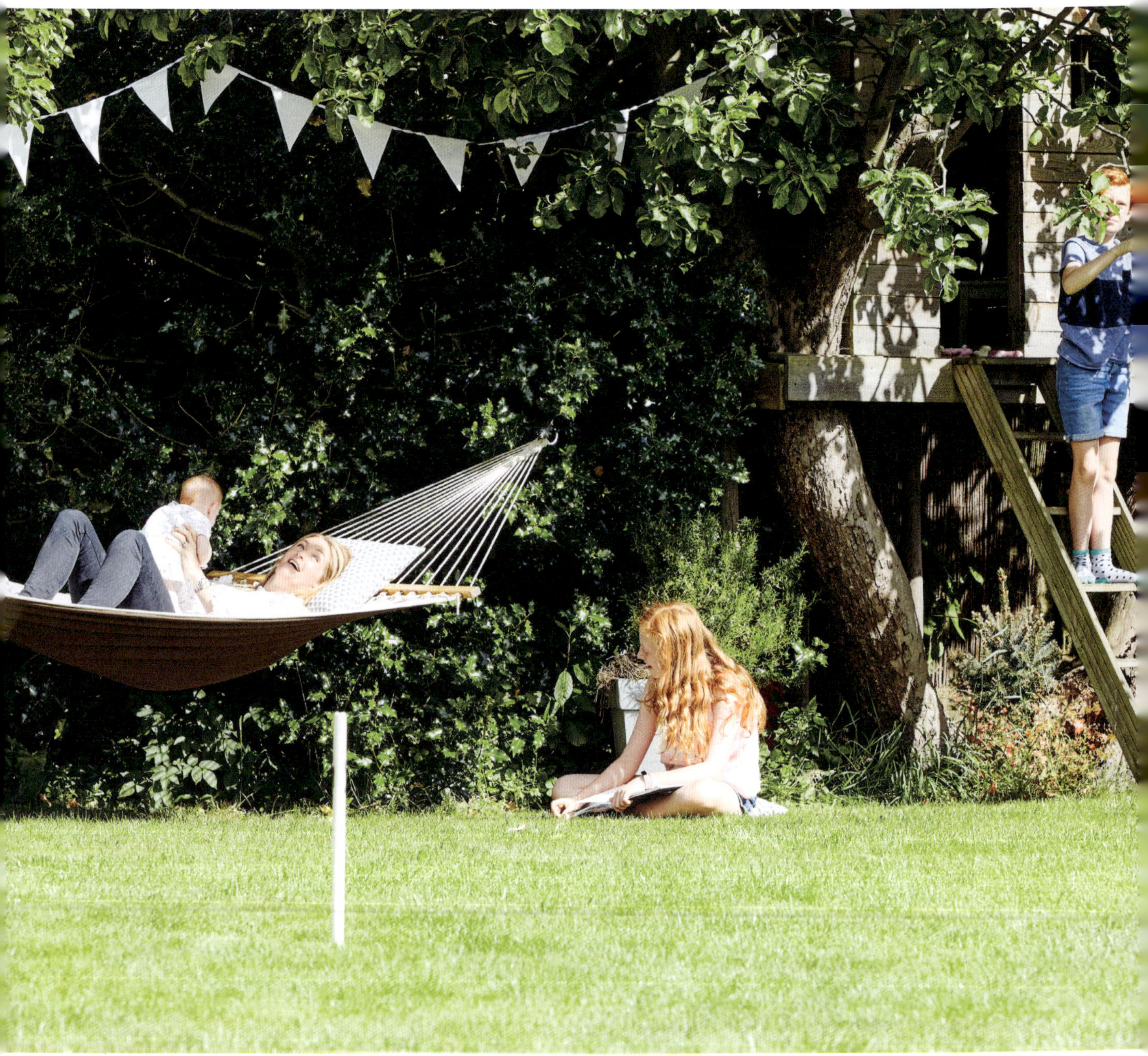

'THE GEORGIANS

got it right,' says Susie. 'They worked out how to bring real tranquillity to our living spaces. The high ceilings, tall sash windows and pleasing symmetry bring such peace, dignity and balance.'

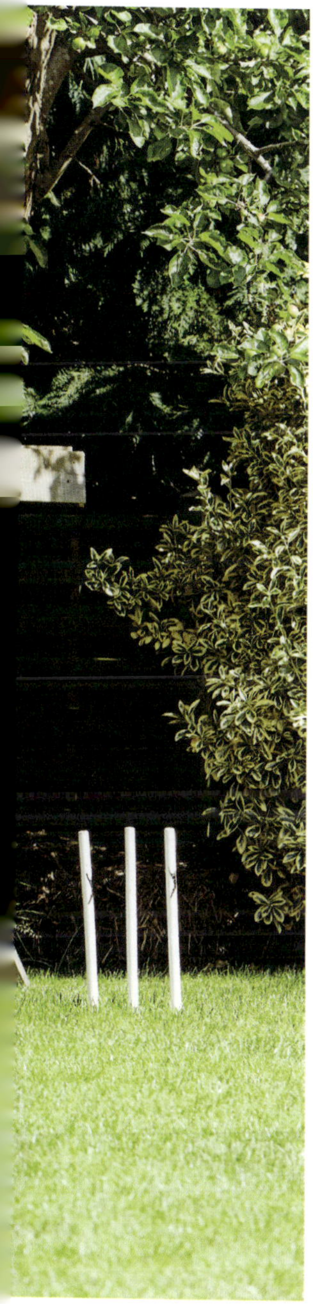

Once in, with toddling Bella and baby Oscar, Chris and Susie were grateful not to have a huge project on their hands. The previous owners had recently updated the house, installing a new kitchen and bathrooms, and redecorating throughout. By simply changing a few superficial details and adding a lick of paint here and a new carpet there, the family were able to settle in.

With great imagination and energy, they set about decorating and furnishing their new home in the original and inspiring way that comes naturally. They love the aesthetic mix of old finds and contemporary pieces. 'It's a big thrill trawling through a junk shop and discovering a one-off piece of furniture with potential,' Susie says. 'And over the years we have bought tons of antique finds and done them up ourselves. The house is littered with pieces we have given a makeover by reupholstering or painting.' The walls too are an inspiration to behold. Susie's paintings beam from the walls, among other vibrant works of art. There is colour and creativity everywhere, and all is calmly displayed against a neutral backdrop.

'As the months turned to years, we had one itch,' explains Susie. They had always dreamt of an open-plan living area where the rooms flowed, and saw a straightforward way to expand the kitchen/dining room and link it to the sitting room. By pushing the terrace back a wonderful space could be created, with garden views and light flooding into the kitchen, via a panel of Crittall windows and an overhead skylight. 'Predictably it took way longer than expected,' says Susie. 'In a moment of overenthusiasm, we had invited our entire family for Christmas.' As the big day approached, they still had no flooring, and tarpaulin was flapping in window-frames. It was only on 21 December that the windows were fitted. 'We pulled it off, albeit with sheets of plastic hanging between the kitchen and the dining room. And the underfloor heating blazing beneath bare concrete kept the older members toasty.'

Since then, there has been one further addition to the home: a new baby, Willow, a blissful plus to family life. This house really does feel the perfect fit for the whole family. It may have bounced out of reach, but once it fell into their hands there was no chance that they were letting it go.

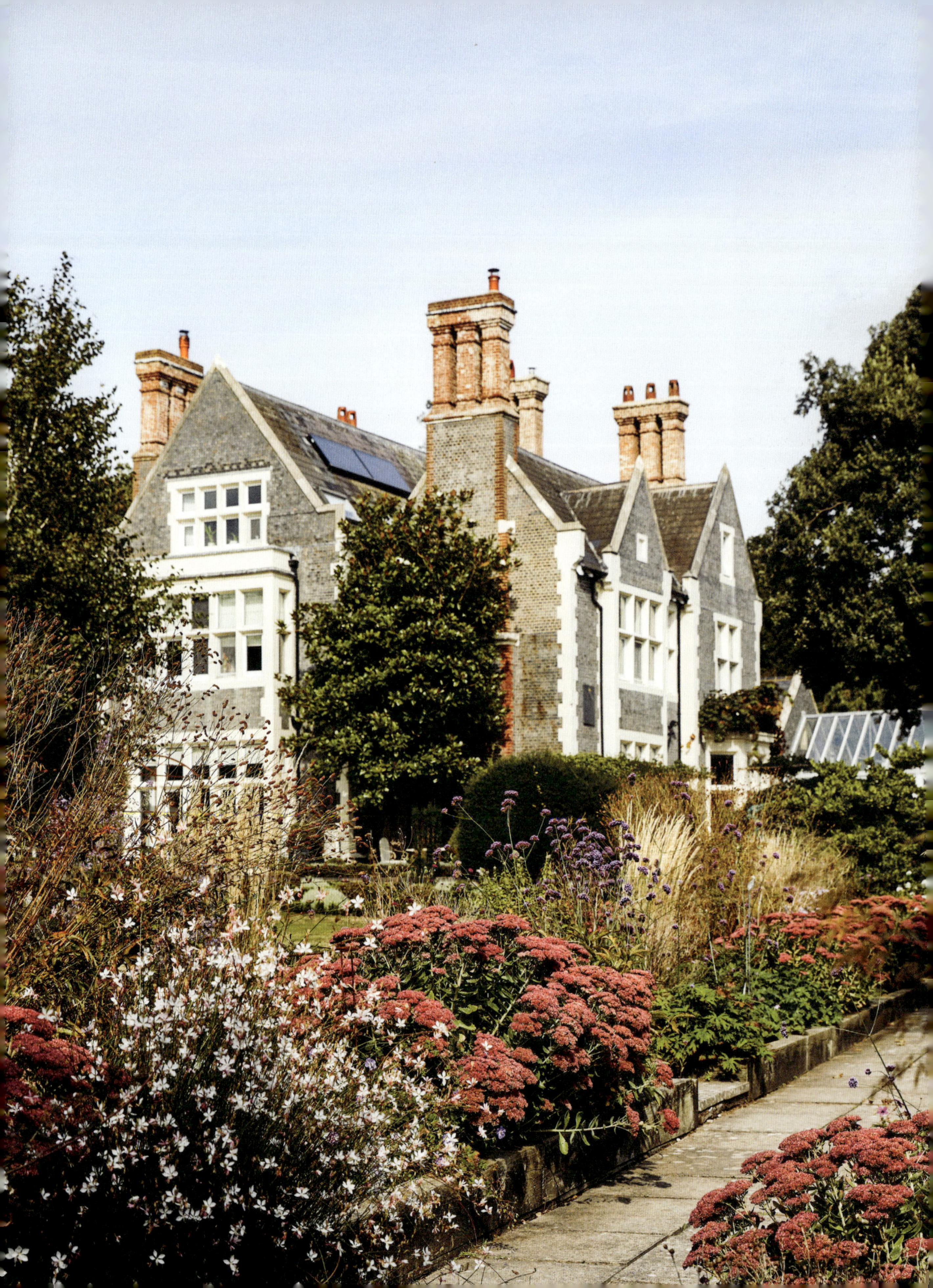

HAPPY HOMECOMING

James Bell's parental home hit the housing market for barely a moment before he, along with his wife Amy and their two daughters, realised just how much they didn't want it to be lost to the family.

On a balmy summer's day in 2004 Amy Culligan married James Bell in a marquee on the sweeping lawns of his stunning family home in the South Downs. James' mother's card to the newly-weds read 'Welcome Home.' 'It seemed curious at the time,' remembers Amy, 'because much as we loved his parents' home, living there ourselves had never occurred to us.'

When Amy had visited James' parents during their courtship, she had been fascinated by its history. Eight acres (a little over three hectares) of land had been given to a newlywed couple, the Whitfields, in 1849, and the proud Mr Whitfield had built the Gothic house on it for himself and his bride. He had designed the gracious rooms with their balanced proportions, high ceilings, wood panelling and ornate plasterwork, and these details proudly stood the test of time. The house had stayed in the Whitfield family for three generations, then changed hands several times during the 1900s. For a time post-war, it was used as a country club.

As a countryside lover Amy had also been truly taken by the position it holds in the foothills of the South Downs – so much so that once she and James had their own children, they had bought a house in a village nearby. 'We would probably have stayed there,' admits Amy, 'if my in-laws hadn't put the family house on the market. We felt such a bolt of sadness at the thought of the house leaving the family that we stretched in every direction to buy it.' She continues, 'We picked up where James' parents had left off, with the house and garden. Both were labours of love for them and likewise for us.'

The pair have worked tirelessly since moving in. 'We loved the essence of the place, and the character that my in-laws had brought, and just wanted to continue helping it evolve with the passing of time,' says Amy. 'Each generation lives slightly differently. When we arrived, the kitchen was more of a functional place, and the drawing room had been where the family gathered. We wanted the kitchen to be the family room.' They took out white MDF units, the dated electric cooker and a lino floor to replace them with a part farmhouse style, part French-style kitchen. Amy found Provençal-inspired blue and yellow tiles from a local dairy that was being sold and based the kitchen colour scheme round these – the summery yellow walls and cornflower blue cooker are a warm colour combination and together with a scrubbed oak table, chairs and dresser complete the welcoming farmhouse feel.

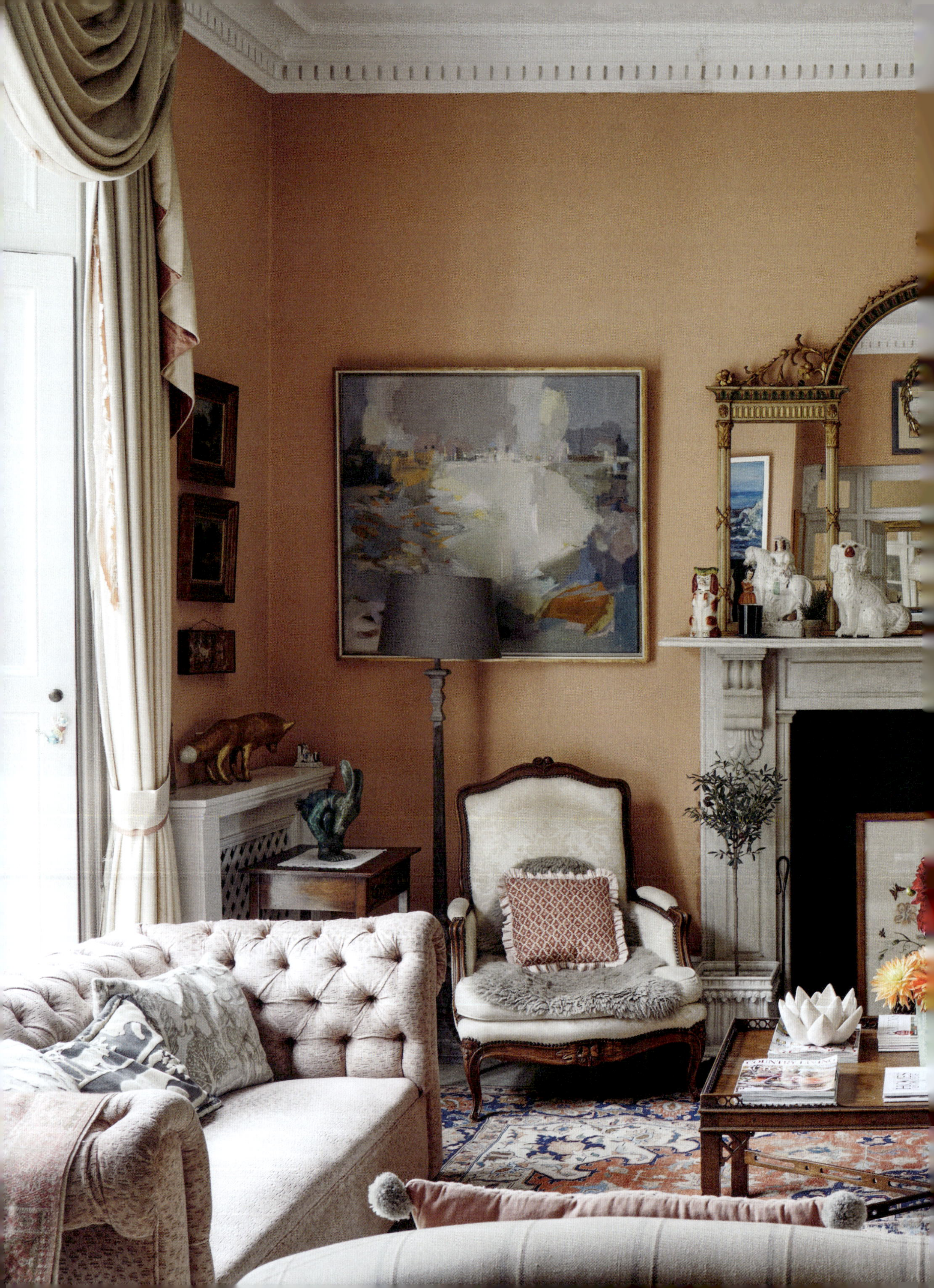
COUNTRY LIVING

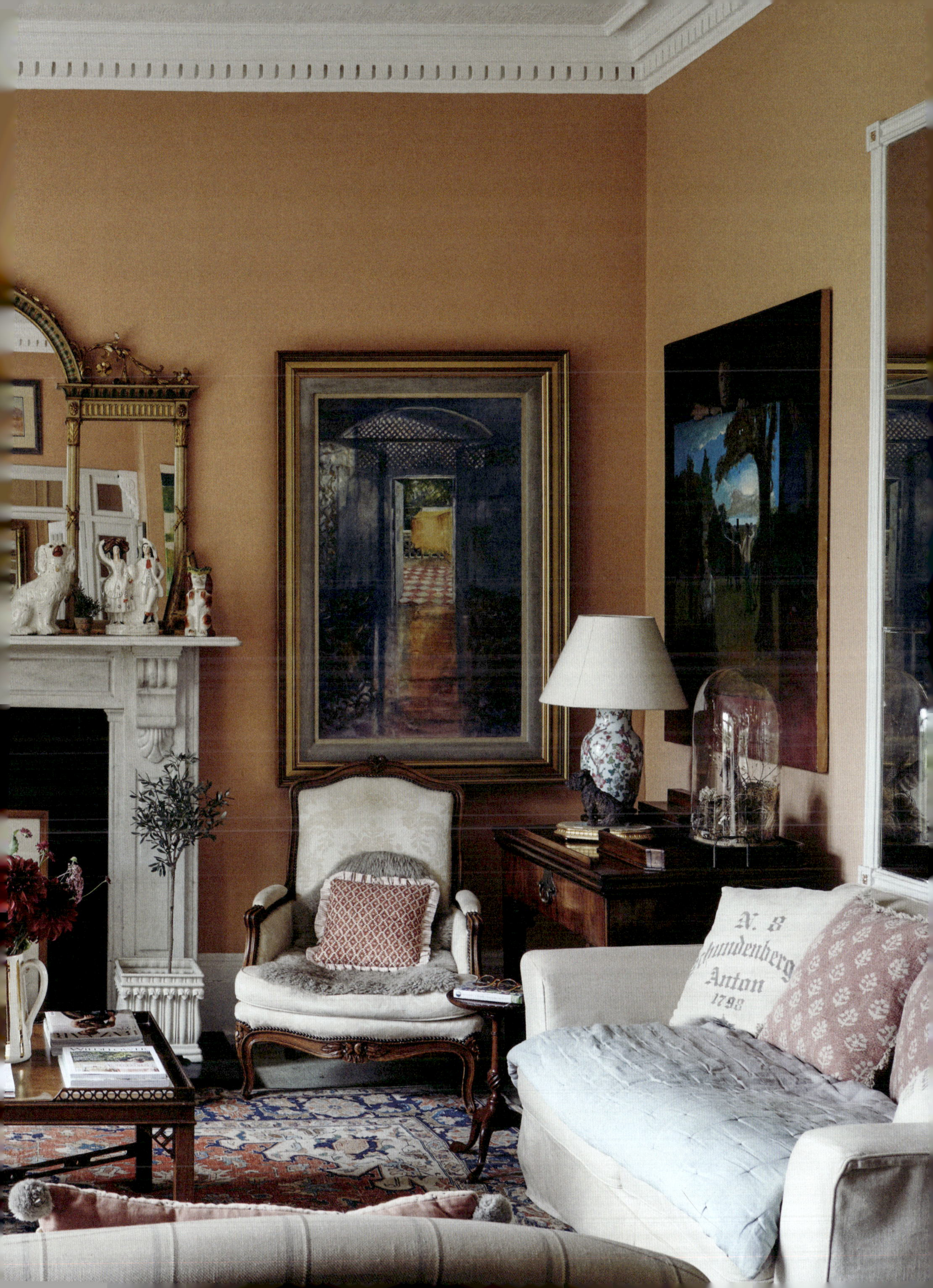
N. 8
Anton
1798

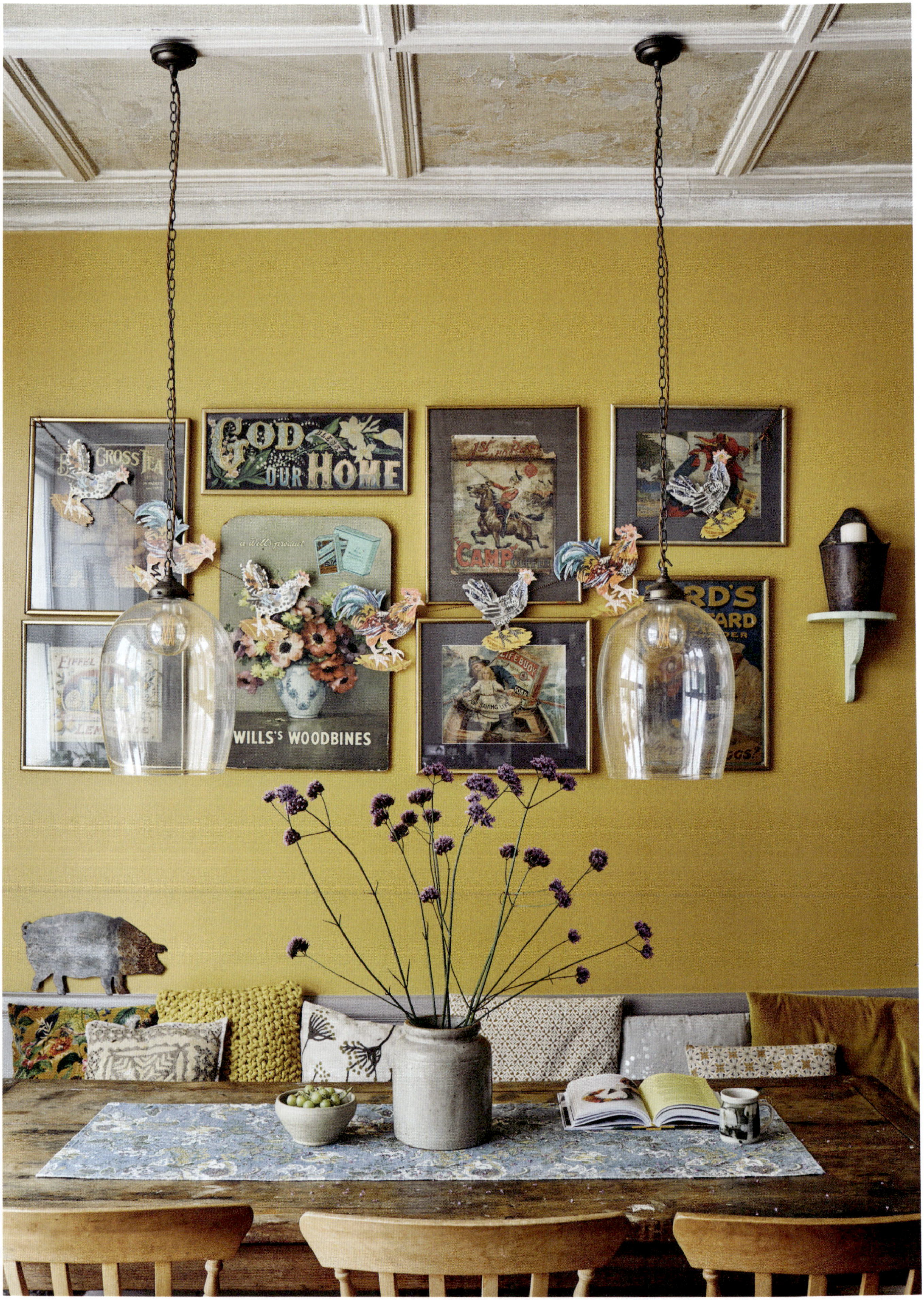
GOD BLESS OUR HOME
a Wills product
WILLS'S WOODBINES
CAMP

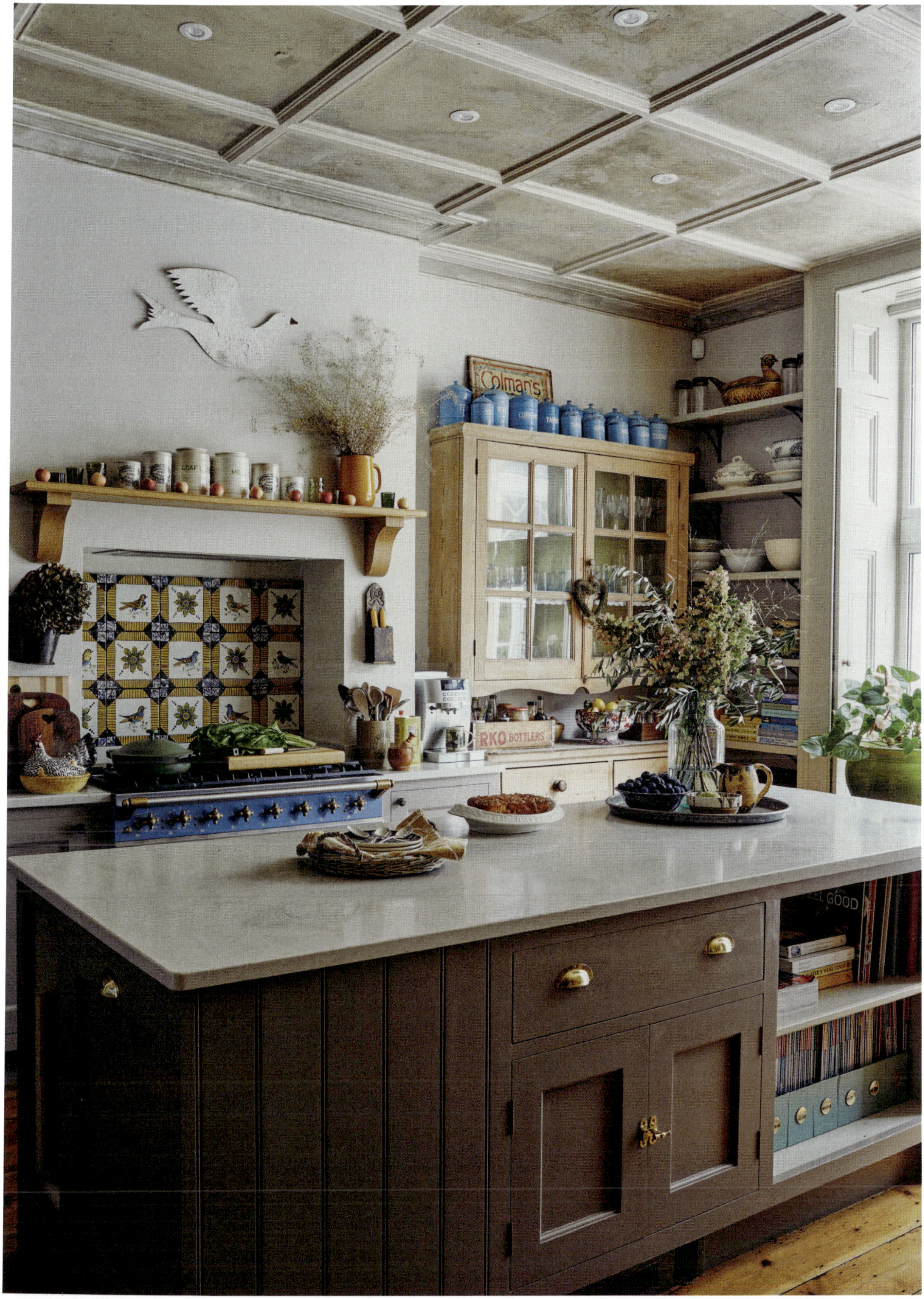
Colman's
RKO BOTTLERS

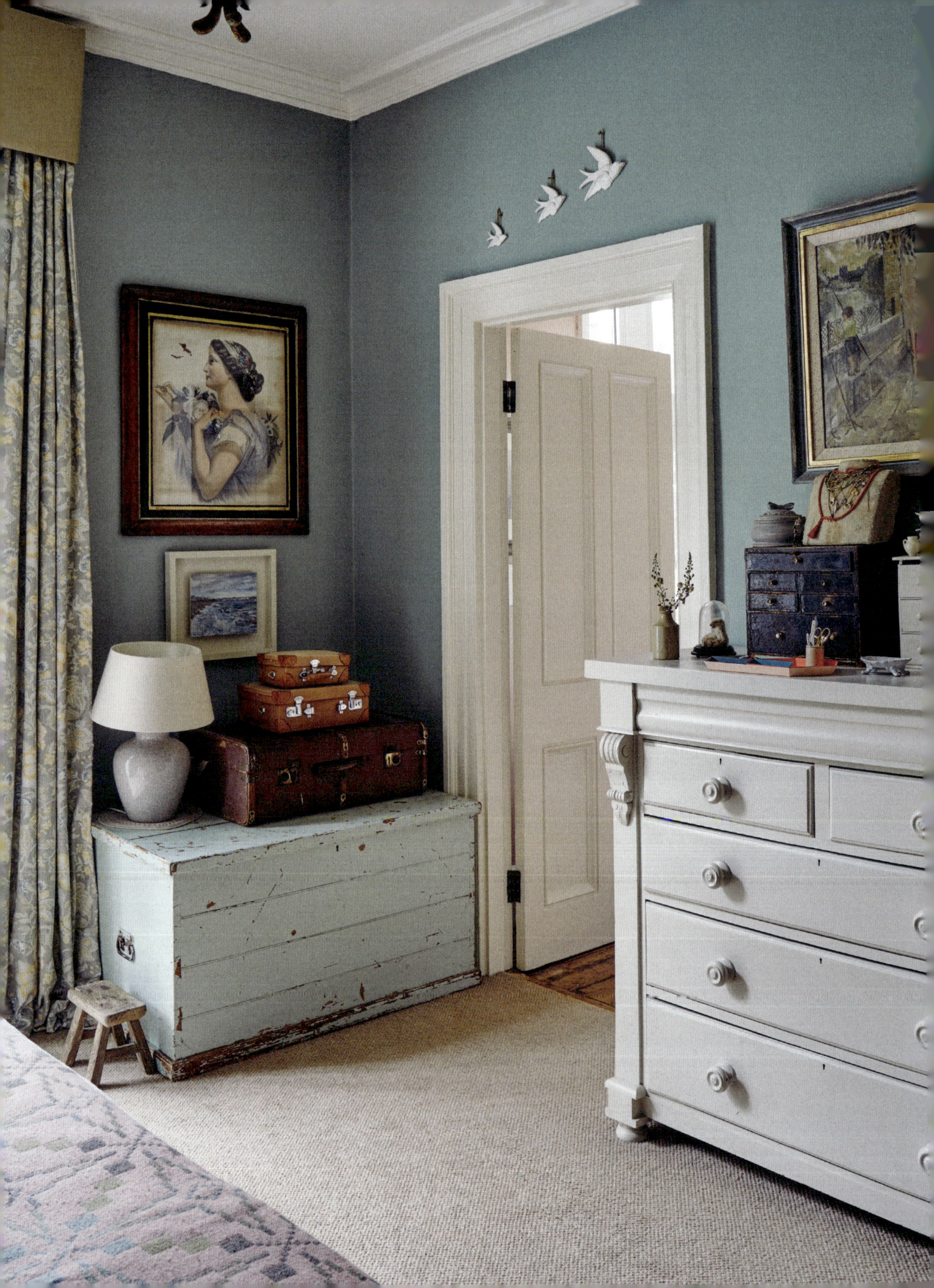

Elsewhere downstairs, the couple have merged their own furnishings with those of their predecessors. 'Fashions come and go,' says Amy, who loves it that the house is continually evolving, rather than changing dramatically. They were grateful to inherit some beautiful furniture, paintings and curtains, which sit comfortably within the walls of the old house. 'Sometimes I find something buried in the cellar that James' parents had tired of, and I bring it back in.' Wall colours are probably the most dramatic change. While her in-laws had opted for pale neutral tones, Amy loves warm and sometimes moodier tones that add depth to the graceful rooms, and adds, 'As the rooms are naturally well lit, they can take some subtly darker colour.'

With slightly heavy hearts about putting an end to an era, Amy and James decided to replace the avocado bathroom suites and pulled up carpets to display wooden floors beneath. Upstairs, they changed surprisingly little else in the six bedrooms other than paint colours, adding some more feminine furnishings for Eliza's and Martha's bedrooms too.

Amy and James' colour, decorating and furnishing choices have brought warmth to the house, and perhaps a loosening of formality. 'We love blending the house and the garden naturally, as my parents-in-law did before us.' A porch built by James' parents has one wall delightfully painted with a fresco of the garden in summer. This space and the conservatory do an excellent job of aligning the interior and exterior. 'The garden is integral to the character of the place,' explains Amy, who loves the outdoor space so much that she now runs gardening courses from here to share the knowledge that she has accumulated.

'Some houses have that "seen it all" character,' laughs Amy. 'We met a lady recently whose parents had spent a night of their honeymoon here when it was a country club. It seems a good place for newly-weds! We hope one day our daughters might tie the knot here, and/or take the house off our hands to continue its journey.'

'I LOVE THE LAYERS

of life that influence and embellish a house. It's a privilege just to be custodians of a house, to do our best to look after it and help it along the way during our time here. With each generation it evolves and gathers character.'

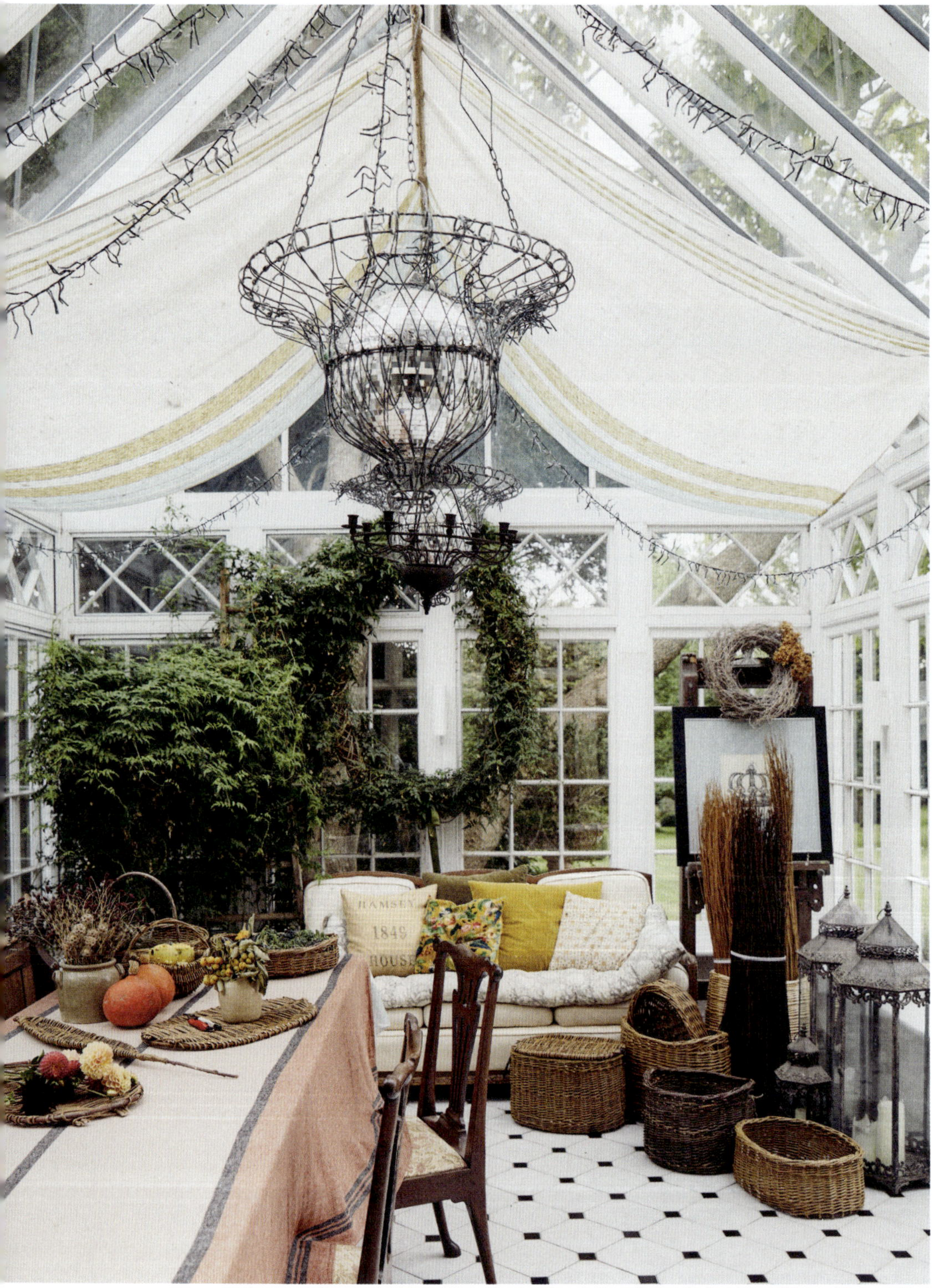

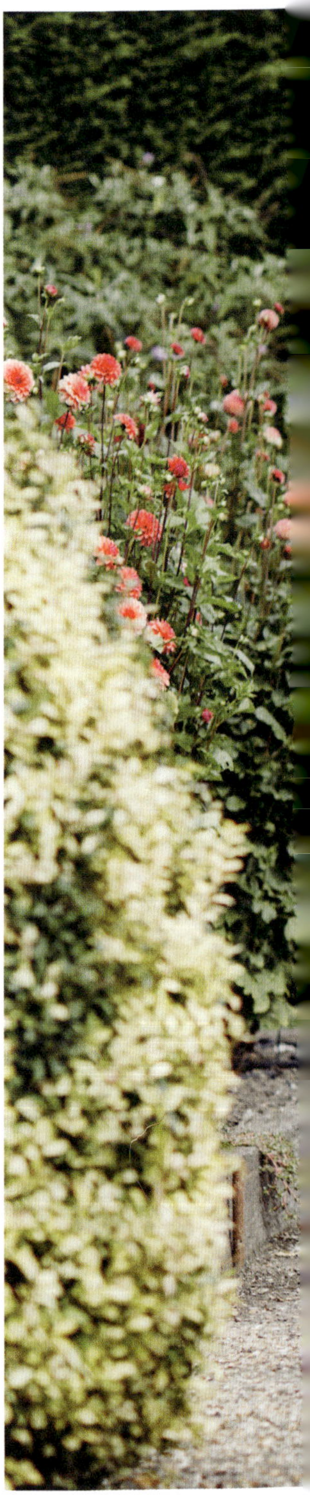

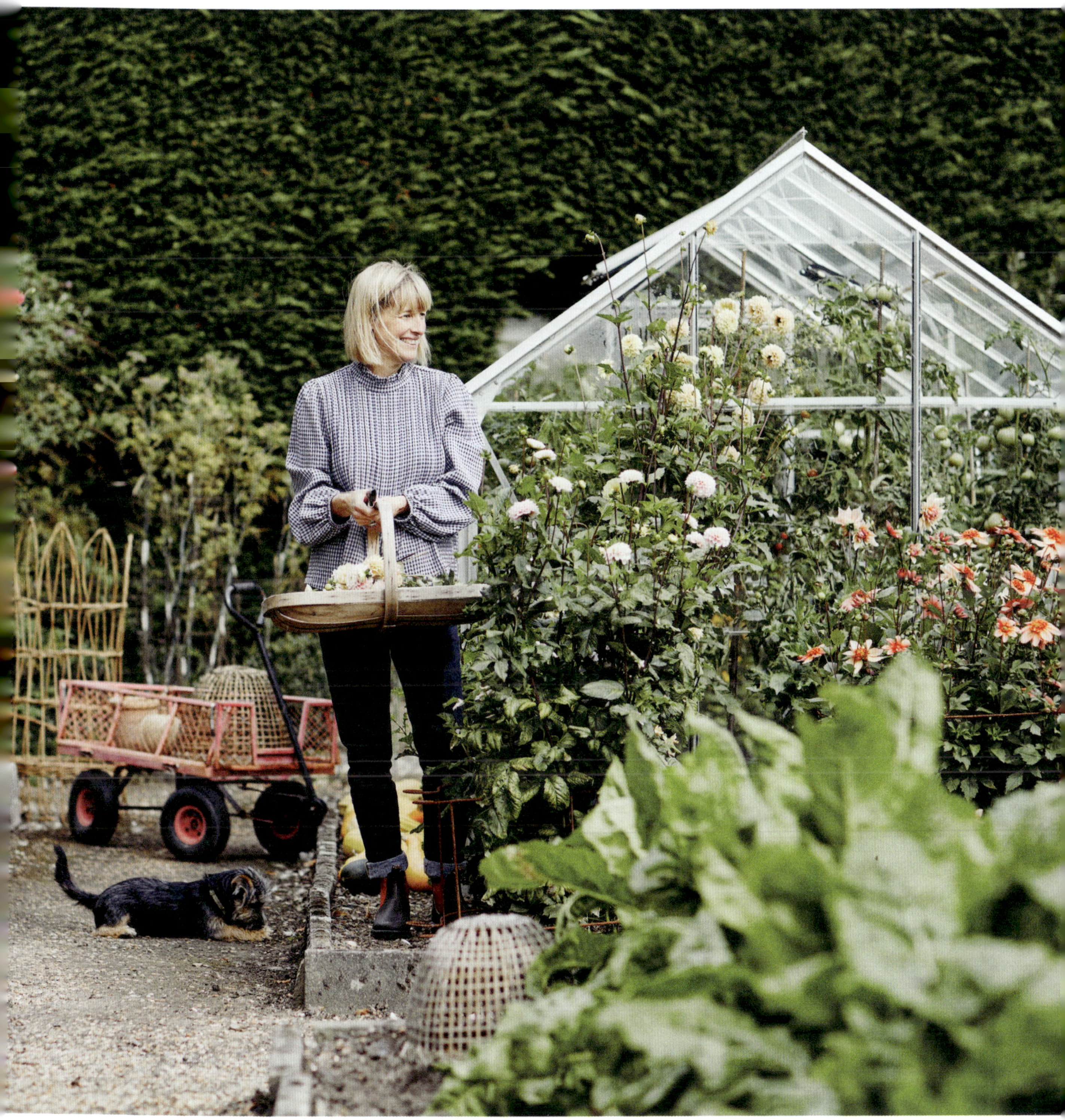

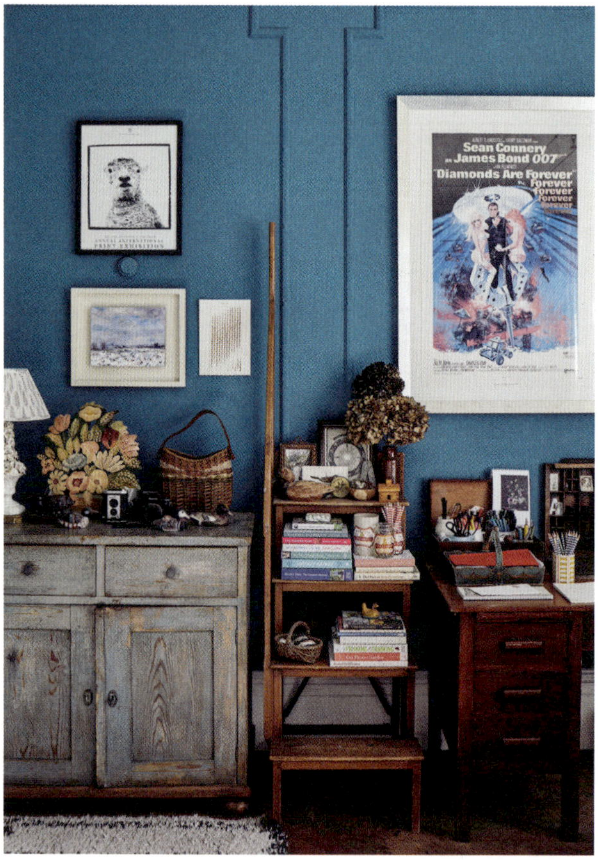

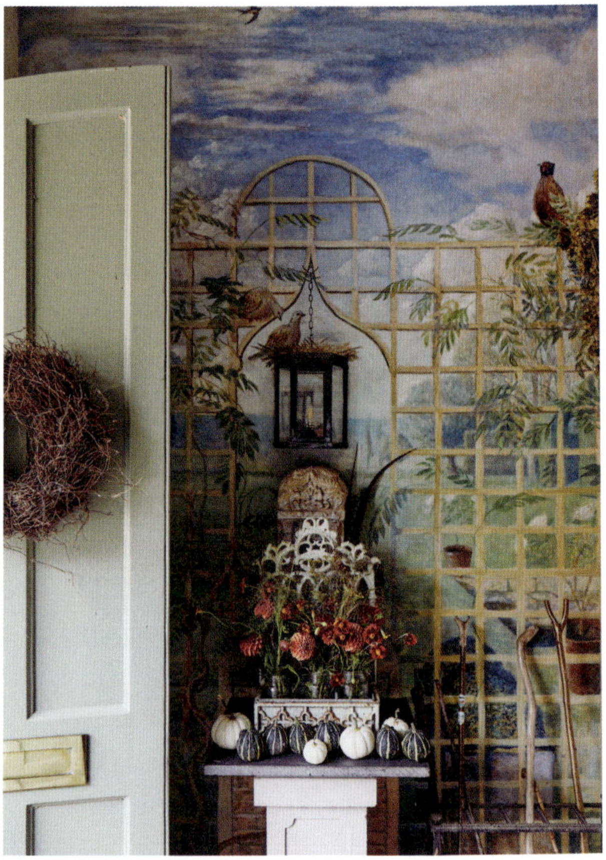

'THE VICTORIAN PROPORTIONS

of the house require large pieces of furniture, great swathes of fabric in curtains, and big paintings to fill the wall space. We were lucky to inherit many lovely family heirlooms. Even if some are a little tired or faded, they are part of the house's story and sit comfortably within its old walls.'

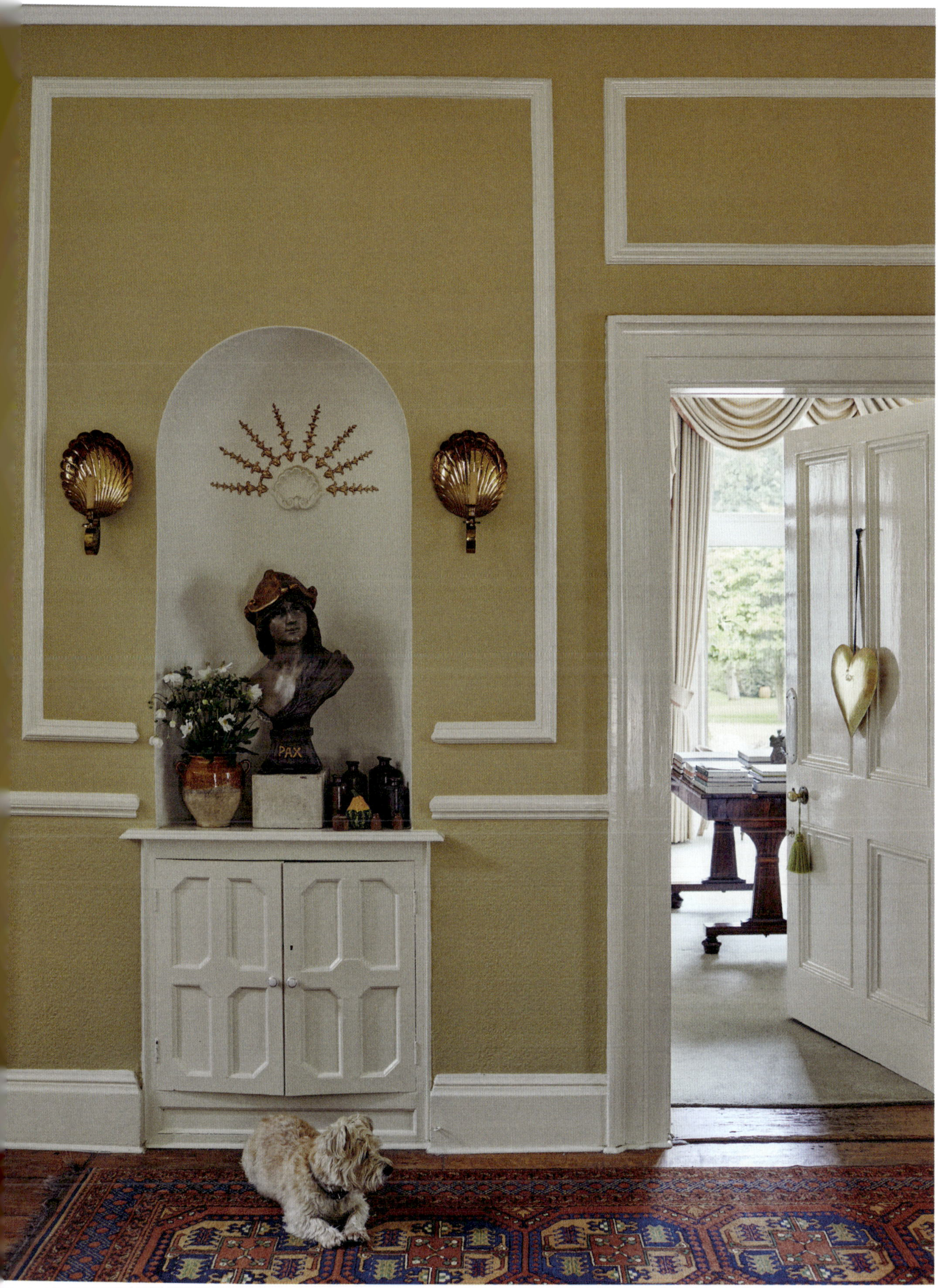
PAX

ORIGINAL STYLE

Cait Swain and Graham Moore have turned a run-down thatched cottage into a stylish and artistic home.

Cait Swain has antiquing in her blood. A glance at her online decorative antiques shop Article 3 confirms her trained eye. Her mother ran an antiques stall in Camden Locks market when she was a child. 'I remember shivering in the early morning gloom as Mum set up her stall for the morning's trade,' recalls Cait. Her father too had a passion for antiques and used to drag the small Cait round the junkyards in search of treasures. A lifetime's interest in antiques and architectural salvage began to develop, as did an eye for a bargain.

It's not any old antique that passes muster for Cait, however. Over the years she has honed her trained eye to find a mixture of the beautiful and the bizarre - her unique skill is in combining the two, often from totally different periods. 'I don't like clutter, but I love anything quirky, beautiful and original,' she says. She keeps a very calm and neutral backdrop and then adds the most unusual antiques and artistic retro finds, which she then combines with contemporary items. She particularly loves finding a piece with interesting texture, in timeworn stone, wood or metal. In a pale, minimalist setting these occasional items add the character of times gone by without the look becoming fusty or cluttered. Her skill is in creating complete harmony between seemingly mismatched items and displaying them artfully in her home.

The house has not always been such a stylish and orderly place. 'When we first viewed it back in 2005 it was "tired", to say the least,' remembers Cait. The previous owners had owned the cottage for twenty-five years and had loved but neglected it. Age combined with harsh winters and its low-lying foundations had caught up with the house, and when Cait and Graham first saw it, they were almost put off by its sorry state. The overwhelming feature was damp. The downstairs floors squelched underfoot; the walls were cold and wet; the bath, showers and kitchen lino were mouldy and the carpets threadbare. The decor too was faded and out of date - mustard walls ran throughout, the bathroom was avocado, and the 1970s kitchen was so out of date that it almost appealed to Cait's retro style, but not quite ... Yet the house had a certain charm to it. There were deep window seats, exposed beams and a big inglenook fireplace. Cait and Graham spotted its potential.

They instantly knew that they would need to gut the place completely and move out during the process. Thankfully there was loft space above the detached garage in the garden. It would eventually be an office, but could in the meantime give them a roof over their heads while they renovated the main house.

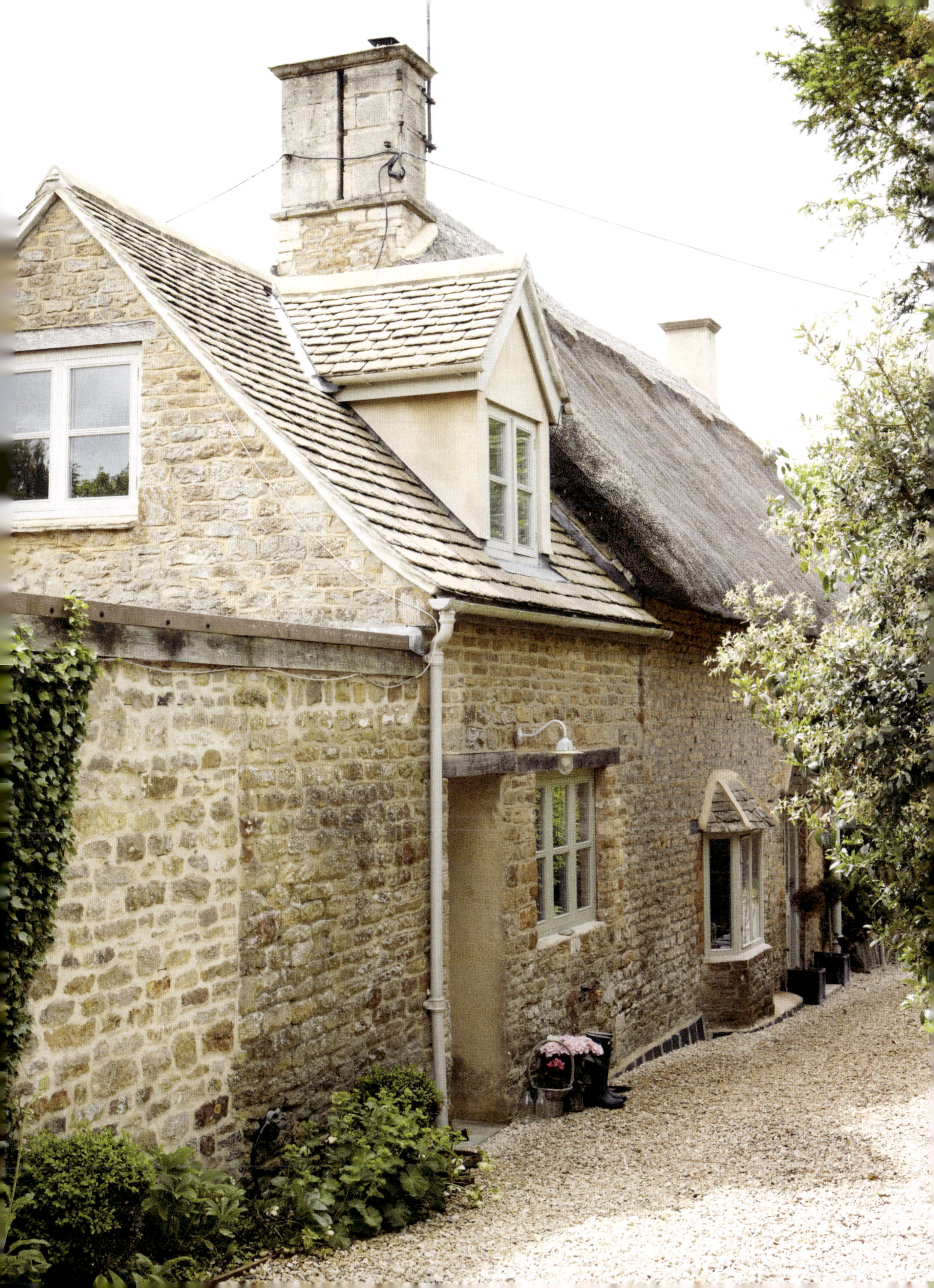

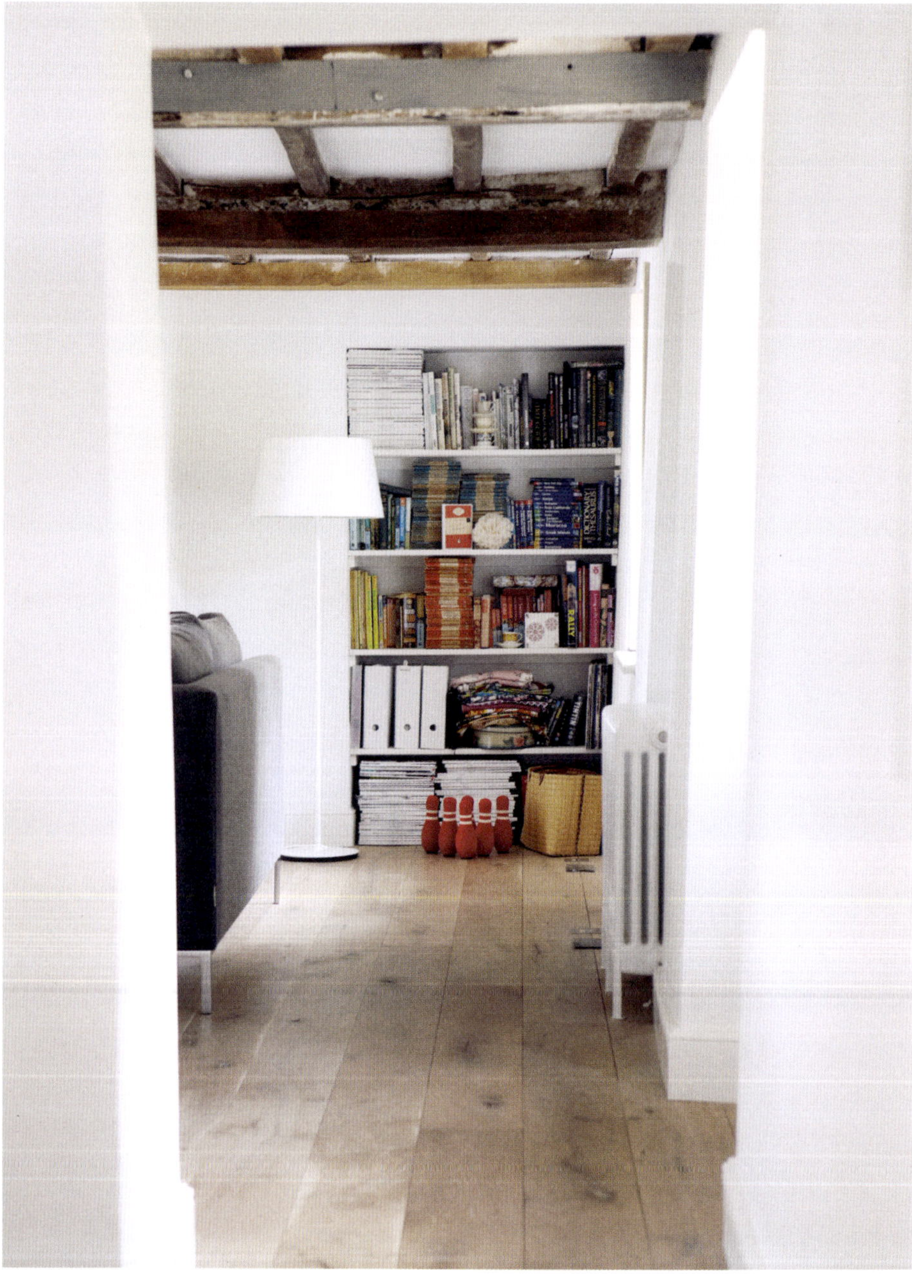

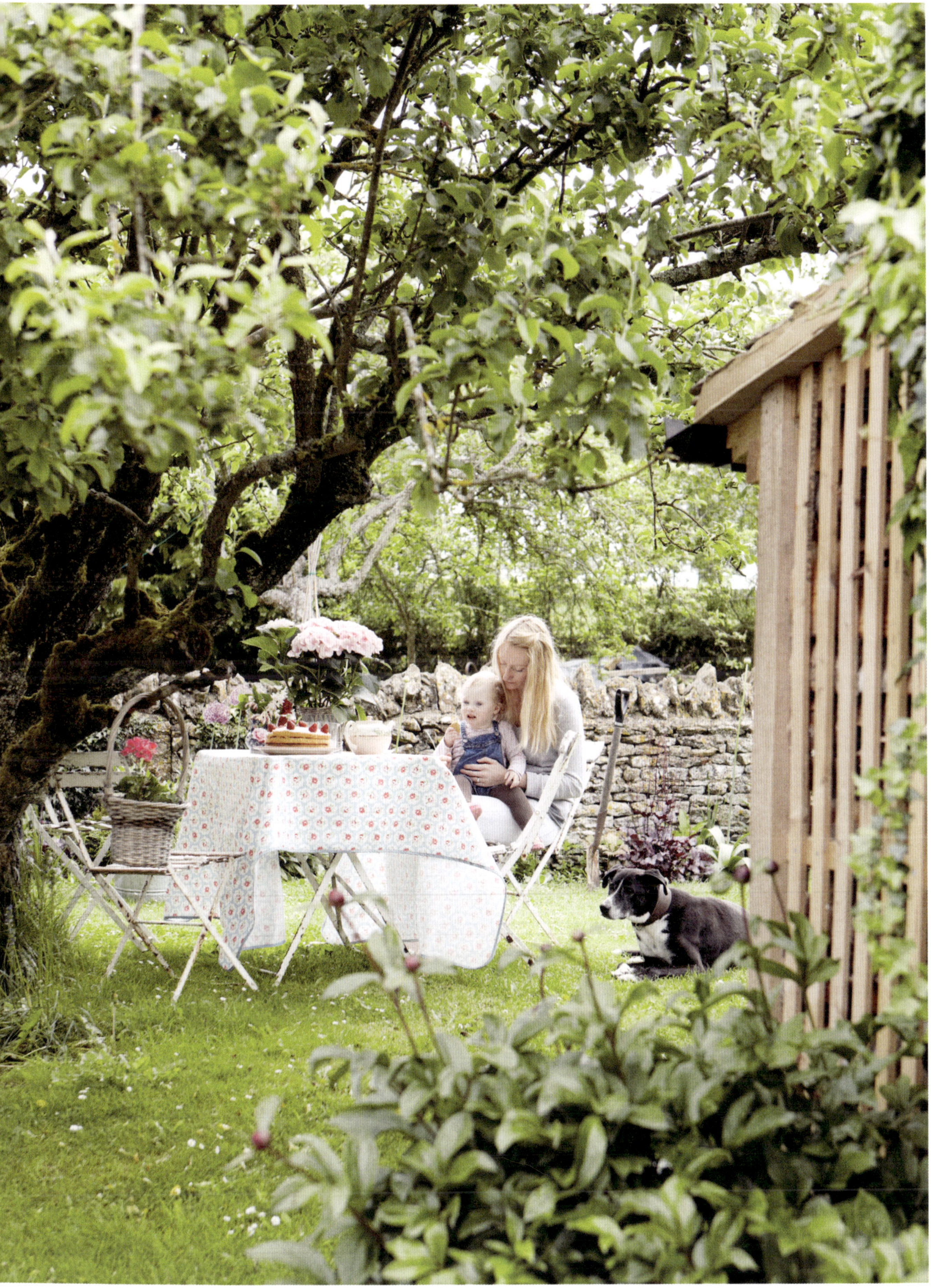

As predicted, many unwelcome surprises came to light when the renovation started. The house needed to be taken right back to its bare bones before work could begin. The electrics and plumbing had not been touched for decades. Shredded electric wires were held together with Sellotape, and in one place an Elastoplast sufficed! On one occasion scalding water came gushing from a cold tap - the water had become charged with electricity due to the haphazard wiring. The plumbing too was on its last legs. While tearing out the bath upstairs, the builders realised that it had been leaking for years and the floor beneath was completely waterlogged. Disaster was narrowly missed when two builders fell through the ceiling, but somehow landed unscathed.

But alongside such dramas came wonderful discoveries, such as a fireplace in an upstairs bedroom that had been plastered over for years, and original floorboards beneath the worn-out flooring. Caitlin and Graham also found ways to create a more liveable space upstairs. Previously a wide staircase had divided, at the top, to access a bedroom with en-suite on either side of the staircase. Each pair of rooms was inaccessible to the other except via the staircase. The couple hadn't yet had their two children but wanted to create a more family-friendly space upstairs. They realised that by narrowing and curving the stairs and incorporating a long corridor they could completely change the layout so it was comprised of three bedrooms and a bathroom, all accessible from the new corridor.

The house was beginning to take shape, and once it had been gutted, tanked, replumbed, replastered and repainted throughout, it became the blank canvas that Cait knew she could work her magic on. Frequent forages to sale rooms, collectors' markets and auctions amassed her larger pieces of furniture, and family heirlooms combined with thrifty finds have made up Cait's unique style. The couple have brought great character and peace to the house and made a truly unique family home.

'MY LOVE OF ANTIQUING

slightly clashes with my lack of love for clutter,' laughs Cait, 'but this doesn't stop me collecting. I just update my displays whenever I'm ready for a change and sell anything on that I've grown out of.'

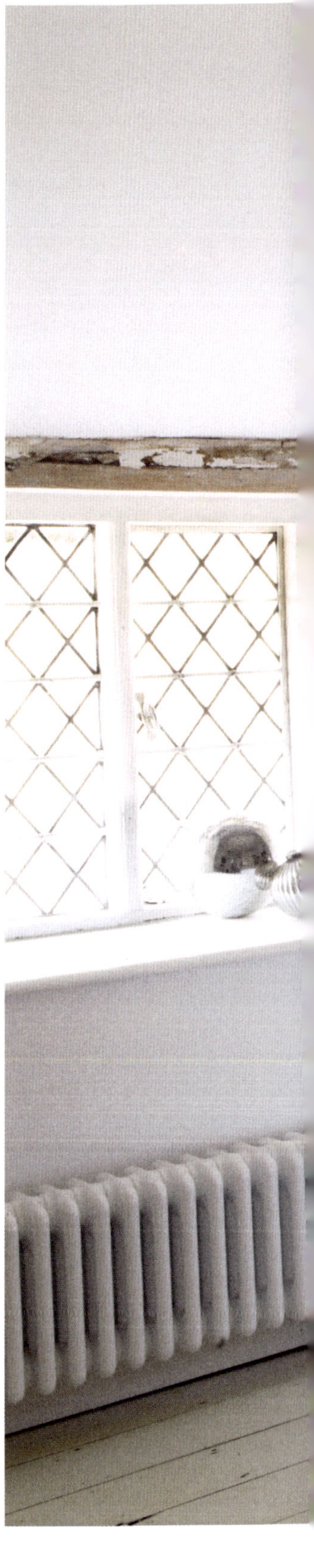

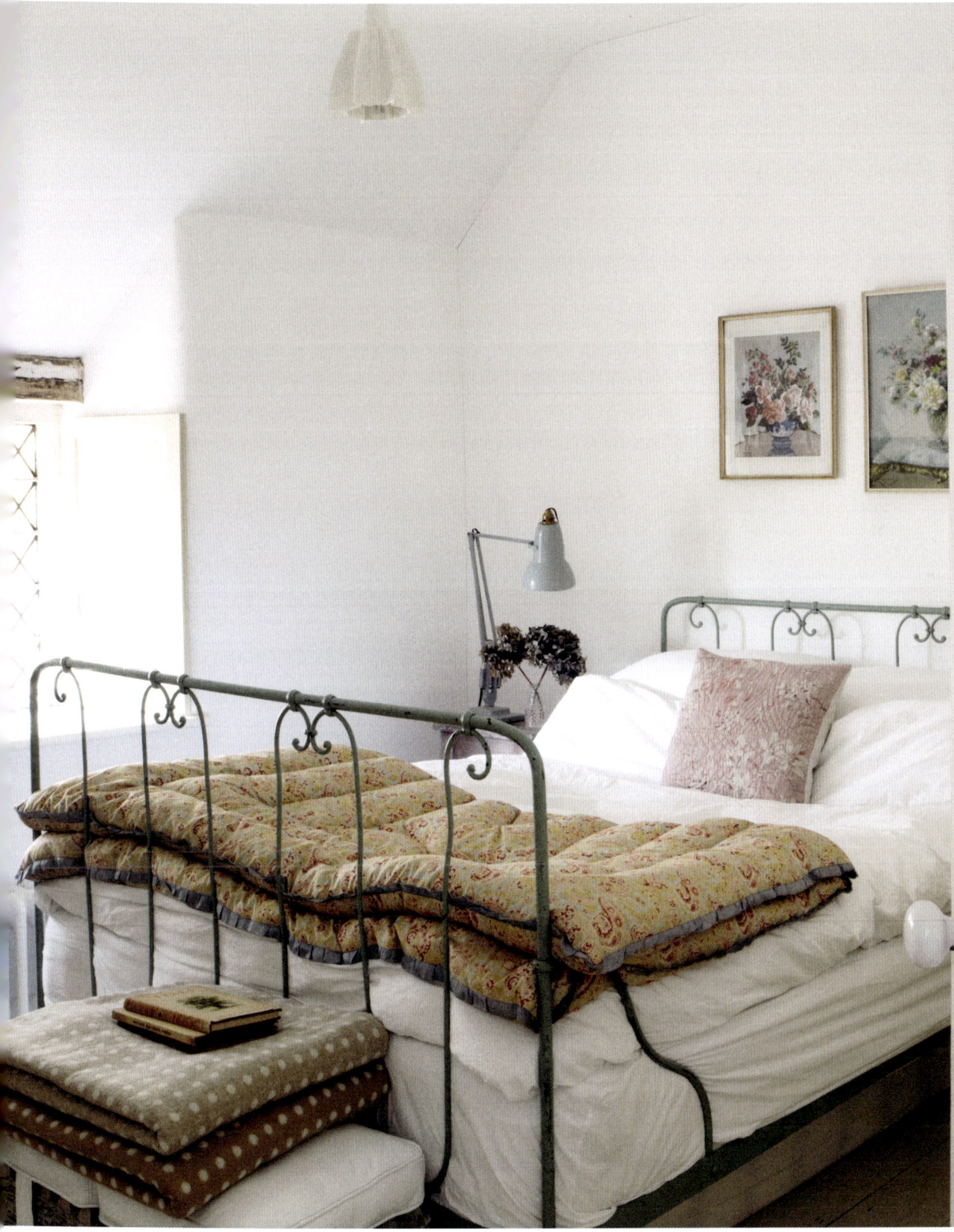

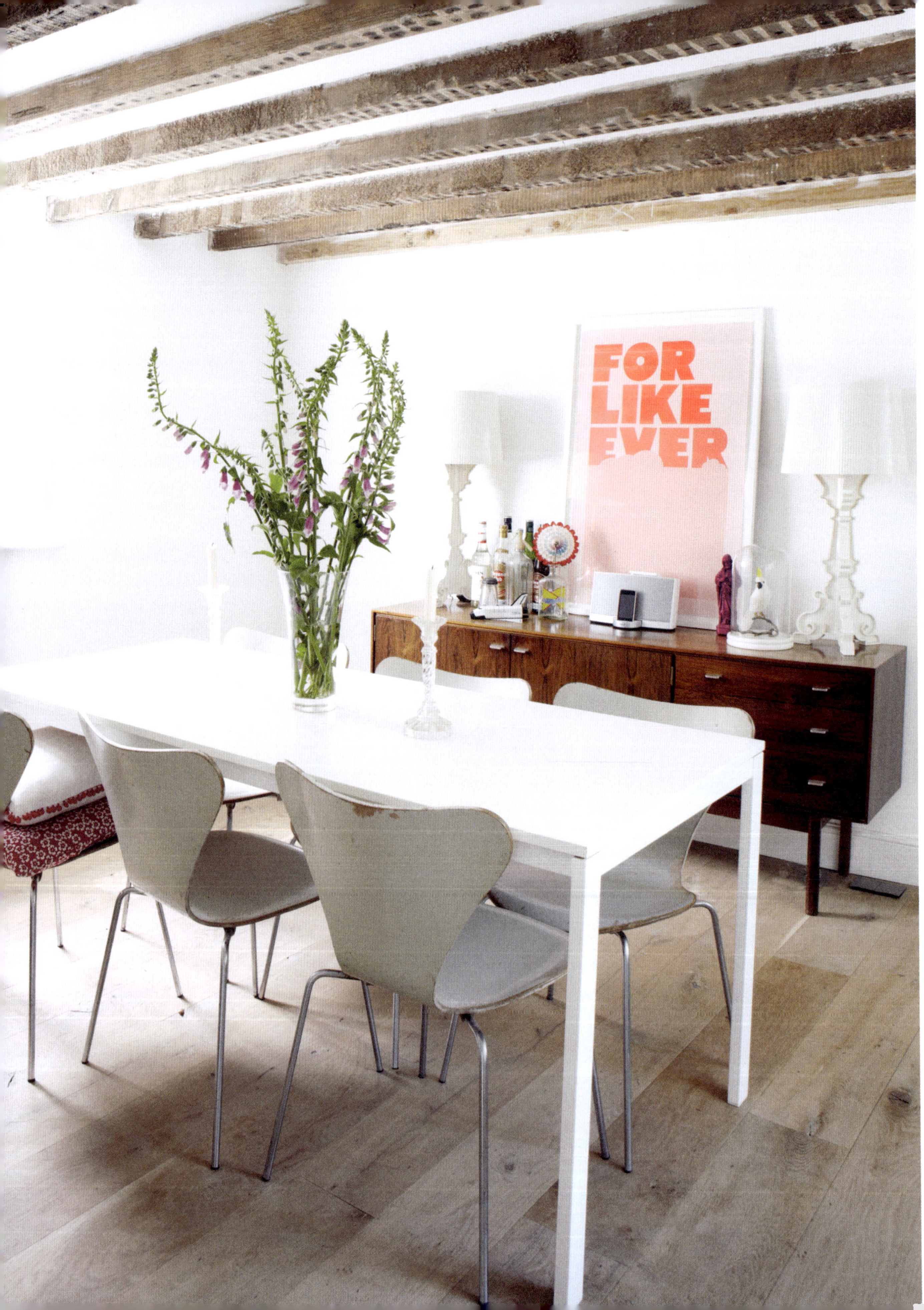
FOR
LIKE
EVER

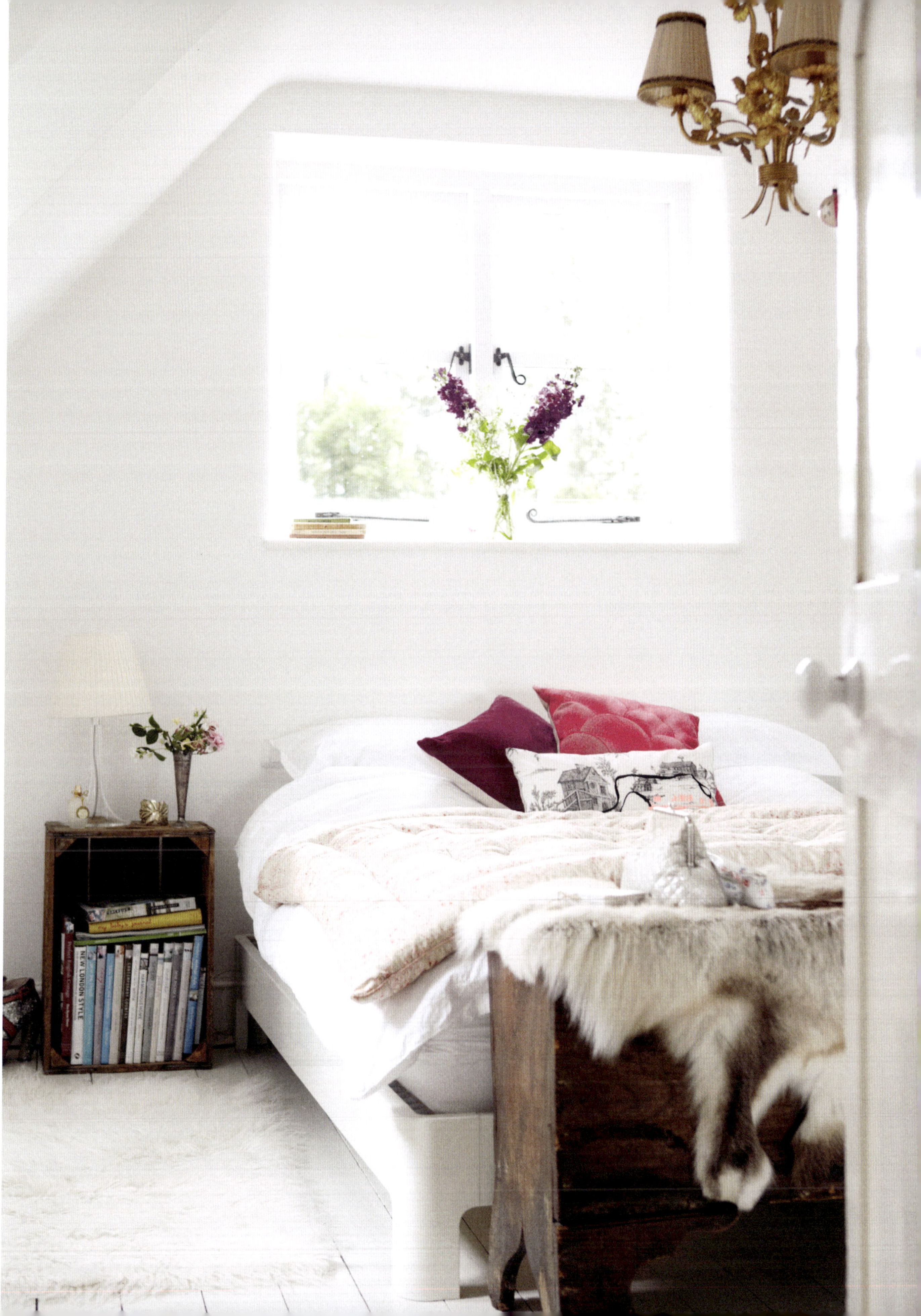
NEW LONDON STYLE

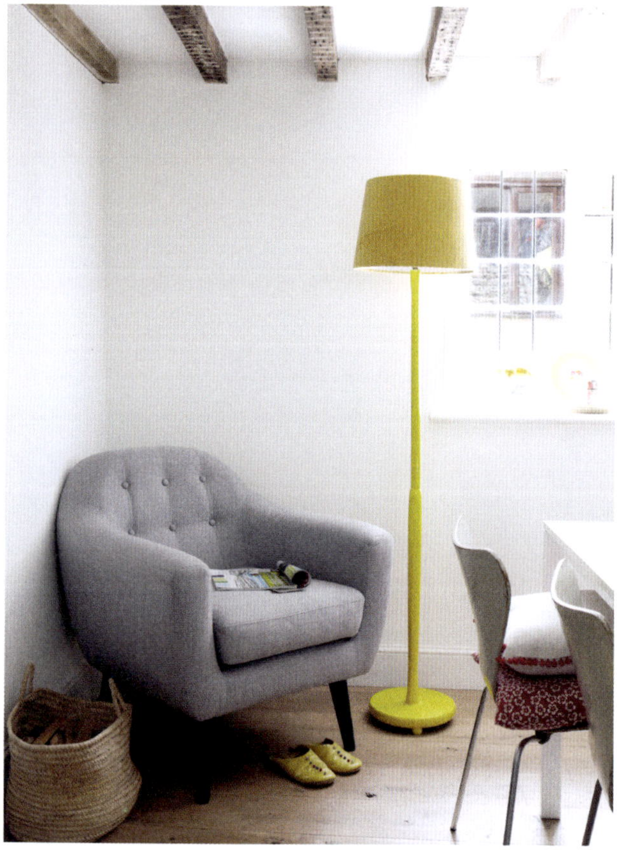

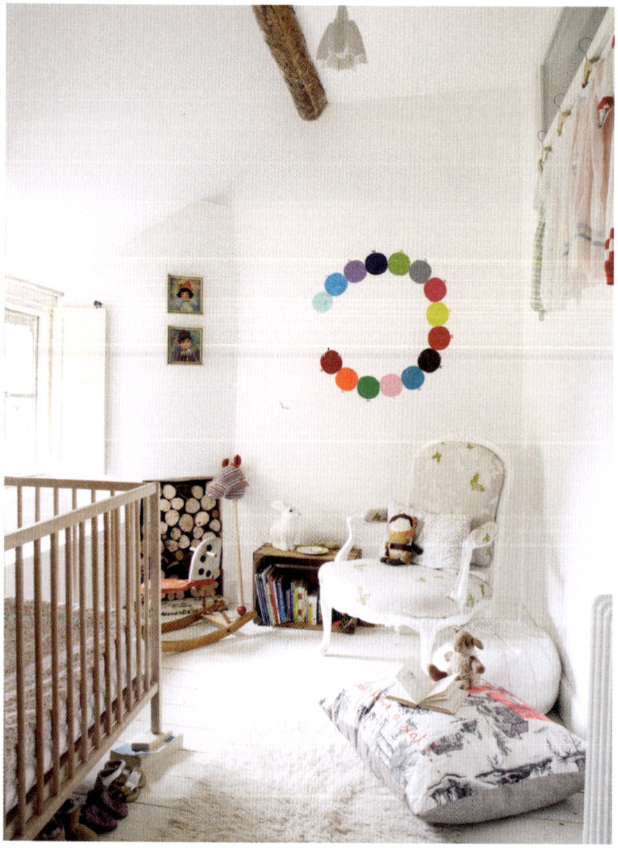

'I CHOSE A PALE BACKDROP

to make the cottage rooms feel light and spacious, and then added a few bold colours. A bright blue stool or a dazzling yellow lamp for character.'

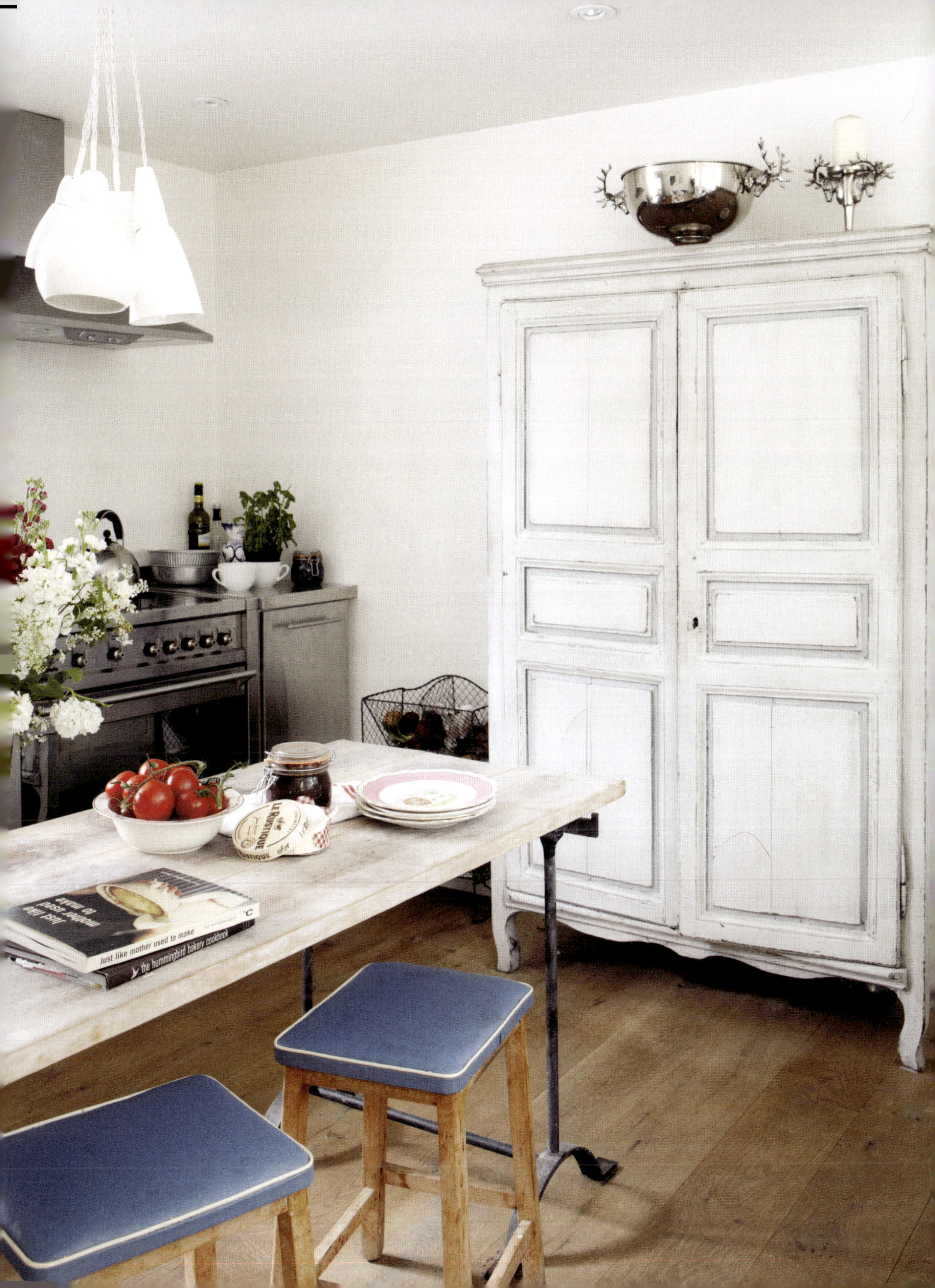

Just like mother used to make
the hummingbird bakery cookbook
LE RUSTIQUE

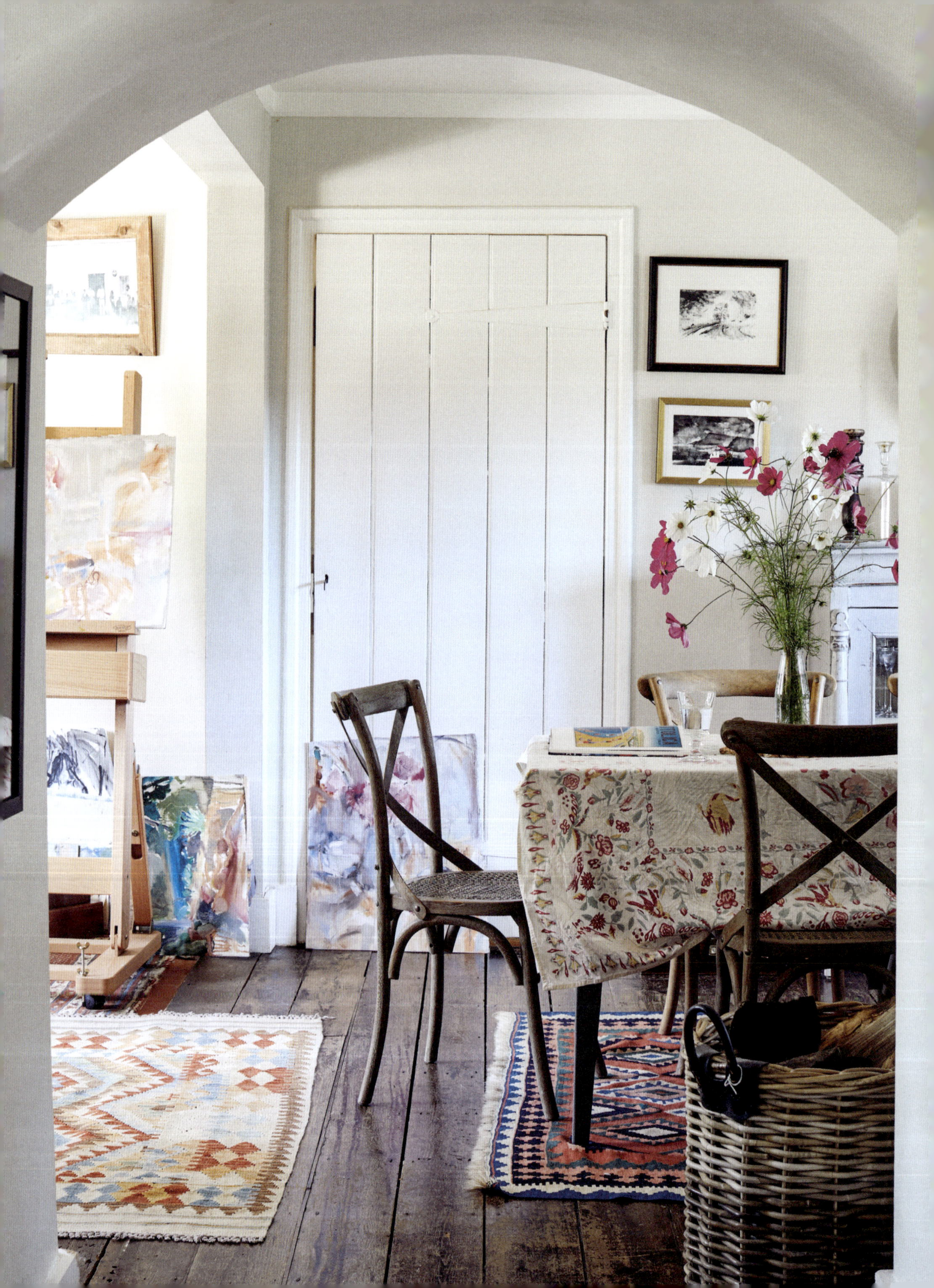

SEASONS OF FRUITFULNESS

An 18th-century cottage in the Oxfordshire Cotswolds, filled with art and antiques, reflects its owners' talents and creativity.

On a summer's day artist and actress Jemma Powell is often to be found at her easel, painting in the garden. Yet it was midwinter that first worked its charms on Jemma and her husband, singer and song-writer Jack Savoretti. Their first winter here brought snow. While others battened down the hatches, Jemma and Jack delighted in it. 'It was nothing like the brown snow of London, but a silent and sparkling world,' recalls Jemma, who felt an elemental urge to capture it on canvas. From then on her inspiration took off, feeding on nature's annual displays.

Jemma was drawn to this area because her grandmother had lived nearby, and later Jemma had studied not far away, at the Oxford School of Drama. Years later, when Jack's music career was taking him all round the world and Jemma was juggling her acting and art careers with motherhood, they felt a pull to move out of the city.

'I couldn't wait to introduce Jack to this familiar turf,' says Jemma. The area duly captured him too: the rolling hills and warm stone were reminiscent of his childhood in rural Italy. 'We rented a tiny cottage for a year,' says Jemma. 'And were lucky when we heard that a lovely family nearby were moving.'

The house suited them perfectly. Once two farm workers' cottages dating back to the 1800s, it had time-worn flagstones, exposed floorboards, wonky walls, original fireplaces and window seats – all elements that whisper of times gone by.

Jemma and Jack knew the house would suit their family fivesome, with its farmhouse kitchen ideal for family mealtimes and its little playroom. It also had a generous dining room, plus a recently added large drawing room perfect for entertaining. There was an entrance hall, downstairs cloakroom, tiny downstairs office and even laundry room (great luxuries after their previous homes). Upstairs were four bedrooms, two with en-suites, and a family bathroom. A perfect layout, with just one or two changes to be made.

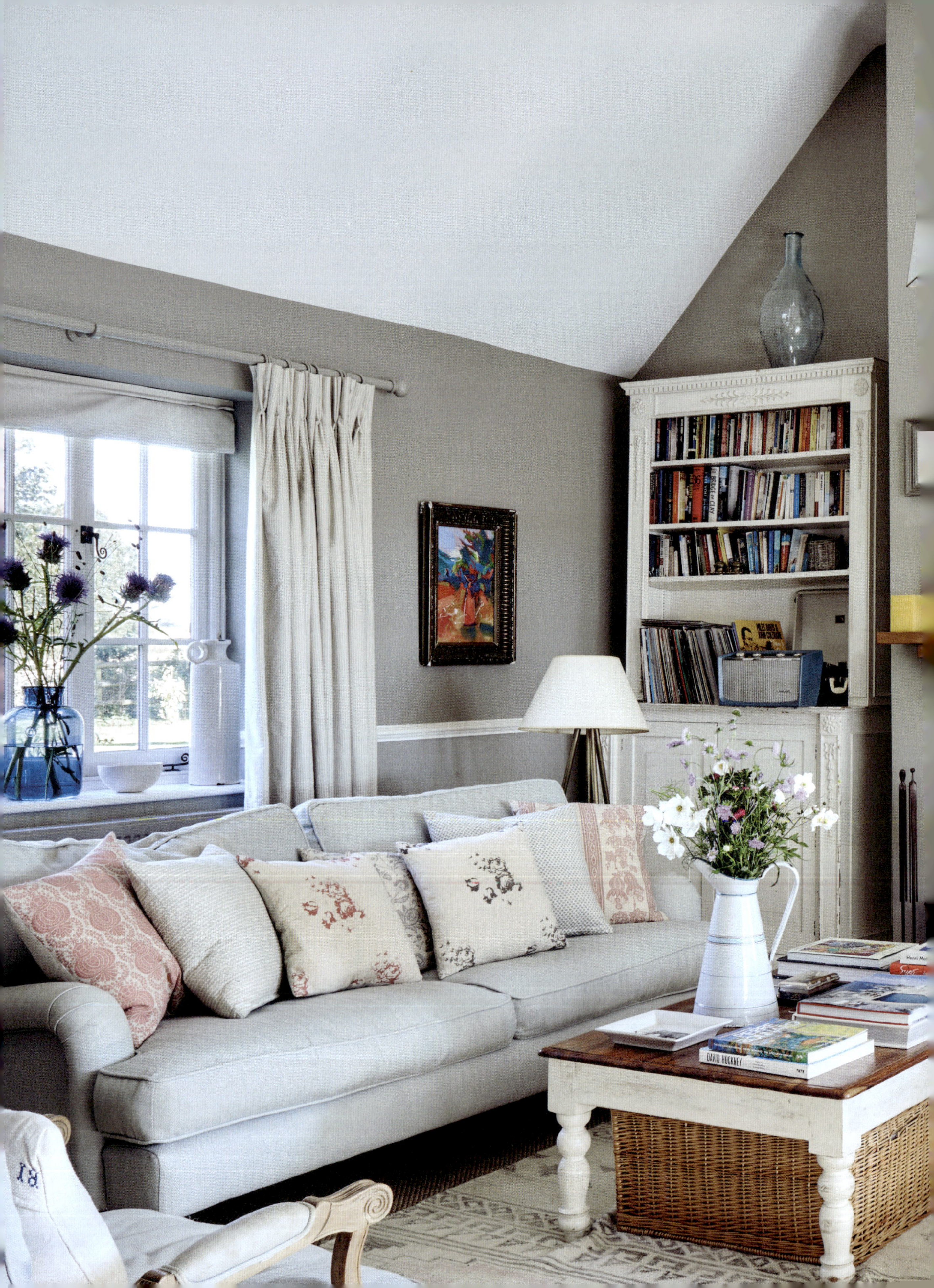
DAVID HOCKNEY

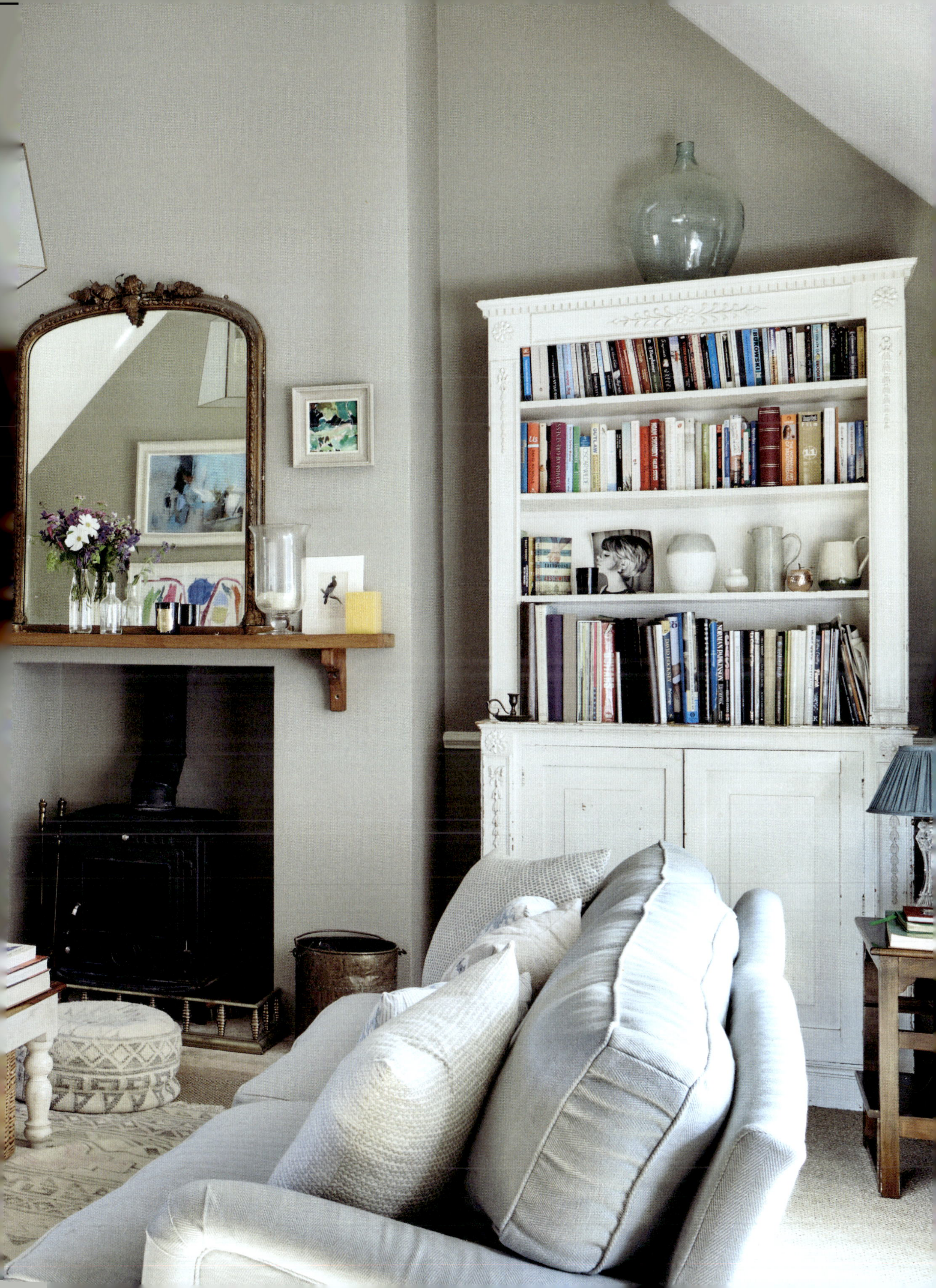
BUKOWSKI
PROMISE OF GREATNESS
OUTLAW
NOAM CHOMSKY
THE WOMAN'S ART OF BREASTFEEDING
The Tattooist of Auschwitz
DAVID HOCKNEY
NORMAN PARKINSON

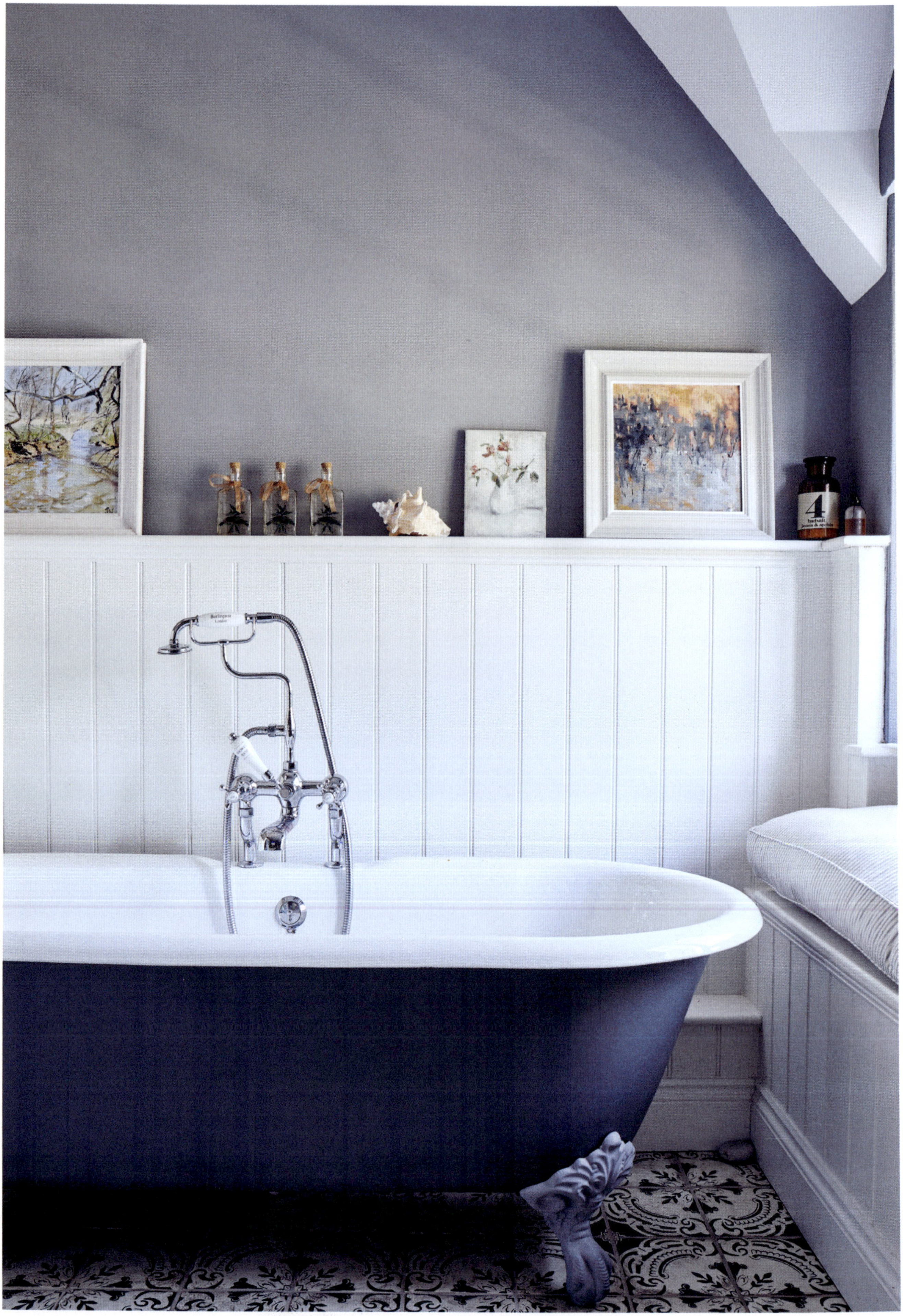

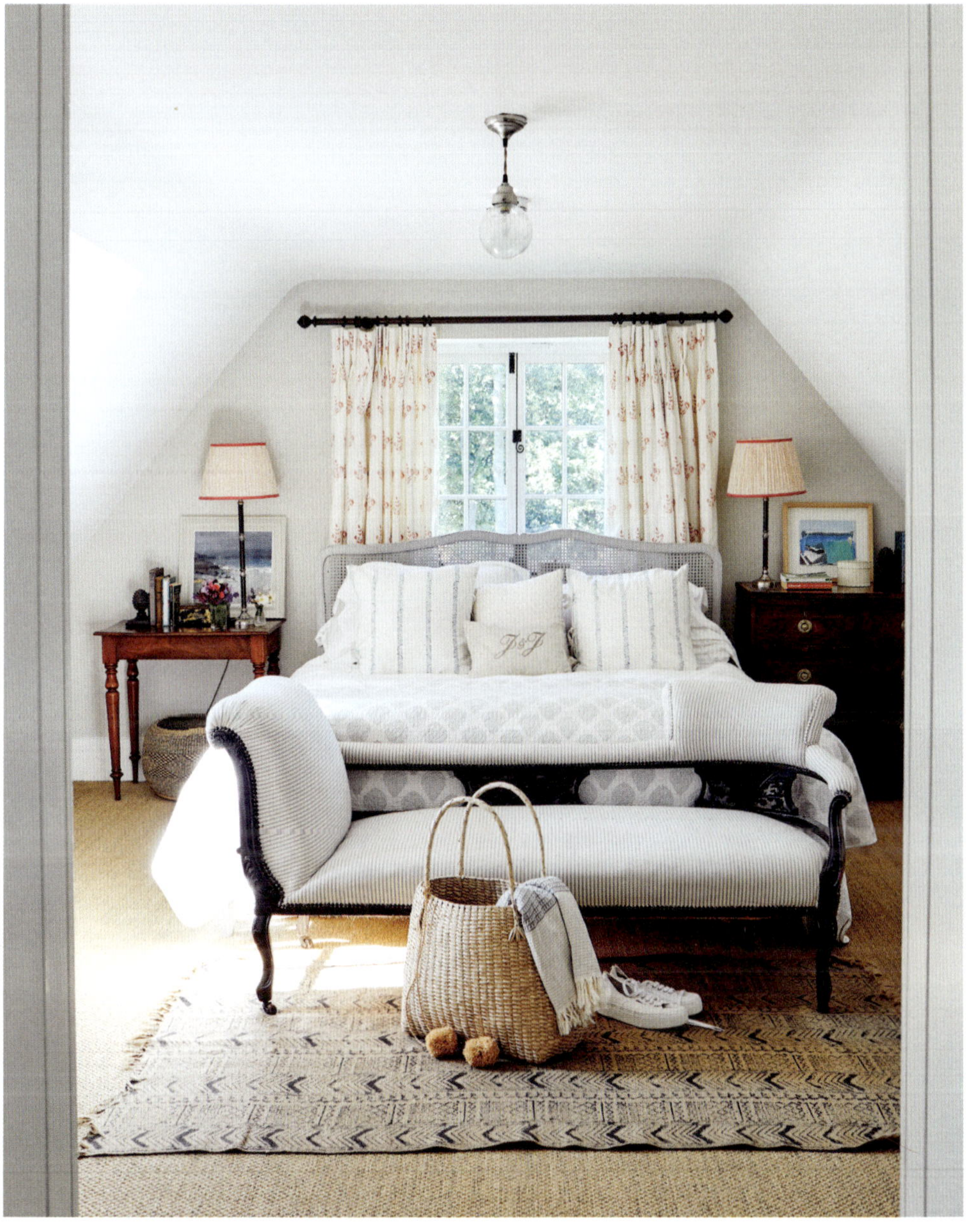

'WE SEEM TO GRAVITATE

to the bathroom,' laughs Jemma. 'We often all crowd in here for kids' bath-time chats. It's probably our favourite room. Even our cockerpoo Maggie's maternal instincts drew her to it; she made a nest and gave birth to six puppies in here!'

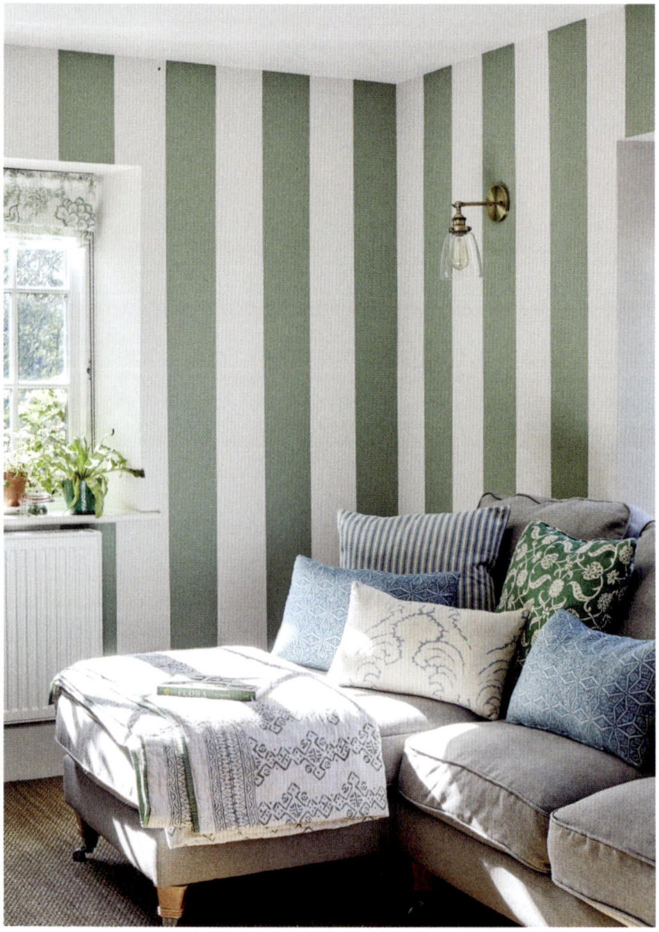

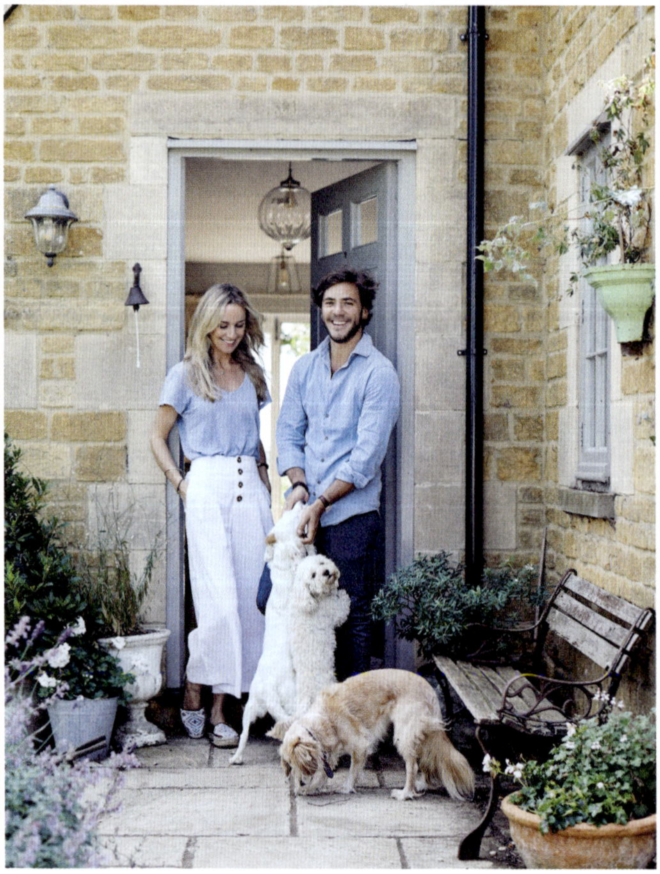

'I THINK THAT *the drawing room sealed the deal when we first saw the house,' remembers Jemma. 'It was added over a century after the original house was built, but adds wonderful space and height, and sits comfortably with the more cottagey side of the house.'*

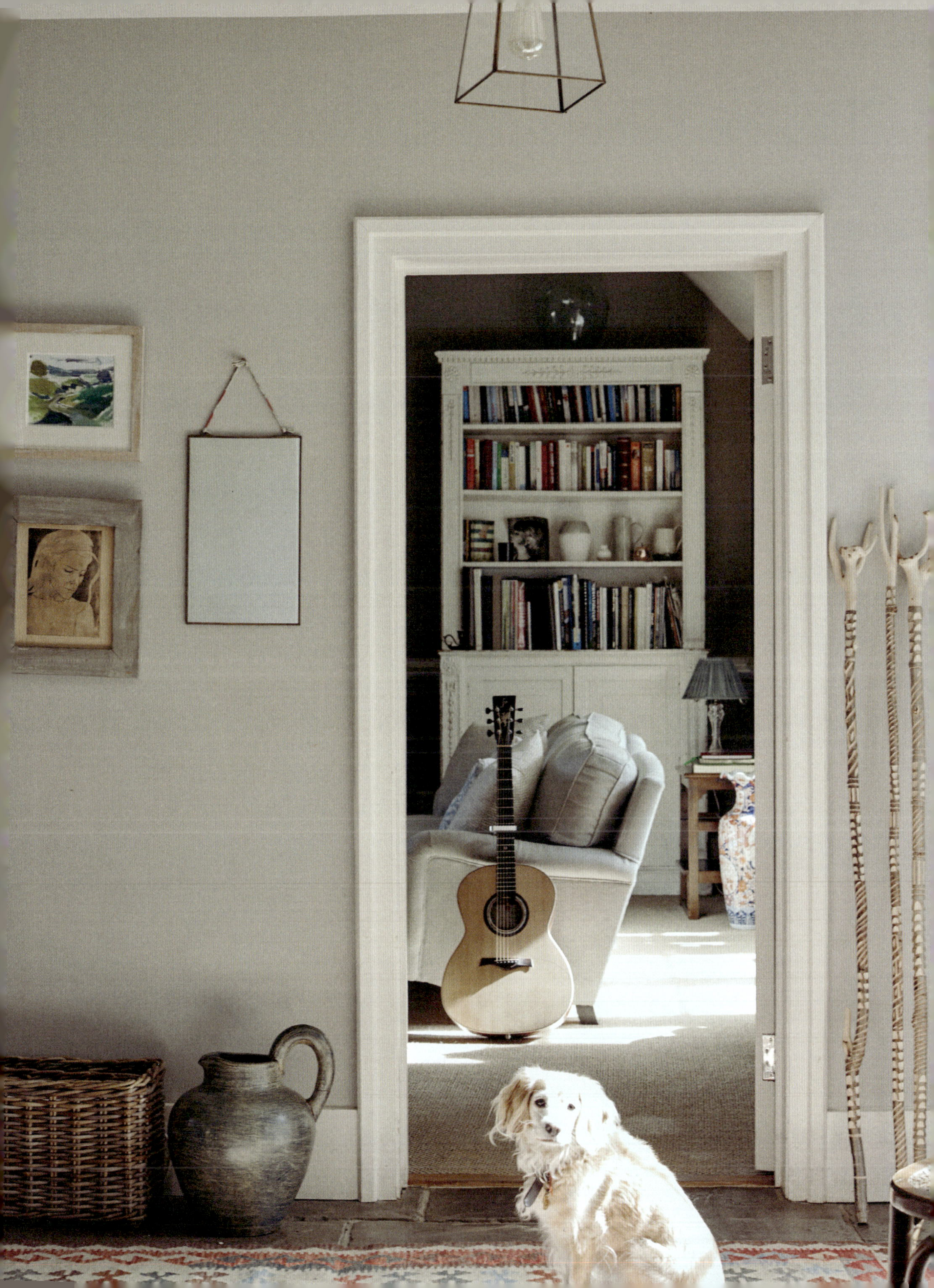

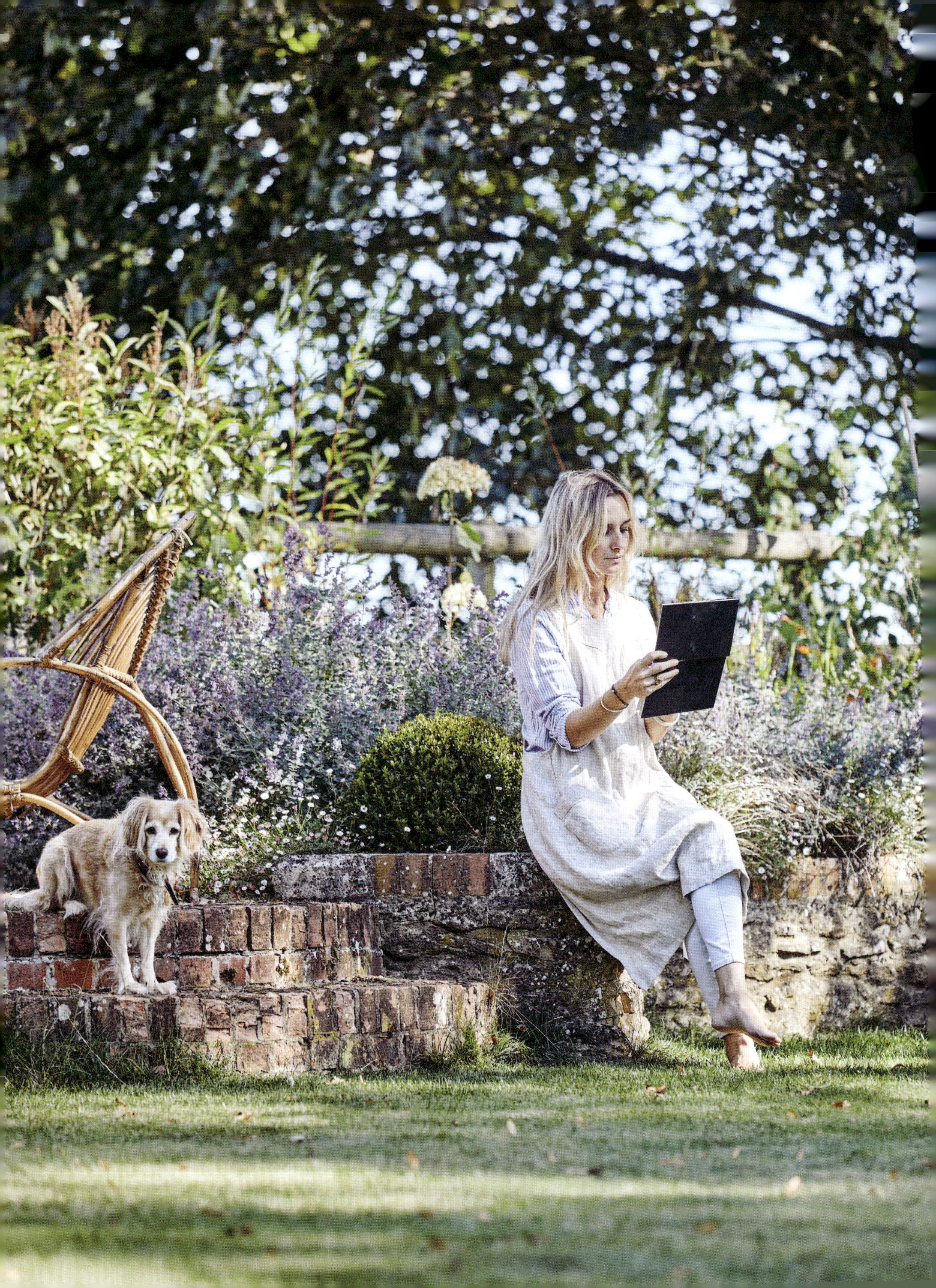

The kitchen was the scene of the first alteration. While characterful, it was a little confined and they decided to knock an archway through to the dining room. The spaces today flow naturally and the layout is perfect for entertaining. They then set about creating a playroom for the children, painting it with green stripes and adding bookshelves and storage.

'We wanted to enhance the Victorian elements upstairs,' says Jemma. So, they pulled up the carpets and found aged floorboards beneath. 'A bit of sanding smoothed them out, and they were as good as, er ... old!' Jemma laughs. They then had wood panelling fitted to complement the original character of the house. 'My pièce de résistance is the bathroom,' admits Jemma. 'We wanted a characterful bathroom and a big bath.' They started from scratch with new units, a claw-footed bath, wooden panelling, a Moroccan-style tiled floor and a squashy window seat.

Jemma and Jack have brought their individual decorating tastes together. Jemma's style is a blend of English country with a whiff of bohemianism. 'I'm a hoarder and would crowd the house with colour, art, ornaments and textiles, if Jack didn't occasionally rein me in,' she admits. Countering her exuberance, Jack prefers subtler colours and cleaner lines, and has an eye for an antique or one-off piece of furniture. Their different styles sit happily in a symbiotic balance.

Alongside the ebb and flow of family life, what resonates throughout the house is creativity. Art in its many forms is everywhere. There are many works by Jemma's favourite artists, augmented by her mother's and of course her own paintings. Music and instruments contribute to the essence too – the sound of Jack practising is a familiar background noise, often with little voices joining in, and so is his warming up his vocal chords in the bathroom.

'There are many elements to family life,' says Jemma, 'and we instinctively knew that this house could accommodate almost every need.' Almost every? 'Well, the dining room doubles up as my studio and a music room.' She gestures to the easels and canvases strewn in artistic abandon at one end of the room, which also houses a piano and Jack's guitar. 'This is where all the magic happens,' she adds. In truth, there's magic in the whole place, where children, dogs and imaginations run free. Though their busy lives take them all round the world, it's quite clear that there is no place they'd rather be.

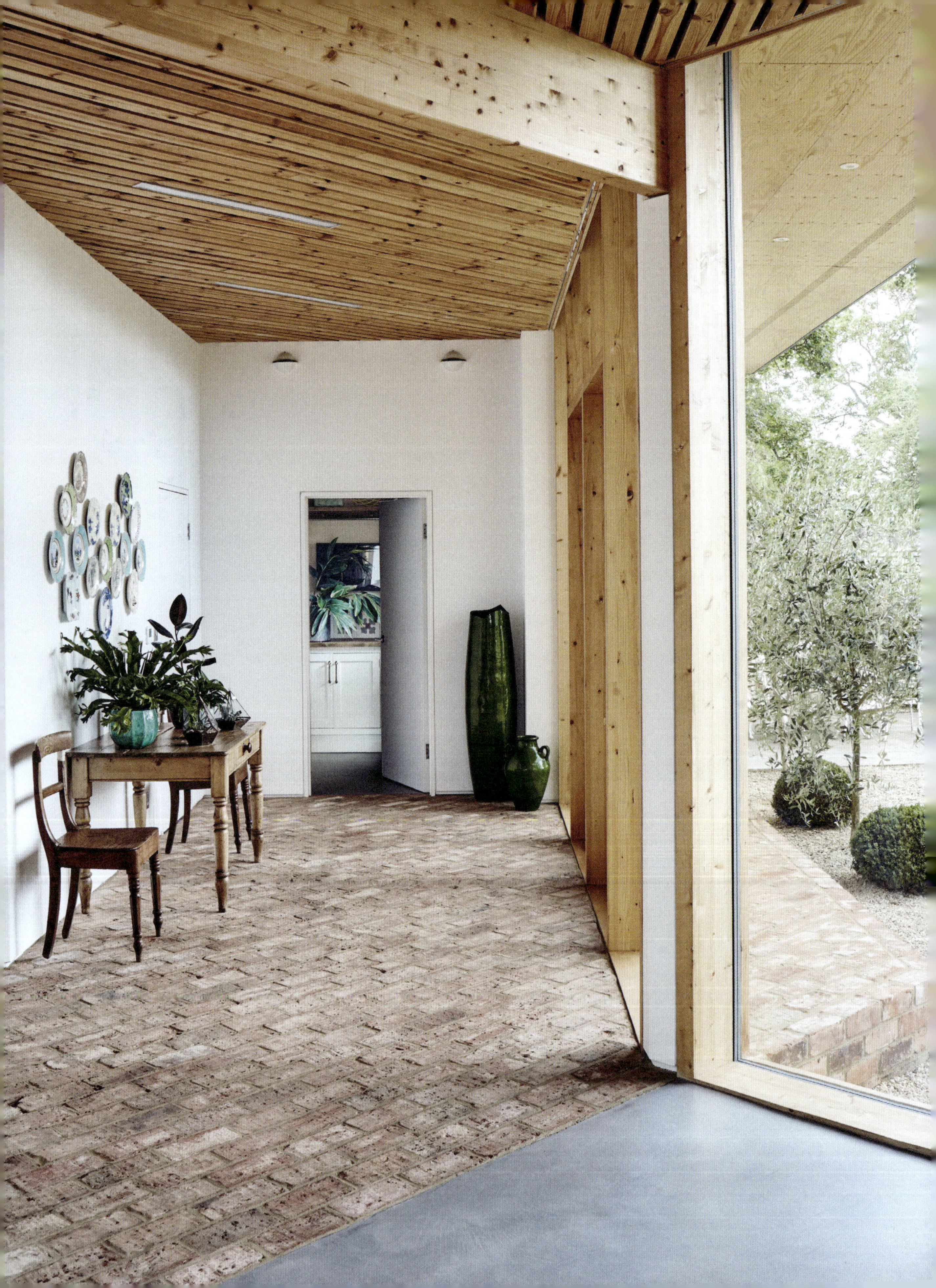

NATURE'S WAY

Bringing a Georgian house up to date in a way that suits family life, as well as taking as little as possible from the environment, has been a true labour of love for Natasha Ginks.

There is no longer any hiding from the fact that the choices we make may have a massive impact on the planet we live on. For many years Natasha Ginks has been a pioneer in how to live more sustainably, and what better place is there to start than the homes we live in? The house that she, her husband and their three children moved into in 2013 has been a demonstration that even old houses can be reworked in an energy-efficient way so that they take little from the environment.

Seven years ago, the Ginks family stumbled upon a wonderful Georgian village house with Edwardian additions, near Oxford. The house had been rented for many years, and not updated for several decades. 'It had a serene character,' recalls Natasha, before adding, 'but was woefully energy inefficient, freezing throughout, with many draughty windows, and little insulation.'

A long journey lay ahead. The kitchen was particularly tired. Tagged onto the back of the house, it was poky and dark, and not in keeping with its gracious Georgian character. 'I was itching to get my teeth into the kitchen,' recalls Natasha, 'but I had to focus on the boring bits first.' They replaced or repaired all the rotten windows as a priority and then moved onto the roof – removing ancient horse-hair insulation and adding sheep's wool and a wood-fibre blend that allows the structure to breathe. 'Man-made insulation overheats buildings,' explains Natasha, continuing, 'contributing hugely to climate change.'

Equally important was finding an energy-efficient way to heat the house. They removed two archaic gas boilers and installed a ground-source energy system. They then focused on upstairs, redecorating the five bedrooms and adding storage. At every turn Natasha used local tradespeople, sustainable building materials and reclaimed timber, low carbon paints and FSC-certified wallpapers, gradually bringing the house back to life while impacting little on the environment.

Meanwhile, Natasha researched kitchens. The outdated one that they inherited had several outbuildings attached to it that offered little value. The Ginkses hoped to extend into this space in a modern and energy-efficient way. 'It needed to be unostentatious externally and subordinate to the Georgian façade of the house,' she says.

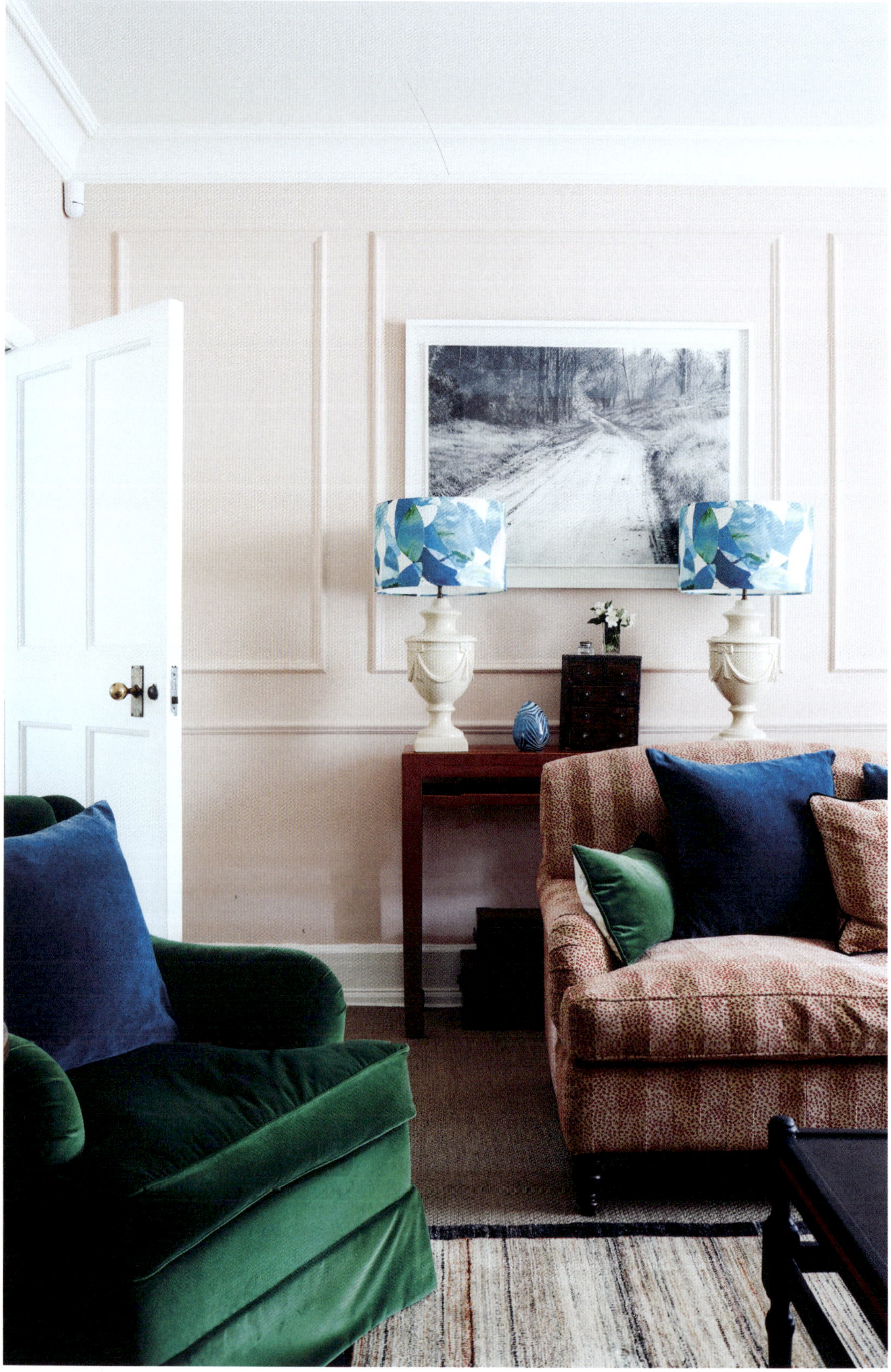

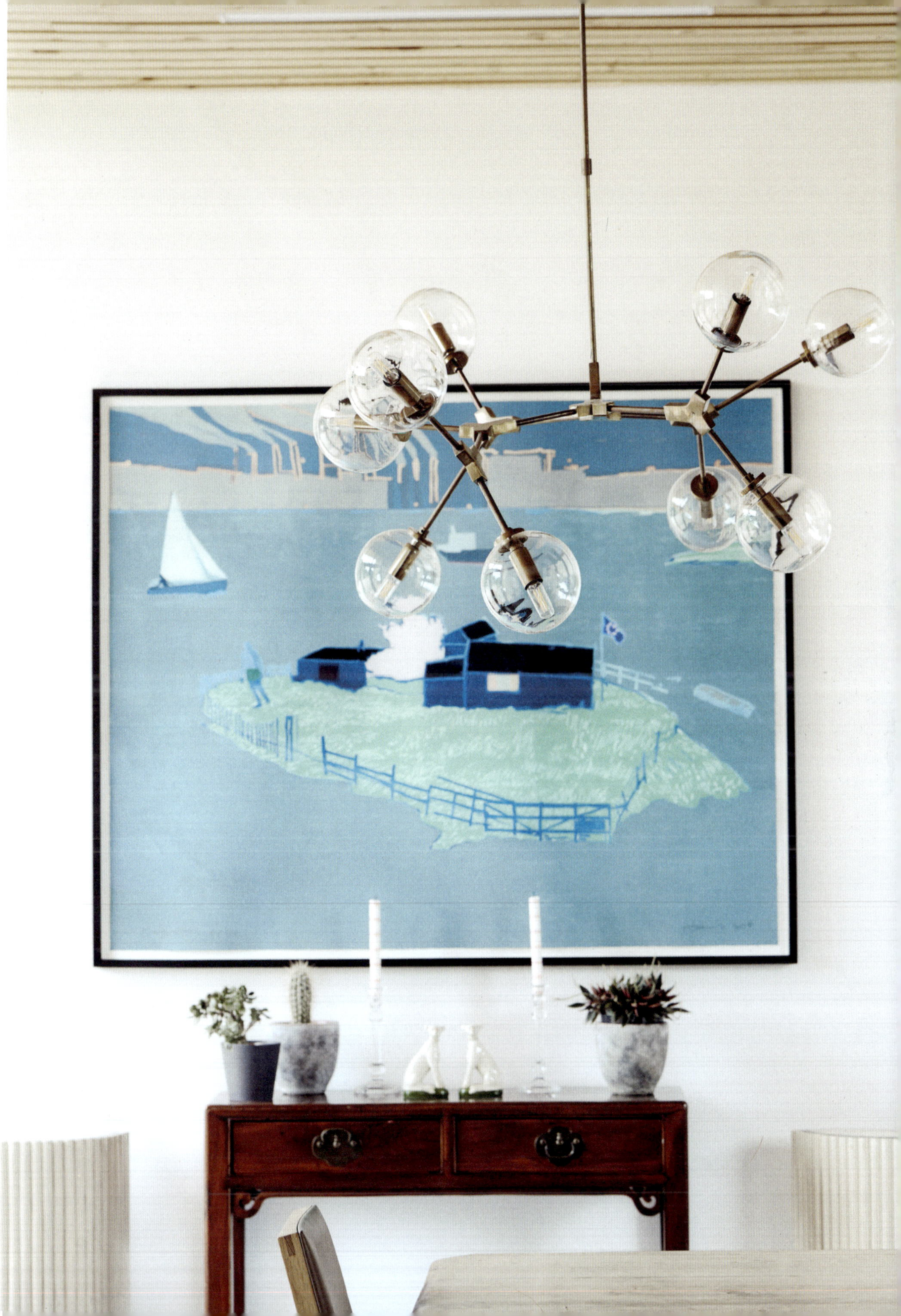

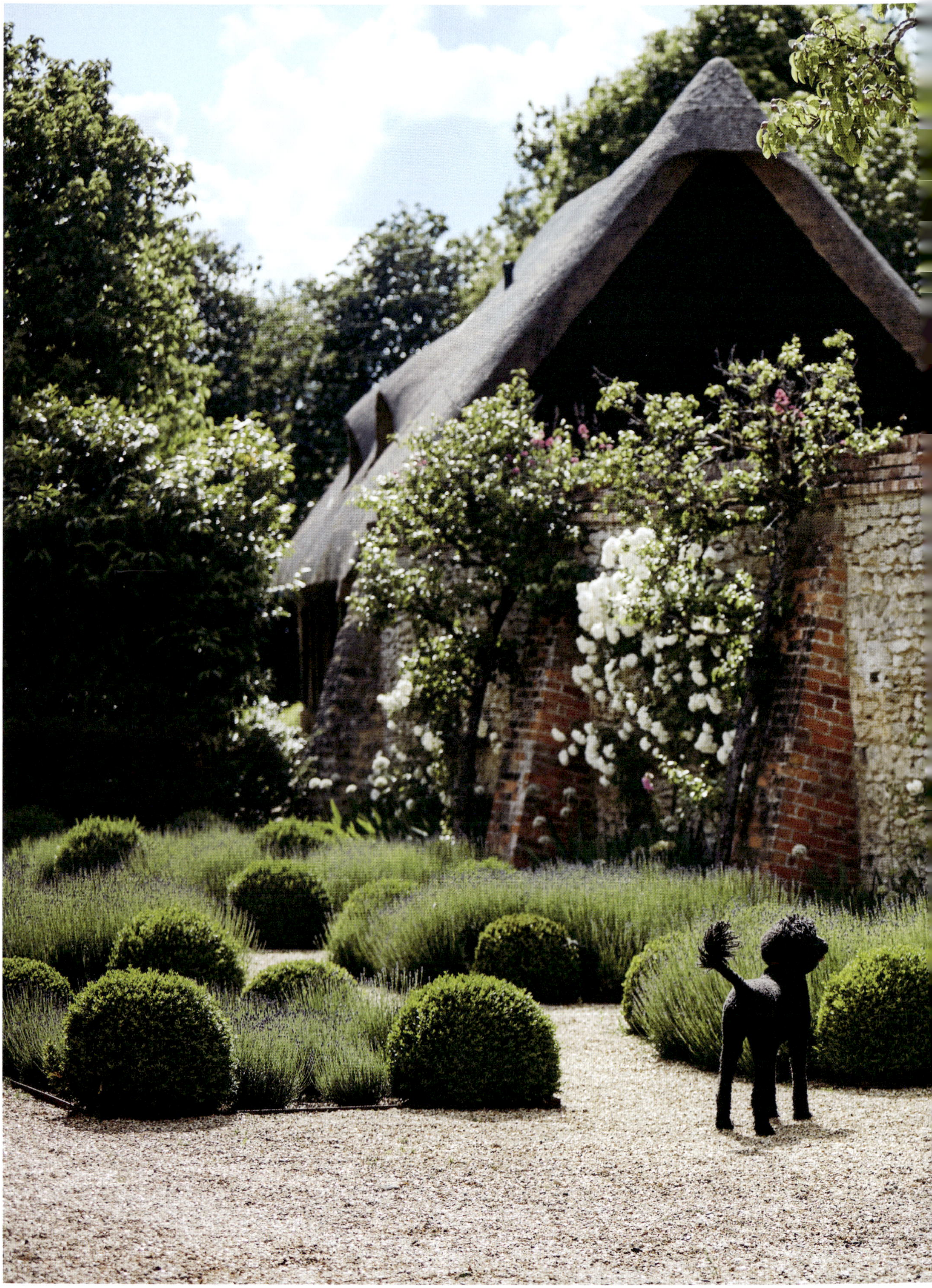

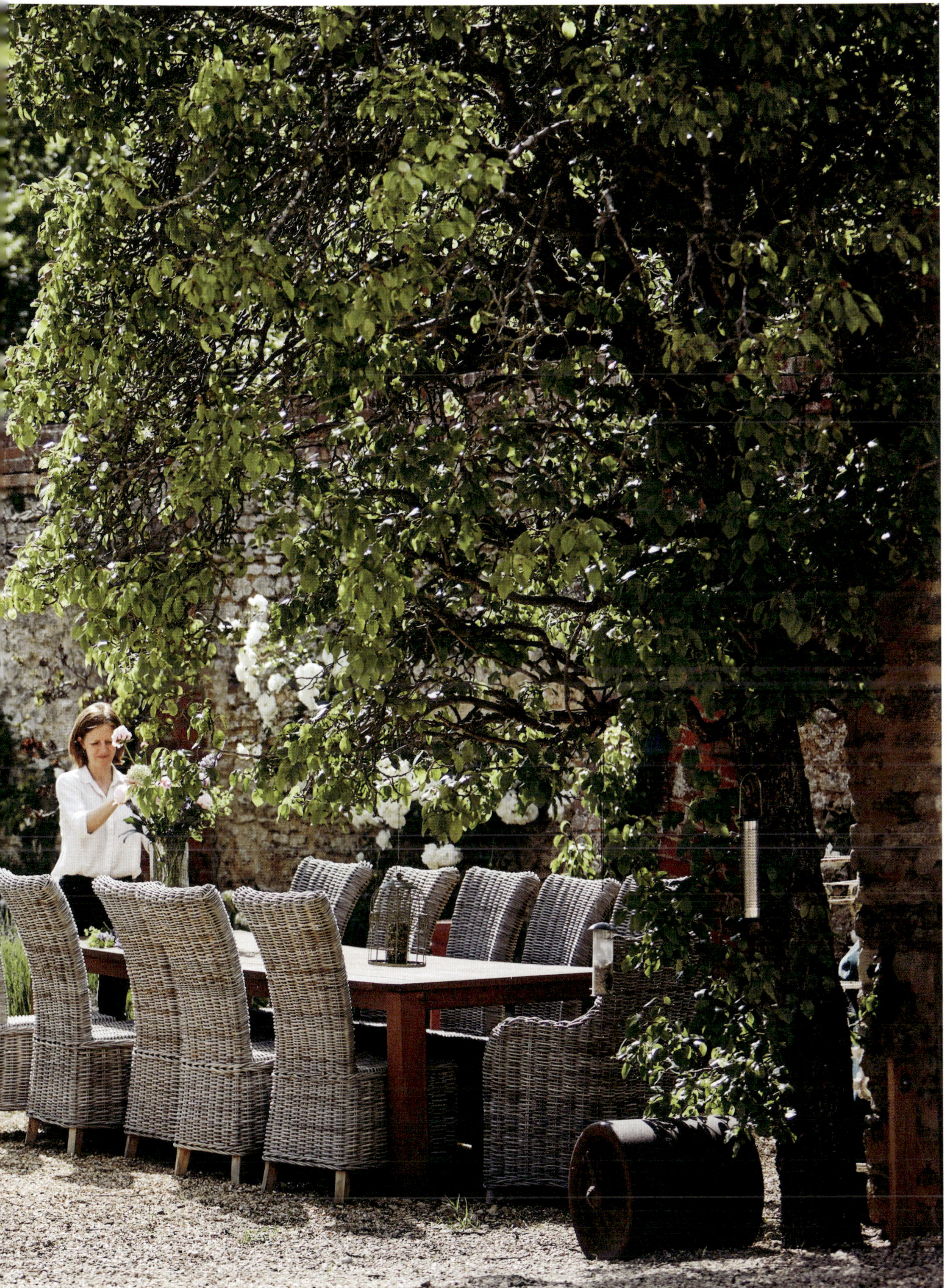

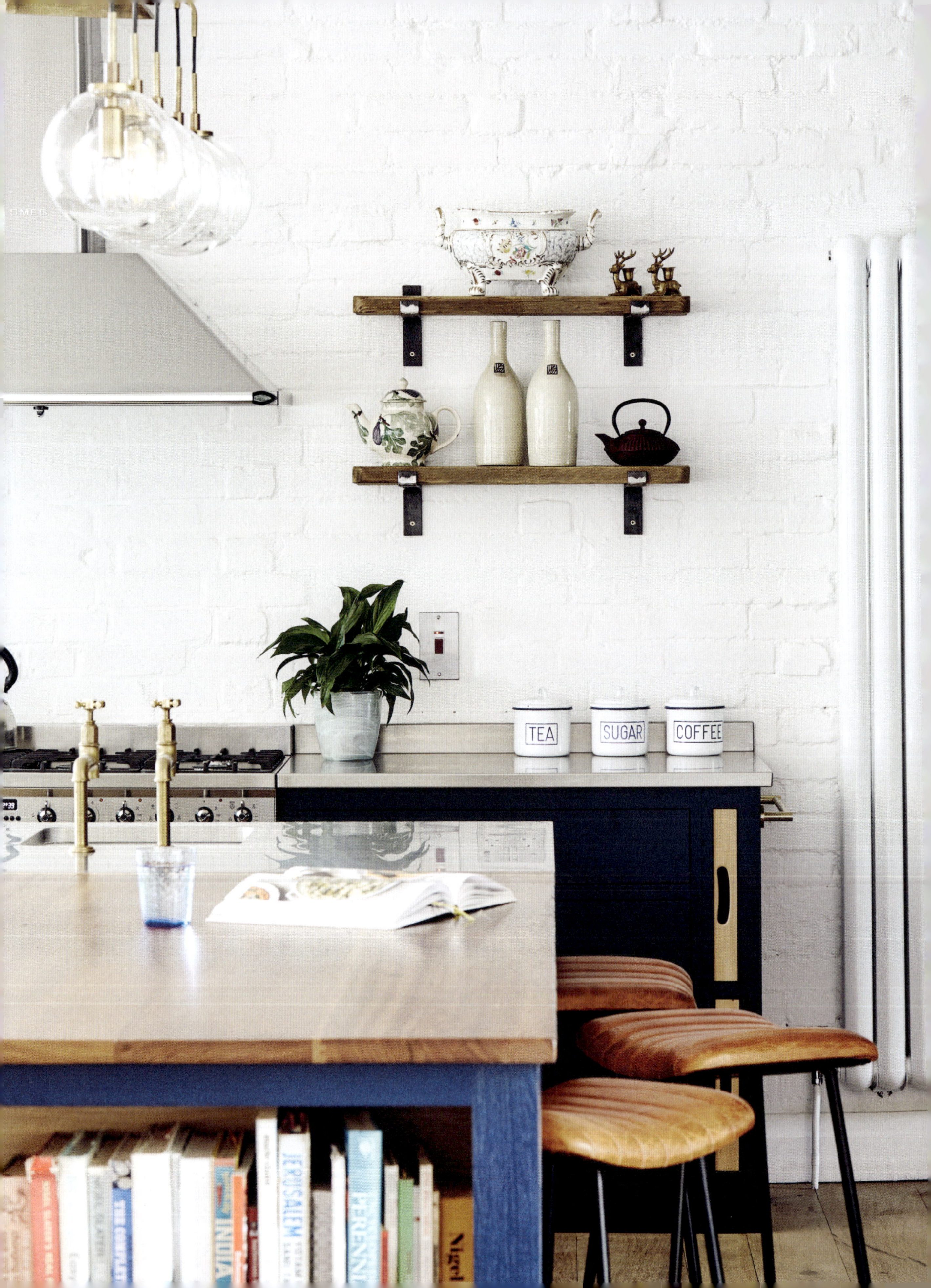
SMEG
TEA
SUGAR
COFFEE
JERUSALEM
INDIA
Nigel

Finally, they found the perfect match architect, Alex Towler, and the kitchen company Sustainable Kitchens. The company's name said it all to the Ginkses, and Alex's knowledge of passive houses (a term used to describe buildings with a rigorously low ecological footprint that require very little energy for heating and cooling) convinced them that he shared their green ideals.

A meticulous plan was conceived. A subtly asymmetrical timber-clad room with floor-to-ceiling windows would replace the former outbuildings. The effect today in the finished space is breathtaking, sleek and modern, with a noticeably calm atmosphere. The temperature is kept constant thanks to a huge mass of wood fibre (Pavatex) which insulates the roof, and the triple-glazed windows. 'This room needs virtually no heating,' reveals Natasha proudly.

The next phase was figuring out how to blend the new and old halves of the room. 'Of course, we wanted to create a beautiful room,' says Natasha, 'but paramount was to do it with minimum impact on the environment.' A stunning, yet unfussy and hard-wearing kitchen has been created. What stands out is the plethora of wood used. From the oak floorboards made from reclaimed beams through shelves that were once scaffold planks, drawers made from fallen wood and the island worktop is a refashioned school science table – it all comes from sustainable sources.

Once the kitchen was complete, Natasha was able to redecorate the rest of the downstairs rooms. These changes were cosmetic and respectful to the house's history. She wanted to make use of all that this generous house had to offer her own family, as well as providing the sustainability for it all to work for future owners for many decades to come. She has since launched Renovate Green, a business helping people to improve their homes while causing the minimum impact environmentally. Her own project proves that this really is achievable. 'There is always a way to bring modern levels of comfort and beauty,' says Natasha, 'and not at the expense of our planet.'

'THE KITCHEN

needs virtually no heating and sustains a similar temperature all year round,' says Natasha proudly. 'Only once or twice, in the iciest depths of winter, have we used the underfloor heating.'

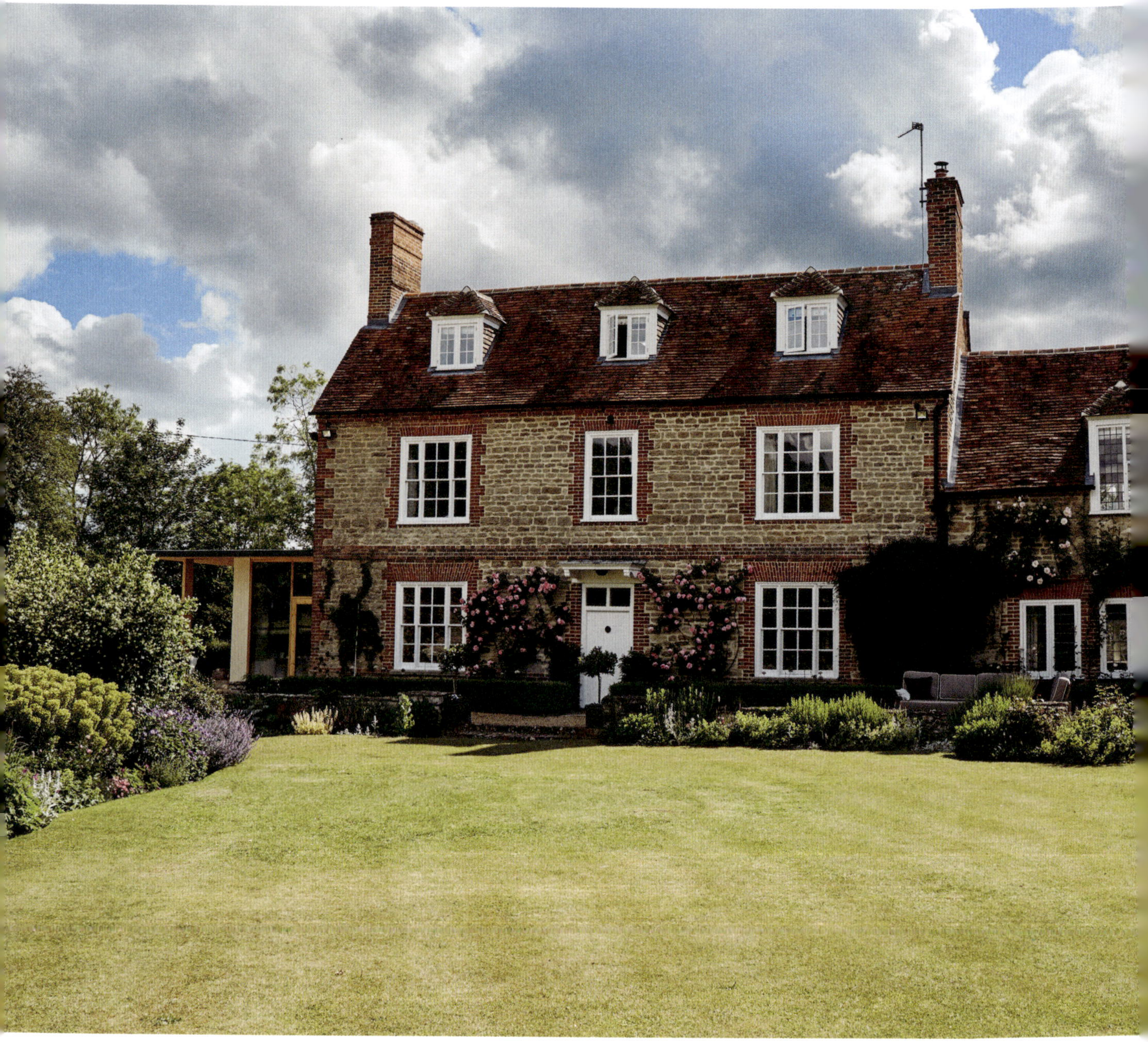

'I PICKED HERITAGE COLOURS

in natural tones when redecorating the house,' Natasha explains. 'I felt the Georgian and Victorian parts needed to blend naturally into the new sustainable house.'

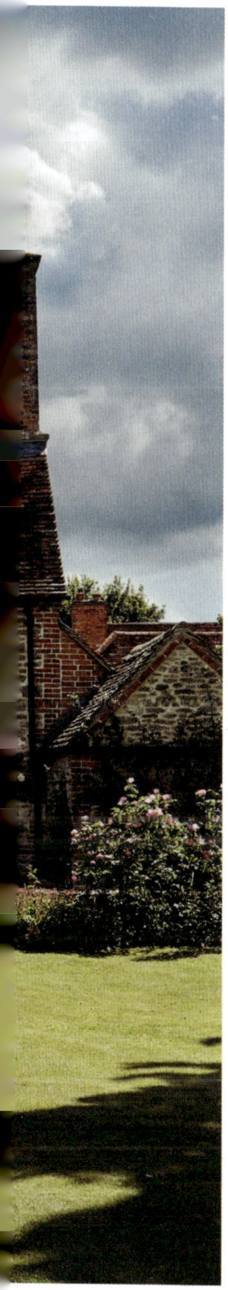

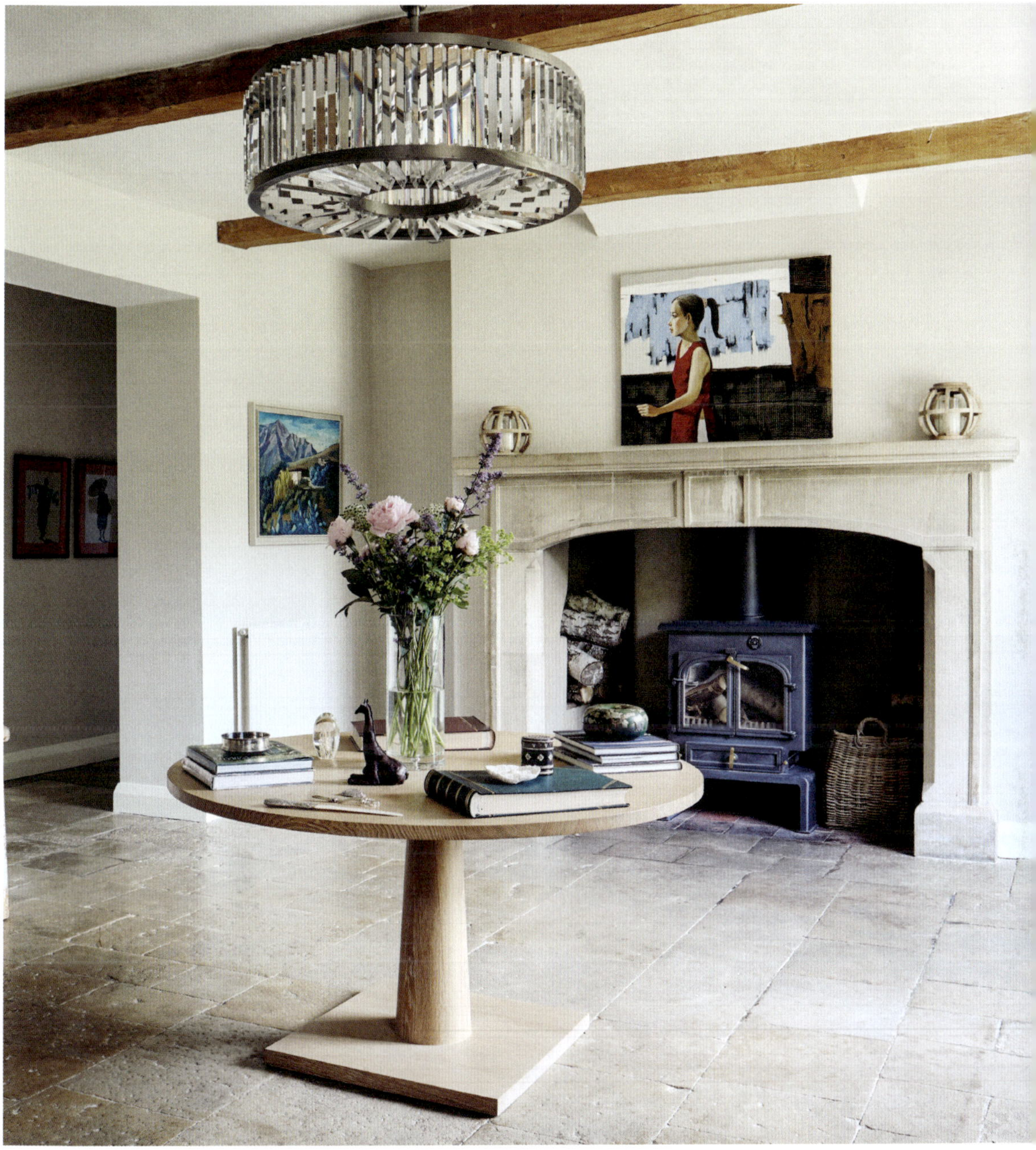

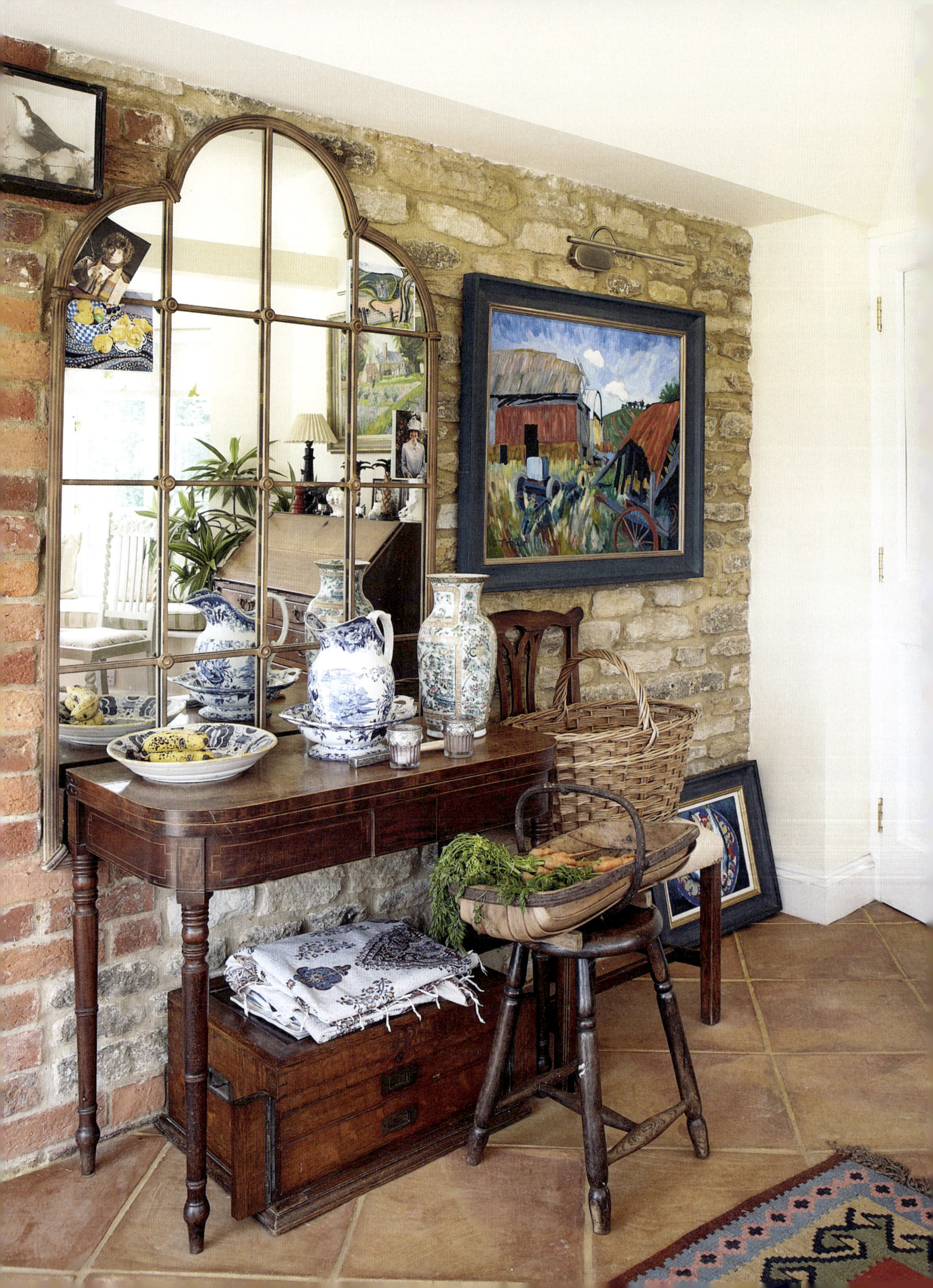

THE ART OF LIVING

When artist Josephine Trotter and her late husband Angus decided to downsize, they needed to look no further than the farm buildings they had lived opposite for forty years.

Josephine Trotter's house is bursting with interest and colour. It's hard to imagine feeling uninspired here. Be it her fuchsia pink bathroom, her floral wallpapers as bright as a garden or her collection of antique teapots, every wall and surface displays a confidence with colour that can come only from the eye of an artist. And to appreciate Josephine's truest passion the onlooker need only stand back and enjoy. Here a London street heaves with jostling crowds, there a cluster of crimson tulips spills from a blue vase. 'A pernicious colour, crimson,' tuts Josephine, who has such empathy with the material she uses that she gives it a wayward nature of its own. It is in harnessing colours and forms that she breathes life into her quite remarkable paintings, which in turn make the walls of her home a pleasure to behold.

Home and art had always lived in a symbiotic relationship in Josephine and her late husband Angus' lives. The pair brought their five children up in a rambling Warwickshire farmhouse. Her studio was there, as well as one of her most significant inspirations, the local landscape. But some years ago Angus suffered a life-changing accident that left him with ongoing back problems. The steep staircases and never-ending upkeep of the farmhouse proved too much for him and they decided to downsize.

They had no inclination to leave the surroundings that had delighted and inspired them for forty or so years, so they decided to look no further than their doorstep, or rather the farm buildings directly opposite. Then home to cattle, hens and horses, and with a dovecote above, these outbuildings offered the solution and, what's more, commanded the same glorious views as the farmhouse.

For the next eighteen months Josephine and Angus watched a transformation take place. The floor was raised in the old cowshed to create an open-plan kitchen and living room, with original beams soaring above. A dividing wall was put up to split the former cowshed from the stables next door. Those were subsequently divided to form the master bedroom and bathroom, plus an office for Angus and a wash/utility room. A flight of stairs leads from here to a spare bedroom above, originally the crowded dovecote dating back to the 1600s. They added a conservatory too.

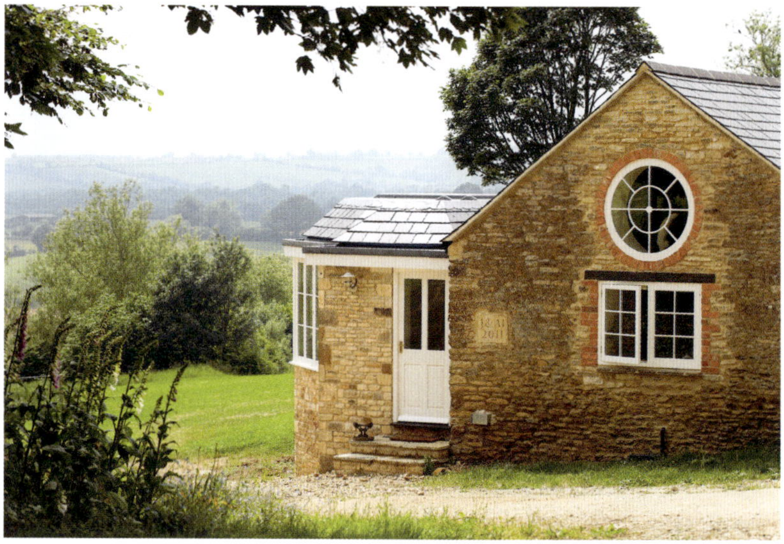

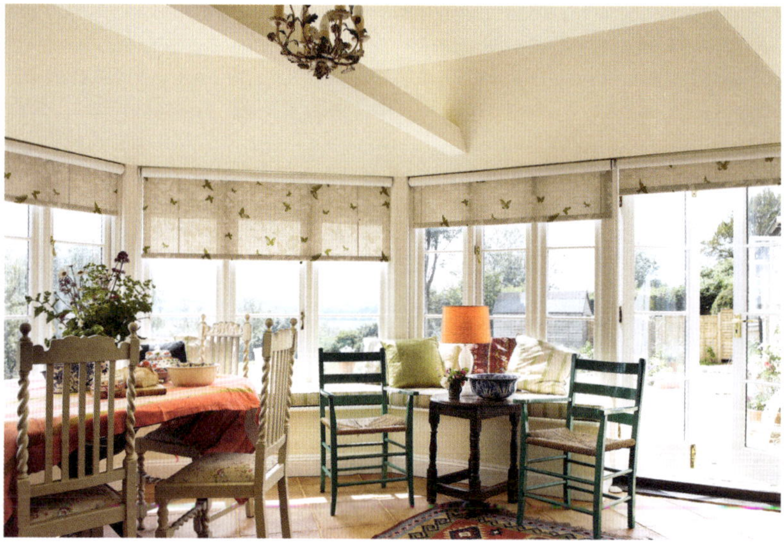

'MY PREVIOUS FARMHOUSE

kitchen was large and busy and red was its noisy colour,' says Josephine. 'In this house I wanted a calmer character, so I chose a backdrop of quieter colours. My paintings and wallpapers add the noise.'

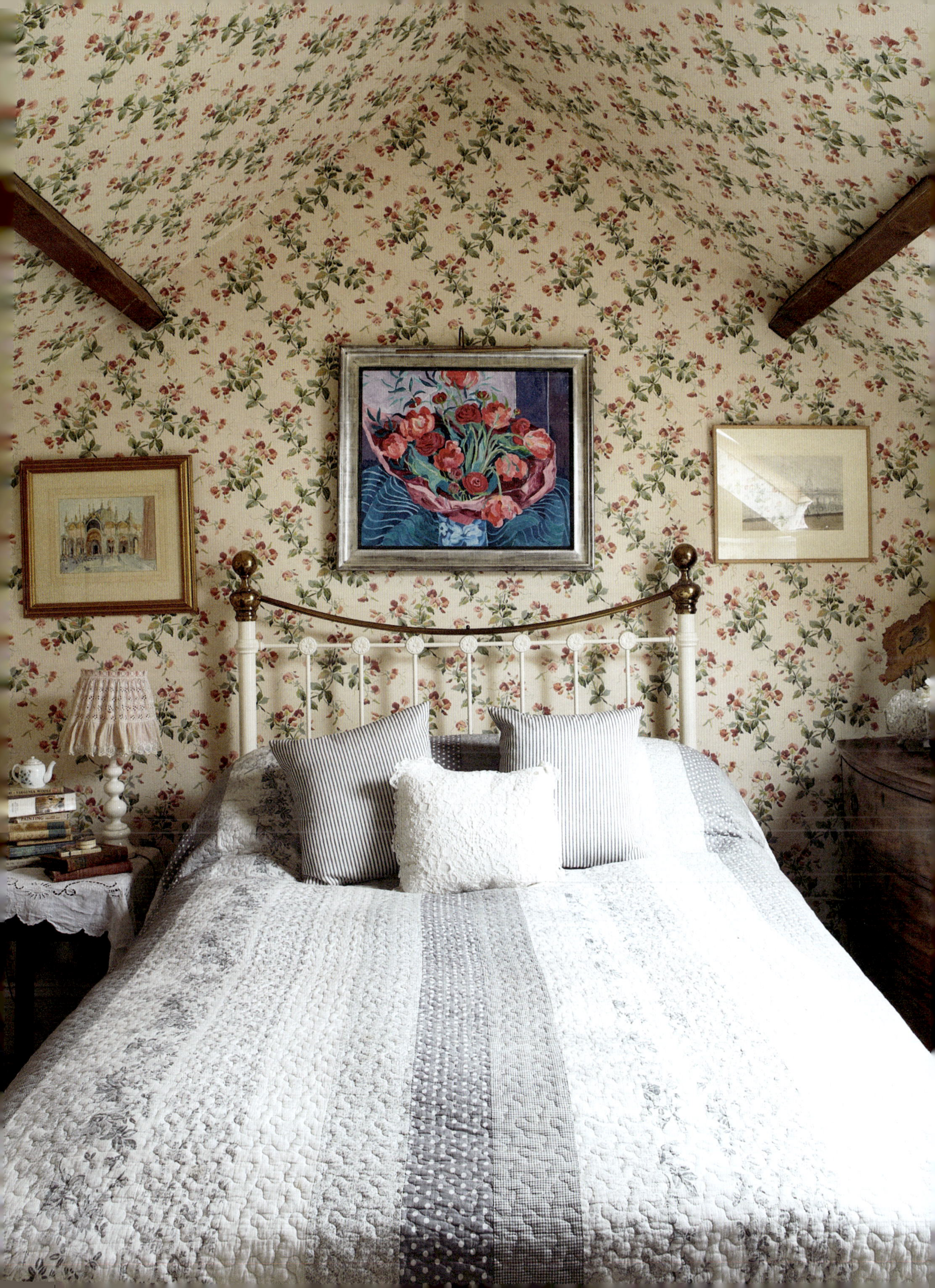

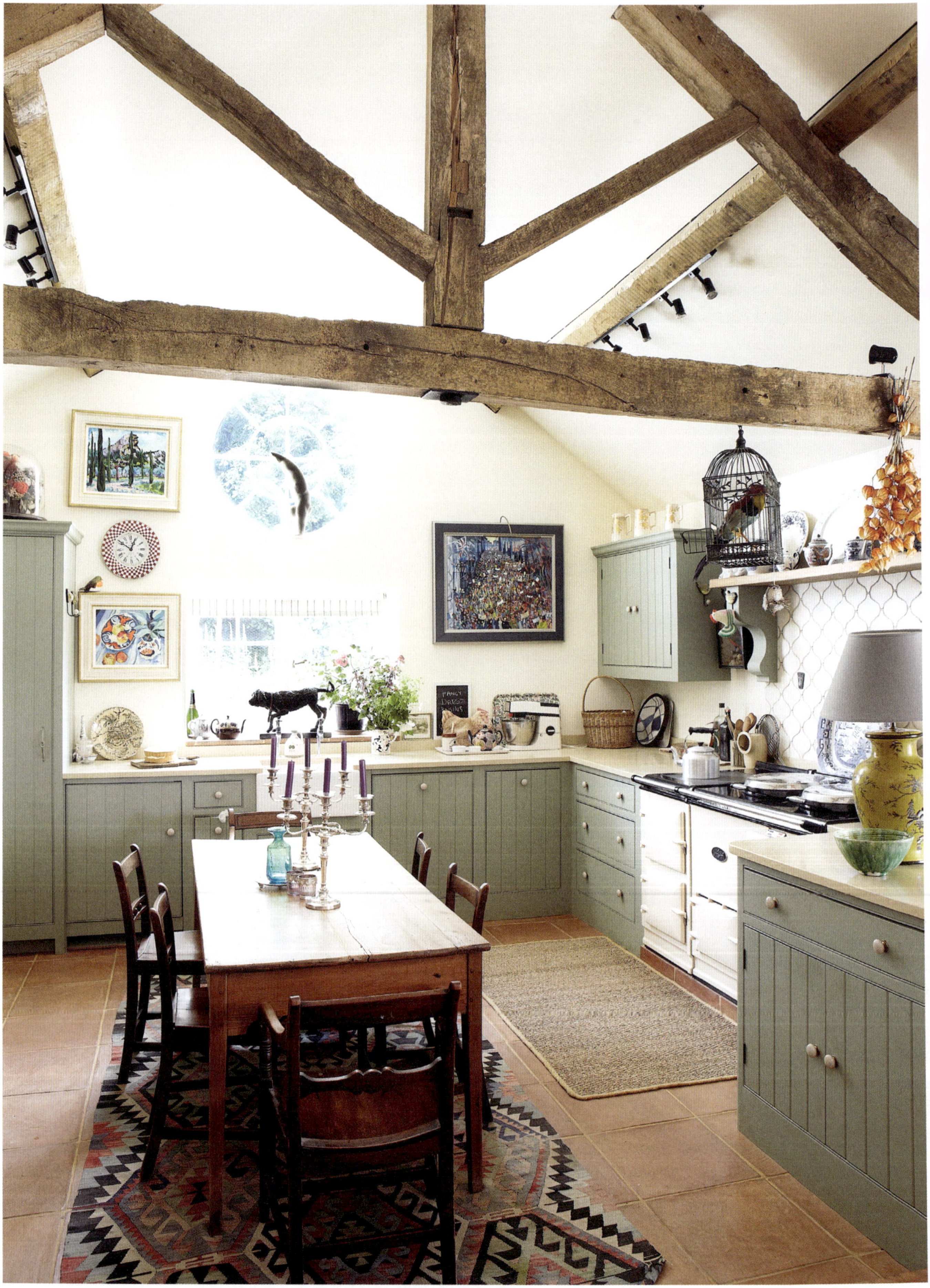

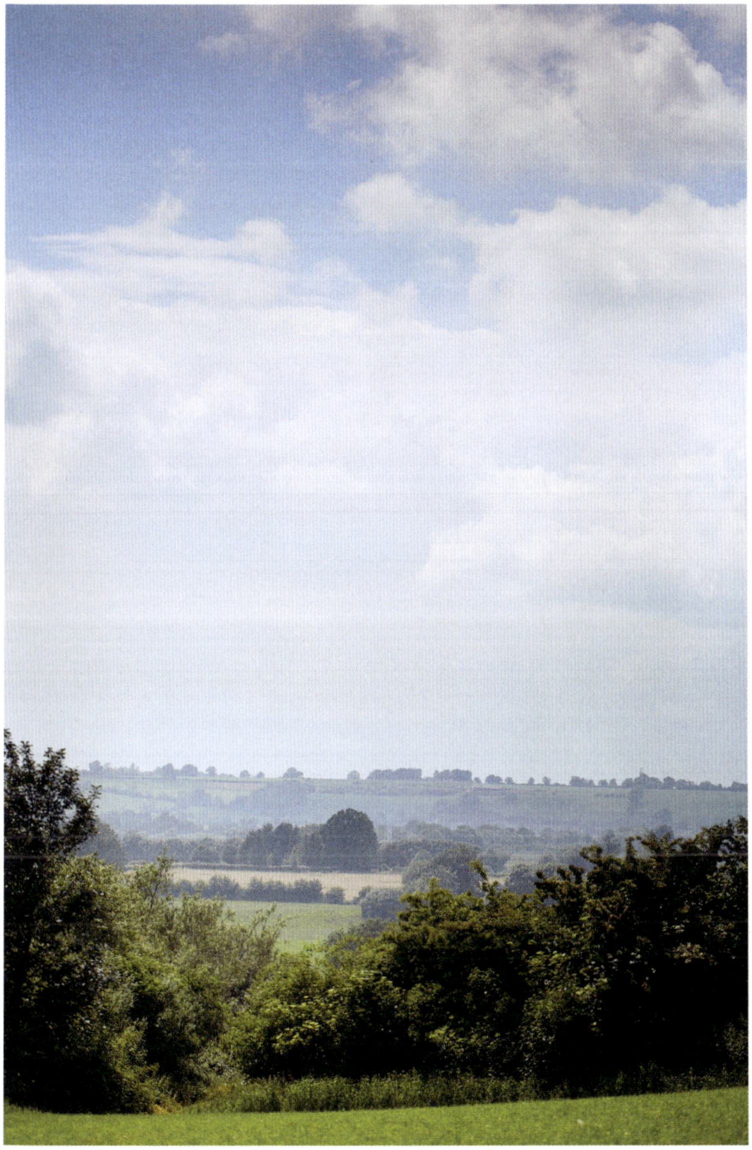

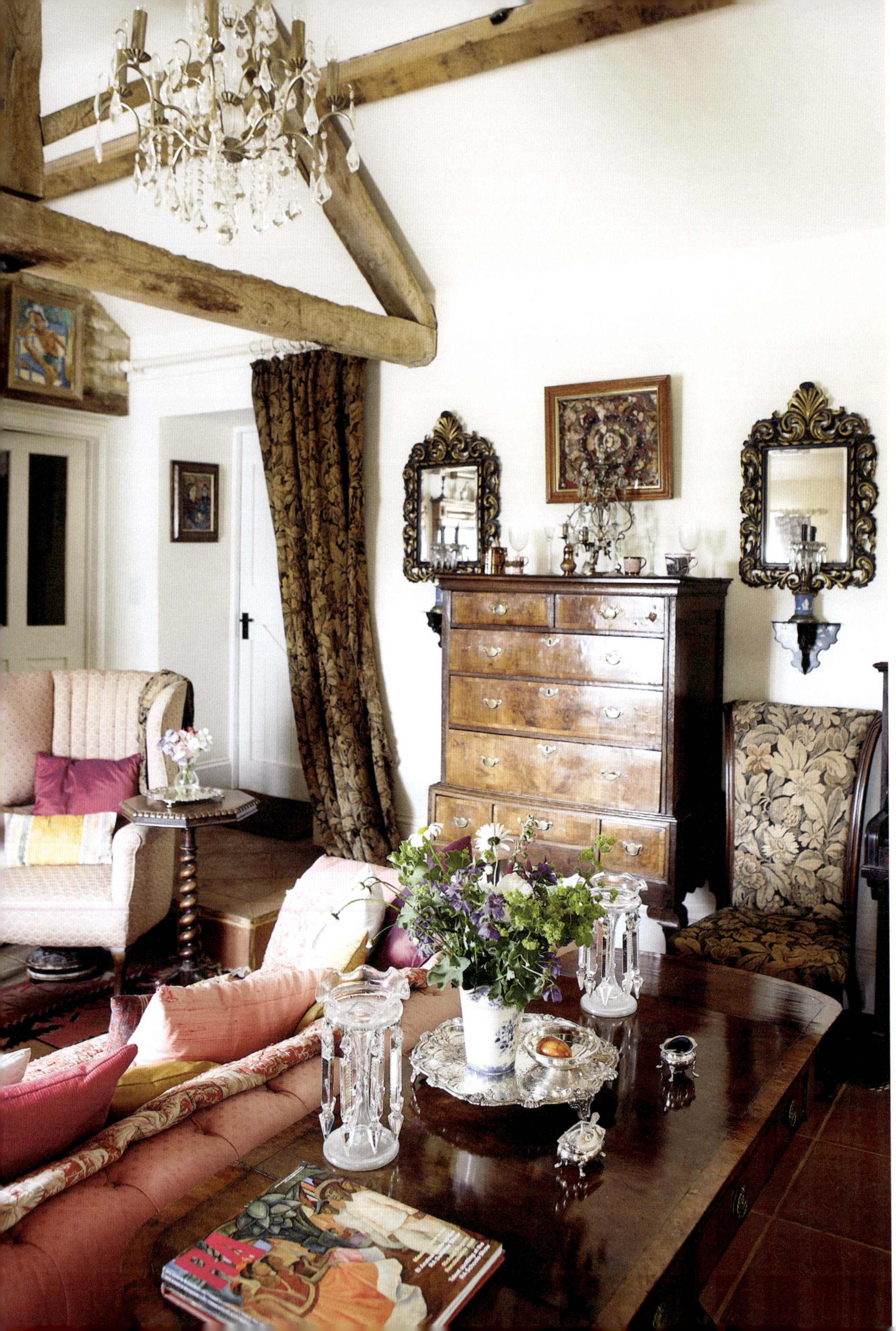
RA

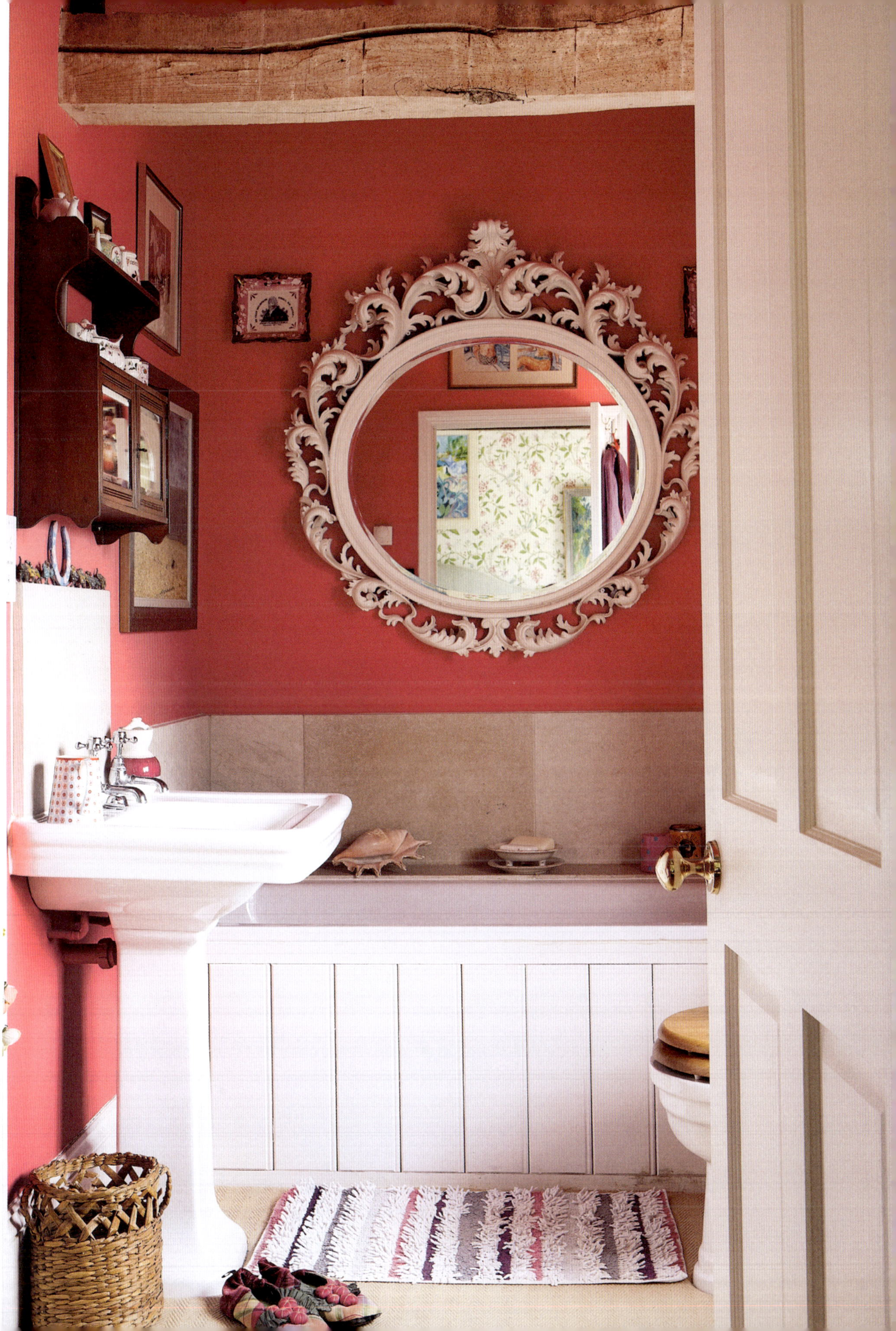

'It was fascinating to behold,' says Josephine, whose pioneering spirit and artistic eye were captivated by the creative process, 'and the craftsmen took such pride in their work.' A process which could have signalled the wistful end of an era became a new beginning. Windows were added, original beams and woodwork were preserved, underfloor heating was installed, and a sympathetic and convenient new home took shape.

When it came to interior design, Josephine and Angus had a much smaller canvas to work with in their new home. 'Naturally we wanted to keep our best-loved treasures,' explains Josephine, so there were countless trips from the old farm to their new house. It was too close to involve removals men and Angus' back was not up to carrying hulking furniture, so they appealed to their family to help them. 'I'll never forget the sight of our poor son-in-law heaving individual drawers full of clothing across the orchard while our "smaller garments" blew about all over the grass,' laughs Josephine.

Of course, they needed new pieces too, and like great travellers - who are often in search of artistic inspiration - they had fun stumbling upon items for their house. The house has evolved into an eclectic combination of old and new finds that sit well with Josephine's exuberant paintings, and everything seems quite at home in this old, yet newly converted farm building.

'What I love is remembering perfectly clearly how the building used to be: the sweet smell of the cowshed, the fluttering activity in the dovecote ... often a memory comes back to me of something that happened here,' Josephine recalls. Angus once reminded her how they had returned from holiday to find that their bloodhound had given birth to seventeen puppies in the old stable - now the downstairs bathroom. And then one morning Josephine woke up and turned to Angus: 'We're sleeping in the hen house,' she said. To which he replied, with some pride, 'Indeed we are.'

'IT MAKES ME LAUGH

that I settle down in the evenings in the old cattle barn,' reveals Josephine. 'The 300-year-old beams above are the only clues to reveal that this room has ever been anything but a sitting room that we stuffed full of our best-loved pieces.'

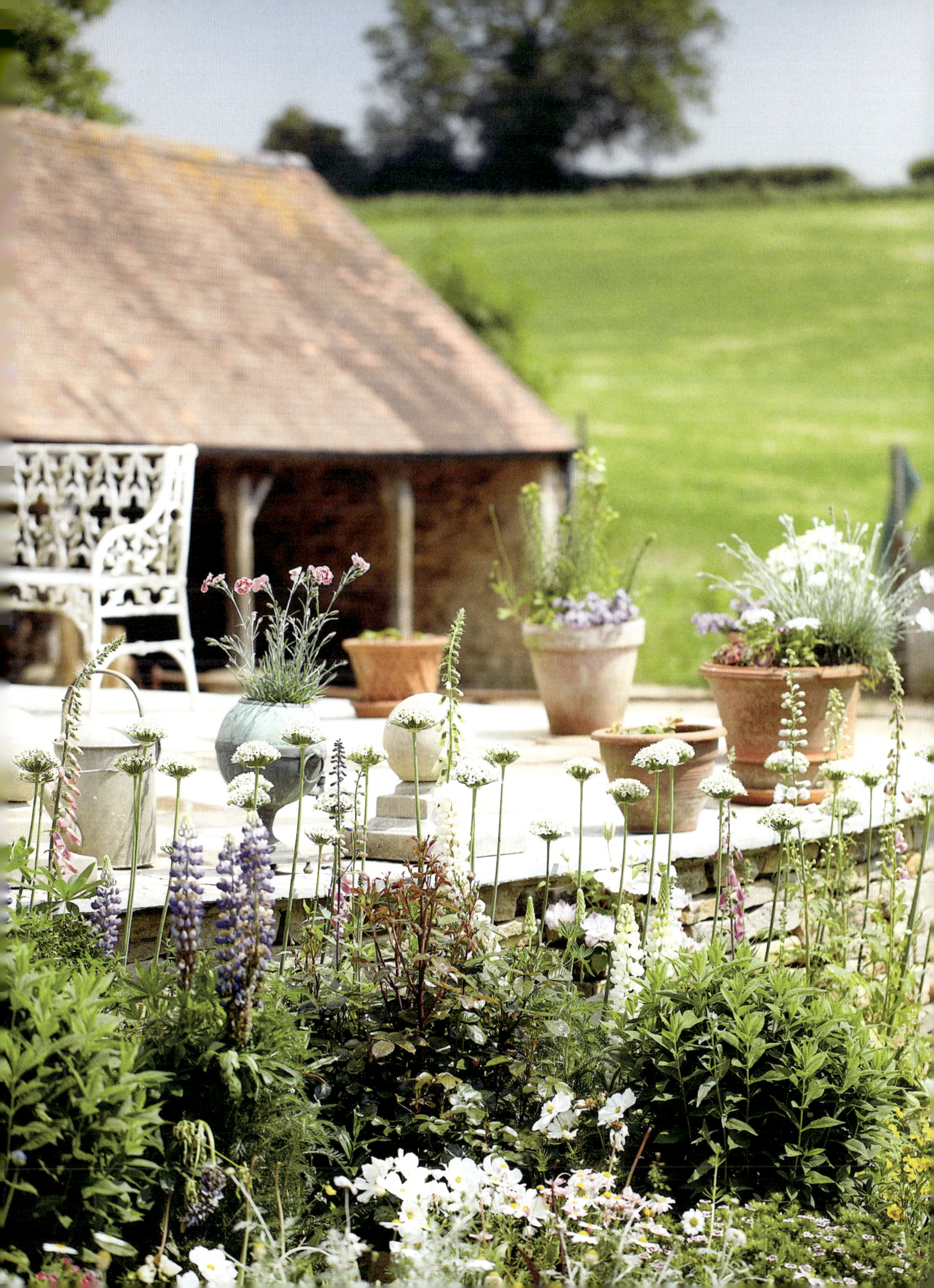

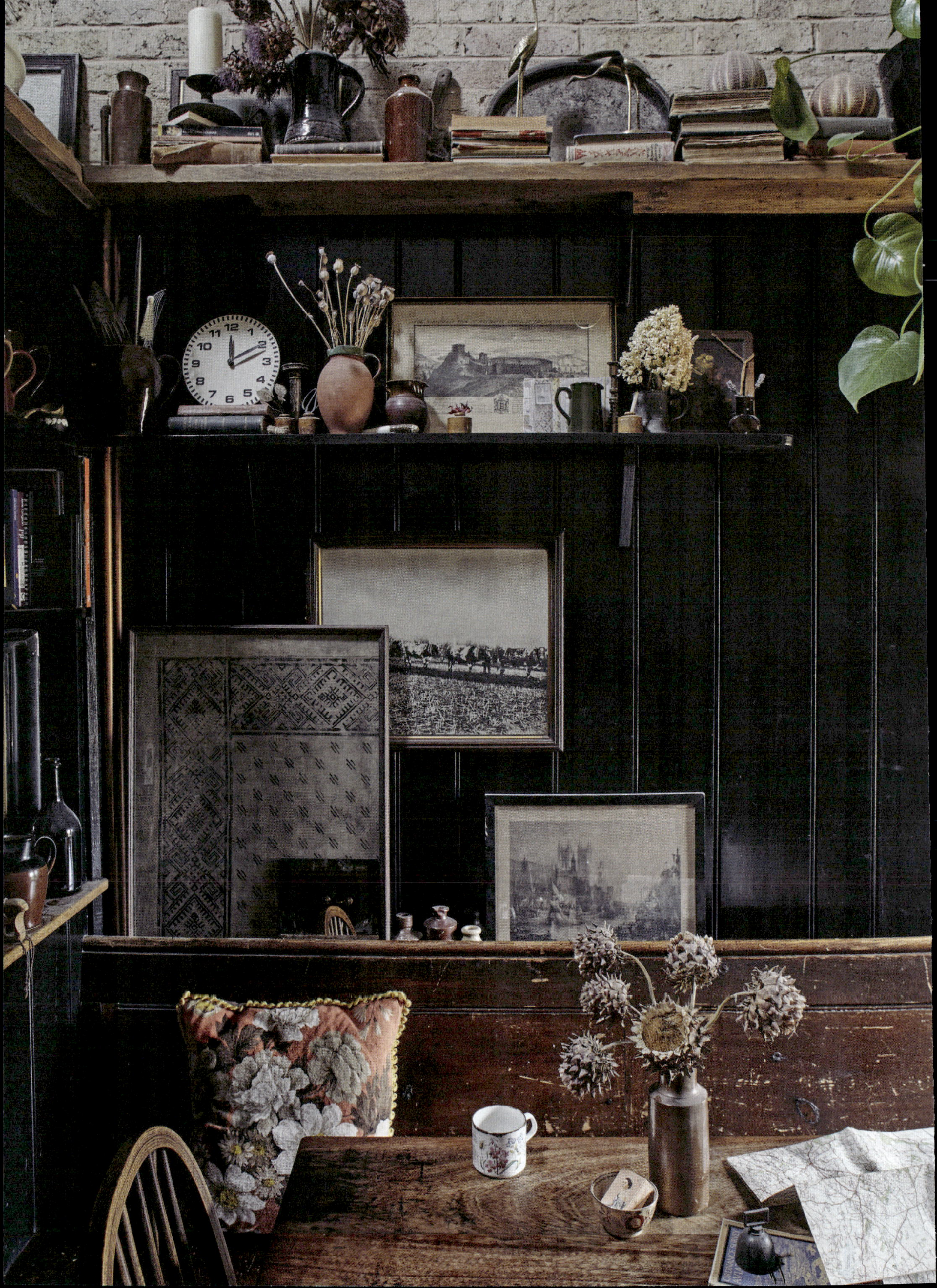

A PERFECT PIGSTY

It was not love at first sight for Elle Kemp when she and her husband Martin Gane first viewed an 18th-century pigsty with planning permission, but over a creative and sympathetic renovation the house worked its charm on them.

'It's a keep-your-shoes-on kind of house,' says Elle Kemp as her two boys give their wellies a cursory stamp on the doormat before hurtling full tilt into their home. It's a great home. Bursting with character, warmth and impeccable retro-rustic style, but strictly no frills. Nor carpets, nor coasters, nor anything pristine. 'We just want to live here, and embrace the marks that life leaves.' Some years ago she'd asked her husband – garden designer Martin Gane – how he'd like the space to turn out. Tired after a long day building and seated by the fireside, cold beer in hand, he'd shrugged off his battered tweed jacket and gestured 'Like this?' Worn, comfortable and natural. So that's where they started.

Elle and Martin had first viewed Longridge Barn in 2012. A 170-year-old pigsty, it was long and narrow, one room thick and one storey high, with mud for a floor. The six individual bays laid out in a row were small, with an outside door opening into each of them and a corridor running along the back. Since it was a listed building, the layout could never be changed. Elle's heart had not instantly sung but Martin (who had once worked as pig farmer in New Zealand) went rather quiet, absorbed in examining various stains on the pigsty walls. 'That's a pig's nuzzle mark,' he'd remarked, 'and this would have been the piglet pen.' Something in Elle shifted ...

'Yep ... We put in an offer,' laughs Elle. 'I was pregnant, and we were living in Stroud town centre in a house opening directly onto a busy road. We wanted to get out into the countryside, but our budget was limited. The pigsty was the only option.' These two are a couple with a great sense of adventure and quiet confidence in their creative ability. They knew instinctively that they would be able to make a home in this quirky space even if its potential might be hard to imagine.

They spent the next six months drawing up plans (and scrapping most of the plans that had already been drawn). And from day one – for almost three years – Martin and Elle saw the project through almost without assistance.

'ONCE THE LONGRIDGE BARN

project was complete, we launched a joint business, Ridge and Furrow, specialising in creating homes and spaces that feel as if they have always been there; well settled and appropriate within their architecture and using sustainable, natural, breathable, reused materials and traditional detailing.'

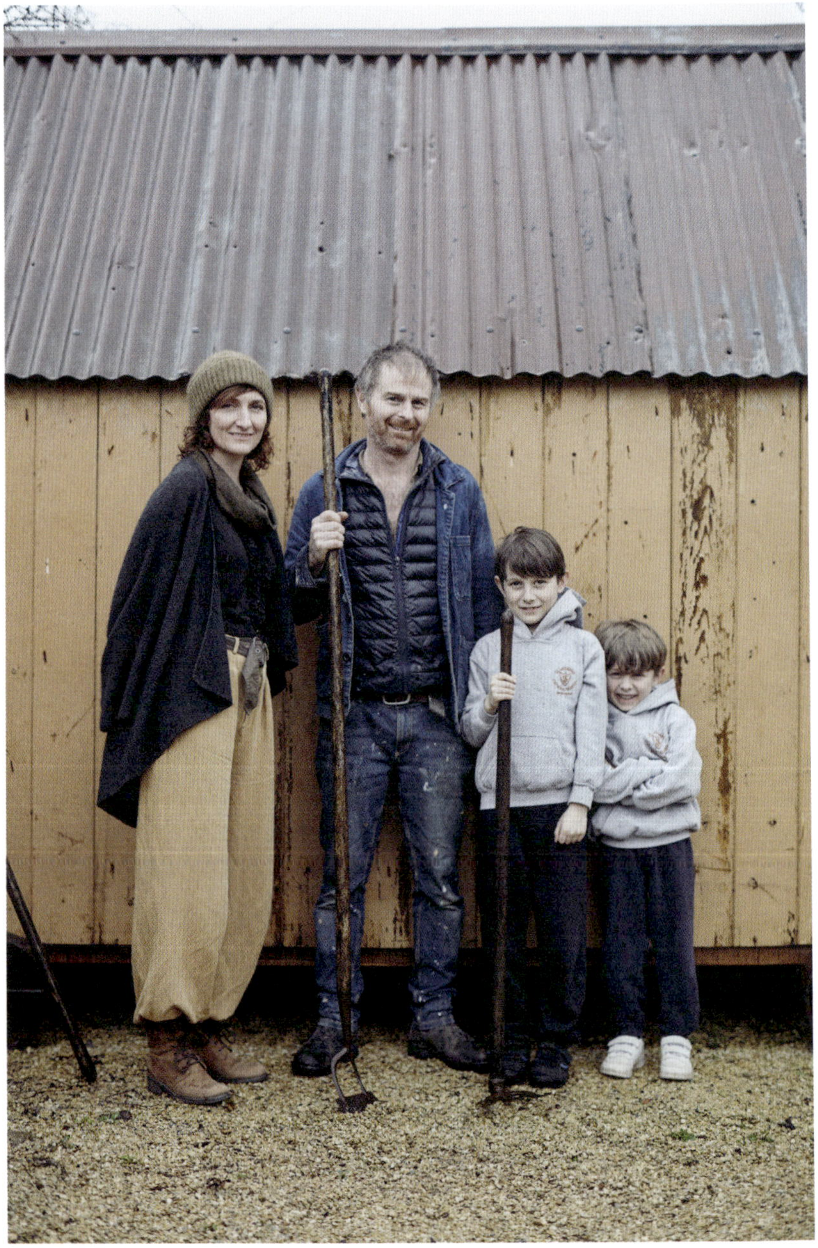

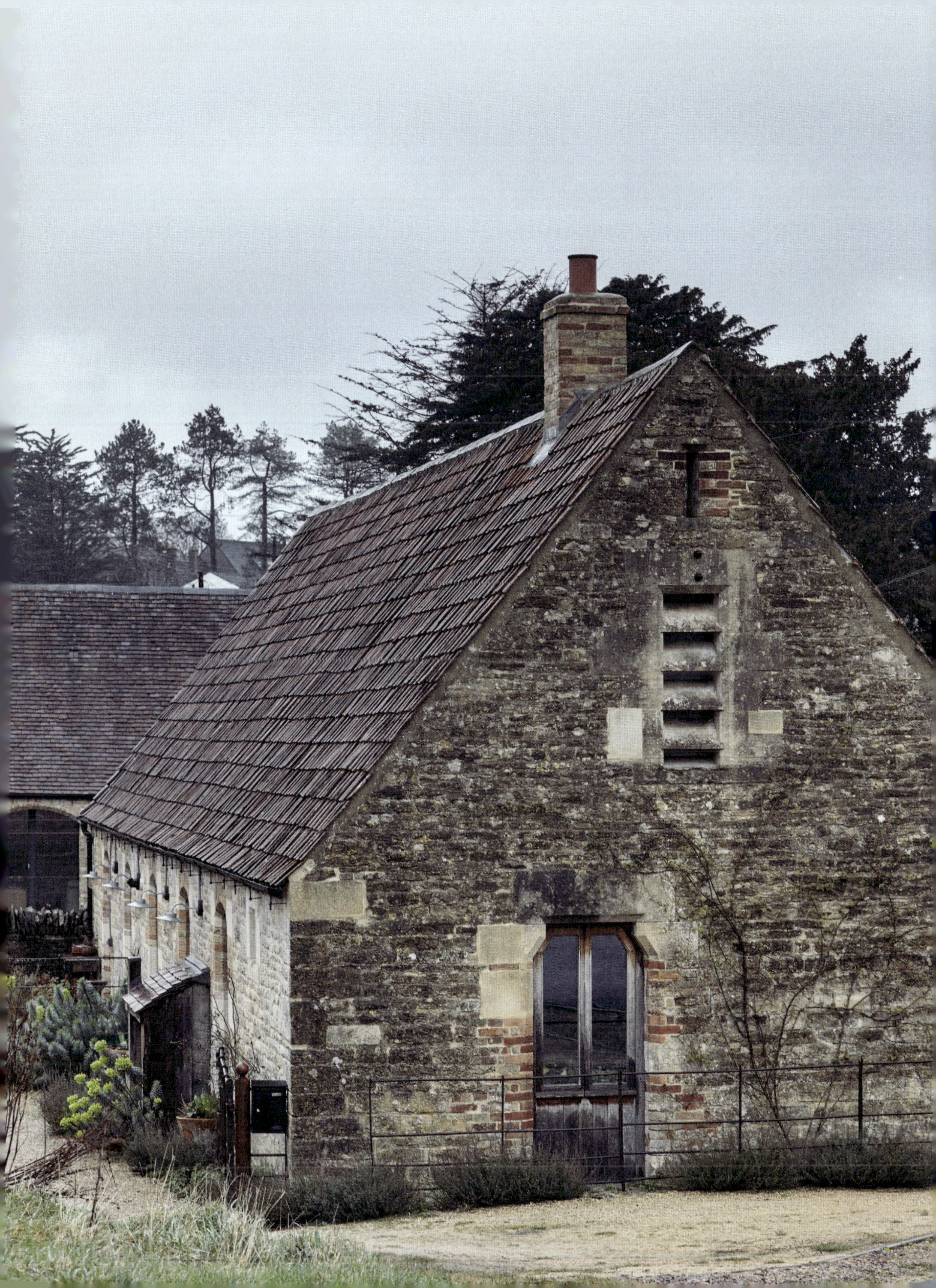

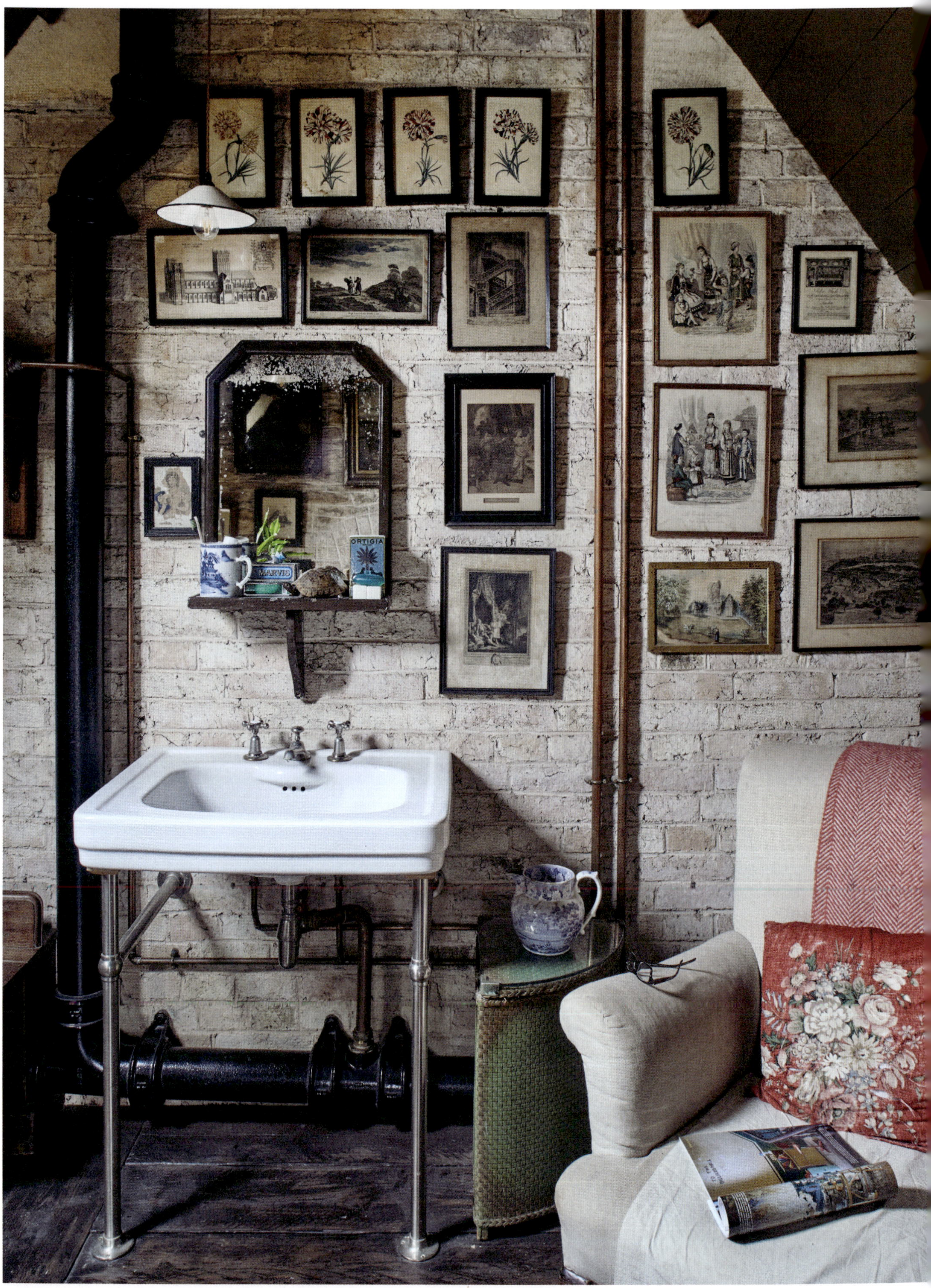
ORTIGIA
MARVIS

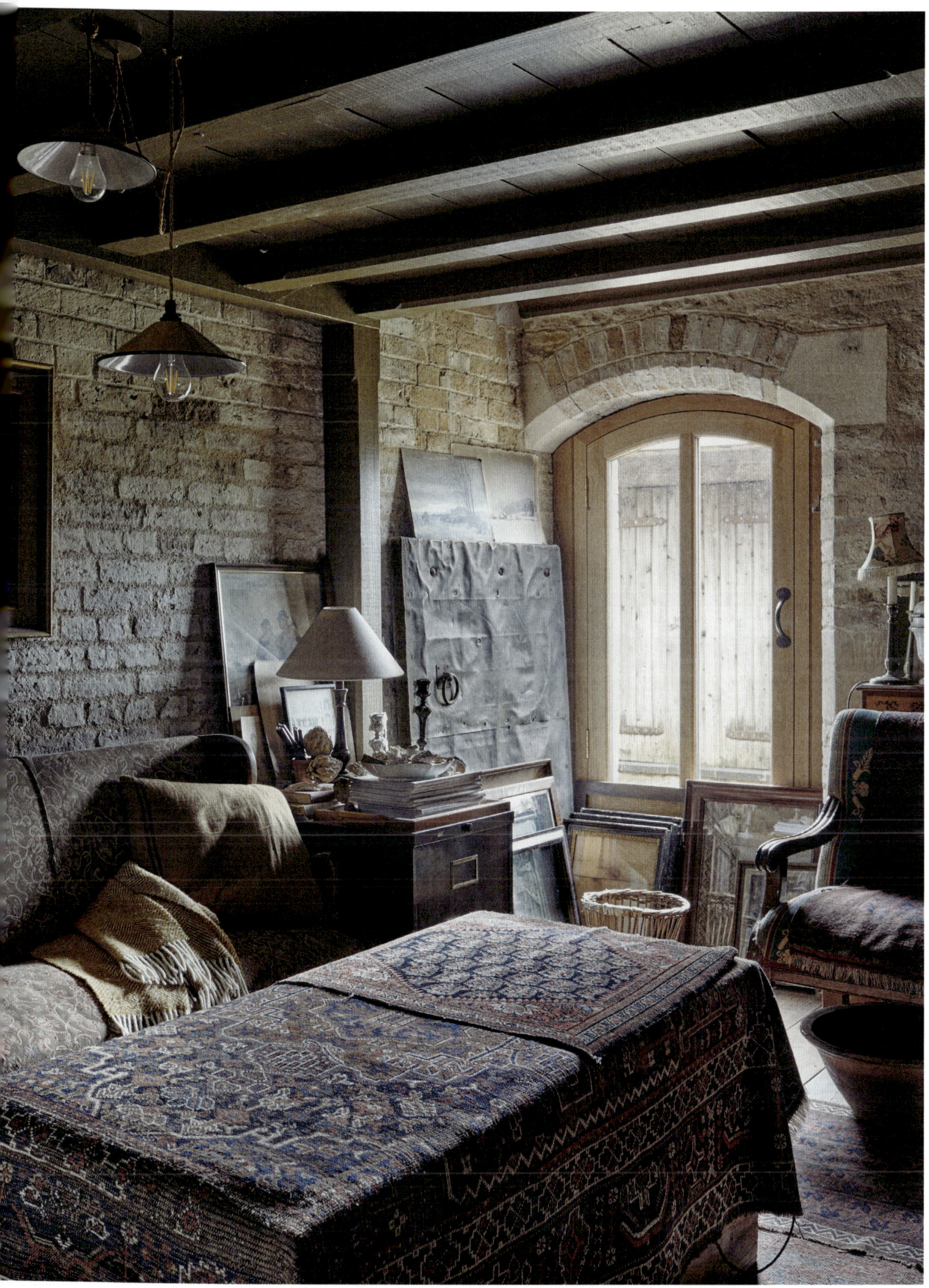

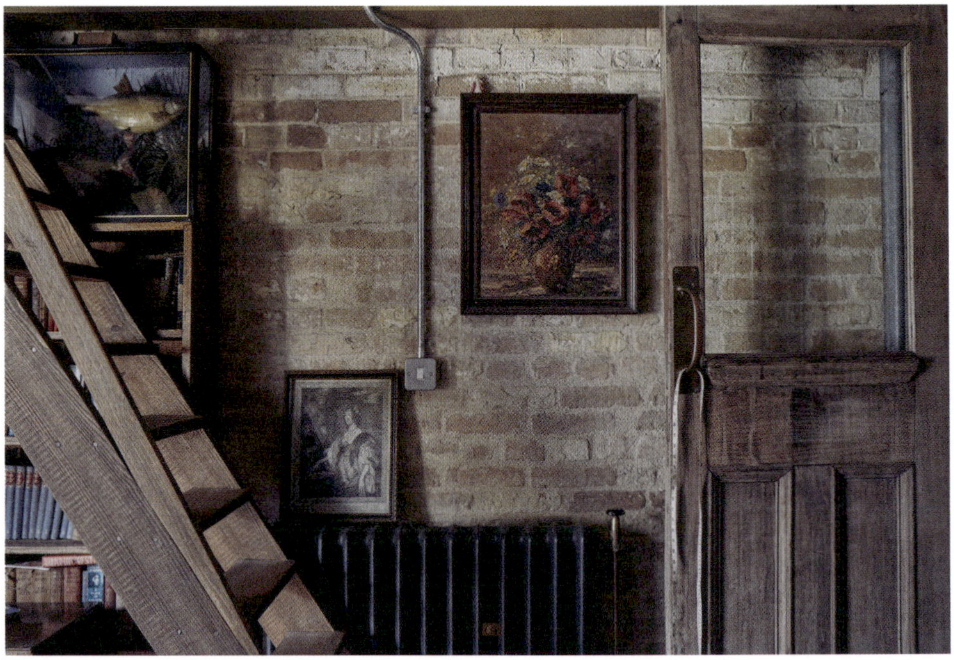

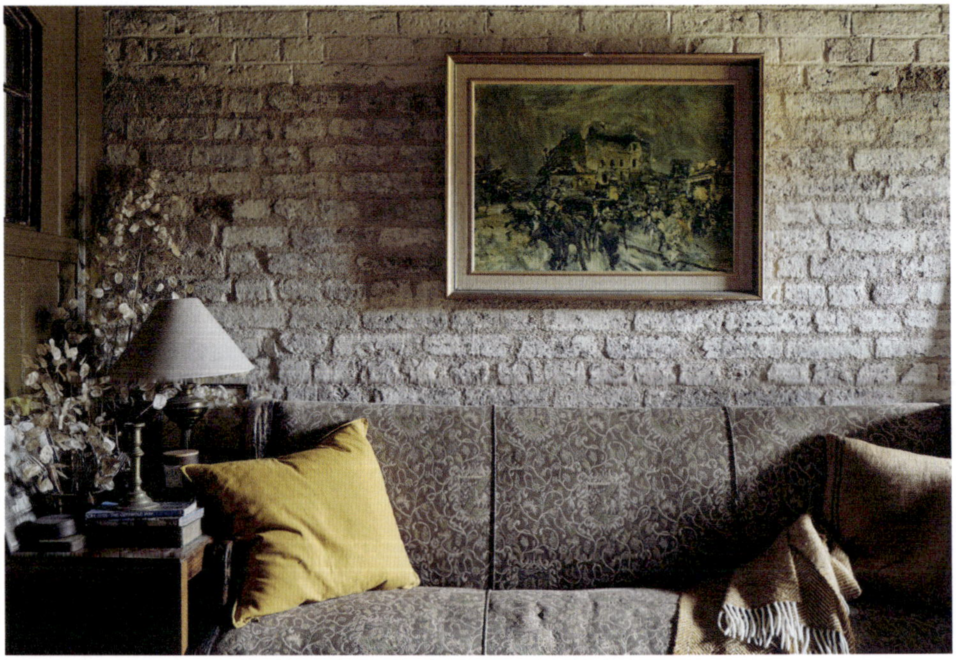

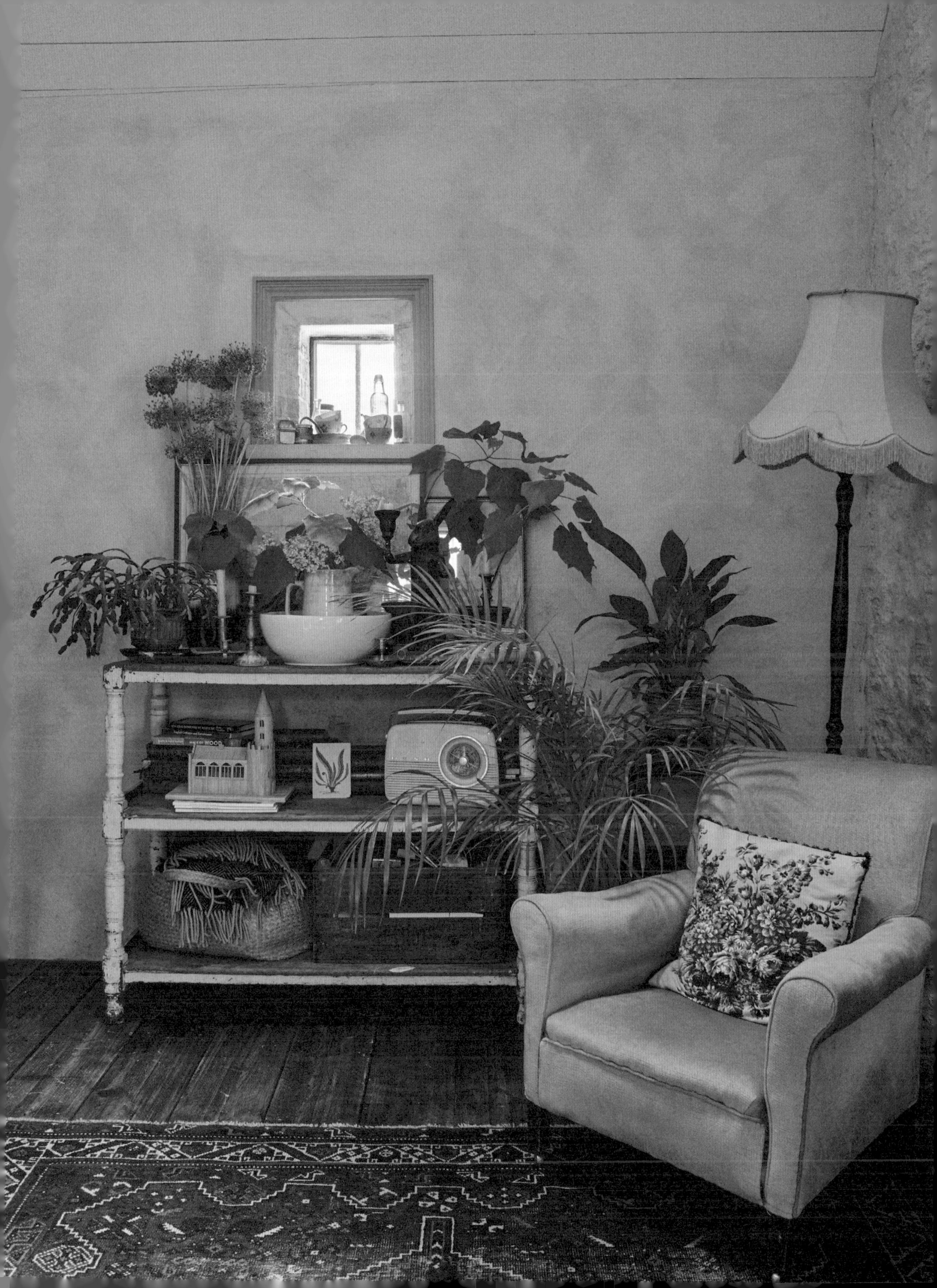

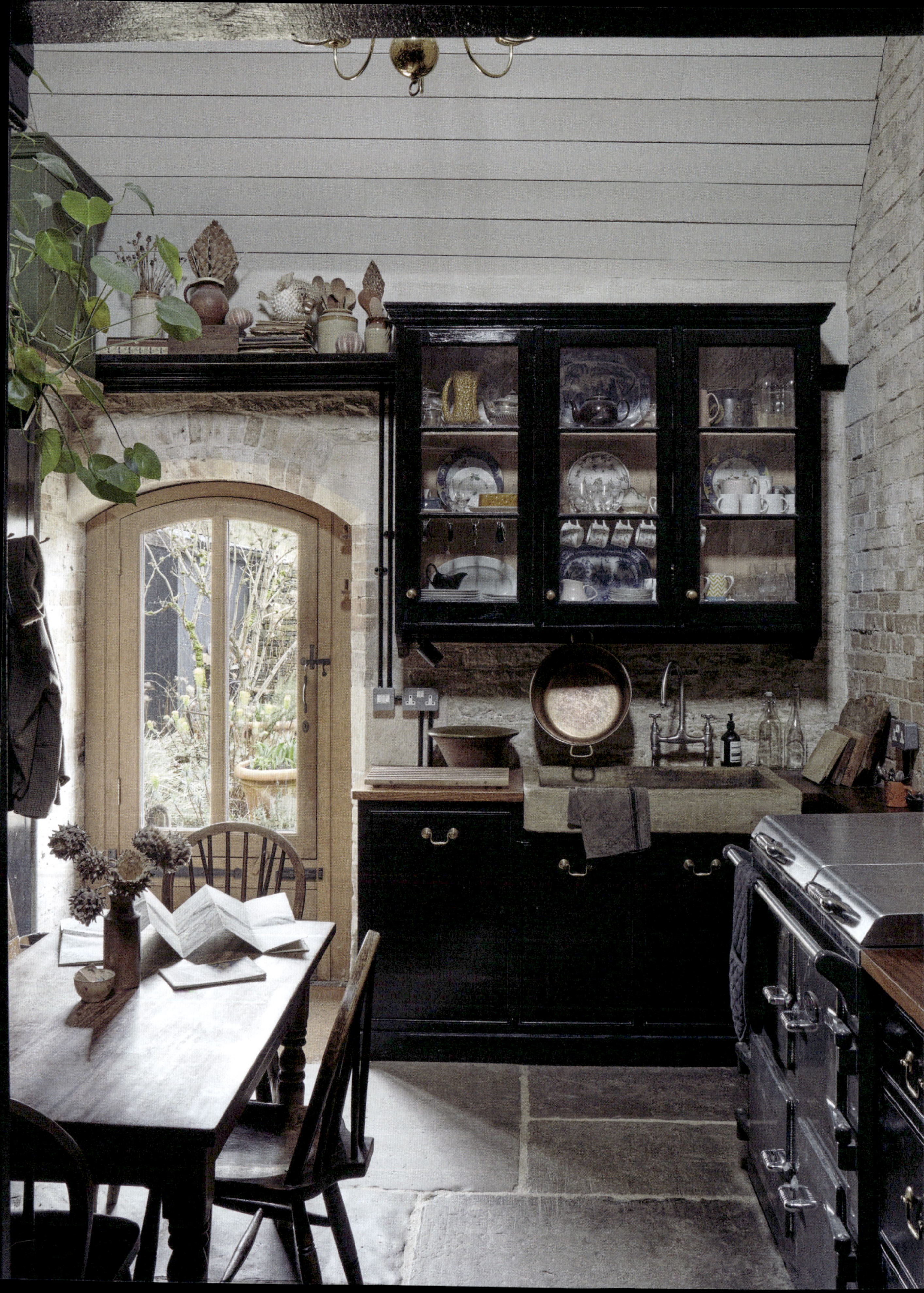

They worked from the ground upwards. For 170 years the whole building had stood on bedrock. To insulate it from ground level and allow the floor to breathe, Martin laid a base layer of blown glass which he describes as 'light as pumice' beneath limecrete. He then laid underfloor heating beneath either York flagstones or wooden floorboards made from reclaimed scaffolding. He could see that the pre-existing plans to plasterboard all of the walls would result in damp creeping in and knew that the walls needed to be breathable, so he stuck with what had worked for all those years and kept all walls exposed. Not a whiff of damp has come in and the rooms today are dry and warm.

Light could have been hard to come by in this long, low house. Doors provided the only daylight along its front face and there were only A4-sized windows along the corridor at the back. Martin and Elle designed doors with as much glazing as possible. As for the internal walls, all were structural and since the building was listed they were unable to build an upstairs floor as a single unit. They left the kitchen and sitting room double height and put in four staircases to access four upstairs rooms - each built as a separate free-standing structure. Building regulations prevented them from creating living space upstairs, but a casual comment from the planning officer hinted that bathrooms don't count as living spaces. So the bedrooms remain downstairs, and offices and bathrooms are reached above.

The whole place creeks with the character of times gone by. Very little is brand new, and Martin and Elle are proud when they find something imperfect to introduce to their home: a cracked sink, a worn armchair or a faded floor rug. Wood is reclaimed, colours are muted and materials are natural. Elle almost scoffs at the idea that she has brought style to the place. 'It's just utilitarian, isn't it?' She allows, 'I've always loved the appeal of a spit and sawdust pub!' The influence is plain to see, for in this well-loved, well-worn place where shoes stay on and people truly relax, the atmosphere does indeed recall the timeless and warm welcome of an old English pub.

To this day Elle marvels that Martin almost entirely single-handedly built this family home. 'On the very first day we met, I mentioned that I'd always wanted to create an utterly unique house of my own, and Martin with gentle gallantry replied, "Well, one day I'll build it for you." And so he did.'

'DESPITE ITS BEING

a humble farm building, we have discovered in the Gloucester archives that Longridge Barn was actually architect designed, by the rather eminent architect Benjamin Bucknell. So, these were probably the smartest styes of their time!' laughs Elle.

SOMETHING OLD, SOMETHING NEW

A place that combines peace and majesty perches high up in the Yorkshire Dales and is home first and foremost to nature, and second to the Leatham family.

Gentle Swaledale doesn't sing its history from the rooftops. It doesn't need to; its timeless beauty speaks for itself. The huge variety of wildlife and nature that thrive on its soaring moorland and in its fertile valleys are oblivious to the fact that they roam, grow, nest and feed among rocks and fossils dating back as far as 300 million years.

Some twenty-five years ago Oliver Leatham discovered this corner of Yorkshire when hill-walking the slopes where a glacier had forged its path over millions of years. The mellow majesty of the landscape captivated him – in particular a sheltered glacial bowl scooped out of the hillside. Held in the bowl was a farmhouse built in the stone that dots the dales and makes up the patchwork of walls that characterise this landscape. Oliver came back many times and, once married, introduced his wife Lucy to the area. Together they would soak up the landscape, nature, wildlife and history of the place. They would often stop to admire the house, Telfit Farm, which blended so well into the landscape that there were days when only a thin plume of smoke gave away its presence.

When Telfit Farm came onto the market for the first time in decades, Oliver and Lucy put in an instant offer. Lucy remembers the joy swelling in her. 'The house had perfect Georgian proportions, and almost every window gazed out onto the landscape,' she recalls. 'It had a palpably peaceful atmosphere. All I could hear were curlews and lambs.' It was, however, quite a project. The house had been divided into two dwellings, homes for the families of two farming brothers who had been born and raised here. The stone staircases and fireplaces, original beams and features had been maintained with care, and Oliver and Lucy wanted to retain such features while securing a future for the house.

'We decided to bring the two halves back together, creating large living spaces that made the best of the incredible views,' explains Oliver. They set about improving the house to make it as comfortable and as liveable in as possible. The downstairs rooms needed expanding in size and reducing in number since the split farmhouse had of course needed two of each room. Two kitchens and a staircase were removed as well as many stud walls. Single-glazed windows and warped, ill-fitting doors were taken out and replaced with double-glazed timber windows and Georgian-style doors, exact replicas of the originals, in keeping with the age of the house. Gradually a spacious, gracious house evolved.

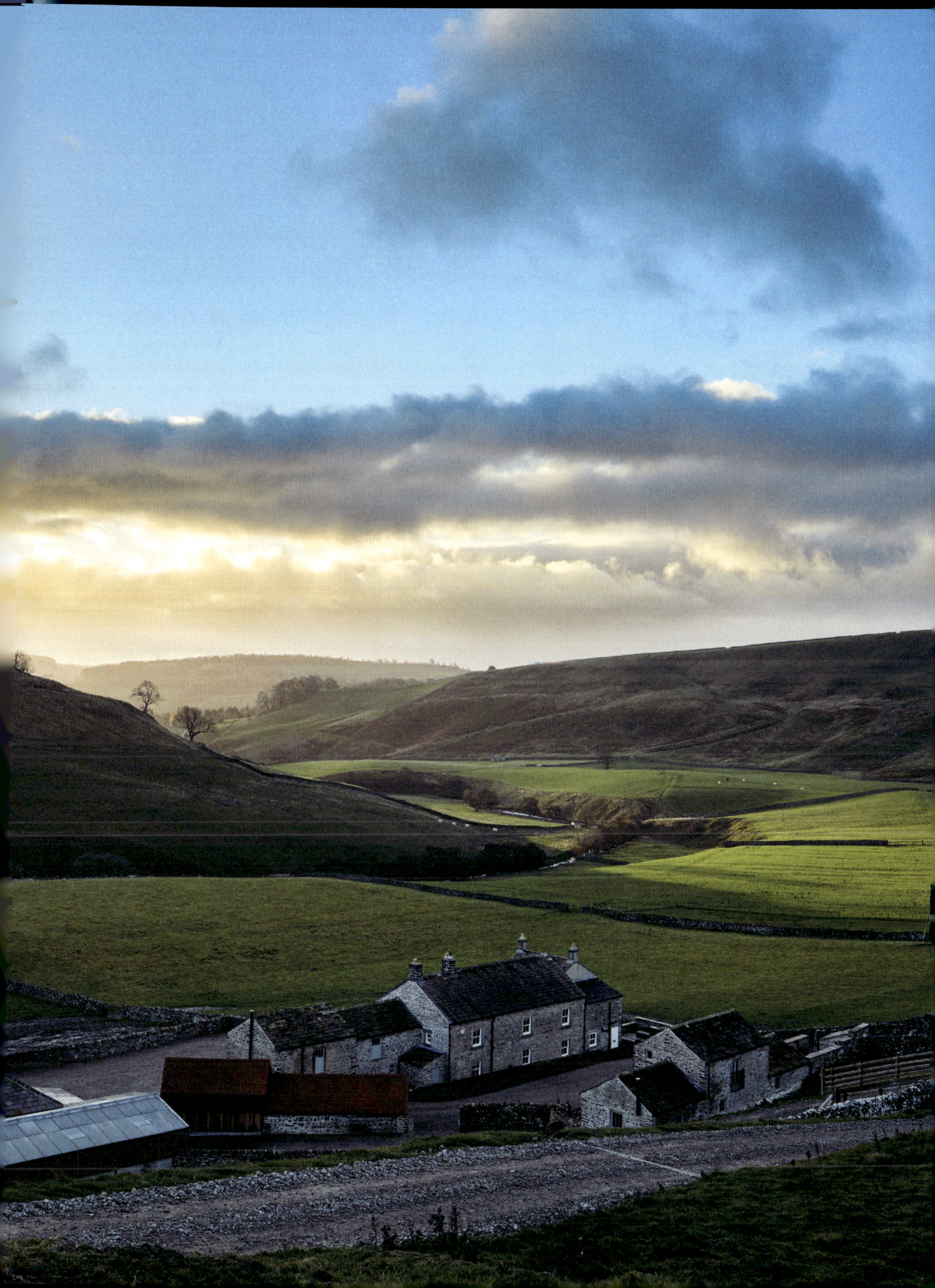

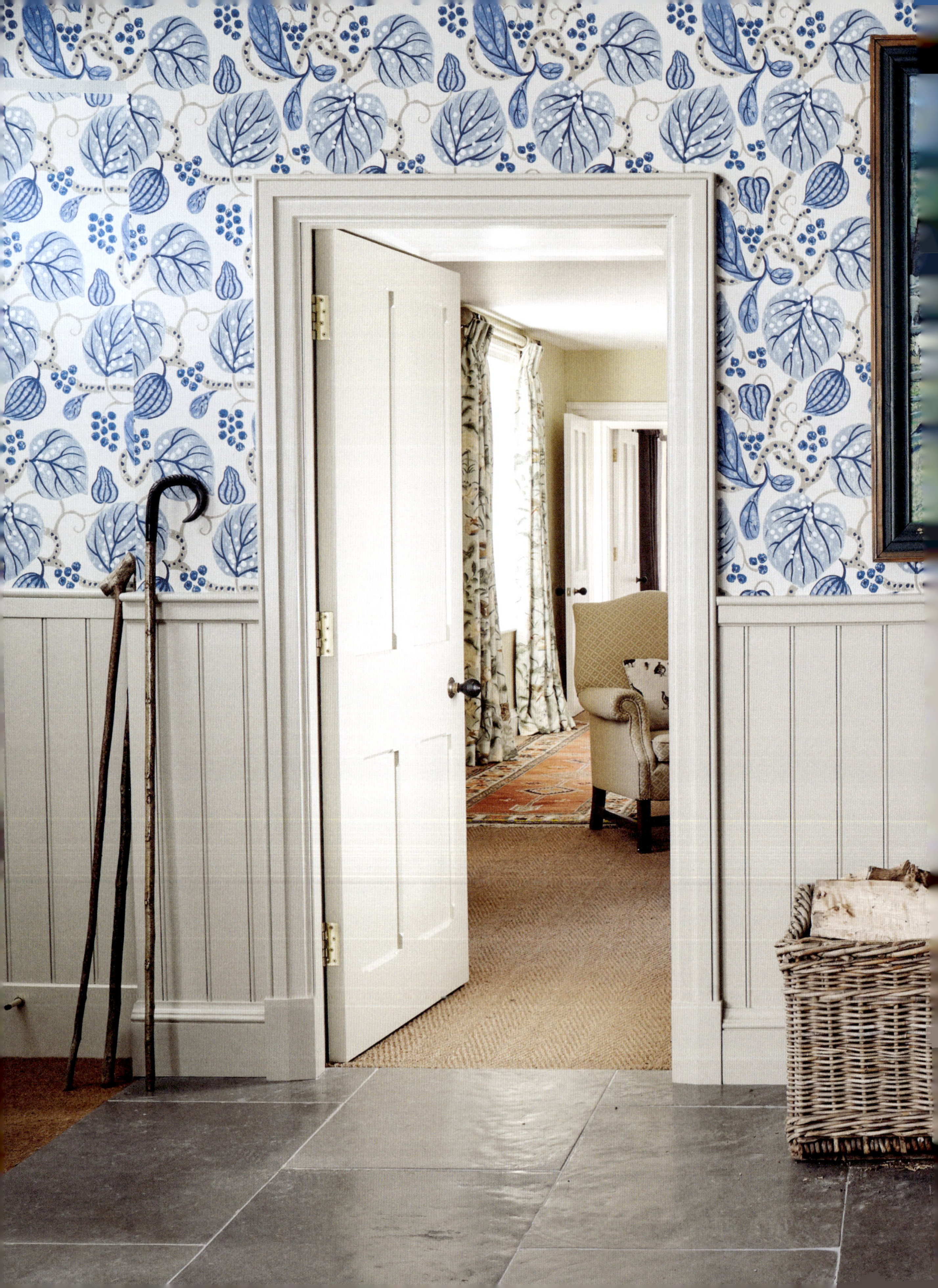

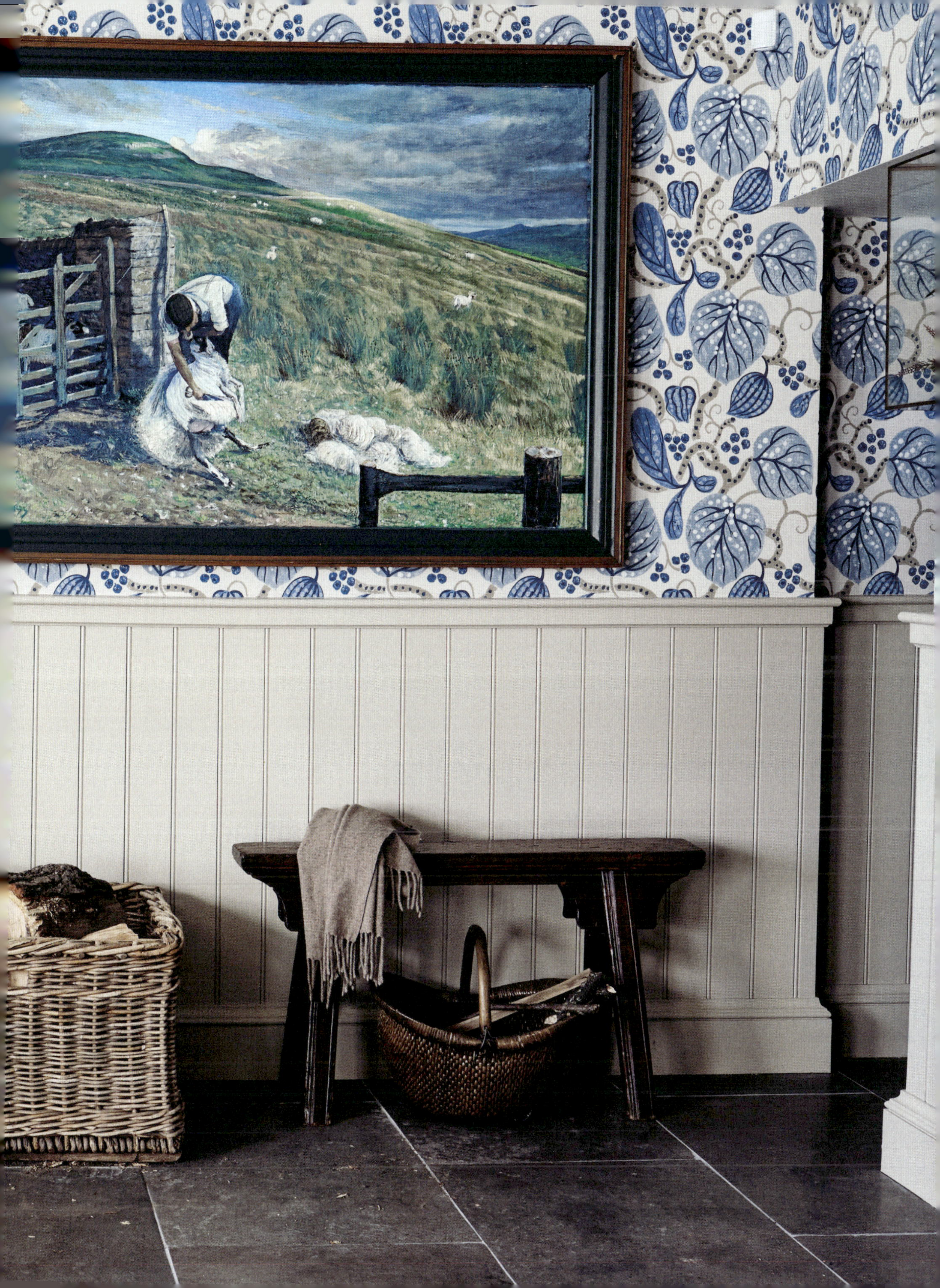

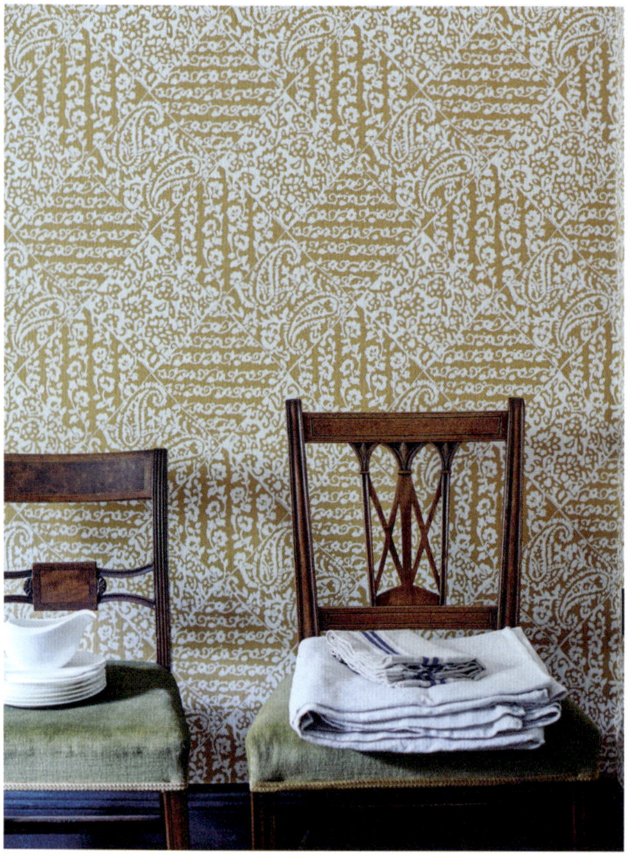

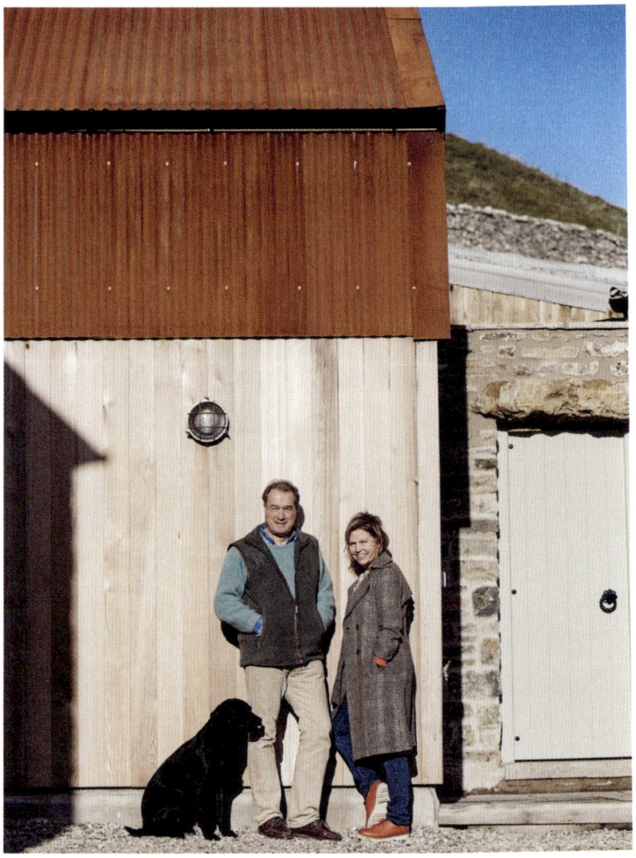

'MOST OF OUR ANTIQUE FURNITURE *comes from the local auctioneers, which means a lot of our furniture has never left Swaledale. The receptionist at the auction room laughed at us on our last visit, exclaiming "I see you've bought my aunt's linen cupboard!"'*

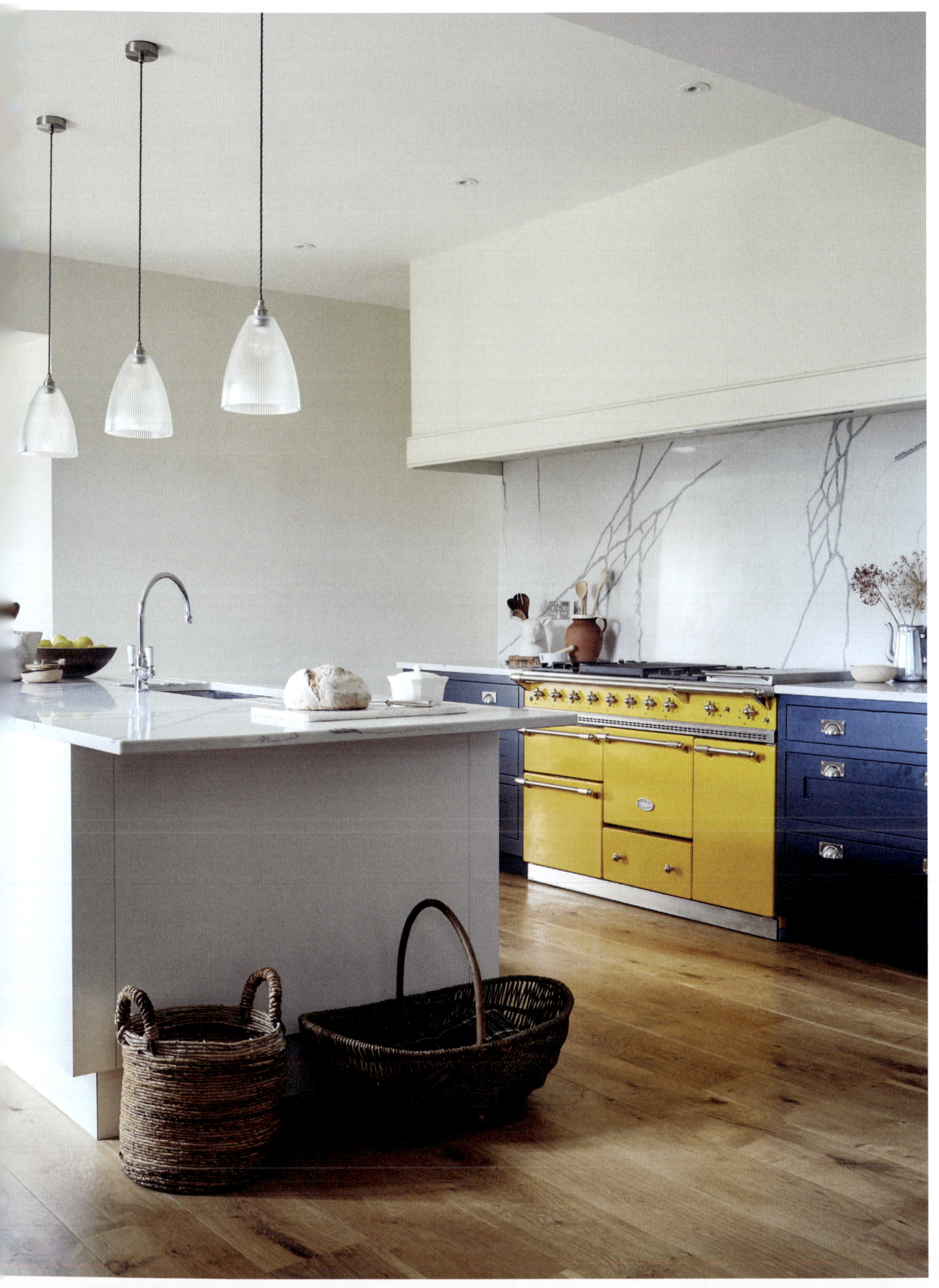

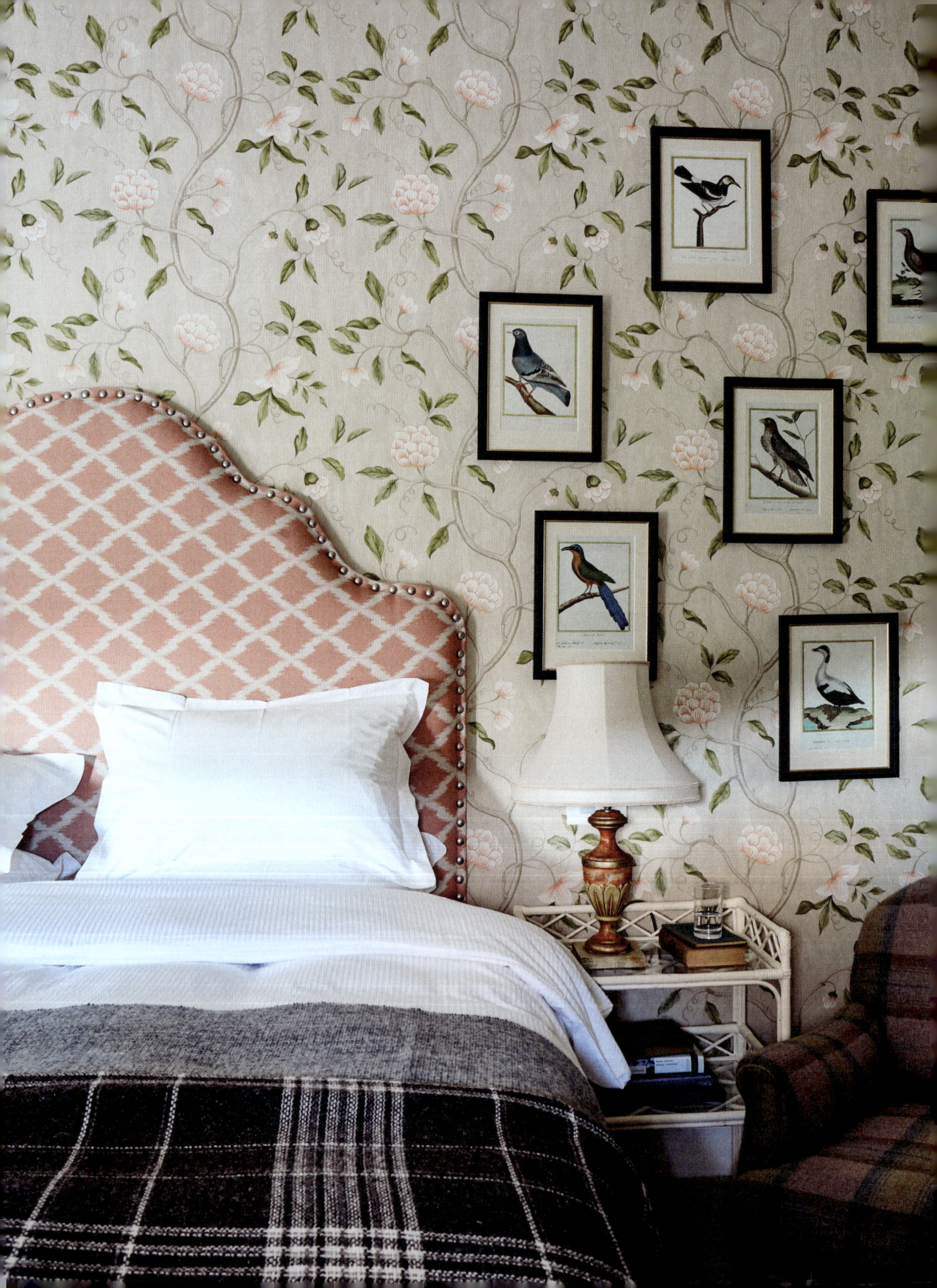

'We wanted to make it up to date without losing its heart and integrity,' explains Lucy, who realised that the way to do this was to mix old and new, majoring in classic style but introducing modern flashes. The new kitchen epitomises this break with days gone by - with navy units and a zingy yellow Lacanche oven taking centre stage. The more traditional dining side of the large room is a respectful nod to the house's heritage. Likewise, the other large reception rooms play with classic and modern furnishings and strike a stylish balance - the entrance hall, for instance, mixes antique furniture from the local auction room with contemporary bright blue floral wallpaper and a comfortable combination of old and new artwork and ornaments. The two sitting rooms have a traditional backdrop and are all about comfort with warm flashes of colour injected by the soft furnishings and artwork. Upstairs likewise is dedicated to relaxation. Eight bedrooms vary in size and aspect, but all share the same understated comfort. They each have a bathroom, and the Leathams again had fun choosing the occasional modern surprise to keep the house up to date.

Nature and wildlife are saluted and celebrated everywhere. Artwork featuring local birds can be seen on most walls, and a huge and glorious pencil portrait of a Swaledale sheep by an artist friend dominates the dining area. 'He may have a long line of ancestors grazing in our fields,' laughs Lucy. It's clear that the family have a deep respect and huge affection for the wildlife that surrounds their home and are an integral part of their world.

The house is a triumph of warmth, comfort and understated style, adapted faultlessly for modern life. It has however remained an intrinsic part of the landscape. Its combination of modesty and luxury sits naturally in this part-rugged, part-mellow landscape. It seems fitting that the house has, in the respectful hands of the Leathams, evolved a little more in its life journey, a blink of the eye in the evolution of the landscape surrounding it.

Telfit Farm is not currently a full-time home to the Leatham family and is available to rent for weddings, long weekends and holidays.

'WE CHALLENGED OURSELVES

to come up with a scheme to decorate in a style that was both classic and country without being too predictable, stuffy or old-fashioned.'

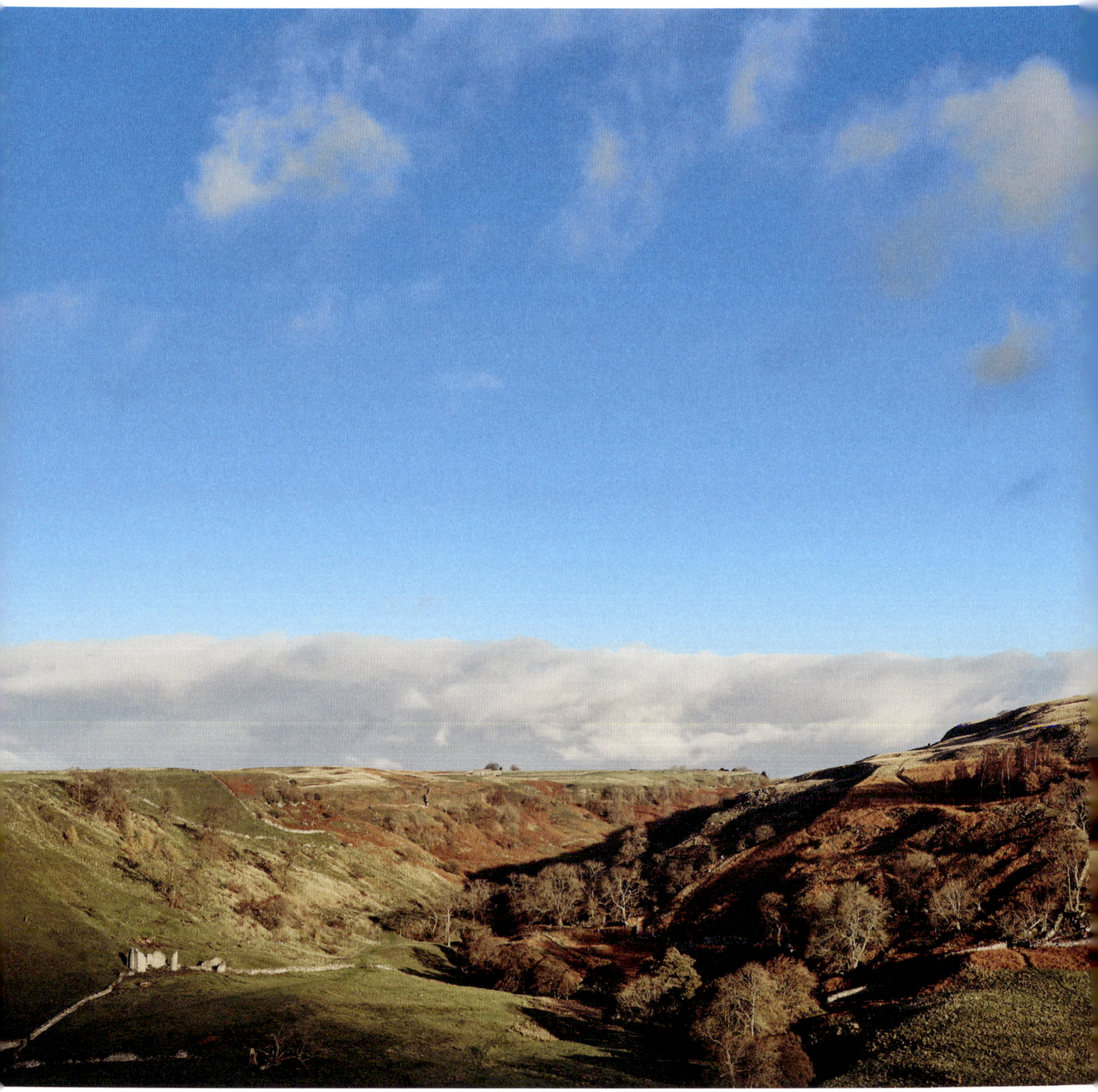

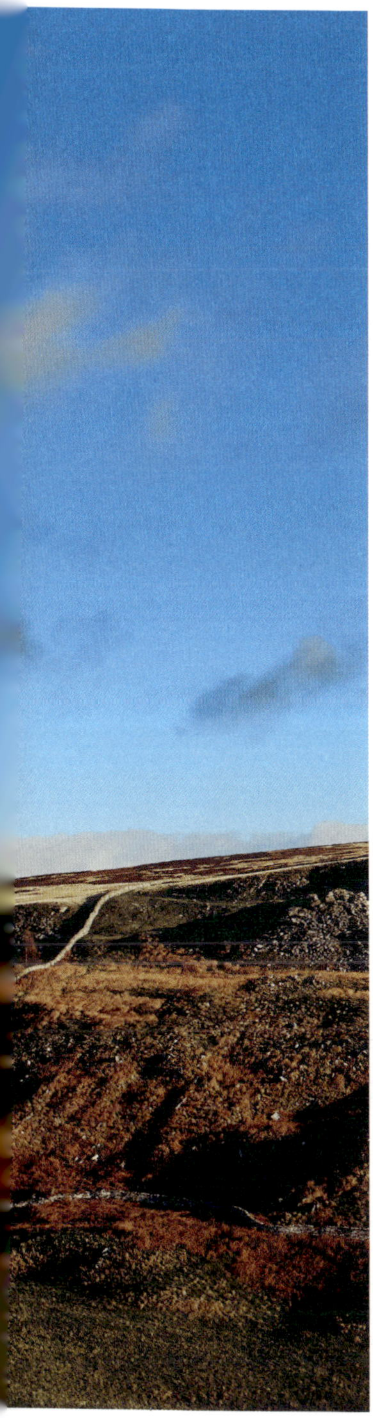
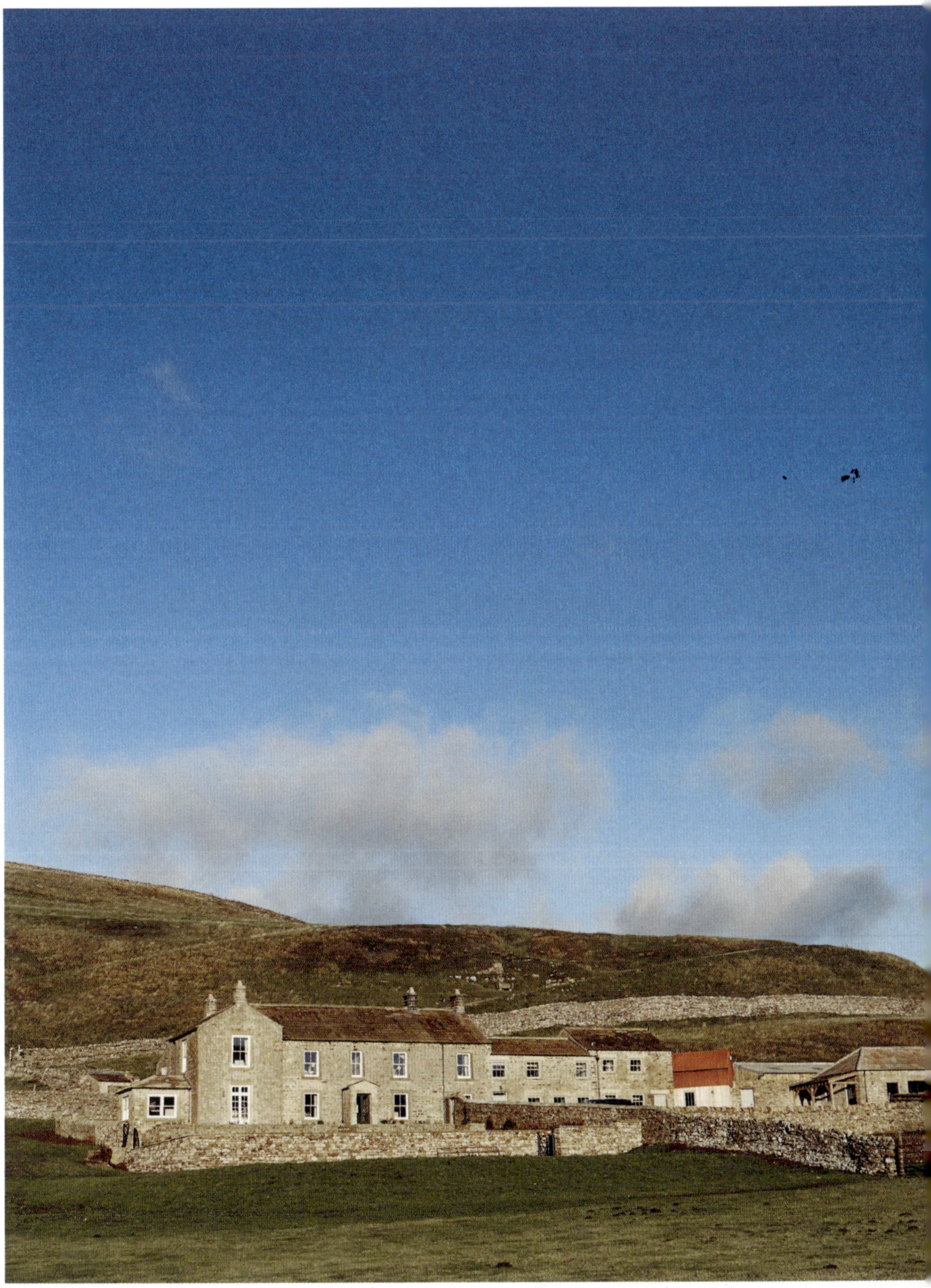

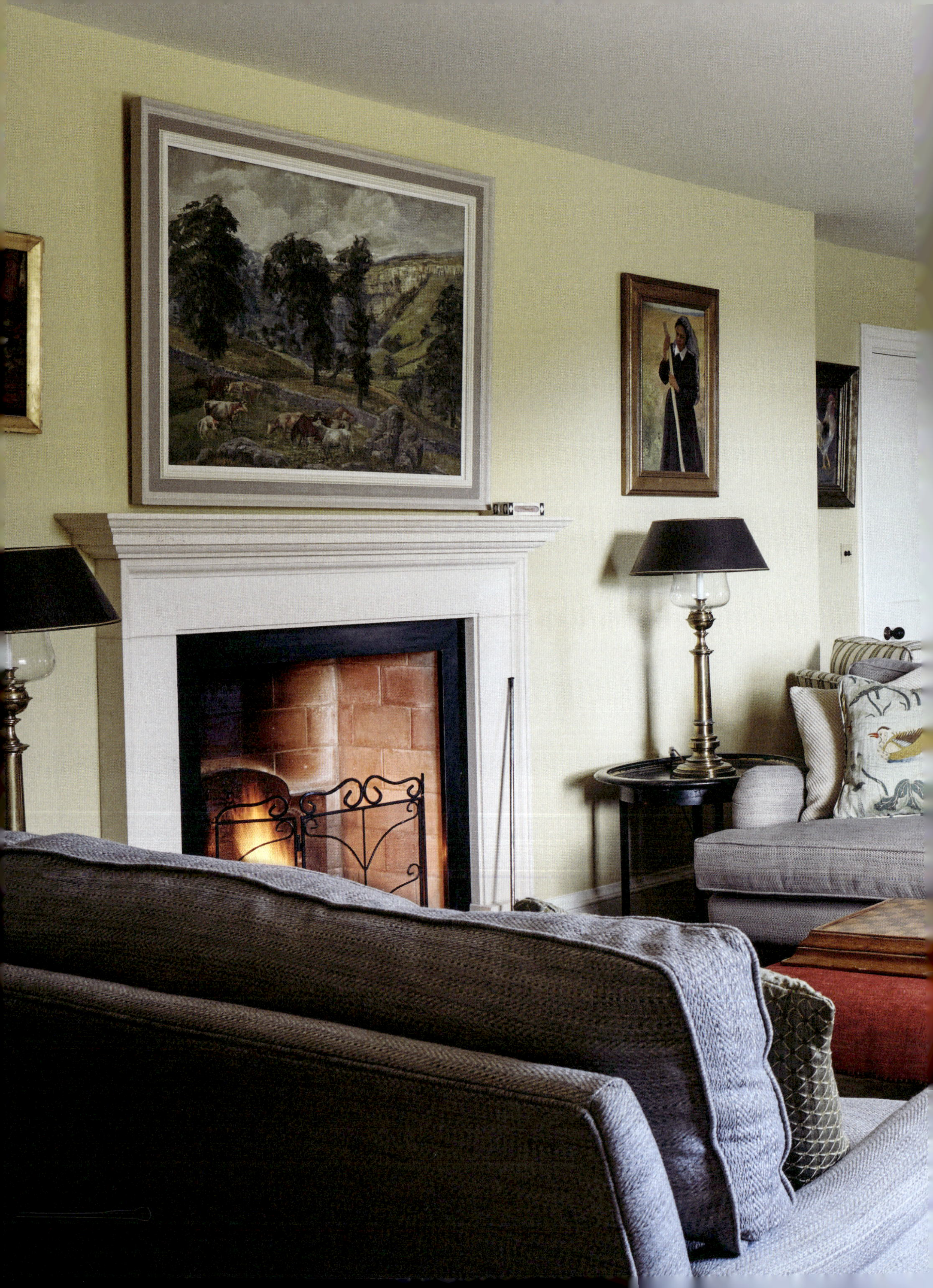

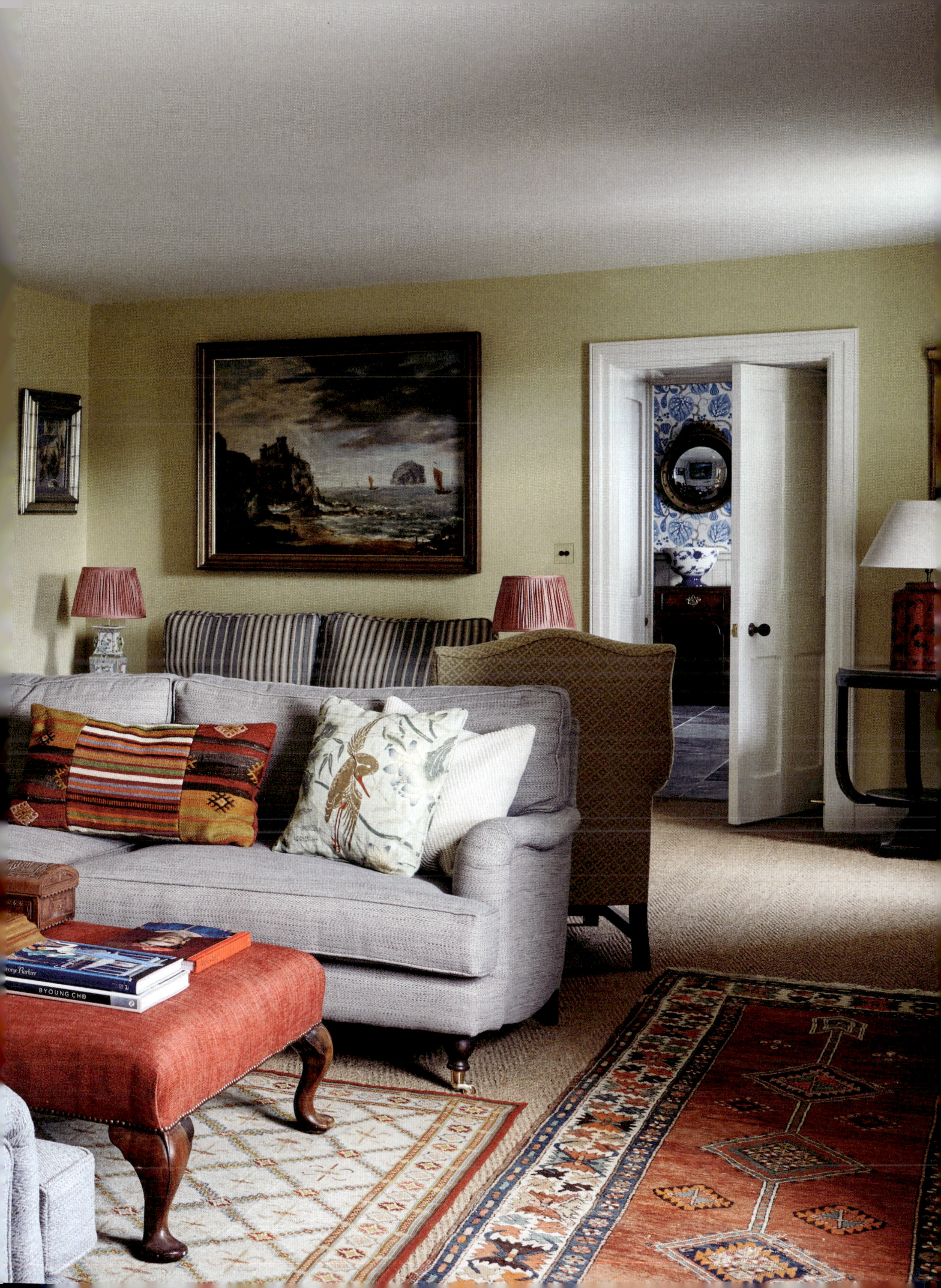
Barbier
BYOUNG CHO

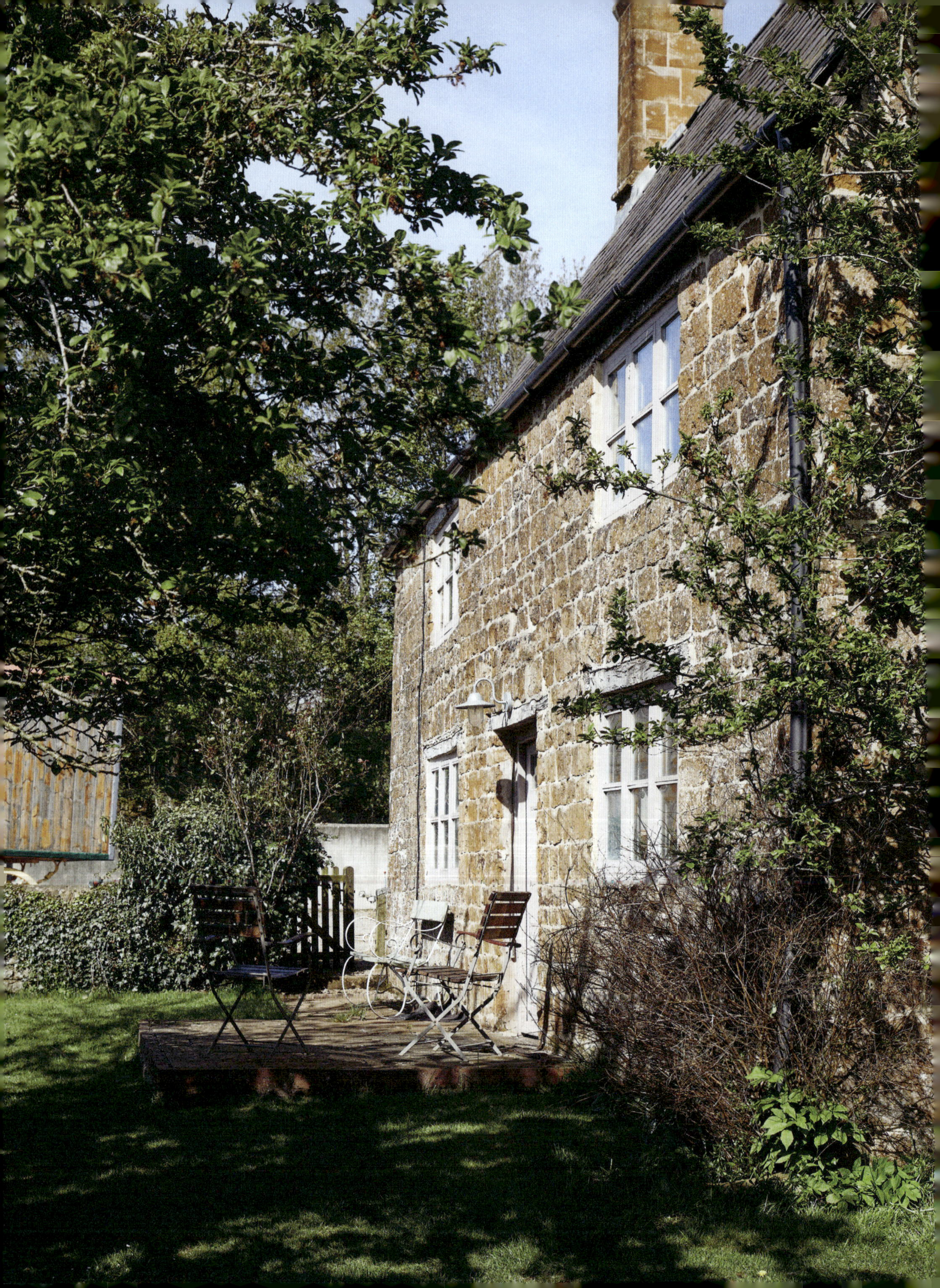

COUNTRY COLLECTIONS

A talented and creative couple have breathed a new life into a 18th-century dairy farm.

Polly McMahon has a passion for collecting. 'I don't just want one of something,' she admits. 'I want as much as I can possibly find.' And a brief look round her home confirms her confession. There's a windowsill crammed with terrier ornaments large and small, a mantelpiece laden with clock faces, a bathroom shelf glinting with dozens of hand mirrors, a basket full of dog collars (for pets, not clergy!) and a cabinet heaving with brown chequered china. The list goes on. But as eclectic - and eccentric - as the collections sound, they are quite at home in Polly, her partner Spike and their daughter Delphi's enchanting and characterful converted dairy farm.

When the family saw the house back in 2009, it was in a sorry state. Its interior had not been touched since the 1960s. Its defining decorative feature was a band of brown gloss paint that ran at waist height round all of the walls, to dog proof the rooms. Aside from a further lick of brown gloss every so often, the decor had not been touched for over forty years. Tired lino and threadbare carpets ran throughout, the walls were chilly and damp, and downstairs was a hotchpotch of dark rooms, curiously encompassing two kitchens as well as two sitting rooms. Upstairs were four outdated bedrooms and a dingy shower room. It was tired, to say the least, but Polly and Spike saw the potential it held, and relished the challenging project ahead.

Polly's expertise and business is in finding unique vintage pieces and selling them in her beautiful gypsy caravan The Totting Wagon (named after the age-old gypsy craft of bringing unloved antique furniture back to life). With this spirit for salvage, Polly was undeterred by the house's ragged appearance. Together with Spike, a master thatcher, she felt sure that they could make it the perfect home for their family and their battalion of pets.

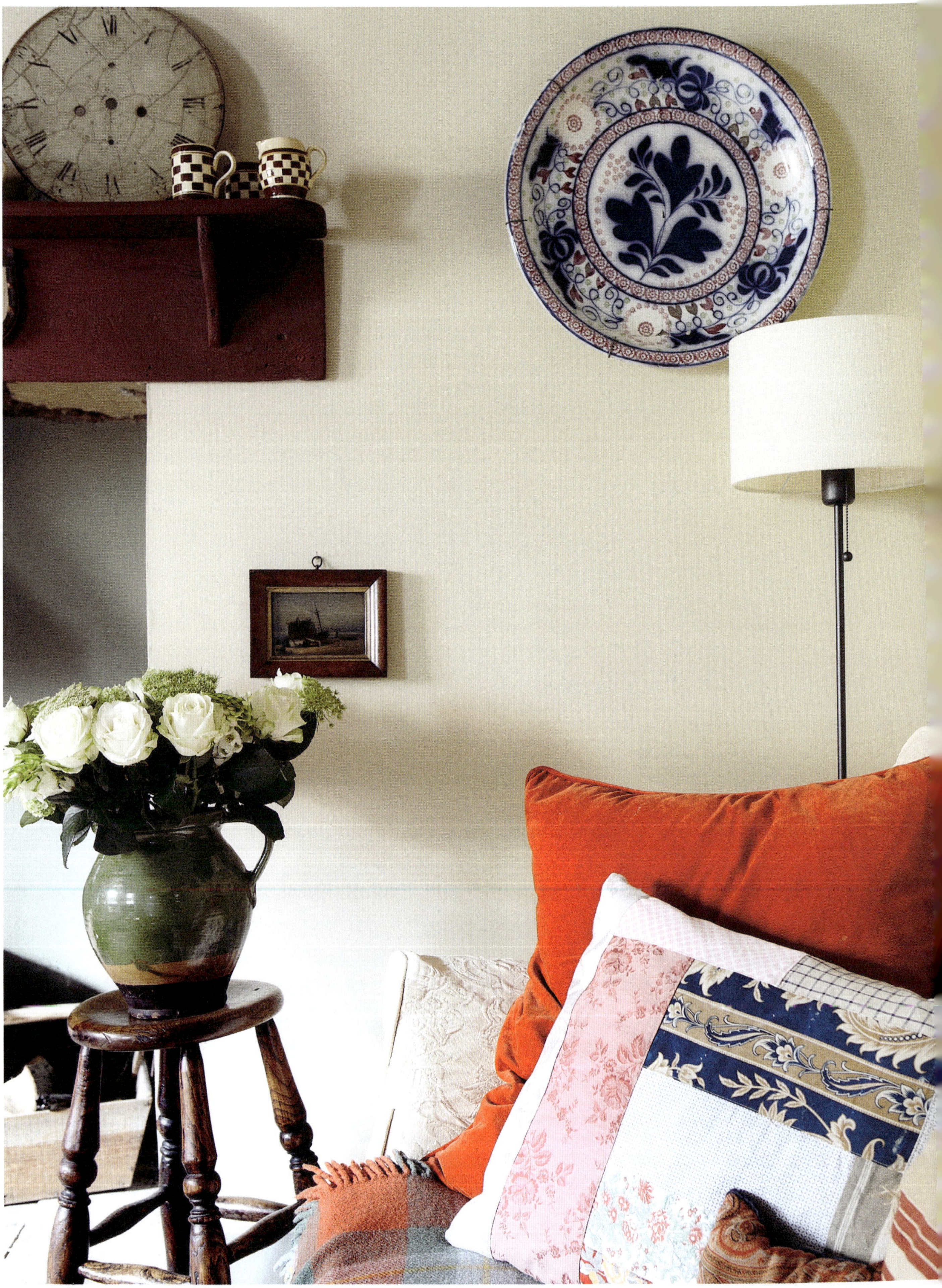

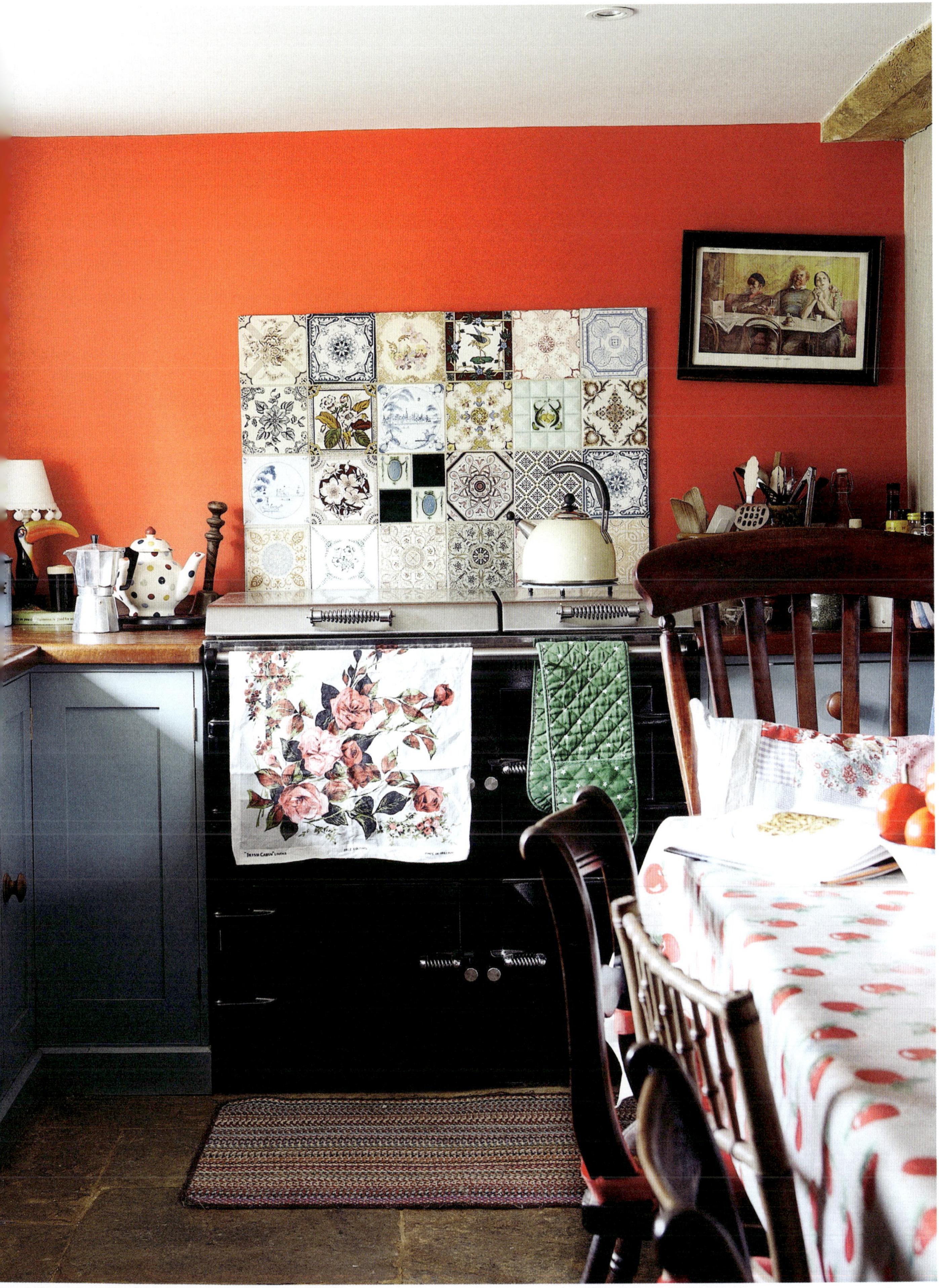

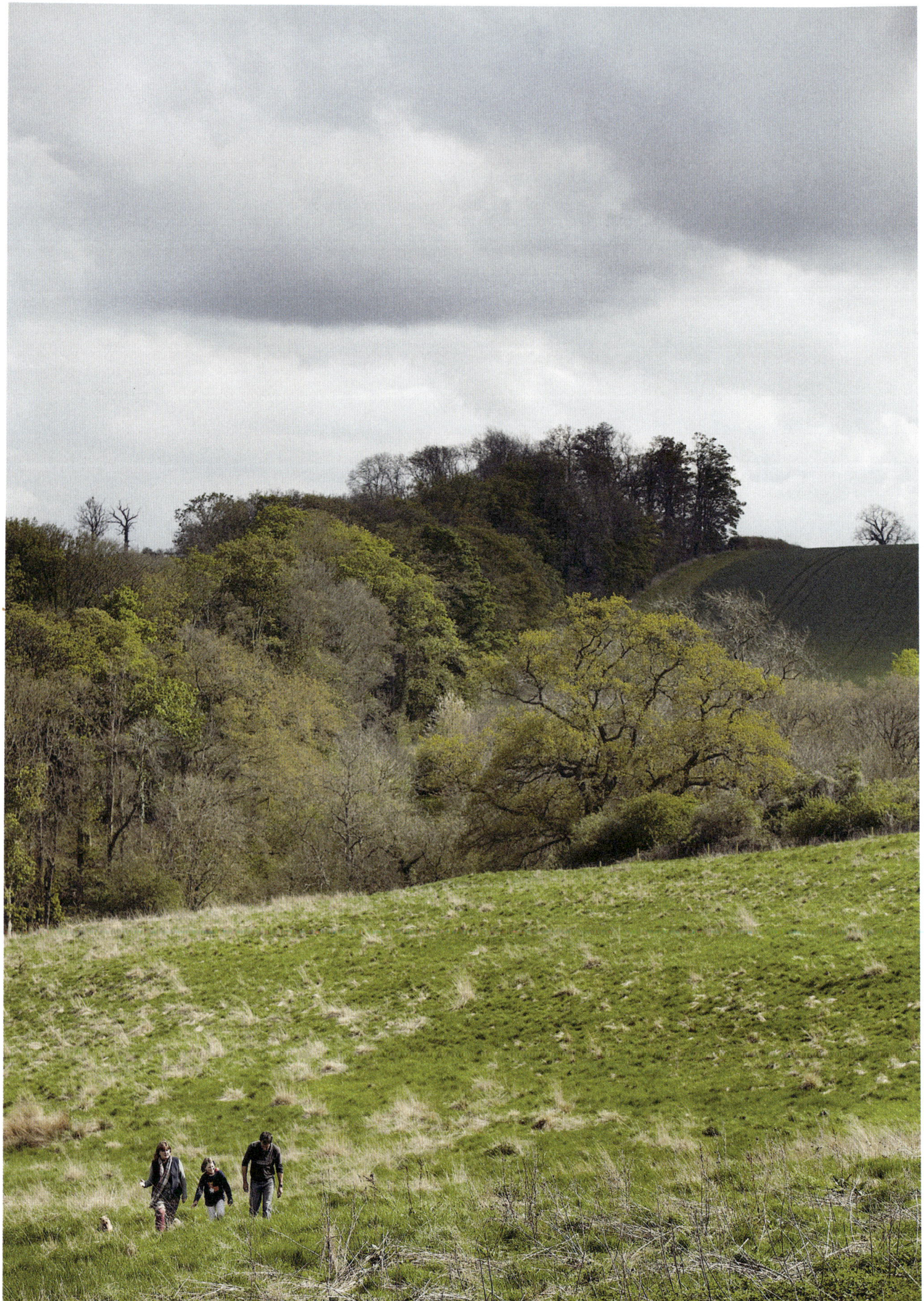

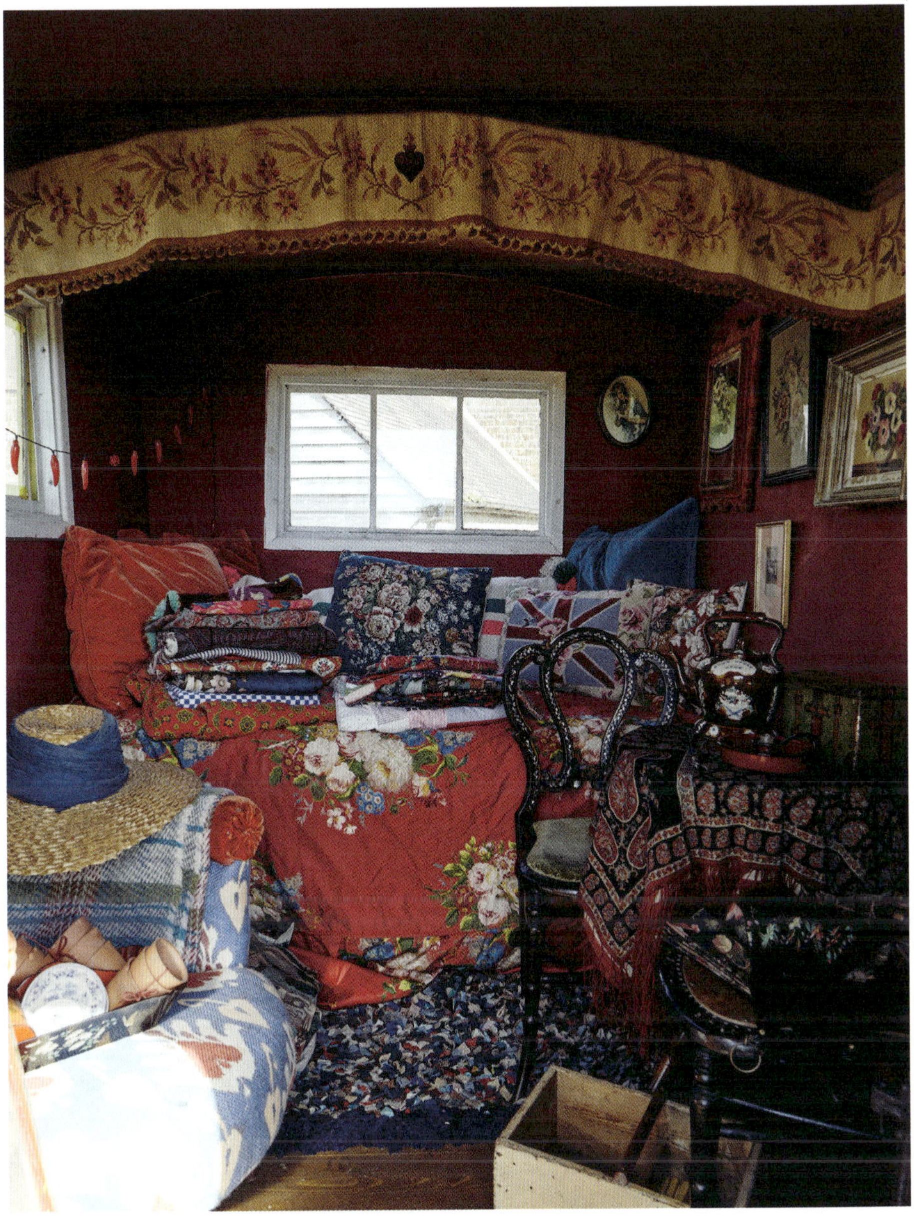

'MY OFFICE IS MY SANCTUARY,'

admits Polly. 'People tease me that it is more of a playroom than a workspace (which I can hardly deny since I do have a dolls' house and a few toys in there), but a lot or work goes on there too and my quirky bits and bobs give me inspiration. On the wall is a huge vintage sign emblazoned "Novelties" and this is what my business is all about.'

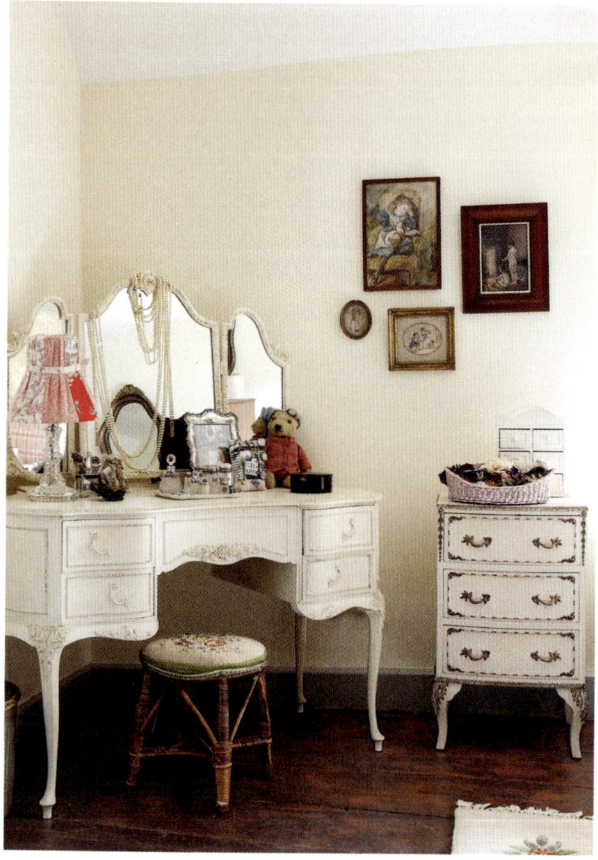

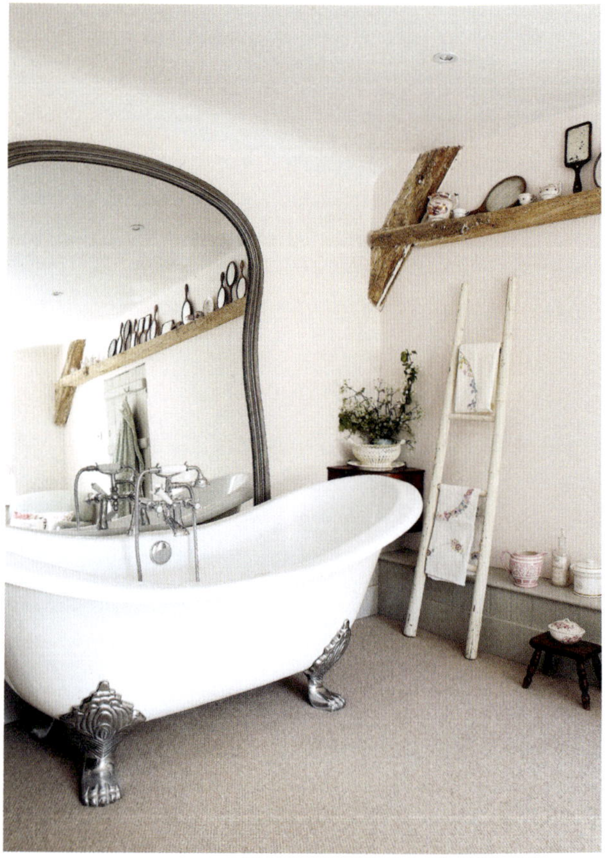

'I'VE BEEN COLLECTING

clock faces for years, in junk yards, flea markets, sale rooms, car boot sales or anywhere I can get my hands on them,' says Polly. 'I have an ever-changing display on the mantelpiece above the sitting room fireplace. To anyone else they probably all look the same, but to me, each has a unique character.'

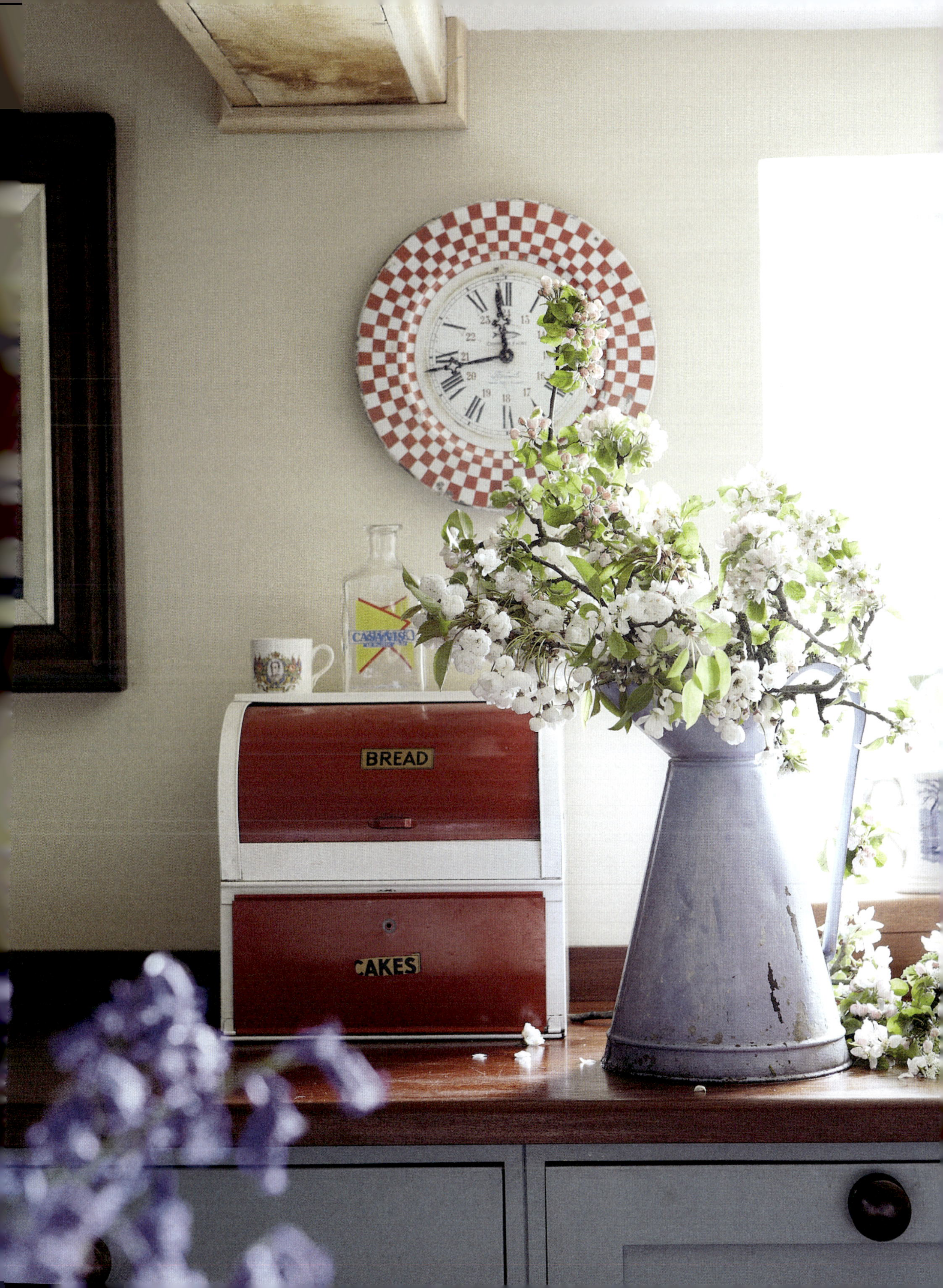
BREAD
CAKES

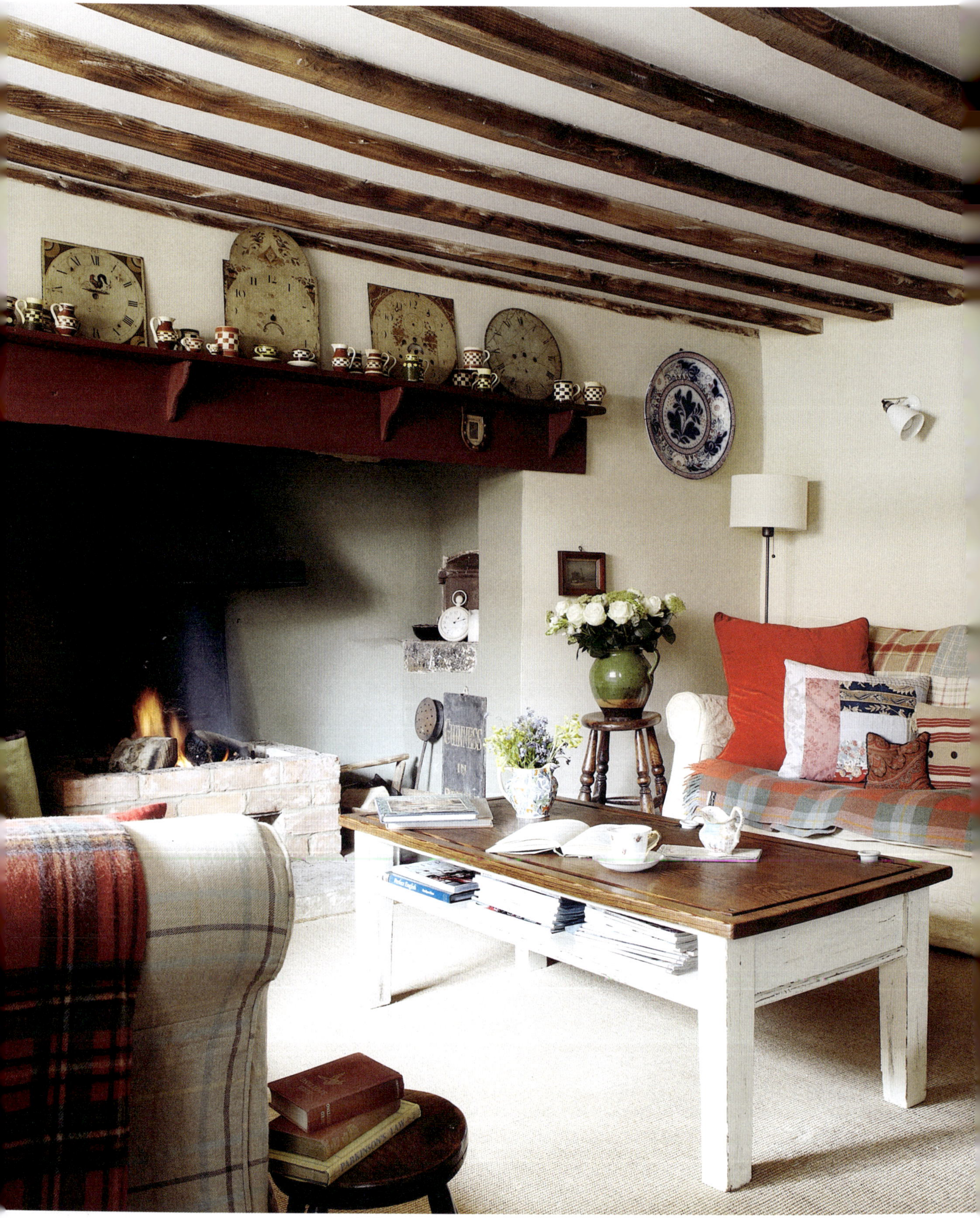
GUINNESS
IN
PARKINSON'S LAW

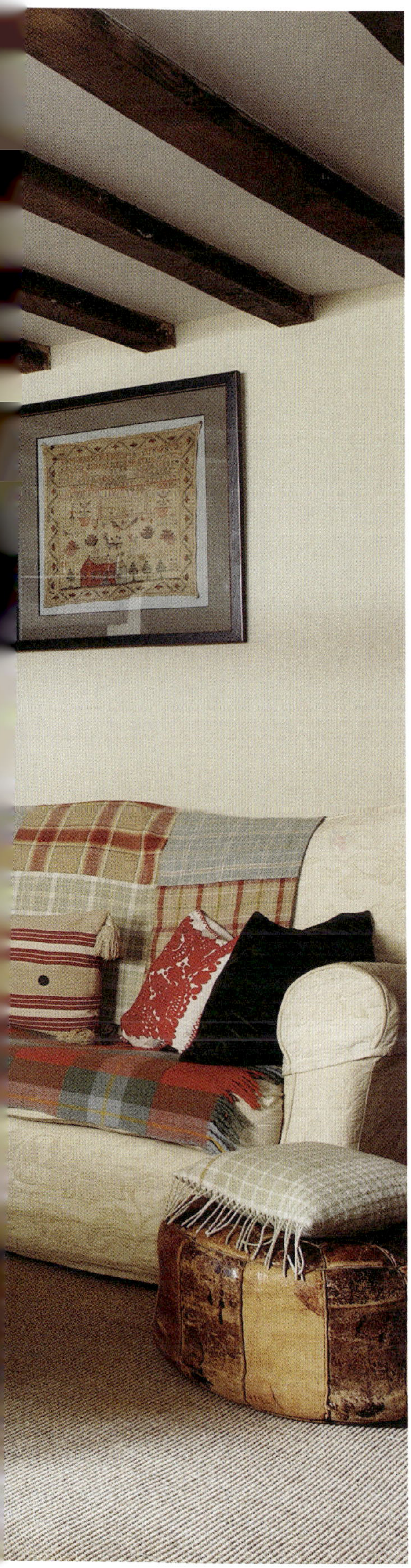

'We knew we had to take the house right back to its bare bones before we could begin to improve it,' recalls Polly. The couple set about stripping walls and hauling up layers of lino and carpets which - to their delight - revealed original flagstones and wooden floorboards that had been hidden beneath for decades. They turned the two sitting rooms at the front of the house into offices for each of them. They then set to work extending the kitchen, thereby losing the two existing higgledy-piggledy kitchens. One of these kitchens made the perfect - and obvious - sitting room, with a huge inglenook fireplace and cosy low beams. The other kitchen ran parallel to a dark corridor, separated by a wall that they took out to create today's spacious kitchen. The downstairs space now flows naturally from one room to the next, and in losing the dark corridors Spike and Polly gained larger, light-filled rooms.

The couple's talents have combined perfectly for converting their home. Spike's building skills have proved invaluable, as has his knowledge of local tradespeople, whom he has called upon throughout the renovation. Polly has a unique flair for finding beautiful antiques and vintage pieces in sale rooms and flea markets, and on eBay, which she displays about their home with casual precision. Every room in the house brims with quirky and wonderful pieces and each room is unique. Polly's favourite is her study, which she refers to as her playroom, a room which blends business with pleasure. It makes perfect sense that, from a room so personal and inspiring, Polly runs her thriving business.

What gives the house its character is that many items within it tell a story. There are family heirlooms that Polly remembers from her parents' and grandparents' homes, and new items that she has stumbled upon or bid feverishly for. The cast-iron bath (it took four burly men to carry it up a narrow staircase) was an eBay bid. Polly was so delighted with it that when it arrived that she was found by Spike, sitting triumphantly and fully clothed in it in the entrance hall before it had been heaved upstairs.

Such one-off finds - combined with heirlooms, antiques and Polly's quirky collections - are quite at home in this 18th-century dairy farm, and add to the feeling that the house has refound its original character. It is hard to imagine that it has ever been anything but the bustling and beautiful family home it is today.

ARTISTIC IMPRESSIONS

A historic house that has grown and evolved over its three decades as home to artist Annabel Playfair and her four children.

Stooped doorways, wonky beams and vast inglenook fireplaces fill Annabel Playfair's 18th-century home with character, and there's a sense of history at every turn. Still, there's a contemporary twist to its light-filled rooms with wide views across a sweep of lawn to the rolling hills beyond. One-off pieces of art are part of a collection built up over the years that is displayed beside a large number of Annabel's own oil paintings. They range from dramatic seascapes to those landscapes stretching from her doorstep, as well as still lifes and vibrant interiors with figures. 'I love colour,' Annabel admits as if sharing a secret, and one look at her paintings, and indeed her home as a whole, makes it clear that she has an exceptional eye for it.

Located in a quiet Warwickshire village, the roomy farmhouse was perfect for a growing family. It also had the bonus of stables, which meant Annabel could relaunch her other great love: horse riding. All of the children subsequently learnt to ride, and blissful childhood days were spent exploring the local countryside on horseback.

The family loved getting to know their new home and her children soon discovered its quirky hidden period features. A hidden salt cupboard was found in an inglenook fireplace in the oldest part of the house; salt was essential for food preservation and was kept there to prevent it from becoming damp. A misshapen 200-year-old door was an air vent to the original pantry. And in the attic, behind generations of wallpaper, they discovered the name of plasterer John Perkins, dated 1793 and written in plaster with his own finger. Beside it were two further signatures and the intriguing words 'We come up here, with candles lit, but do not need them, not a bit.'

Though the house retained its charm, it was beginning to show its age. With her creative talent, Annabel was just the person to breathe new life into it and to adapt its living spaces to suit modern family living. While the house was cosy and characterful, there was no large living space and the kitchen was small and dark. 'I'd always dreamed of creating a large eat-in, live-in kitchen,' says Annabel. An oak-framed extension completed in 2001 gave her exactly that – with a huge table in the middle, a cosy area with sofas round a fireplace and a ceiling soaring into the rafters, it serves every purpose. A similarly sized extension added space to the living room, joining it to a stable that has subsequently been turned into a spare bedroom. Moving the main staircase opened up the hallways and brought more light to this central part of the house.

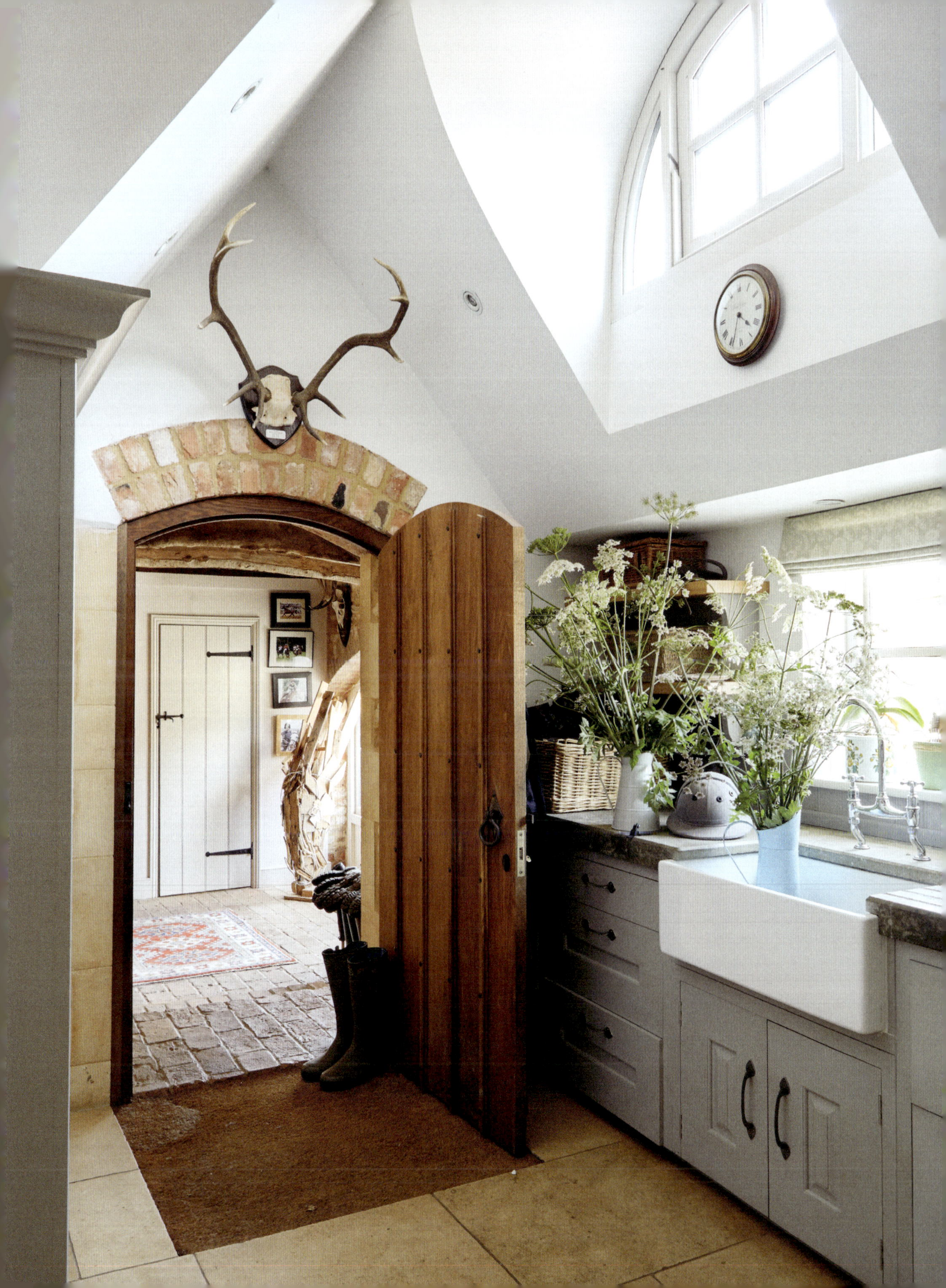

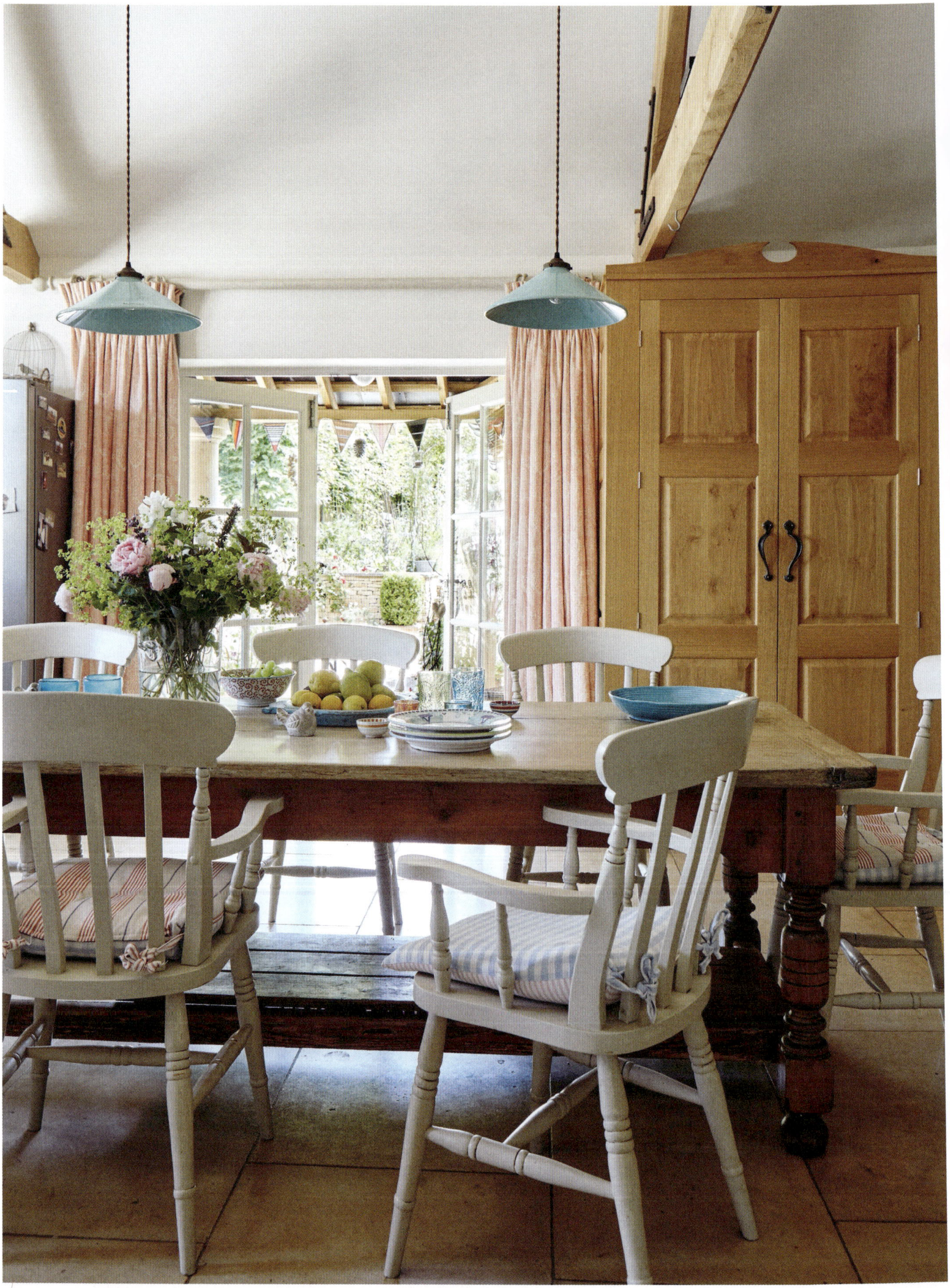

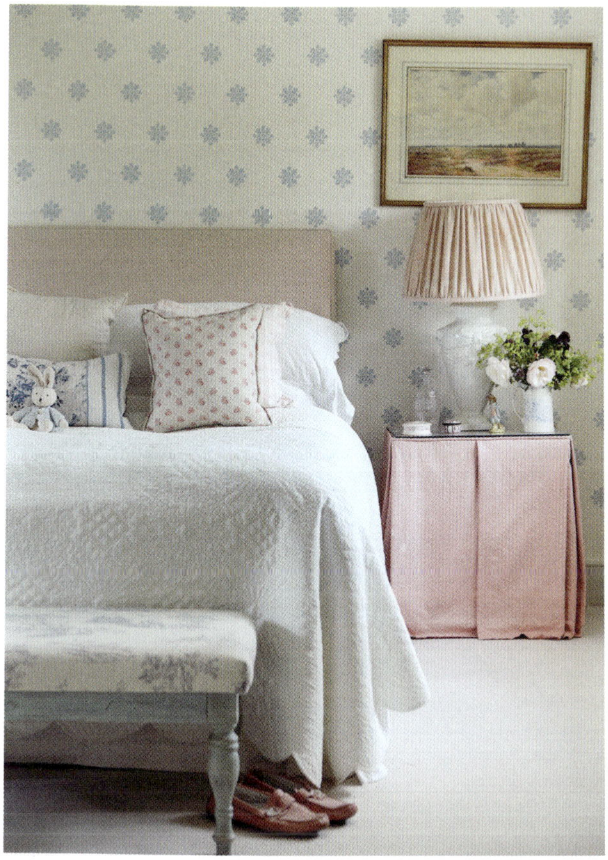

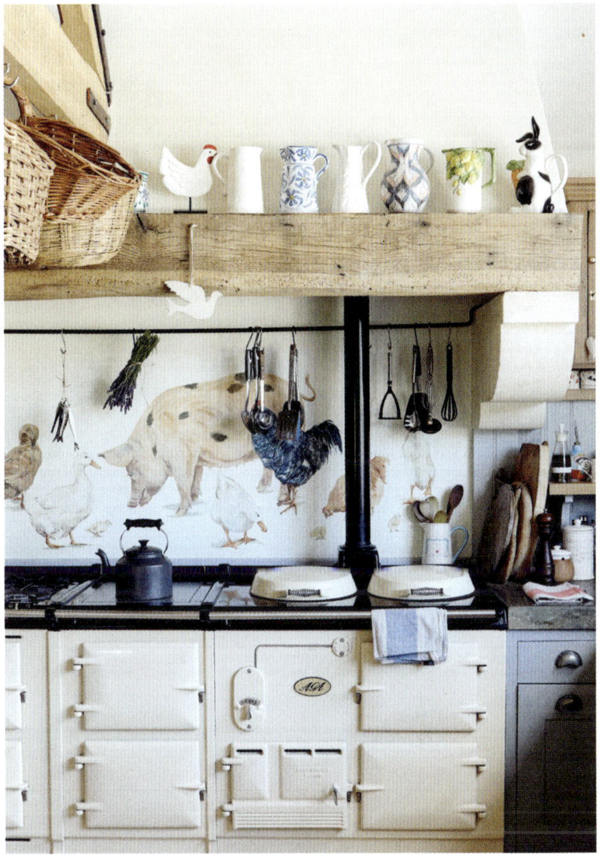

'WHAT I LOVE

about this house are the enormous fireplaces. Such a large space needs them, and I have made them a focal point in all of the rooms and had two new ones installed too.'

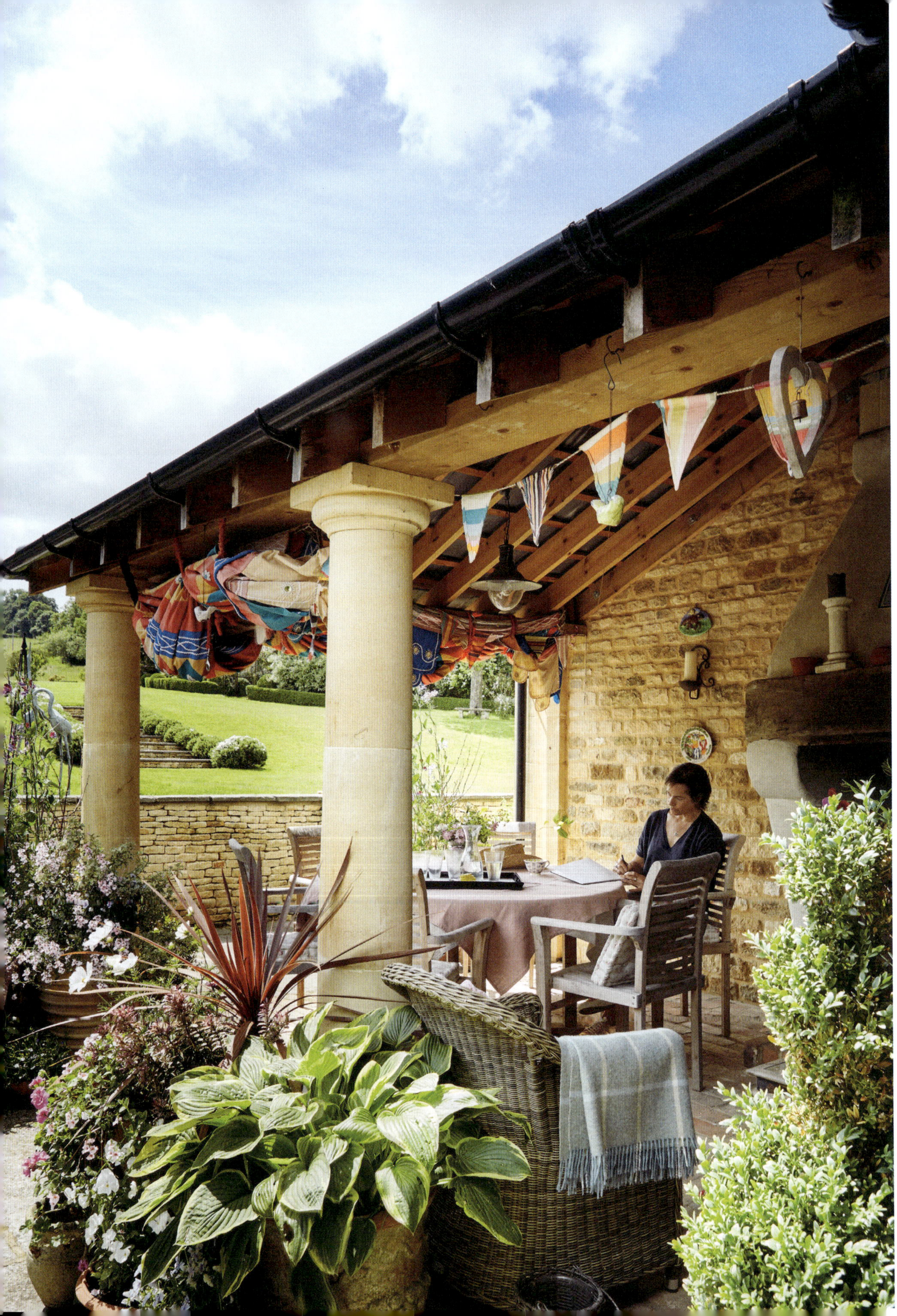

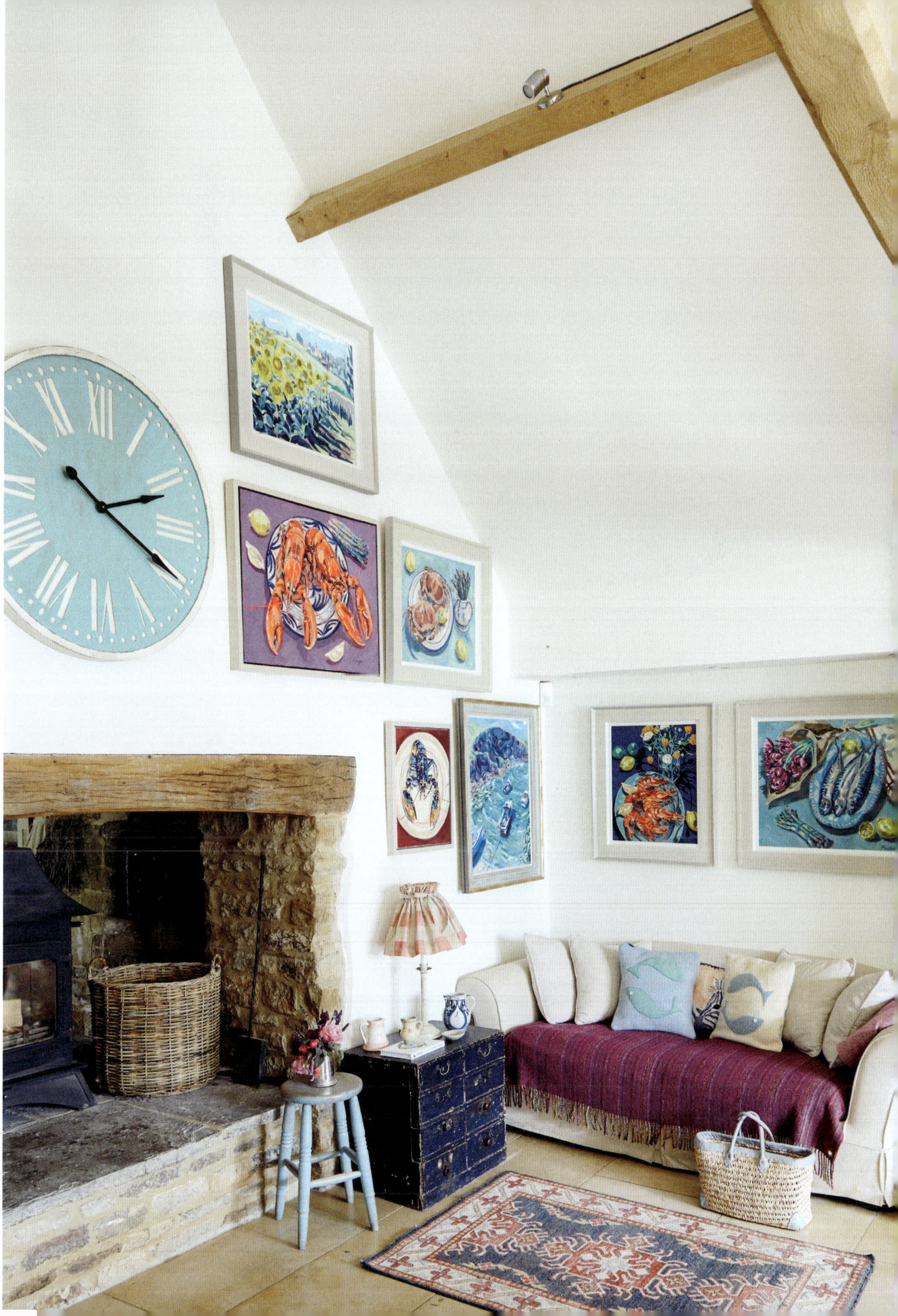

'Light became quite a preoccupation over the next decade,' says Annabel, who despite loving her home was frustrated that most windows faced north. 'Not one room made the most of the southerly views of the garden and countryside beyond.' However, four small children, two dogs and several horses left no time for further home improvements, so it wasn't until 2010 that she embarked on a second project.

A spacious garden room was added at the back of the house, surrounded by windows and topped with a roof lantern. Even in mid-winter this room is filled with light and kept cosy by its enormous log fire. Next came Annabel's most inspired home improvement yet: an undercover loggia, accessed through french doors from the kitchen. Here - beneath climbing jasmine, roses and sweet peas - are sofas, a swing seat and a large dining table, along with an open fire.

As life has calmed down and the children have grown up, the balance has shifted again. Annabel has experienced a surge of creativity. Her painting has taken off, and her output in recent years has been prolific - so much so, that she, with great nostalgia, decided to turn two of her much-loved stables into a studio. A riding accident has put an end to Annabel's equestrian days. But when one door closes, so another opens. Is it fanciful to imagine that her outpouring of creativity is linked to this comforting place, where once Annabel tended her beloved horses? A hard link to prove, but there is certainly something powerful spurring Annabel Playfair on.

'DESPITE MY NATURAL LEANING *towards colour, I kept my backdrops – walls, flooring and curtains – fairly neutral. This was to make the rooms lighter. I then added masses of colour in paintings, ornaments, rugs and cushions.'*

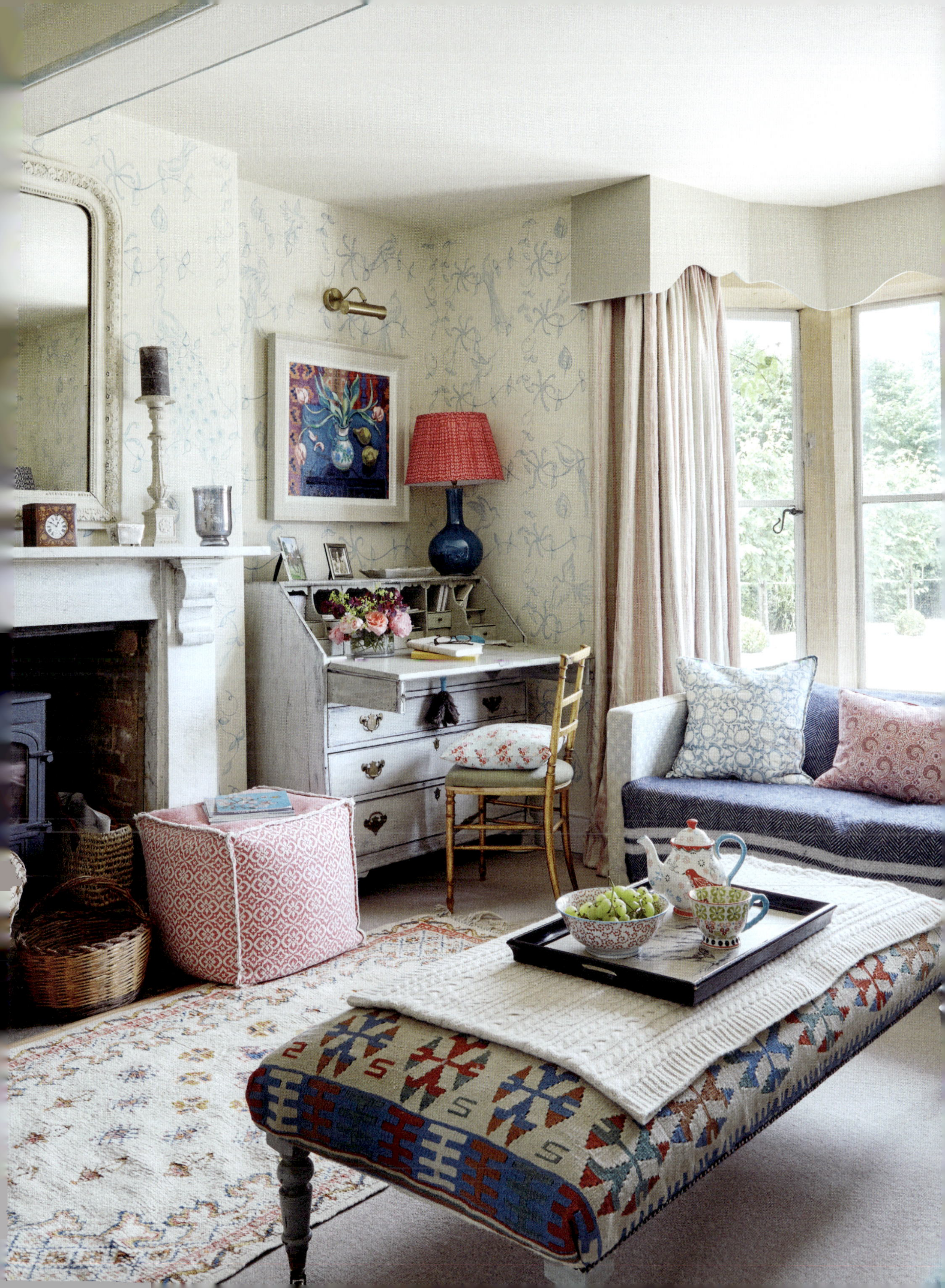

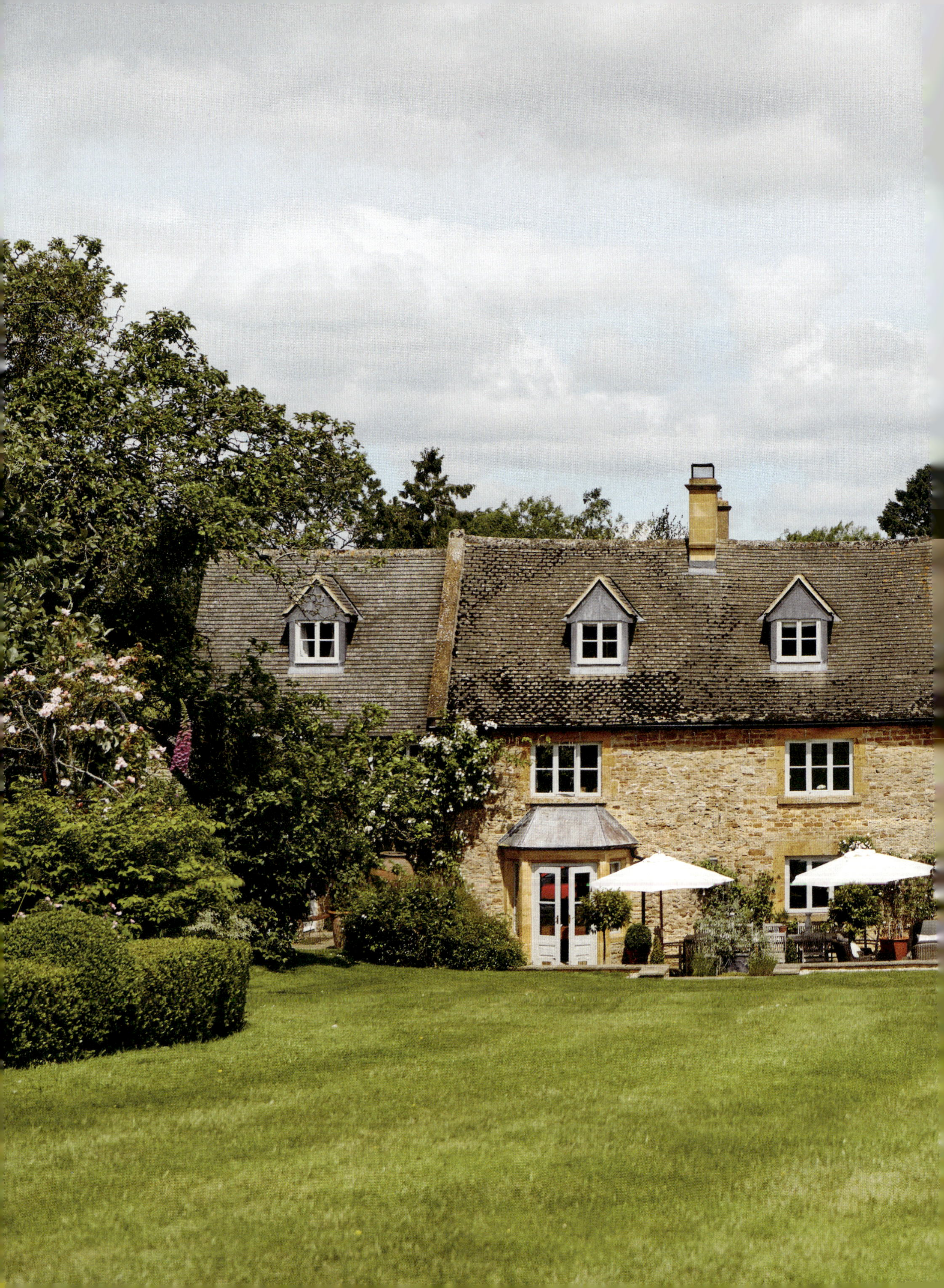

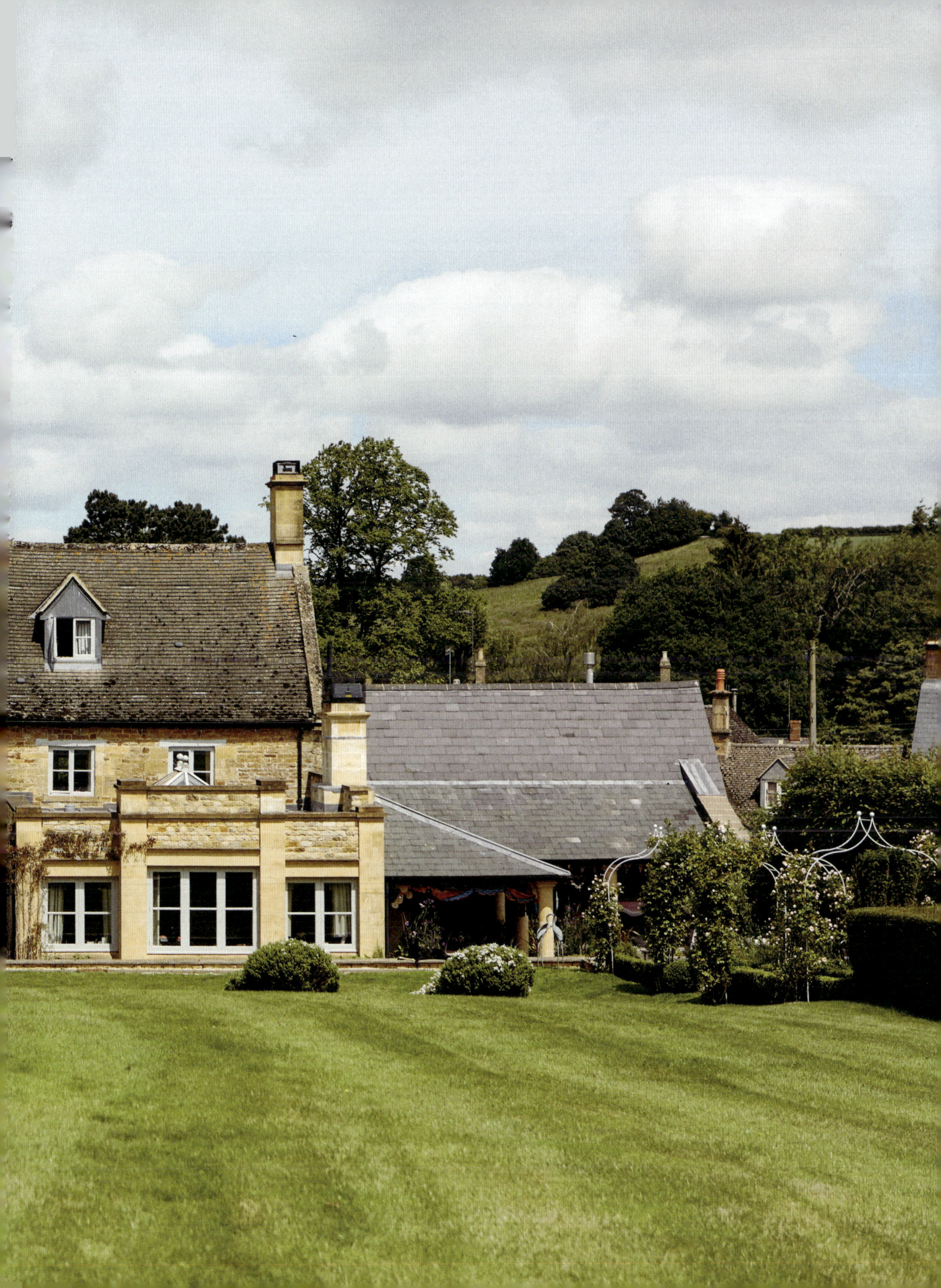

CREDITS

Alice Clark, www.willowonthefarm.co.uk, *@thewillowonthefarmnursery*
Amy Bell, www.hamseybelle.co.uk, *@hamseybelle*
Annabel Playfair, www.annabelplayfair.co.uk
Brent Darby, *@brentdarbyphotography*
Caitlin Swain, article3interiors.com, *@article3interiors*
Charlotte Colville
Elle Kemp, www.ridgeandfurrow.co.uk, *@ridge_and_furrow*
Fiona Carlton Paget, www.fionapagetgardens.co.uk, *@fionacpaget*
Harriet Orr-Ewing, www.taitchorrewing.co.uk
Heloise O'Hagan, www.heloiseohagan.com, *@heloiseohagan*
Henny Haworth-Booth
Holly Clements, *@hambledonhome*
Isabelle Alton, Garden design, taitchorrewing.co.uk
Jemma Powell, www.jemmapowell.com, *@powell.jemma.art*
Josephine Trotter, www.josephinetrotter.com, *@josephinetrotter_artist*
Kate Pinnock, *@myoldpub*
Louisa Butters, www.scarlettbrooksbankinteriors.co.uk, *@scarlettbrooksbank.interiors*
Miranda Gardiner, www.twocabins.com, www.mirandagardiner.com, *@mirandagardiner*
Natasha Ginks, www.renovategreen.co.uk, *@renovategreen*
Oliver and Lucy Leatham, www.telfitfarm.co.uk
Polly McMahon, *@thetottingwagon*
Susie Evans-Pollard, *@susannahtaylor_*, *@susannahtaylorstudio*
Tim Whittaker, *@timjohnwhittaker*
Wendy Sandford
Wink Colville, *@winkcolville*

Texts: Wink Colville
Photography: Brent Darby
Book Design: Elise Castrodale
Editing: First Edition Translations

Sign up for our newsletter with news about new and forthcoming publications on art, interior design, food & travel, photography and fashion as well as exclusive offers and events.

If you have any questions or comments about the material in this book, please do not hesitate to contact our editorial team: art@lannoo.com

© Lannoo Publishers, Belgium, 2023
D/2023/45/452 - NUR 450/653
ISBN: 9789401489973
www.lannoo.com

All rights reserved. No part of this publication may be reproduced or transmitted in any form or by any means, electronic or mechanical, including photocopy, recording or any other information storage and retrieval system, without prior permission in writing from the publisher. Every effort has been made to trace copyright holders. If, however, you feel that you have inadvertently been overlooked, please contact the publishers.